Creating Value with
Science and Technology

Creating Value with Science and Technology

Eliezer Geisler

Q

QUORUM BOOKS
Westport, Connecticut • London

Library of Congress Cataloging-in-Publication Data

Geisler, Eliezer, 1942–
    Creating value with science and technology / Eliezer Geisler.
      p. cm.
    Includes bibliographical references and index.
    ISBN 1–56720–405–8 (alk. paper)
    1. Science—Social aspects. 2. Science—Economic aspects. 3. Technological
innovations—Social aspects. 4. Technological innovations—Economic aspects. I. Title.
Q175.5.G427   2001
303.48′3—dc21   2001019189

British Library Cataloguing in Publication Data is available.

Library of Congress Catalog Card Number: 2001019189
ISBN: 1–56720–405–8

First published in 2001

Quorum Books, 88 Post Road West, Westport, CT 06881
An imprint of Greenwood Publishing Group, Inc.
www.quorumbooks.com

Printed in the United States of America

The paper used in this book complies with the
Permanent Paper Standard issued by the National
Information Standards Organization (Z39.48–1984).

10 9 8 7 6 5 4 3 2 1

For my son, Dan

CONTENTS

LIST OF FIGURES

PREFACE

Everybody knows that science and technology (S&T) creates value for the economy and for society, and this book is about why it is so difficult to show that this is true. Everybody knows that the 21st century will be the century of technological marvels, but how do we document this beyond disjointed anecdotal evidence? We are increasingly becoming a society dependent on technology. Few people know how to design and operate complex technological systems, and the vast majority has simply resigned itself to knowing very little about the working of these technologies. We not only depend on science and technology, we also are inherently convinced that it greatly contributes to our way of life. This book is therefore about how to support these convictions. While enumerating the difficulties in making the claim that S&T creates value, this book also brings about some comfort to the perennial sentiment of the love-hate relationship that humans have had with S&T for millennia.

In a marvelously lucid book which he completed the year before his death in 1997, Donald Stokes argued that science and technology, particularly in the United States, are in a state of drastic change.[1] He contended: "The compact between science and government...has come unstuck, and the scientific and policy communities are actively canvassing for the terms of a fresh agreement" (p. 2). Stokes then proceeded to argue for a more precise link between fundamental science and its use in technological innovation. By offering a more dynamic approach, Stokes suggested that there is much more of a fusion of science and technology than the prevailing paradigm had allowed us to accept.

Although Stokes provided a convincing discourse to his arguments, the theoretical foundations to his departure from the extant approach were conspicuously absent from his narrative. In this post-cold-war era, combined with the increased complexity of the universe of science and technology, there is an emerging environment much more conducive for the strengthening of the link between science and technology. The separation of the components of the innovation process into self-contained and independent stages that serially interlink may increasingly be under attack as an artificial form of analysis. Some science is now viewed as driven by technology, and the neat flow from basic research to technological innovation is being challenged.

This *internal* link between science and technology is not sufficient to evoke a change in our paradigmatic view of the innovation phenomenon. There is also the need to view the consequences of science *and* technology. That is, the *external* impacts. Why is this necessary?

If basic science is the purview of the intellectual curiosity of researchers, then they may conduct their endeavor in partial or total disconnect from their socioeconomic surroundings (assuming that someone in these surroundings is willing to foot the bill). But, if technological innovation and applied use of their findings are also contemplated, and become part of the empirical equation, then such use has its genesis in sponsors and potential users in society and the economy. Hence, if science and technology are strongly linked, they are also strongly linked to potential users and their organizations.

This is the issue of concern to philosophers of technology. Traditional views considered science and technology to be a custom-made entity, with its own essence that influences the economy and society to which it is generated and evolves. Such a perspective served two purposes. One was the ability to measure, with relatively fewer constraints, the effects of individual technologies on economic welfare and social institutions. The other was the use of such an approach to further political views that regarded technological progress as either a beneficial or, alternatively, a destructive social and economic force.[2]

Considering S&T as an independent and self-propelled force largely ignores the complexity of the process that links S&T with society and the economy. S&T without coordinated utilization, and the political and social forces that govern such utilization, remains an isolated activity that leads to nowhere. Derek de Solla Price commented on the scientific apathy of ancient Hellenistic scholarship.[3] Science was to them pursuit of knowledge in its logical or rational framework, without attempts to transform it—through calculations and empirical applications—into useful technologies. Science thus became a scholastic activity of manipulation of arguments, with little, if any, connection to social and economic activities.

A different philosophy argued for S&T to be explained only in the context of its social connection. S&T is reduced to a strict relationship between a given technology and its social and economic impacts.[4] This approach also allows its proponents to demonstrate the effects from an individual technology (device or artifact) on selected social and economic dimensions. In this context it was also possible to argue that certain political interests are at work in determining the generation, progress, and, in particular, the utilization of the technology. As with the philosophy that viewed technology as having an "essence" and being an autonomous force, proponents of the society-technology nexus also used their construct to support their preferred political positions. Some take the logical leap, for example, that since the existing oligarchies of big business subjugate technologies to their own interests and to the continuation of their power, there is a need to counteract this force by a more democratic and popular "control" over the technology.[5]

However we choose to view the link between S&T and society/economy, such a connection is complex and a two-way street. Social and economic interests and forces help to shape the allocation of resources to S&T and the process of its generation and progress. These forces also help to determine the utilization of the subsequent technological innovations.

By the same token, S&T creates effects and impacts on society and the economy. Some of these impacts are intended, others are unintended consequences, often to the detriment of the social/economic forces that originally helped to shape S&T.

The problem, then, is one of evaluation. However strong the internal or external linkages, the key to our understanding of the phenomenon of scientific and technological innovation is in adequate evaluation of the process and its consequences.

But, as I will explain in Chapters 5, 9, and 10, the evaluation of S&T should focus on the value created with S&T. Although the evaluation effort is constrained by the motives behind the evaluation, biases of evaluators, and the methods used in it, the ultimate outcome from evaluation of S&T should provide some measurable assessment of value generated for recipients and users of the technological innovators. Without such value S&T would indeed be reduced to nothing more than infinite dialogues and unusable interaction.

Whatever political position one assumes regarding the recipients of such value and their use of it to satisfy their unique objectives, this book focuses on the exploration of the process by which we measure this value. This book is not devoid of an underlying ethical position of the value created by S&T and its uses. On the contrary, I espouse a very clear position that S&T produces substantial value to society and the economy and that certain market and political mechanisms are better suited to exploit S&T for the welfare of larger portions of society.

For almost two decades I have attempted to study and comprehend the nature of this phenomenon. My research and consulting activities emphasized the link between science (research) and technology. I have searched for theories and evaluation methodologies that would serve as a basis for research into this complex phenomenon. In this endeavor I came across theories of the firm, theories of organization, economic theories, and sociological theories. The diversity of these theories and the interdisciplinary nature of the topics in science and technology hindered a focused approach. Each theory seems like a force pulling in a separate direction, with its specific terminology and agenda. For managerial purposes many authors have oversimplified the phenomenon, so that science and technology are reduced to a single definition or purpose.[6]

WHY THIS BOOK?

I became convinced that there was a need to identify and assemble the various theories and models that had served as foundation for studies of evaluation of science and technology. I also became convinced of the need to assemble the knowledge about how S&T creates values, what types of value are created, and what means are available to measure it. This is an inter-disciplinary field of study, where students of management, economics, organization, marketing, finance, and engineering have traditionally congregated to evaluate S&T. Each formulated a distinct theoretical background and used different methods for evaluation. I felt there were some common elements in these theories that somehow connected them to the phenomenon and to each other, hence offering the basis for establishing the value from S&T. This book is an attempt to frame these theories and models to explain their similarities.

Then the book offers a discussion of the evaluation of S&T, and attempts to answer the questions: Why evaluate? What is evaluation? and, What are the theories and models that govern evaluation of S&T? This will be followed by the questions: How indeed does S&T create value for the economy and for society? Therefore, do we currently possess adequate analytical and evaluative tools to establish the link between S&T and value created in the economy and society? Finally, what types of value are created by S&T, and how can we evaluate them?

Much of the scholarly effort in the evaluation of S&T has been dispersed and disjointed. Michael Porter and Scott Stern suggested in 1999 that there is a way to measure a "National Innovation Index," computed on the basis of indicators such as international patents, national investments in R&D, and expenditures for higher education as percent of the gross domestic product.[7] Porter and Stern went on to use this index in their analysis of international economic competitiveness of nations.

However, such a link between innovation and level of national competition is but one example of empirical applications of evaluation models that generate far-reaching implications for S&T policy, yet are not adequately anchored in theoretical foundations. The models thus employed vary by the kinds of measures and indicators they utilize, but leave much to be desired in their conceptual background. What is the connection between investments in S&T and national (or firm) competitive position? This book attempts to establish the conceptual and methodological basis answering such questions as: What is the connection between S&T and society and the economy? How is value created from S&T and how can we adequately measure and assess it? What constitutes value from S&T and who are the beneficiaries?

This book assembles the theories and models currently used in evaluation of S&T, so that the link between S&T and value is better identified. It emphasizes the conceptual frameworks on which empirical applications of measures are conducted. However the main contribution of the book is in developing the outcomes from such evaluations in the form of the value created for social and economic institutions. As I continue to elaborate in Chapter 5, the "technohuman condition" is explored in this book. Crucial questions are asked, and I attempt to procure some answers, from the literature as well as my own interpretation of the phenomenon of S&T and its outcomes.

What value is created by S&T? Is such value adequate enough to assess S&T as a worthwhile human activity? How best can we measure and evaluate the value created by S&T? Who influences the generation and the utilization of S&T, and who benefits from the value it creates? Finally, what are the shortcomings and harmful side effects from S&T, and are they favorably balanced by the benefits that the economy and society has accrued from S&T?

WAKE-UP CALL

This book is a wake-up call for academics, industry executives, and government officials. By showing how value is created with S&T, this book also points to the "real" value created, in terms of its contributions and the ability we have to identify, measure, and assess such contributions. As discussed in this book, perhaps there are various types of value, organized in some hierarchy of importance, for each stage of the S&T-society/economy nexus.

This book not only attempts to clarify the parameters and conditions that lead to value creation from S&T, but also brings to the attention of the readers the deliberate importance of such value. What constitutes "real" value from S&T and what are its implications? This is the crucial issue of our times, and this book is a contribution to this discourse.

AUDIENCES

This book is about the evaluation of S&T and values it generates. Thus, it is written for three complementary audiences. The first is scholars, researchers, and other people interested in the theory and methodology that drives studies of S&T. This group includes researchers in the general area of evaluation, and those in the focused area of management of research and development (R&D), engineering, and technological innovation. They are dispersed among many disciplines, from sociology to economics, from industrial engineering to marketing and production (new product development).

The second audience is composed of managers of R&D and S&T, and policy-makers in government and industry. They have been involved with evaluation of S&T and wish to better understand what the contributions are that S&T provides. This is not simply intellectual curiosity, but a need to jusitfy effort in S&T.

The third audience is the public at large, particularly the informed and knowledgeable reader. Increasingly people find themselves faced with advances in science and technology that encompass all aspects of our lives. Technological innovations are emerging in medicine, transportation, telecommunications, and education, to cite just a few socioeconomic areas. S&T is changing the way we live our lives, and will continue to do so at an ever-increasing pace.

Informed readers wish to gain additional knowledge about the process of S&T, and what value this effort creates. Perhaps the combination of knowing what changes S&T brings with knowing how to assess its value may bring about a sense of less bewilderment in such a dynamic and uncertain world.

WHAT THIS BOOK IS ABOUT

This book articulates the foundations of the evaluation of science, technology, and innovation and explores the value that they create. In 1980, Alan Kantrow suggested that there is a critical link between technology and strategy, and it is up to corporate managers to see it.[8] He went on to elaborate the risk involved in technological innovation and the enormous resources devoted to this activity. Therefore, Kantrow correctly argued that the commonsense thing to do is to consider technology as an integral part of strategic thinking.

This book is about the commonsense approach to S&T and innovation. The complexity of the process of innovation and the various approaches to evaluate its activities and outcomes may be based on a set of sensible theories. Similarly, conceptual frameworks that are used to describe and assess technological innovation are anchored in some fundamental notions of organization and management. These fundamentals are elaborated in this book.

This book reflects my bias as a student of organizations. The problem of the evaluation of S&T has been a constant companion in my scholarly work over the years. In my own research and while consulting for industry and governments, I continually expanded the conceptual foundations of my work and that of my colleagues to include methods that would measure the outcomes, the benefits, and the overall value of technological innovations. My interest in this issue has permeated every report and study of S&T that I was able to accomplish. My experience and my biases are therefore also responsible for any errors and omissions in this book.

HOW THE BOOK IS ORGANIZED

This book is organized into four parts. The first provides a historical background of how S&T developed during the 20th century with both industrial and public investments. This part also describes the recent trends by which industry and government have cooperated to further advance the state of S&T. This first part ends with a personal note about the theme that runs throughout the book and my views of the impacts and evaluation of S&T.

Part II describes the theoretical foundation for evaluation of science and technology. First the nature of the S&T phenomenon is detailed in Chapter 5. The "technohuman" condition receives special consideration and is explained. Chapter 6 lists and discusses theories of technology. This is followed by Chapter 7 which is devoted to theories of knowledge and the knowledge-driven society. Finally, the concepts and notions used in evaluation of S&T are defined in Chapter 8.

Part III is dedicated to a discussion of evaluation, and the evaluation of research, development, and innovation. This part discusses the methodological aspects of assessing the creation of value from S&T.

Part IV provides the essence of the book. It describes the impacts of S&T on society and the economy, and the ways and means to evaluate such impacts. Chapter 13 starts by discussing the models of innovation, considered to be the phenomenon through which S&T impacts social and economic organizations.

Chapter 14 describes the link between S&T and economic progress. The chapter offers my views and a model of how economic value is created with S&T. Chapter 15 explores the foundations and processes by which companies create economic value with S&T. Chapter 16 continues this line of analysis in the issue of how society creates and exploits value from S&T.

Chapter 17 is a comprehensive discussion of ethical issues, controversies, and current concerns regarding S&T and its consequences. This is followed by the final chapter, Chapter 18, as a summary, epilogue, and my observations about the future.

So the organization of this book follows the logic of successive questions: (1) What are the factual dimensions of S&T activities and investments in the recent past? (2) What are the theoretical bases for assessing the value of S&T? (3) What is evaluation, what are its boundaries, and how does it apply to the various components of the innovation phenomenon?, hence based on the above, (4) What is the value created by S&T for the economy and to society, and what are some of the ethical implications of such value?

ACKNOWLEDGMENTS

It would have been impossible to write such a book as this without the inputs from my teachers, colleagues, friends, students, and, of course, my family. I am particularly grateful to Al Rubenstein, Don Campbell, Charles Thompson, and Ron Kostoff. I benefitted from the work of my students, Nuttaphon Chetiyanointh, Tom Bajek, and Devangi Shah, who assisted in the data collection for the book. M. Zia Hassan was helpful in his support of my writing effort and I owe a special debt of gratitude to him. I am also grateful to Joel Goldhar and Gerald Hoffman. Several grants from the National Science Foundation have supported the research on which this book is based.

I want to especially thank Eric Valentine, my publisher, for his continuing support, and my editor, Katie Chase. Janet Goranson and Jean Waschow prepared this manuscript. Their immense talent made this book possible. I owe them my sincerest gratitude.

Finally, to my family, and especially my wife, Betsy, for her unflinching support and encouragement, I am deeply thankful.

NOTES

1. Stokes, D., *Pasteur's Quadrant: Basic Science and Technological Innovation* (Washington, D.C.: Brookings Institution Press, 1997).

2. Such "extremist" views are illustrated in the work of such philosophers as Herbert Marcuse. See Marcuse, H., *One Dimensional Man* (Boston: Beacon Press, 1964).

3. Price, de Solla D., *Science Since Babylon* (New Haven, CT: Yale University Press, 1961).

4. See, for example, Feenberg, A., *Critical Theory of Technology* (Oxford: Oxford University Press, 1991). Also see Feenberg, A., *Questioning Technology* (London: Routledge Kegan, 1999).

5. See, Veak, T., "Whose Technology? Whose Modernity: Questioning Feenberg's Questioning Technology," *Science, Technology and Human Values*, 25(2), 2000, 226-237. Veak uses the Internet as an example for such popular forces *vis-à-vis* existing powers.

6. For example, Kenneth Arrow argued that the activity of invention is geared toward the production of *information*. Other economists have suggested that science and technology is one aspect of the firm's effort at creating wealth. Management scholars emphasized the efficiency and strategic impacts of S&T.

7. See their conclusions in Buderi, R., "In Search of Innovation," *Technology Review*, November-December, 1999, 4-8.

8. Kantrow, A., "The Strategy-Technology Connection," *Harvard Business Review*, July-August, 1980, 6-21.

PART I

HISTORICAL BACKGROUND

Let both sides seek to invoke the wonders of science instead of its terrors. Together let us explore the stars, conquer the deserts, eradicate disease, tap the ocean depths, and encourage the arts and commerce.

John F. Kennedy
(1917-1963)
Inaugural Address, January 20, 1961

1

INDUSTRIAL SCIENCE AND TECHNOLOGY: A HISTORICAL PERSPECTIVE

In the continuing effort to institutionalize the generation and application of science and technology which became prevalent after the Second World War, industrial companies assumed a leading role in this phenomenon. Although scientific developments had been formal activities in many industries since the latter part of the 19th century, the pace of growth in such activities has been unprecedented in the latter half of the 20th century.

In the second part of the book there is a concise definition of what constitutes science and technology, and what is included in the term research and development (R&D). In this chapter, however, science and technology is considered an activity that encompasses much of the innovation continuum—from exploratory research to commercialization of innovations.

This chapter provides a historical perspective of the development and growth of science and technology in industry, and, in particular, in American industry. As a bedrock for American scientific and technical innovations, industrial laboratories have grown dramatically in the second half of the 20th century. This chapter briefly traces the reasons and trends of such growth.

TRENDS OF GROWTH

The national science and technology system in the United States currently has over 15,000 laboratories, of which the vast majority are owned and operated by industrial companies.[1] Although several major American companies have established a substantial national and global presence since the early part of the 20th century (for example, General Electric, Bell Laboratories, Westinghouse, and Eastman Kodak), the phenomenal growth in size and depth has bloomed in the latter half of the century.[2]

Figure 1.1 shows the pattern of growth in expenditures for industrial R&D, and the source of the funds, for the period 1960-1997.

In the decade of the 1960s, total investments in industrial R&D rose by almost 40 percent. In the decade of the 1970s, this rise was only 13 percent. But, during the 1980s, despite the recession in the early part of the decade, industrial R&D grew by over 50 percent (all in constant 1987 dollars).

The unparalleled growth of industrial science and technology in the past four decades was not only in terms of the size of economic investments. There was also a growth in the corporate culture that made innovation a desired term in corporate parlance. Once the link between the R&D function of the firm and its commercial side was firmly established, innovation became a recognized force in corporate success and in its market competitiveness. Moreover, this recognition was not limited only to the major corporations, but filtered down to smaller companies, who then adopted this same attitude toward research, science, and technology.

Concomitantly, the rise of science and technology in corporate esteem also helped to foster academic interest in the topic. Studies of the economic and efficiency aspects of corporate R&D began to emerge in the mid-1960s, ultimately leading to the intellectual area of exploration commonly known as "Management of Technology."

Historically, then, this book is a continuation of the trend of systematic studies of the phenomenon of S&T and corporate R&D. Although in size of investments, corporate research has been about half of the total national effort in science and technology, companies nevertheless have been more active in their effort to assess these investments and to identify their impacts and benefits. The historical context of the development in corporate R&D offers a potential explanation to the focus on evaluation of S&T and the theoretical foundation that underlies these activities.[3]

PERIODS OF GROWTH AND CONTRACTION

In the second half of the 20th century it is possible to identify distinct historical periods in the development of industrial science and technology.[4] Three factors helped to determine the rate of growth of industrial R&D: (1) economic vitality of the marketplace, (2) federal investments, and (3) internal recognition of R&D as a major success factor for corporate survival.

Based on these factors, there are five historical periods of note. In conceptualizing these arbitrary historical partitions, I have ventured to provide the temporal as well as logical backgrounds for the use of certain evaluation approaches, such as resource allocation and project selection models. There

**Figure 1.1   Expenditures for R&D by Industrial Companies by Source of
Funding for the Period 1960-1997, in Constant 1987 Dollars**

(millions of constant 1987 dollars)

Year	Total	From Federal Government	From Industry	Share of Federal Government
1960	38,585	21,554	17,031	55.86%
1961	39,365	21,616	17,749	
1962	41,033	22,338	18,695	
1963	44,912	22,206	19,706	
1964	47,108	26,199	20,910	
1965	48,634	25,940	22,694	
1966	51,677	27,133	24,544	
1967	52,693	26,224	26,469	
1968	53,503	25,613	27,890	
1969	53,425	23,913	29,512	
1970	49.983	20,756	29,227	41.52%
1971	48,057	19,340	28,717	
1972	48,979	19,250	29,729	
1973	50,131	18,402	31,729	
1974	49,530	16,864	32,666	
1975	47,683	16,012	31,671	
1976	49,918	16,579	33,338	
1977	51,633	17,036	34,597	
1978	53,436	16,761	36,675	
1979	56,497	16,308	39,189	
1980	60,290	17,785	42,505	29.50%
1981	63,910	19,008	44,902	
1982	68,217	20,359	47,858	
1983	73,031	21,898	51,133	
1984	80,287	23,799	56,488	
1985	87,263	26,836	60,427	
1986	88,293	26,444	61,849	
1987	89,804	28,401	61,403	
1988	91,772	28,469	63,303	
1989	91,449	26,415	65,034	
1990	89,966	24,613	65,353	27.35%
1991	84,486	19,173	65,312	
1992	86,931	21,588	65,343	
1993	88,530	22,859	65,670	25.82%
1994	89,130	21,612	67,518	
1995*	91,380	20,483	70,897	
1996*	93,103	20,313	72,790	
1997*	95,807	22,478	73,329	23.46%

Sources: National Science Foundation, Science and Engineering Indicators-1993 and
1996. Estimates. Source: *R&D Magazine*, 1995-1998.

is a link between historical trends, as encapsulated in a given period, and the focus that evaluators of the phenomenon tend to select for their assessment.

Formation (1900-1959)

The first period was an era of formation of the R&D function in American corporations. Following the examples of corporate giants such as Standard Oil of New Jersey, Du Pont, Westinghouse, AT&T, and General Electric, other manufacturers formed and institutionalized their R&D activity as an on-going function in these companies. As commented earlier, the two world wars were also motivators in this phenomenon. Together with support from the government, there was also the opening of international markets and military (then civilian) cooperation among nations, industries, and individual companies. By 1960, investments in corporate R&D in the United States amounted to about $40 billion (in constant 1987 dollars). The share of the federal government in this effort was about 56 percent, due to the massive investments in the Second World War, and the continuing involvement of federal interests due to the cold war.

This period was characterized by the establishment of intracompany R&D units and by the beginning of federal participation in the corporate R&D effort. It was also a period in which procedures and processes began to appear, and in which the distinction between military and civilian R&D was formalized.

Transition (1960-1967)

In this short period of the 1960s, there are two converging and inter-related phenomena. For their part, American federal obligations had dramatically increased, in view of the space endeavor and the war in Vietnam. Industrial investments in R&D had also increased by 55 percent, about 8 percent per year. This was not only a period of growth, but also a transition toward dependency on federal contracts. Such transitions facilitated the creation of the giant aerospace corporations and fostered a link between the military and industry.[5]

Moreover, with capital and contracts ubiquitously available, and a prosperous economy, American industrial companies expanded their R&D into high-risk, exploratory, and emerging technologies. Defense requirements for new and advanced weapon systems and new and advanced materials are among the main illustrations of the changing landscape of industrial R&D in this period. Total expenditures for basic research almost tripled during this period, largely due to federal investments.[6]

Figure 1.2
Periods of Growth and Contraction in the History of U.S. Corporate Science and Technology in the 20th Century

PERIOD*	MAIN CHARACTERISTICS
I. Formation (1900-1959)	• Establishment of procedures and processes for corporate R&D • Increased role of federal investments • Organizational distinctions between military and civilian R&D
II. Transition (1960-1967)	• Sharp increase in federal support of industrial R&D • Increased dependency on federal contracts • Expansion into emerging technologies • Concentration of R&D in a few dominant industries
III. Stabilization (1968-1983)	• Decline in federal support • Industry picks up the slack with increased funding of its R&D • Balance sheet of competitiveness
IV. Renewal (1984-1993)	• Renewed funding by federal government in the defense area • Increased deregulation of industry • Internal reorganization by industry • Move towards globalization • Making R&D more relevant and accountable
V. Contraction and Reorientation (1994-)	• Reorientation of R&D and closing corporate research laboratories • Downsizing, globalization, and outsourcing • Emerging industries and companies

Boundary dates for the historical periods are arbitrary.

This period is also characterized by the formation of the R&D intensive industries that have since dominated the industrial R&D scenario in the United States, and indeed the world. Industries such as machinery, transportation (including aerospace), electrical and electronic equipment, chemicals, and scientific instruments have emerged as the leading industries in R&D funding. Figure 1.3 shows the trend by which these industries grew in their importance and share of the industrial R&D they came to control.

Stabilization (1968-1983)

In this brief historical overview, the third period in the evolution of U.S. industrial R&D is the period of stabilization, which occurred between 1968 and 1983. The period is mainly characterized by the end of the Vietnam War, and by a reduction in federal investments in industrial R&D. From slightly over 40 percent in 1970, federal support dropped to under 30 percent in 1980. Nevertheless, industrial companies picked up the slack and increased their funding of R&D throughout the period (in constant 1987 dollars). After a hiatus in the mid-1970s, following a sharp decline in federal support, industrial companies increased their share of R&D to a stable level of about 70 percent.

Figure 1.3
Share of Selected Industries in Total Funding of U.S. Industrial R&D in the Period 1960-1967 (Machinery, Transportation, Electrical/Electronics, Chemicals, and Scientific Instruments)

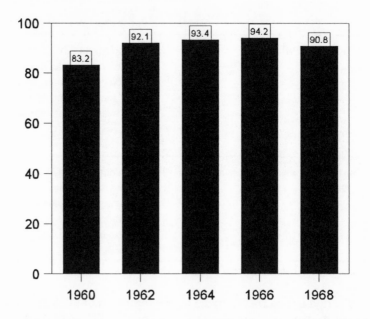

Source: National Science Foundation, *Science Indicators-1982*, Washington, D.C., NSB-83-1, pp. 282-283.

This is also a period in which American industrial companies began flexing their muscles in the continuation of a global expansion. Driven by rapidly increasing competition from foreign products at home (such as automobiles, electronics, and machinery), American industry reconsidered its priorities. Solutions were sought as companies began their soul-searching. By this time, the role of science and technology was firmly recognized as a potential solution to the decline in world competitiveness.

Renewal (1984-1993)

Two important phenomena occurred during the period 1984-1993. Following the recession of the early 1980s, the remainder of the decade was the "Reagan years," as President Ronald Reagan sharply increased the budget for defense. Yet motivated by threats of foreign competitors at home and abroad, American industrial companies continued to increase (in real terms) the funding of their R&D activities.[7]

This they did with three very distinct changes when compared to the previous period. First, American companies began their recovery from the damage they had suffered from foreign competition by fomenting internal reorganization. At first the guiding principle was quality improvement and the establishment of total quality management programs. R&D had a crucial role in this effort. Processes, methods, and testing apparatus and techniques came out of the R&D units in many corporations, thus contributing to a more timely and less eventful transition to a quality-oriented regime, in both manufacturing and services.

Reengineering appeared around the end of this period, signaling dramatic corporate changes. Both programs led to the emergence of a new culture in the American corporation. This culture was now predicated on the need for structural reorganization and on the imperatives of close examination of corporate functions and activities, and the necessary accountability of each in the broader chain of relevant events in the corporation.

Thus, the corporate R&D function was mobilized to provide support for the reengineering program, and, at the same time, underwent a comprehensive analysis of its relevancy and effectiveness. The predictable results were a shift toward highly relevant, short-term, product-oriented R&D.

The other distinct change during this period was the massive deregulation of American industry. The Reagan administration accelerated the rate of de-regulation of such industries as transportation and telecommunications, lead-ing to the breakup of AT&T. Deregulation also included the relaxation of many regulatory pressures. In the 1970s, many executives in the chemicals industry, for example, complained that a good portion of their R&D was actually geared toward meeting or anticipating regulatory demands. To some extent, deregulation had changed the playing field, thus theoretically freeing some R&D to be directed toward strategic and product-oriented innovation.

However, a side effect of deregulation was the breakup of a major company and the effective dissolution of its corporate lab. With the breakup of AT&T, Bell Labs lost a giant sponsor. As the birthplace of numerous inventions and innovations in physics, optics, and telecommunications, Bell Labs (currently roughly transformed into Lucent Technologies) lost much of its power and its luster.[8]

Finally, the third change was the massive impact of automation and information technology on American industry. Felt principally in manufacturing, these improvements generated highly efficient production systems, which allowed U.S. companies to expand their operations globally. This included the move of R&D to foreign countries.

Construction and Reorientation (1994-)

The fifth period covers the second half of the decade of the 1990s. In this period, industrial R&D in the United States has begun a stage of reorientation, characterized mainly by the following events. First, there has been, and to a degree continues to be at the time of the writing of this book, a contraction in industrial funding for R&D. Although in real terms the dollar expenditures show an increase in funding, the rate of the increase has slowed to that of the stabilization period of the 1970s.

But, more important, there has been a radical shift of the R&D portfolio from basic research to product-orientation, and from central corporate laboratories to divisional laboratories.[9] As the focus moved from the central laboratory, the divisions now had more control over which R&D to fund. They largely preferred "relevant" research with short-term results and with much less risk.[10] This led to the closing of central corporate laboratories of major corporations, such as Xerox and Arco Oil. The joint effects of reorientation, downsizing, globalization, and outsourcing corporate R&D have reduced the concentric power of the large corporate R&D capability.[11]

It is important to note here that the rush to mergers and acquisitions in this period did not result in the pooling of R&D resources by the merging companies. The celebrated mergers of such companies as Bell Atlantic and Nynex, and SBC Communications and Pacific Telesis Group, in 1996, have not produced the much needed strengthening of their corporate research laboratories.

A third event which, to an extent, is defining the transition to the 21st century is the emergence of new and revitalized industries, and a growing phenomenon of heavy investments by these companies in R&D. In 1997, for example, companies such as Microsoft of Redmond, Washington, and Intel of

Santa Clara, California, increased their funding of R&D by 67 percent and 40 percent, respectively.

A more dramatic trend is seen in smaller companies in the so-called high technology industries. Calgene, of Davis, California, quintupled its R&D budget in 1996. As a leading agricultural bio-technology company, Calgene exemplifies the trend. Similarly, Biogen of Cambridge, Massachusetts, a bio-pharmaceutical company, also dramatically increased its R&D investments in the late 1990s.

This trend of construction and reorientation has been radically influenced by two seemingly distinct developments: the new "executive culture" of linking technology to corporate success and the emergence of the field of knowledge management. Both of these have shaped, and are continuing to impact, the type and growth of industrial science and technology in the United States.

The new executive culture is based on the model of integrating technology with the commercial processes of the company. Iansiti and West, for example, defined technology integration as "the approach that companies use to choose and refine the technologies employed in a new product, process, or service"[12] (p. 69). This new perspective has contributed to redesigning the landscape of the management of industrial science and technology.[13] Closer linkage to the commercialization process means a much higher degree of relevancy of the research performed—at the expense of more fundamental and corporate-wide programs. This trend is hardly new, as I had written a commentary on it as early as 1995.[14]

Shortsightedness and the regulation of the R&D function in the firm to essentially technical support for manufacturing and marketing are the two major threats to industry from this new executive culture. In their desperate search for improved competitiveness and more efficient commercialization of new products and processes, companies have run the risk of mortgaging their future and their sustained survival.

This perspective rests on two important premises. First, that technology is a capability or competency in the firm (rather than a function), and second, that the way R&D was practiced in the 1970s, and even the 1980s, is beyond the means of the companies of the late 1990s and early 21st century, due to their highly dynamic and competitive business environment. No other example better illustrates these premises than the semiconductor and computer industries.[15]

In the 1990s, therefore, the age of the corporate research facility, laboring in a relatively glorified isolation, was over. The move was toward dedicated, also distributed, and product-oriented teams. They were designed to encapsulate the linkage between R&D and the commercialization processes in the firm. At this point in the book, I have listed this development as part of the trend in the late 1990s. Later in the book, this discussion will be enlarged within the context of commercialization and technology transfer within the industrial company.

The emergence of the field of knowledge management has contributed to the belief that companies possess the tools to integrate, better channel, and better utilize their intellectual capital, including R&D. Spurred by the rapid development of information technologies and their ubiquitous use in industrial applications, the academic and practical interest in knowledge management has dramatically increased.[16] As the proliferation of intranets and the Internet affected intra- and intercorporate communications, integration of R&D with commercial activities became much more feasible and less onerous.

Cooperation, Consortia, and Networks

Finally, a trend that accompanied the reorientation of industrial R&D was the growth in number and categories/types of technology cooperation, consortia, and networks among industrial companies. What had begun in the mid-1980s as a movement to forestall the Japanese market superiority in particular industries (such as in computers and integrated circuits) continued to expand in the 1990s. From dedicated consortia such as SEMATECH and MCC, companies moved to a continuing string of forming technology-based cooperative efforts and networks.[17]

Such cooperation and networking programs were established among companies in the same industry, as well as across industries. At the end of the 1990s, it was not uncommon to have large companies in the computer or electronics industries maintain a complex web of dozens of cooperative programs with most of their competitors, its vendors, and other companies across related industries. Such programs have contributed to the ability of American industry to reorient its R&D investments and to restructure its processes. Outsourcing of technology became more commonplace, thus diminishing even further the traditional role of the internal R&D function in the industrial firm.[18]

SUMMARY

The brief historical review of how U.S. industrial R&D has evolved provided only a cursory description of the intricate processes in the development of this function. Clearly, industrial R&D today is an institutionalized activity in most corporations. As a percent of sales, some industries expend in excess of 20 percent on their R&D, whereas 4 percent is an average in the less R&D-intensive industries.

The financial picture notwithstanding, and regardless of the continuous transformations of this activity, industrial R&D in the United States is a well-established and recognized capability of the firm. Overall, the 20th century has witnessed the growth of industrial R&D from an activity of tinkering with inventions, to a more than $100 billion constellation of laboratories and entrepreneurial effort. These have led to the present era in which industry is highly innovative, agile, and competitive.[19]

This historical perspective provides a substantive background to the conceptual and theoretical foundations described later in the book. The growth and current trends of S&T as a critical activity in the economy clearly show the need to evaluate the outputs and benefits from this activity. Furthermore, since S&T is such a major component of corporate activity, its evaluation must be anchored in solid conceptual framework.

NOTES

1. There are over 700 federal R&D/technology laboratories, and about 15,000 industrial laboratories. A simple count is somewhat deceiving, due to the trend in the 1990s, in which American companies began to internationalize their R&D. Essentially, many American companies "outsourced" their R&D to foreign countries and foreign companies—not always their own subsidiaries. See, for example, Bowker, R. (ed.), *Directory of American Research and Technology 1999* (New York: R. R. Bowker, 1998).

2. For the early attempts of hegemony of American companies in the global marketplace, and the history of the larger American manufacturers, see, Hounshell, D., and Smith, J., *Science and Corporate Strategy: DuPont R&D, 1902-1980* (Cambridge: Cambridge University Press, 1988). This is an absorbing book. The authors had access to DuPont executives and records, thus they were able to compile an engaging history of the giant manufacturer. Their focus was on the policies, boardroom decisions and processes, and strategies of the company during its "boom and bust" periods of this century. Also see, Reich, L., *Making of American Research, Science, and Business at GE & Bell, 1876-1926* (Cambridge: Cambridge University Press, 1985). Reich has provided a solid history of the origins and development of the research arm at General Electric and American Telephone and Telegraph (AT&T). Reich's book is a fascinating historical account of the struggle of individual technologists in setting up and in fostering the research laboratory in a large corporation. By highlighting the evolving culture in the company—in which science and technology were gradually linked to business interests and successes—Reich was able to create a story that transcends the more historical development of corporate R&D laboratories.

3. See, for example, Gray, C., *Technohistory: Using the History of American Technology in Interdisciplinary Research* (New York: Krieger Publishing Company, 1995).

4. As mentioned before, research and development and science and technology are used interchangeably in this first part of the book.

5. See, for example, Foerstel, H., *Secret Science: Federal Control of American Science and Technology* (Westport, CT: Greenwood Press, 1993). The author advances the thesis that federal influence on American science (particularly in industry) is harmful to the full exploitation of the outputs from R&D. Foerstel has maintained that the defense-oriented agencies of the federal government are obsessed with secrecy, hence severely limiting technology transfer within companies and between federal laboratories and industry. I disagree with his thesis in my discussion of federal laboratories in Chapter 2.

6. Source: National Science Foundation, *Science Indicators-1982* (Washington, D.C., NSB 83-1, Appendix Table 2-7) p. 239.

7. See, for example, Afua, A., and J. Utterback, "Responding to Structural Industry Changes: A Technological Evolution Perspective," Working Paper, Sloan School of Management, MIT, 1995; and, Utterback, J., *Mastering the Dynamics of Innovation* (Boston: Harvard Business School Press, 1994).

8. See, for example, Shooshaw, H. (ed.), *Disconnecting Bell: The Impact of the AT&T Divestiture* (New York: Elsevier Science, 1984). Also see, Cole, B. (ed.), *After the Breakup: Assessing the New Post-AT&T Divestiture Era* (New York: Columbia University Press, 1991).

9. For a comprehensive and insightful description of the structure of U.S. industrial R&D in the decentralized structure of large American companies, see Rubenstein, A. H., *Managing Technology in the Decentralized Firm* (New York: John Wiley & Sons, 1989).

10. See Geisler, E., "When Whales Are Cast Ashore: The Conversion to Relevancy of U.S. Basic Research and Universities," *IEEE Transactions on Engineering Management*, 41(1), 1995, 3-8.

11. Another consequence has been the focusing of R&D assessment in terms of efficiency and cost-effectiveness.

12. Iansiti, M., and J. West, "Technology Integration: Turning Great Research into Great Products," *Harvard Business Review*, 75(3), 1997, 69-79.

13. See, for example, Jolly, V., *Commercializaing New Technologies: Getting from Mind to Market* (Boston: Harvard Business School Press, 1997).

14. Professor Jolly of Lausanne's International Institute for Management Development has written a book that characterizes the new perspective. He has proposed the transformation of the corporate R&D function into small, quasi-independent units, linked to the products and processes that are potentially favored by the marketplace.

15. Geisler, 1995, *op. cit.* Also see Buderi, R., *Engines of Tomorrow: How the World's Best Companies Are Using Their Research Labs to Win the Future* (New York: Simon & Schuster, 2000). Buderi argued that some individual companies are at the forefront of their industries, thanks to their R&D effort. Buderi is an excellent raconteur of these selected cases of success, but he fails to establish a sound relationship between R&D and the commercial success of these companies (IBM, Siiemens, NEC, GE, and Bell Labs).

16. See, for example, Iansiti, M., *Technology Integration: Making Critical Choices in a Dynamic World* (Boston: Harvard Business School Press, 1997). Also

see Brown, J. S., *Seeing Differently: Insights on Innovation* (Boston: Harvard Business School Press, 1997).

17. For example, see Davenport, T., and L. Prusak, *Working Knowledge: How Organizations Manage What They Know* (Boston: Harvard Business School Press, 1997). Also see Allee, V., *The Knowledge Evolution: Expanding, Organizational Intelligence* (New York: Butterworth-Heinemann, 1997).

18. See, for example, Gibson, D., and E. Rogers, *R&D Collaboration on Trial: The Microelectronics and Computer Technology Corporation* (Boston: Harvard Business School Press, 1994).

19. The role of technology-based consortia, cooperative programs, and networks is further discussed in Chapters 2 and 3 of this book.

2

PUBLIC INVESTMENTS IN
SCIENCE AND TECHNOLOGY

One can only marvel at the legendary laboratory of Los Alamos where the first atomic bomb was produced. But we readily forget the vast network of technology laboratories that are a national patrimony in the United States. This network is an array of over 700 different R&D/technology laboratories funded by the American taxpayers. Although other countries such as the United Kingdom, Russia, Japan, and Germany have national research centers in the areas of energy, defense, and health, the American federal laboratories are a unique phenomenon.

The federal laboratories are spread over all regions of the country and represent a major intellectual and economic force in many states (e.g., New Mexico, Illinois, and California). Almost every department of the federal government has one or more technology institutes. A high concentration of large laboratories is found within the federal Departments of Defense (DOD), Energy, Agriculture, Health and Human Services, Commerce, and Transportation. The space agency (NASA) and the Environmental Protection Agency are not directly subordinated to a given department, but rather are stand-alone agencies, each with a network of dedicated laboratories.[1]

FUNDING THE LABORATORIES

The network of federal laboratories has mushroomed in the period after the Second World War.[2] In the late 1990s, the 726 laboratories routinely consumed a substantial portion of the American federal investments in science and technology.

Figure 2.1 shows the internal R&D budgets of the top 40 laboratories in 1995. The first 25 laboratories, commonly referred to as "superlabs," consume about half of the annual federal budget for R&D. However, in addition to *internal* R&D, many laboratories contract out much of their R&D activities. The National Institutes of Health had, in the late 1990s, an annual budget of around $1 billion, but spent over $10 billion in contracted research. The total funding of the federal laboratories (internal R&D *and* contracts) averaged annually around $40 billion. Of this total, funding for defense-related R&D consumed about 35 percent of the budget, followed by health with 25 percent, energy with 20 percent, and NASA with 20 percent.[3]

Funding of the national laboratories is intricately tied to their mission and outcomes. However needed for the accomplishment of the objectives of their parent agencies, the national laboratories also enjoy wide public support. For example, in the issue of technology maturation, some researchers have argued that in the mid-1990s, the DOE laboratories had been working on alternative energy R&D programs, which these researchers deemed to be "largely incompatible with the nation's energy policy."[4]

In general, the American taxpayer is largely unaware of the subtleties of funding the national laboratories. There is, however, an aura of vitality that, in the mind of citizens, seems to be attached to these laboratories. There is also a sense of "public good" that Americans seem to associate with their federal laboratories. For instance, laboratories that support the environmental protection mandate, space exploration, or the development of new weapons for national security are viewed as a positive outlet for funding with tax dollars.[5]

In the evaluation of public R&D and technology, congressional committees that oversee funding of agencies and their laboratories are much more critical and discerning. These committees routinely scrutinize the funding patterns of laboratories, with emphasis on their relevance to the overall mission of the parent agency and according to criteria of the laboratories' performance. Although the allocation of resources to the parent agencies and laboratories is a complex process of politics, regional preferences, and other factors, lawmakers are also concerned with international competition. Since the 1970s, they have continually recognized that in Western Europe and Japan science and technology are openly and tenaciously supported by public funding. Thus, scrutiny of funding the national laboratories is attenuated by the desire to maintain American competitiveness at home and in international markets.[6] In a different venue, the scrutiny of national laboratories is also moderated by the long-held belief that, through their outcomes and the value they create, national laboratories not only support

Figure 2.1
Top Federal Laboratories in 1995

	Laboratory	Parent Agency	FY-95 Internal R&D Budget* (in billions)	Total
1.	Goddard Spaceflight Ctr.	NASA	1.25	
2.	National Institutes of Health	HHS	1.20	
3.	Sandia National Labs	US DOE	1.20	
4.	Los Alamos National Lab	US DOE	1.00	
5.	Lawrence Livermore	US DOE	0.906	
6.	Idaho National Eng.	US DOE	0.836	
7.	Agricultural Research Serv.	USDA	0.688	
8.	Lyndon B. Johnson Space Ctr.	NASA	0.660	
9.	Oak Ridge National Lab	US DOE	0.572	
10.	US Geological Survey	D of Int.	0.571	8.883
11.	Phillips Laboratory	USAF	0.550	
12.	Naval Research Lab	US Navy	0.507	
13.	Naval Air Warfare	US Navy	0.501	
14.	Marshall Space Flight	NASA	0.492	
15.	Lewis Research Center	NASA	0.490	
16.	Air Force Flight Test	USAF	0.482	
17.	Naval Surface Warfare	US Navy	0.411	
18.	Natl. Oceanic & Atmospheric Adm		0.400	
19.	Ames Research Center	NASA	0.372	
20.	Jet Propulsion Lab	NASA	0.368	
21.	Pacific Northwest Lab	US DOE	0.350	
22.	Argonne National Lab	US DOE	0.325	
23.	Langley Research Center	NASA	0.300	
24.	Surface Warfare: Dahlgren	US Navy	0.296	
25.	US Army Research Lab	US Army	0.284	15.011
26.	Natl. Inst. of Stds. & Tech.	D Comm.	0.265	
27.	Brookhaven National Lab	US DOE	0.261	
28.	Airforce Develop. Test Center	US AF	0.238	
29.	Lawrence Berkeley	US DOE	0.224	
30.	Naval Air Warfare Weapons Div.	US Navy	0.212	
31.	Wright Laboratory	USAF	0.208	
32.	US Army R&D & Engineering	US Army	0.207	
33.	Naval Undersea Warfare	US Navy	0.193	
34.	Cmd., Control., & Ocean Surv.	US Navy	0.161	
35.	Waterways Experiment	US Army	0.160	
36.	Natl. Renewable Energy Lab	US DOE	0.130	
37.	Armstrong Lab	USAF	0.135	
38.	Rome Laboratory	USAF	0.130	
39.	Air Warfare: Warminster	US Navy	0.108	
40.	Savannah River	US DOE	0.105	17.748

Source: *Technology Transfer Business*, Summer, 1995, pp. 38-46.

*These numbers are in-house R&D budgets. NASA and DOE do not routinely track their R&D by internal versus external budgets. Military laboratories routinely track their internal R&D as distinguished from externally contracted. These numbers also reflect some of the recent cuts in the budgets of the laboratories. The authors of this list in Technology Transfer Business surveyed directors of laboratories to obtain the unpublished data on internal R&D budgets.

their parent agencies, but also contribute to the larger benefit of the public. The following sections address this issue.

MISSION AND OUTCOMES

It seems logical that spending an excess of 40 billion tax dollars annually on a network of R&D/technology laboratories will require justification beyond merely national pride and a sense that public value is being generated. Historically, the laboratories were created to support the mission of the parent agency.

For example, the Agricultural Research Service (ARS) established its six-year implementation plan of 1984-1990 to reflect the following objectives. First, to "maintain emphasis on mission-oriented fundamental, long-range, high risk research."[7] Second, and more specifically, to "emphasize research approaches directed toward increasing efficiency of operation and quality of products, reducing the use of non-renewable resources (soil, water, fuels) and increasing the dollar value of agricultural products."[8]

Traditionally, ARS is perhaps the oldest research system in the federal government. It evolved from the agricultural stations and the system of agents who have assisted American farmers for over a century. The mission of ARS has also evolved to include research on conservation and to support the national agricultural policy.

By comparison, the National Institute for Occupational Safety and Health (NIOSH) is a relative newcomer to the federal network of laboratories. NIOSH was created in 1970, when Congress passed the Occupational Safety and Health Act. The act called for the establishment of the Occupational Safety and Health Administration (OSHA) as an enforcement agency of standards for the workplace. NIOSH was created to carry out the research function for maintaining a healthy and safe work environment.

Interestingly enough, unlike the case of the ARS and defense and energy laboratories, NIOSH is subordinated to the federal Department of Health and Human Services (DHHS), whereas OSHA is part of the Department of Labor. The mission of OSHA is: "to save lives, prevent injuries, and protect the health of America's workers."[9]

The mission of NIOSH is to: "Provide national and world leadership to prevent work-related illness, injury, and death by gathering information, conducting scientific research, and translating the knowledge gained into products and services."[10] The mission statements for the enforcement and the research arm are similar, but the administrative disjointment provides a certain flexibility to the research laboratories. This separation may also prevent potential conflicts of interests between the organization that sets the standards (through scientific research) and the one that enforces them.

However, the missions of ARS and NIOSH reveal a phenomenon that is quite prevalent among federal technology laboratories. This is the "mission-outcomes dilemma," which may be operationally defined as the gap between what is expected of the laboratory and its actual outcomes.

What is expected of the federal laboratories? As their mission is closely tied to the mission of the parent agency or to a national goal or policy (as in the cases of NIOSH, NASA, and EPA), this mission becomes a lofty vision of grandiose national proportions. When one reads the mission statements, one wonders about the link between research outcomes and what the laboratory is expected to accomplish.

The public laboratories do support, via the outcomes from their research and development, some of the more inscrutable and politically charged national objectives. The laboratories are aware of the fact that their performance is not enough, and that in order to accomplish their mission they need the cooperation of other entities (industry, their parent and other government agencies, and the scientific community). This dilemma was a factor throughout the 1990s in the rise of such issues as commercialization and technology transfer.

COMMERCIALIZATION OF PUBLIC-SECTOR TECHNOLOGY

If the federal laboratories are viewed as more than simply research support of their parent agencies, then the discussion about them and their value to the country invariably moves to a different level. In the early years after the Second World War, the laboratories were created and imbued with the mission to provide scientific and technical support to government departments and agencies. This meant that the laboratories were engaged in dedicated research, designed to explore fundamental questions in the specific disciplines related to the mission of the agency. The portfolio of research projects selected by the laboratories was directed internally, without much thought about the possible dissemination to outsiders, besides a select group of scientists in the disciplinary area.

The changing policy toward commercialization began in the 1970s, and received legislative cogency in the early 1980s. These periods of transformations and tribulations are summarized in Figure 2.2.

Figure 2.2
Historical Periods of Transformation in the Approach Toward
Commercialization of Outcomes from the National Laboratories

HISTORICAL PERIODS*	MAIN CHARACTERISTICS
I. Mission Oriented (1945-1974)	• Inwardly directed science and technology • Little or no incentives or directions for commercialization
II. Awareness (1975-1980)	• Awareness of accumulated capital of public technology • Initial formation of technology transfer programs
III. Formalization through Legislation (1981-1989)	• Congress legislated technology transfer in 1980, 1986, & 1988 • Dilemma of the Reagan mandate • Initial evaluations
IV. Accountability & Reformulation (1990-1999)	• Post cold-war climate leads to pressures to commercialize • Technology transfer assumes its own momentum • Cases of success and failure
V. Identity Crisis (2000-)	• The "privatization" debate • Structural uncertainty • Emerging new formats

Boundary dates for the historical periods are arbitrary.

Mission-Oriented (1945-1974)

The first period, between 1945 and 1974, was characterized by adherence to the mission of the parent agencies. It was essentially an "in-house" operation, where the contributions from the laboratories were assessed from the viewpoint of the federal constituencies.

Awareness (1975-1980)

The late 1970s were a period of awakening. This was due primarily to the increased emphasis on federal support for social issues, coupled with concerns and questions about massive programs such as space and defense technology, which seemed to provide little, if any, spin offs to civilian and social causes of urgency.[11] Doubts about the social legitimacy of massive investments in federal R&D/technology began to emerge. Questions such as: "Did we *really* need to spend $10 billion to put a man on the moon?" became commonplace, helping to somewhat erode public support for such programs. Combined with the end of the war in Vietnam, questions began to emerge concerning the massive investments in defense-related technology.

On both sides of the debate, the issue led to demands for, and attempts to, justify such investments. An attractive compromise seemed to be the "spinning-off" of existing technologies in the federal arsenal (and those to be generated by the network of laboratories) to industrial and other social recipients. This intensified the phenomenon, variably named "technology transfer," "commercialization," and, in the case of defense, "technology conversion" and "technology reinvestment." The culmination of this trend of increased awareness to the possible utilization of federal technology for social and economic purposes led to the establishment of the enabling legislation of the 1980s.[12]

Formalization (1981-1989)

Formalization through legislation was the main aspect of the period 1981-1989. The Stevenson-Wydler Act of 1980 was followed by the Federal Technology Transfer Act of 1986. Stevenson-Wydler instructed federal laboratories to create specialized offices for technology transfer and to carry out this function. In 1986 legislation was expanded to facilitate technology transfer and provide incentives to federal employees engaged in such activities. In 1989, the National Competitiveness Technology Transfer Act (NCTTA) provided laboratories with the tools to undertake cost-shared collaboration with industry. The legislation removed some of the obvious barriers to such an effort, particularly such issues as intellectual capital and industry's ability to benefit from public technology.

Yet the national laboratories had to contend with a dilemma of choosing between their portfolio and the need to commercialize their outputs. Simply put, the Reagan administration, in its pursuit of cold-war policies, did not encourage technology transfer, particularly in defense and other sensitive areas of federal R&D. At the same time, this administration also pursued a policy of more freedom from regulation and support for private industry. Within this policy, the administration strongly encouraged federal laboratories to concentrate on exploratory and high risk technologies, and avoid any R&D that would compete with private industry. Such a choice of an R&D portfolio made commercialization even more difficult, because it helped to intensify the gap between outcomes from public laboratories and the needs and willingness of private companies to adopt such outcomes.

The director of a large national laboratory expressed this dilemma in an interview conducted in the late 1980s. "I would tell my managers to go on and perform technology transfer, but to not let me catch them doing it!," he said with all seriousness.[13] The dilemma was also exacerbated by evaluations of failures in the effort to commercialize. However, the trend had been set, enabling legislation was in place, and the national laboratories had to continue and even accelerate their technology transfer activities.

Federal funding for public R&D followed the purpose of these policies. Total obligations for the Department of Defense (in constant 1987 dollars) rose by 78 percent in the period 1980-1987. In 1987 the defense expenditures peaked. For the decade 1980-1989 defense expenditures for R&D, in constant 1987 dollars, rose by 75 percent, or 61 percent of total federal obligations to all agencies in 1989.

By the same token, during the Reagan years (1981-1988), obligations for socially related R&D also increased sharply. The Department of Health and Human Services (DHHS) had its obligations for R&D rise by 48 percent (in constant 1987 dollars), while obligations for the National Institutes of Health (NIH) increased in this period by 50 percent. By comparison with defense, in 1989 the DHHS and NIH combined obligations for R&D amounted to 24 percent of the total for all agencies. In terms of public investments in technology, the Reagan administration had delivered on both "guns" and "butter."[14]

Accountability (1990-1999)

The 1990s were a period in which two converging phenomena occurred. First, the end of the cold war propelled a climate of reduction in public support for investments in defense, including defense-related technology. Second, with increased accountability and scarce resources, the federal establishment was also influenced by the reengineering phenomenon that private industry had embraced. Thus, accountability has generated reformulation of priorities in public investments. Pressures to commercialize the pool of public technology have gained popularity, eventually evolving into a debate about the future and ownership of the national laboratories.

The key topic was the idea of "privatization" of some or all the federal laboratories. The primary target was energy laboratories. Although, as shown in Figure 2.3, the obligations for the Department of Energy have decreased between 1981 and 1991 by almost 20 percent (in constant 1987 dollars), there emerged some critics, primarily in industrial circles, who advocated privatization.

Yet even the more vocal critics of the federal laboratories did not go as far as to advocate dismantling the system. On their part, directors of the labora-

Figure 2.3
Federal Obligations for Total R&D, By Agency, for Selected Years

(in billions of constant 1987 dollars)

Agency	1980	81	82	83	84	85	86	87	88	89	90
All Agencies	42.2	42.5	43.5	44.5	46.4	51.2	52.9	55.2	54.9	56.7	56.4
Dept. of Defense	19.8	21.2	24.6	26.4	27.9	31.6	33.9	35.2	34.1	34.7	33.0
Dept. of Energy	6.7	6.3	5.6	5.2	5.1	5.2	4.8	4.7	4.8	4.7	4.9
Dept. of Health & Human Services	5.3	5.0	4.7	5.0	5.3	5.7	5.8	6.6	6.9	7.3	7.4
National Institutes of Health	4.5	4.2	4.1	4.3	4.6	5.1	5.1	5.8	6.0	6.2	6.3
NASA	4.5	4.6	3.6	3.0	3.1	3.5	3.5	3.7	4.1	4.9	5.8

Source: National Science Board, *Science and Engineering Indicators-1993*, Washington, DC, NSB 93-1.

tories went on the defensive by emphasizing the ability of their current format—to contribute to the American competitive position. Alan Schresheim, director of Argonne National Laboratory, exemplified such pronouncements when he argued in 1991 that "the national laboratories are a reservoir of scientific and technological talent that can help America compete in international markets."[15] Similarly, accounts of successful stories of commercialization of publicly-supported technology began to emerge.[16]

Arguments for radical changes in both ownership and mode of operation of the national laboratories were based in part on the lack of substantial success stories of commercialization and technology transfer. I disagree with Foerstel, for example, who argued that the federal government's obsession with secrecy severely hindered commercialization.[17] Inadequate transfer also occurred in such areas as agriculture and environment, where secrecy was not an issue.[18]

Identity Crisis (2000-)

Although the call for reformulation of the network of federal laboratories peaked in the mid-1990s, I believe that there has been little erosion in public support for federal science and technology. The debate on privatization generated a climate of uncertainty within the laboratories. Yet, due perhaps to the public's disfavorable view of corporate restructuring, coupled with the economic growth of the late 1990s, the support for public investments in technology has not eroded in any meaningful way.

Other factors for continuing support may include the well-publicized successes of the space shuttles and the space station, coupled with continuous increases in public investments in R&D directed toward medical technology and other socially preferred causes.

SUMMARY

The trends in public investments in the federal network of laboratories reflect the nation's wishes and expectations. In the years since the Second World War, the American taxpayers have invested over a trillion dollars in this network. The agreed-upon allocation of these dollars to certain categories of expenditures seems to closely follow the general mood in the nation regarding preferences in the allocation of the federal budget. It boils down to the priorities in channeling tax dollars to activities of urgency in the given budget period.

In the final analysis, although the trends showed fluctuations to one side or another, Americans had a consistent view toward public science and technology. Over the second half of the 20th century they have opted to invest—almost equally—in defense-oriented technology (and similar areas such as energy and space exploration) and in socially oriented technology (e.g., health, environment, and transportation).

NOTES

1. See, for example, Bozeman, B., and M. Crow, *Limited by Design: R and D Laboratories in the US National Innovation System* (New York: Columbia University Press, 1998). This is a comprehensive book authored by two knowledgeable scholars in the study of federal laboratories. See, in particular, chapter 3, "A Snapshot of US R&D Laboratories in the National Innovation System: Structure, Output, and Design."

2. The terms *federal, national,* and *public* laboratories are used here interchangeably.

3. See Kassicieh, S., and R. Radosevich, *From Lab to Market: Commercialization of Public Sector Technology* (New York: Plenum Press, 1994).

4. Radosevich, R., and S. Kassicieh, "The King Solomon Role in Public-Sector Technology Commercialization," in Kassicieh and Radosevich, 1994, *op. cit.*, p. 17.

5. See, for example, Link, A., "Evaluating the Advanced Technology Program: A Preliminary Assessment of Economic Impacts," *International Journal of Technology Management, Special Issue on Industry-Government-University Cooperation*, Vol. 8, 6/7/8, 1993, 726-739.

6. See, for instance, Committee on Science, Engineering, and Public Policy, *Science, Technology and the Federal Government: National Goals for a New Era* (National Academy of Sciences, National Academy of Engineering, Institute of Medicine, Washington, DC: National Academy Press, 1993).

7. USDA-ARS, *The Mission of Science and Education Administration: Agricultural Research* (Washington, DC: September 1980) p. 12.

8. *Ibid.*

9. See the website of the agency at <http://www.OSHA.gov>.

10. See the website for NIOSH at <http://www.colc.gov/niosh>.

11. For example, see Mechlin, G., and D. Berg, "Evaluating Research—ROI Is Not Enough," *Harvard Business Review*, 58(3), September-October, 1980, 93-99; and Salasin, J., *The Evaluation of Federal Research Programs*, MITRE Technical Report, 80W129, June 1980. Also, National Aeronautics and Space Administration, *Useful Technology From Space Research*, Technology Utilization Program, Washington, DC, 1968; and Saunders, N., *Overview of NASA/OAST Efforts Related to Manufacturing Technology*, NASA Technical Memorandum, TMX-73583, November, 1976.

12. See, for example, Galvin, R., "Forming a World-Class Future for the National Laboratories," *Issues in Science and Technology*, Fall 1995, 67-72; also see Hecker, S., "Retargetting the Weapons Laboratories," *Issues in Science and Technology*, Spring 1994, 44-51.

13. Private communication to the author.

14. National Science Board, *Science and Engineering Indicators-1993*, Washington, D.C., NSB 93-1.

15. Schresheim, A., "Toward a Golden Age for Technology Transfer," *Issues in Science and Technology*, Winter 1991, 52-58.

16. For example, Ross, S., "DOE's Energy Technology Program Yields Commercial Inventions," *Technology Transfer Week*, 2(12), 1998, 6-10.

17. Foerstel, H., *Secret Science: Federal Control of American Science and Technology* (Westport, CT: Greenwood Publishing Group, 1993).

18. Similar arguments regarding secrecy can also be found in Kassicieh and Radosevich, 1994, *op. cit.*

3

DEVELOPMENT OF PARTNERSHIPS

In the late 1980s, and more intensely in the 1990s, a wave of partnerships engulfed American science and technology organizations. Similar to the strategic partnership and cooperative programs that industrial and service companies had embraced, science and technology did not lag behind.[1]

Industrial cooperation in R&D and technology became a reality due to several legislative and regulatory activities that attenuated the fierce anti-monopoly laws. As competition from abroad stiffened, American lawmakers and their advisors began to realize that intense competition among American companies might not yield the best atmosphere for the generation of commercial products that would have enough attributes to be globally competitive. They also realized that the process of commercialization within individual companies might not be efficient enough to produce the necessary degree of exploitation of the vast array of knowledge embedded in industry, government, and universities.[2]

Based also in part on the lessons learned from Japan and European countries, American companies and government policy-makers concluded that in order to accelerate the application of R&D into marketable products, a certain degree of cooperation would be useful.[3] In particular, the emphasis was on precompetitive cooperation, whereby the time to market would be shortened by joint effort at the R&D stage of the process. Such a strategic solution to America's competitiveness weakness was seen as a creative way to sustain a bridge between the Reagan-Bush policy of economic conservatism, and the

Clinton administration's desire to have the government play a more drastic role in industrial policy.

Support for cooperation thus emerged over the two-decade period from various quarters of industry and government. As federal laboratories had been confined to concentrating on exploratory research, they were also encouraged to transfer to industry technology they had already accumulated. Thus, the three components of science and technology—industry, government, and universities—embarked on a process of trying to collaborate within and among each other.

In 1984 Congress passed the National Cooperative Research Act (NCRA) and within a year almost 50 consortia had been formed. By 1998 over 400 consortia had registered with the government, involving some 3,800 domestic companies, 800 foreign companies, over 220 universities, and 40 federal laboratories. Areas of technical cooperation included microelectronics, computer science, telecommunications, medical technology, automotive, material sciences, manufacturing, and transportation.[4]

CONSORTIA AND CRADAs

Two major instruments that facilitated cooperation in R&D and technology are the consortia model for companies and government, and the creation of the Cooperative Research and Development Agreement (CRADA) for government laboratories. Both instruments have legal and organizational qualities that have enabled otherwise competitive entities to engage in cooperative efforts.

Consortia are a form of cooperation in which companies institute *formal* networks, designed to exchange, transfer, and create specific technologies and their ultimate commercialization. Two examples come to mind. The first is the Microelectronics and Computer Technology Corporation (MCC), founded in 1982 by a group of 16 companies. This was an R&D consortium, in a very specific area of cooperation, formed under the specter of threatening Japanese superiority in microelectronics and computer technology.

The second example is SEMATECH (Semiconductor Manufacturing Technology Initiative), established in 1987, with the purpose of joining corporate and government know-how to develop tools and equipment for the manufacturing of semiconductors. The aim of SEMATECH was to ultimately restore to the United States the leadership position in manufacturing, in general, and, in particular, the computer field. Thus, 13 corporate members of the Semiconductor Industry Association (SIA) formally created the consortium in May, 1987. In December of that year Congress had approved federal funding of 100 million dollars for the consortium. In 1988 the consortium was established in Austin, Texas. By 1993, the mission of this consortium was modified to help "solve the technical challenges required to keep the United States number one in the global semiconductor industry."[5] In the decade that followed, there have been successes and disappointments in the performance of MCC and SEMATECH.

Cooperative Research and Development Agreements (CRADAs) are an instrument developed by the government to allow federal laboratories to collaborate with industry and universities. Such collaboration was based on the main purpose of transferring federal technology. In order to circumvent issues of proprietary technology and the need for competitive bidding for any government goods and services, CRADA became a legal and organizational tool that allowed federal laboratories to establish cooperation with selected companies, without the trouble of general bidding.[6] Other constraints, such as transfer of patents to private companies and the noncompetitive use of federal installations for profit-seeking enterprises, were also addressed by CRADA. These instruments were so successful that they formed the backbone of the organizational aspects of cooperation between federal laboratories and other parties. In fact, much of the assessment of the success of such cooperation continues to be measured as the number of CRADAs signed.[7]

SUMMARY

Cooperation and consortia in science and technology are still a major force in the American as well as the global environment of technology. Although informal cooperation among scientists has always been a mainstay of scientific progress, the trend in the last two decades of the 20th century has been to create and sustain *formal* collaborative entities. The jury is still out for many of these cooperations and partnerships. In part, a shared charac-teristic—at least in the beginning—has been high expectations for a short term flow of positive results. Historically, however, these partnerships have adapted and modified their goals and structure—as political, economic, and technical changes reconstituted the landscape of American and global economies.

In the final analysis, partnering in science and technology has not been a story of great successes nor of unbearable failures. Constrained by design and factors of economic, political, and legal realities, partnerships have now become a different, yet increasingly popular organizational mechanism to advance the creation and commercialization of technology.[8]

NOTES

1. See, for example, Geisler, E., "On the Importance of University-Industry Government Cooperation: A Global Perspective," *International Journal of*

Technology Management, 8(6/7/8), 1993, 435-439. Also see Betz, F., "Academic/ Government/Industry Strategic Research Partnerships," *The Journal of Technology Transfer*, 22(3), 1997, 9-16.

2. See, for example, Kozmetzky, G., "Prologue," in: D. Gibson and E. Rogers, *R&D Collaboration on Trial: The Microelectronics and Computer Technology Corporation* (Boston: Harvard Business School Press, 1994), pp. xxiii-xxvi.

3. See Okimoto, D., T. Sugano, and F. Weinstein, *Competitive Edge: The Semiconductor Industry in the U.S. and Japan* (Stanford, CA: Stanford University Press, 1984). Also see Ledeboen, W., and T. Gorter, "ESPRIT: Successful Industrial R&D Cooperation in Europe," *International Journal of Technology Management*, 8(6/7/8), 1993, 528-543.

4. See Gibson and Rogers, 1994, *op. cit.*, pp. 21-22, and Myata, Y., "An Analysis of Cooperative R&D in the United States," *Technovation*, 16(3), 1990, 123-131. Also see Geisler, E., "The Metrics of Intersector Technology Cooperation," *INFORMS*, Seattle Meeting, Fall 1998, October 25-28, 1998.

5. Gibson and Rogers, 1994, *op. cit.*, p. 505.

6. See, for example, Joly, P., and V. Mangematin, "Profile of Public Laboratories, Industrial Partnerships, and Organization of R&D: The Dynamics of Industrial Relationships in a Large Research Organization," *Research Policy*, 25(5), 1996, 901-922.

7. See Souder, W., "Getting Together: A State-of-the-Art Review of the Challenges and Rewards of Consortia," *International Journal of Technology Management*, 8(6/7/8), 1993, 784-801. Also see Sultan, F., and L. Chan, "The Adoption of New Technology: The Case of Object-Oriented Computing in Software Companies," *IEEE Transactions on Engineering Management*, 47(1), 2000, 106-126.

8. See Geisler, E., "Intersector Technology Cooperation: Hard Myths, Soft Facts," *Technovation*, 17(6), 1997, 309-320.

4

A PERSONAL VIEW

Historically the development of large-scale science and technology in human affairs in general, and in the United States in particular, has been a process of growth, learning, and adaptation. In the 20th century, and more so in the second half of the century, science and technology rose to a level never before achieved by any human endeavor in such a short period of time. Science and technology became a major area of investment and a powerful force in society and in the economies of the United States and of the rest of the world.

There are two interrelated questions that beg to be asked: (1) Is science and technology shaping our world today, and especially, will it shape it in the years to come? and (2) How can we evaluate the value created by science and technology?

Some scenarios of the 21st century have advocated a substantial role for S&T in shaping social and economic conditions in the United States and the rest of the planet.[1] Regardless of how powerful their role is in the future of human affairs, science and technology have been transformed into a force well beyond the confines of the laboratory, not only because of the massive investments in such activities, but also because of the outcomes and benefits from them.[2] There seems to be a phenomenon in which S&T has an internal dynamic that allows for growth and evolution. With large-scale organizational configurations in all sectors of the economy, S&T thus develops by sheer magnitude of its size and corresponding influence.[3]

In the final analysis, S&T in the United States and other developed countries will be assessed not only on its own growth and sustainability, but primarily on its outcomes and other impacts—including negative effects on people, organizations, and the environment. The total assessment would be a balancing out of all that S&T has accomplished, as well as its future impacts. Yet the long road for such an evaluation starts with the understanding of the conceptual and theoretical foundation for the assessment, and with the set of tools we possess for evaluating the value that S&T creates.

The theme that runs throughout this book is a reflection of my own beliefs and biases. It considers S&T, on balance, a positive influence on the economy and society, and a force that has contributed to better living conditions for a growing portion of the world's population. The theme also heralds the notion that such positive influences will continue in the foreseeable future, and that the value created by S&T outweighs the negative side effects that S&T may generate.[4]

Another aspect of this theme is the belief that we possess an adequate toolbox of ways and means to measure and evaluate the impacts from S&T on society and the economy. As we proceed in the following chapters, I unfold the theoretical bases for evaluation of S&T, and the various dimensions of value that S&T creates will begin to emerge and will be described.

I believe that S&T has generated—and will continue to do so—a vast array of valuable outcomes for society and the economy of all nations. Although some countries have benefitted more readily and to a greater extent from such value, the impacts from S&T nevertheless reverberate throughout the world. Values from S&T have impacted, and will continue to impact, rich and poor nations alike.

I believe that S&T has generally produced value that can be measured in terms of goods, services, knowledge, and overall has extended human capabilities and human abilities not only to survive, but also to improve living conditions for the present generations and for those that will follow.

Moreover, as S&T has permeated almost every aspect of the human condition, our currently available evaluation frameworks and instruments may not be able to entirely capture all the benefits accrued from S&T. I believe that even if we are able to assess only a small portion of the value generated by S&T, the investments in S&T may have been worthwhile. To consider the 21st century without the accomplishments from S&T and the value thus created is to me unimaginable.[5]

Historically, we are essentially in the beginning. We have only recently begun to systematically address the results from the magnificent growth of S&T in our own life-time. The generation of this writer, and even younger generations, are both historical eye-witnesses and judges of the tremendous transformations that have accompanied the growth in S&T. The long march begins with the theoretical foundations of evaluating this phenomenon.[6]

In Part II of this book I discuss the theoretical foundations of measuring and evaluating S&T. These chapters are the prelude to a detailed look at the evaluation of research, technology, and innovation that are given in Part III.

NOTES

1. See, for example, Coates, J., and J. Contes, *2025: Scenarios of US and Global Society Reshaped by Science and Technology* (New York: Oak Hill Press, 1996); and Davies, O., and M. Cetron, *Probable Tommorrows: How Science and Technology Will Transform Our Lives in the Next Twenty Years* (New York: St. Martin's Press, 1997).

2. In 1998, for example, American industry invested $143 billion in R&D. Federal investments were $63 billion and universities and other not-for-profit organizations invested over $10 billion in R&D. In 1999 federal expenditures for R&D rose by almost 2.5 percent over 1998. The optimistic overall national S&T plan at that time called for an increase of 32 percent for the period 1999-2004.

3. See Hameri, A., "Innovating from Big Science Research," *The Journal of Technology Transfer*, 22(3), 1997, 27-36.

4. I refrain from advocating that these are the components of a thesis, since the book does not offer an empirical testing of a thesis nor of any testable hypotheses. Rather, my views are embedded in the main theme of the book, that S&T does create value to society and the economy, and that such value can be adequately measured and evaluated.

5. Some philosophies of technology abhor the notion of modernity and aspire to "simpler" times and less technology-laden social organizations. See, for example, Feenberg, A., *Alternative Modernity: The Technical Turn in Philosophy and Social Theory* (Berkeley: University of California Press, 1995). Such approaches notwithstanding, the theme in my book favors the view that S&T has had, and will have, meaningful and positive impacts on the human condition. Hence, any philosophy that advocates society and economy devoid of S&T (as we experience its effects today) administers erroneous conclusions that are heralded by false prophets. See, for example, Stoll, C., *Silicon Snake Oil: Second Thoughts on the Information Highway* (New York: Doubleday, 1995). Also see Lash, S., B. Szersnyski, and B. Wynne (Eds.), *Risk, Environment, and Modernity: Towards a New Ecology* (London: Sage Publications, 1996).

6. See, for example, Saviotti, P., and E. Elgar, *Technological Evolution, Variety, and the Economy* (London: Cheltenham, 1996). Also see Burgelman, R., and R. Rosenbloom (Eds.), *Research on Technological Innovation, Management, and Policy: Volume 5* (London: JAI Press, 1994), and Carlsson, B., and R. Stankiewicz, "On the Nature, Function, and Composition of Technological Systems," *Journal of*

Evolutionary Economics, 1(2), 1991, 93-118. Also see Grupp, H. (Ed.), *Dynamics of Science-Based Innovation* (Berlin, Germany: Springer, 1992).

PART II

THEORETICAL FOUNDATIONS

All theory, dear friend, is grey, but the golden tree of actual life springs ever green.

Johann Wolfgang von Goethe
(1749-1832)

5

THE NATURE OF THE PHENOMENON

What is science? What is technology? Although in Chapter 8 I do my best to describe these concepts, I really don't know how to precisely define them. If science is the pursuit of knowledge, what then is technology? Is it the lifting of the space shuttle on the way to the stars, or the roar of destructive ballistic missiles in military arsenals? Or, is it perhaps the transplant of a liver into the body of a tiny baby, and by saving its life, hence creating the utmost good in human interaction? Is technology simply a needful tool, or is it perhaps more than just the means to achieve a certain goal?

In the examples above it seems to me that technology reflects both good and evil that people and their organizations do. So, perhaps technology is more like art, an extension of our imagination and creativity, and perhaps even more so, an extension of our reach and capabilities.

Technology may be much more than just the know-how we accumulate on a given topic or in a certain discipline. It's an extension of humanity—which is essentially the theme of this book, more aptly described in Part IV. As such, technology has a *utilitarian* aspect, as well as *artistic* and certainly *idealistic* properties.

For want of a better definition, science and technology is idealistic because it reaches beyond its immediate utility as knowledge and tools to accomplish tasks.[1] It's more in the form of the reach in search of dreams.

When humanity is defined by its weakness and lack of ability, science and technology fills the need to achieve those things that human beings cannot, because of their physical or mental constraints. But humanity is also defined by its dreams and aspirations, where science and technology becomes the means to greatness. This is reflected in, or perhaps even shapes, our civilization, art, culture, and clearly our beliefs about our world. The more we can achieve, and the more we find ourselves in control of our physical environment (through science and technology), the more our view of the world changes. Our drive pushes technological frontiers, which in turn drive our motivation.

Are we in a vicious circle of an ever-lasting climb up the technological ladder? Clearly, the impacts of scientific and technological achievements and our ever-changing view of our world are *cumulative*, hence much more powerful than we can imagine in a cursory analysis of the moment. In essence, if science and technology is our creation, we and it are one entity. The bond between creators and creation is such that systemic perturbations by either component will drastically affect the entire system.

Much of humanity's education of its young has been the transfer of technology. We teach the next generation scientific and technological knowledge—its basics, its spirit, and its nuances. Technology is thus manifested in how to hunt, run, rest, work in a team, gather, compete, distinguish between nourishing and poisonous plants, learning how animals behave, or how to successfully conduct mergers and acquisitions of large companies.[2]

The need to maintain, record, enrich, and ultimately transfer such scientific and technological knowledge was, and is, a matter of survival. To a large extent, the transfer process was the progenitor of writing, culture in general, artistic expression, and the reach for posterity. Perhaps paintings in caves served all of the above needs, as today's computer programs do.

So what is the phenomenon that we are exploring in this book? It's a multifaceted, yet rather simple process by which science and technology (however defined) intimately interacts with all aspects of humanity. We may view this interface as that of instruments, capabilities, goals in themselves, or what transpires when human beings make things happen. The focus of this book is how do we theoretically support our evaluation of whatever happens and what are the impacts that we can identify. The phenomenon we wish to measure for the purpose of evaluation is the way human beings create science and technology, put them to use, and are impacted by so doing.[3]

THE TECHNOHUMAN CONDITION

Since antiquity, but especially during the 20th century, individual human behavior and well-being, as well as those of our institutions, have been drastically shaped by science and technology. It wasn't until the 1950s that we began a systematic study of the impacts of technology on social systems. Eric Trist and his colleagues at the Tavistock Institute in England coined the notion of "sociotechnical systems."[4] This notion introduced a new perspective of technology's impacts in work organizations. Whereas earlier the prevailing view considered people to be extensions of machines, hence to be studied as individuals and strictly controlled in this mode, the new approach advocated the power of the sociotechnical group and workers as complements to the technology.

Today the notion that technology and social groups are intertwined seems evident. However the integration of technology into managerial thinking and organizational design was a slow process. Although S&T today is a ubiquitous presence in almost every facet of organizational life, many managers and other participants in work organizations still have difficulty in changing their mind-sets and in fully accepting S&T as an integral component of the social fabric of work organizations.[5]

With the concept of the "Technohuman Condition" I have extended the notion of sociotechnical systems. S&T impacts have progressed beyond their effect on work groups and the design of organizations. Such progression is shown in a rough historical context in Figure 5.1.

The figure portrays four distinct periods or phases. The first period is preindustrial revolution, in which the main effects of S&T on the human condition was in large-scale efforts of institutions and states. S&T primarily influenced the conduct of war, the building of roads and cities, and the development of commerce and geographical exploration. Little, if any, influence was directed at the personal lives or interests of individuals.

The emphasis shifted during the period of the industrial revolution. S&T primarily impacted production systems and the distribution of the outputs from this turn of events. As production of goods increased, so did the need for continuing the flow of S&T to maintain this pattern of economic progress. Production and its associated services thus dominated the technohuman condition.

In the postindustrial revolution, the technohuman condition now focuses on both work and personal behavior. S&T has been diverted toward the needs of individuals. Although large-scale efforts such as defense remain as major recipients of S&T, personal needs have advanced to a position of almost equal importance. This trend is seen in the allocation of S&T resources to social needs, chief among them, health S&T.

However, this pattern of the effect of S&T on the human condition is much more visible in the developed and richer countries, and to a much lesser extent, in the developing world. In these emerging countries the focus of technology is on large-scale state-controlled effort and production systems in a move toward modernization. Less attention is given to targeting technology toward uses in response to needs of individuals.

Figure 5.1
A Framework for the Development of the Technohuman Condition

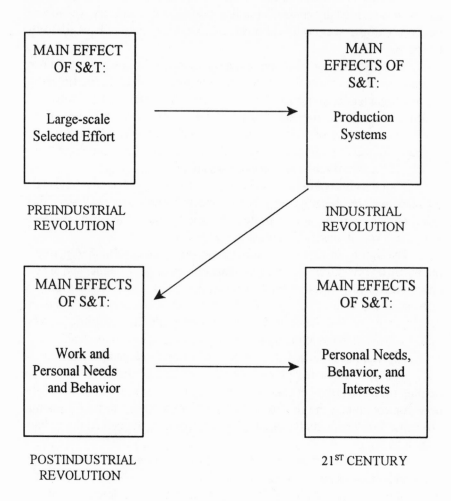

As we progress toward the 21ˢᵗ century, the emphasis will be shifting toward impacts of S&T on personal needs and interests, hence toward radical changes in personal behavior.[6] Impacts from S&T will probably reverberate throughout every aspect of daily life. Indeed, the trend seems to have progressed from technology's influence on overall economic and social phenomena to a shift toward how individuals live their lives, how they play, reproduce, create, and even work.

Contributing Factors

There are three stages or factors that have contributed to the present and perhaps will even contribute to the future states of the technohuman condition. As the model of this condition shows in Figure 5.1, there has been a shift toward individual impacts at the level of everyday existence. So, in large measure, the factors that impinged upon this condition have also promoted this shift.

Enabling factors are the first group that can be identified. These are factors that have contributed to the formation of the background circumstances that facilitated the impacts of S&T on human activities. Among these factors are historical trends of cumulative investments in S&T, the growing desire of citizens to enjoy the benefits from S&T, and the cumulation of outcomes and benefits from S&T effort.

Participating factors influence the technohuman condition by contributing to the shifts within the process of this condition over long periods of time. These factors include developments in industrial and commercial patterns of progress; social policies and regulatory developments and changes; and overall cultural shifts that favor the generation and implementation of S&T in the broader aspects of the human experience.

Amplification factors are the third type that include factors influencing the actual usage, adoption, and application of the outcomes of S&T. Among these factors are management policies, strategies, and philosophy regarding the role of S&T in their organizations; attitudes of the general population toward usage of the outcomes from S&T; and improved measures used to evaluate and assess the benefits accrued from S&T. Figure 5.2 summarizes the various factors.

Consequences

The importance of this trend in the technohuman condition is in the consequences from such a shift on how people deal with the new focus of S&T. As more facets of their daily existence are increasingly shaped by technological developments, the general reaction is a mixed bag of fear, uncertainty, shock, surprise, wonder, and enjoyment. For every person who is truly flabbergasted by S&T there is the little boy who enjoys electronic games or the patient recovering from a procedure that was utterly unforeseeable only a short number of years earlier.[7]

Both positive and negative consequences seem to emerge from the technohuman condition. These consequences in effect characterize this condition, so that the *net effect* constitutes an argument for praise or criticism of the condition at any given point in time.[8]

Figure 5.2
Factors Contributing to the Technohuman Condition

TYPE OF FACTORS	FACTORS AND THEIR MAIN CONTRIBUTION
ENABLING FACTORS	• **Cumulative investments in S&T** – create background for S&T exploitation – allow for variety in S&T outcomes • **Desire to enjoy benefits from S&T** – creates positive mood and support for S&T • **Cumulation of outcomes from S&T** – allows for different uses and cross-fertilization of ideas and outcomes
PARTICIPATING FACTORS	• **Developments in industry and commerce** – need to improve productivity, quality, efficiency, and demand for products and services • **Social policies and regulations** – create need to comply with social and political exigencies via S&T outcomes • **Cultural shifts** – create climate that favors broad application of S&T outcomes
AMPLIFICATION FACTORS	• **Management policies, strategies, and philosophies** – amplify utilization of S&T by encouraging technical solutions to problems • **Attitudes of general population** – amplify acceptance of S&T outcomes as routine components of everyday life • **Improved measures for evaluation** – amplify usage by providing better means for assessment and justification for S&T

SUMMARY

The technohuman condition is the circumstances that characterize the impacts of S&T on human activities and on human life. This notion of the technohuman condition is useful in explaining the phenomenon of the relationship between S&T, society, and the economy. The notion offers a conceptual as well as a temporal framework for the evaluation of S&T impacts.

What, then, is the nature of the phenomenon? It's the context and content of the ways and means by which S&T impacts the human condition and in which value is created. In this book I consider the investments in S&T, the public support for it, and the modes of evaluating its outcomes. I also approach the phenomenon from the perspective of the theoretical basis for S&T and its outcomes.

In the latter part of the book I examine the social and economic impacts of S&T and the mode of evaluating them. I focus on the value that S&T thus creates for the human condition.

In summary, this is a book about the phenomenon of S&T and its contributions to human activities and the quality of life. Its main theme is an optimistic outlook on what S&T has already contributed and will continue to contribute to humankind.

NOTES

1. The terms *technology* and *science and technology* are used interchangeably throughout the book. Because science and technology are intricately related in the form of a process of innovation, the impacts and effects of technology are also counted as impacts of science and scientific discovery. See, for example, Teece, D., "Capturing Value from Knowledge Assets: The New Economy, Markets for Know-How, and Intangible Assets," *California Management Review*, 40(3), 1998, 55-79.

2. See, for example, Simpson, D., J. Walker, and J. Love, *The Challenge of New Technology* (Boulder, CO: Westview Press, 1987). Also see Ballard, E., *Man and Technology: Toward the Measurement of Culture* (Pittsburgh, PA: Duquense University Press, 1978). Ballard discusses the issue of "technism," and suggests that "technological man" has denied the human condition of finiteness, by perhaps aggrandizing the potential accomplishments of technology. Ballard also hastens to suggest that his views are not technophobic but call for harmony between human frailty and technology's preponderance. Ballard's essay is illustrative of the continuing discussion of the phenomenon of science and technology and its role in human activities.

3. See, for example, Dean, J., "Building the Future: The Justification Process for New Technology," in J. Pennings and A. Buitendam (Eds.), *New Technology as Organizational Innovation* (Cambridge, MA: Ballinger, 1987). Also see Kanter, R., *The Change Masters: Innovation for Productivity in the American Corporation* (New York: Simon and Schuster, 1983).

4. See the original publication: Trist, E., and K. Bamforth, "Some Social and Psychological Consequences of the Long Wall Method of Coal Getting," *Human Relations*, 4(1), 1951, 3-38. Also see Emery, F., and E. Trist, "The Causal Texture of Organizational Environments," *Human Relations*, 18(2), 1968, 20-26; and Trist,

E., "The Sociotechnical Perspective," in A. Van de Ven, and W. Joyce, *Perspectives on Organization Design* (New York: John Wiley & Sons, 1981) pp. 20-53.

5. See, for example, Bohme, G. and N. Stehr, "The Knowledge Society: The Growing Impact of Scientific Knowledge on Social Relations" (Boston: Kluwer Academic Publishers, 1986). Also see Aldrich, H., "Technology and Organization Structure: A Re-examination of the Findings of the Aston Group," *Administrative Science Quarterly*, 17(3), 1972, 26-43.

6. See, for example, the popular publications, such as Toffler, A., *The Third Wave* (New York: Simon & Schuster, 1982). Also see Wyke, A., *21st Century Miracle Medicine: Robosurgery, Wonder Cures, and the Quest for Immortality* (New York: Plenum Press, 1997). See in particular some interesting predictions in Hackney, R., and D. Dunn (Eds.), *Business Information Technology Management: Alternative and Adaptive Figures* (New York: St. Martin's Press, 2000); and Baker, R., *Sex in the Future: Ancient Urges Meet Future Technology* (New York: Arcade Publishing, 2000). Also see Ellis, D., M. Campbell, and D. Crandall, *Technology and the Future of Health Care: Preparing for the Next 30 Years* (New York: American Hospital Publishing, 2000); and O'Hanlon, M., *Technological Change and the Future of Warfare* (Washington, DC: Brookings Institution Press, 1999).

7. This and similar issues are further discussed in Chapters 14 and 15.

8. See, for example, issues such as the "digital divide" and similar topics in the evaluation of the technohuman condition. See Bolt, D., and R. Crawford, *Digital Divide: Computers and Our Children's Future* (New York: TV Books, L.L.C., 2000). Also see Kosko, B., *The Fuzzy Future: From Society and Science to Heaven in a Chip* (New York: Crown Publishing Group, 1999). In this book Kosko extends the concept of fuzzy logic to potential applications in various fields such as smart cars and power plants, to the far-extended conclusion and prediction of digital machines encapsulating human consciousness, thus leading to the much-desired human immortality. Also see Cetron, M., and O. Davies, *Probable Tomorrows: How Science and Technology Will Transform Our Lives in the Next 20 Years* (New York: St. Martin's Press, 1999); and see Teich, A., *Technology and the Future*, 8th ed. (New York: St. Martin's Press, 1999).

6

OVERVIEW OF RELEVANT THEORIES

Science and technology affect almost without exception all aspects of human activities. Every organization and institution in the fabric of society and the economy benefits from S&T or is impacted by it to some degree. Theorists of S&T have long reasoned that it is in the organizational and institutional manifestations of such impacts that S&T can and should be studied.

This chapter follows two distinct perspectives in the approach to S&T, and particularly to technology. Organization theorists have addressed the role of technology as a dimension in the structure and performance of organizations. This constitutes a distinct collection of theories. Second, researchers in the area of the management of technology, sociology, and economies have also addressed the role of technology, but in the macro-context of society and the economy. Both perspectives are discussed in this chapter.

TECHNOLOGY IN ORGANIZATIONS

Textbooks in organization theory and organization behavior discuss technology as a dimension in the analysis of organizations. Theories in this context capture the concept of technology primarily as it relates to work processes and tasks. Joan Woodward discovered a link between the technology of operations and the firm's structure.[1] She classified work technology as one of three types: unit, mass, and process, in an ascending state of complexity. Thus, structural dimensions such as centralization, formalization, vertical differentiation, and complexity vary according to the type of work technology employed by the firm.[2]

Another view of technology as a dimension of the organization was proposed by Perrow.[3] In his scheme, technology is defined as actions by workers in the organization, who transform raw material into some form of a product or service. The variability of the task faced by the worker (i.e., has few or many exceptions) is one dimension of technology. The other is the degree to which the task (or problem) faced by the worker is analyzable, so that search procedures for the adequate tools can be formalized, standardized, or routinized. The intersection of these two dimensions produces four types of technology: craft, routine, nonroutine, and engineering.[4]

Thompson offered a view of technology as a core asset of the organization.[5] His model was the precursor of the concept of "core competencies" of the firm, which was heralded in the literature almost a generation later.[6] In Thompson's view, the "core technologies" of the organization encompassed the most valuable assets, which therefore needed protection from environmental pressures. Organizations thus construct layers of "buffers" between these technologies and the external world of competitors, regulators, and other threatening entities. Examples of such technologies are the operating room in a hospital, or the process of making pharmaceuticals.[7]

Thompson also classified organizational technologies as long linked, mediating, or intensive. The determining factor for the classification is the degree of interdependence (a concept similar to that of a value chain, where a change in one component perforce creates changes in another component).

In a refinement of Woodward's concepts, Hickson and his colleagues at the University of Aston in the United Kingdom have related "operations technology" to structural variables.[8] Their findings suggest that operations technology variables are related only to structure variables that are centered on the workflow. They also found that the larger the organization, the smaller the effect of technology on structure. Their finding that all types of production systems are present in every size range seems to contradict Woodward's initial conclusions.

A more comprehensive model was suggested by Scott, who combined the dimensions used by previous researchers.[9] He measured technology along the dimensions of *complexity*, *uncertainty*, and *interdependence*. He also linked his model to the processing of information, by suggesting that an increase in each dimension would increase the amount of information necessary to accomplish a given task.

Technology in organization analysis was also viewed as a *social* variable. The "sociotechnical theory" has argued that there is a strong relationship between technical and social subsystems in organizations.[10] So the introduction, for instance, of a new technology (production or information) would create disequilibrium in the existing social structure that determines the efficacy and configuration of work flows and methods.

Orlikowsky offers an excellent summary of the main findings in the study of technology in organizations.[11] Technology is a major influence on how work is accomplished and on how the organization configures itself to perform. At the same time, this influence is also shaped, to a degree, by members of the organization and their social interactions. Therefore, although technology is a major force in organizations, there is much that they can do to influence the direction of this force and its effects.

TECHNOLOGY AND CHANGE

Most of the studies listed in the previous section considered technology in terms of its influential presence in the life of the organization. They emphasized the ways in which technology impacts workflows and the products or processes of these flows. The driving force in the methods employed by such models was the desire to classify technology and its components.

An insightful addition to our understanding of technology was the generation of models of technological change. Following Schumpeter's concept of "creative destruction,"[12] Tushman and Anderson introduced the concept of "technological discontinuities."[13] They argued that technology progresses through a series or succession of cycles, where the start of each cycle is marked by a phenomenon of discontinuity. Following this, there is the emergence of a dominant design, which they define as the standard for technology in the marketplace. Based in part on methods and rationale developed by technological forecasters, theorists of technological discontinuities have considered them as revolutionary innovations that extend the limits of the technology they replace.

Technological breakthroughs are mediated by certain limits, such as those inherent in the physics of a phenomenon (e.g., engine efficiency), or in their economic, social, or organizational aspects. The model of discontinuity is a process model that describes the stages of the dynamics of discontinuity, and the emergence of the dominant design.

But, although insightful in explaining the emergence of new technologies and the process by which they replace existing ones, this model relates to product and process technologies, perhaps more so to product technology, as dominant designs are more often illustrated by products (e.g., Model T automobile, IBM 360 computers, and Microsoft Windows 95/98). To apply this model to process technology or to administrative or knowledge technologies would create some grave barriers to the integrity of the concept.

For example, how would we translate dominant designs to knowledge technology? Also, how would the dynamics of the process of cycles and continuities apply to organizational and other nontechnical dimensions of adoption and substitution processes? Geisler and Heller have studied adoption of new medical technology in healthcare organizations.[14] They identified the following factors in the adoption process of new technologies: quality, performance, ethics, cost, projected benefits, liability, and strategic considerations.

TECHNOLOGY AND KNOWLEDGE

A different approach views technology as knowledge within the organization.[15] In a logical departure from theories of technology and information (such as Perrow and Scott), knowledge is considered a form of technology. Hence it is viewed as a resource and a core competence.[16]

Geisler approached this topic from another perspective.[17] He suggested that knowledge in organizations may be classified into high-level constructs and operational knowledge. In order for an organization to function and survive in a competitive environment, it must arrive at a workable match between the two types of knowledge. So resources are therefore organized in an adequate configuration to achieve such a convergence. Technology is embedded in both types of knowledge and serves to contribute to the workability of a successful configuration of resources.[18]

Although in their infancy, theories of knowledge and its processes and impacts are a unique view of technology. They bring to the topic a mixture of information, theory, strategy, and group and individual behavior (including managerial cognition). Again, technology is viewed in a duality of roles, embedded in the knowledge systems themselves, and in the individuals and groups who operate within the organization.

SUMMARY OF TECHNOLOGY THEORIES

However we define it, technology is a central element of the organization. It enables members to do their work and it is embedded in products, processes, and skills and know-how that are needed to manage the organization.

From attempts at taxonomy to the view of technology as a dynamic process, theorists have shown us that this phenomenon is inherent not only in how we make things (artifacts, machines, products), but also in the way we *organize* ourselves to enable us to make things. Because of this duality, technology remains a somewhat fuzzy concept. We know enough at this juncture to manage it with an acceptable level of knowledge, perhaps because we have gained much understanding of its complexity and its uncertainty. Figure 6.1 summarizes some of the theories that have contributed to this knowledge (all of the theories listed have been cited previously in this chapter, except Leonard-Barton[19]).

Figure 6.1
Duality of the Construct of Technology in Organizations and Selected Theories

Theory	Technology as Embedded in Products, Processes, & Outcomes	Technology as Embedded in the Structural Configuration of Organizations
PERROW	Variability and search in transforming raw materials to accomplish tasks	Routine and nonroutine types of structural match: organic model of group and managerial behavior
THOMPSON	Long-linked, mediating, and intensive	Due to inclement environment, "core technology" requires protection, hence layers of functions serving as "buffers"
SCOTT	Amount of information needed for performing tasks	Contingency model of complexity, uncertainty, and interdependence: variation in structure to accommodate flow and processing of information
TUSHMAN & ANDERSON	Technology embedded in "dominant design"	Structure varies to fit strategic configurations that are a function of the evolution of "dominant design"
ORLIKOWSKI	New technology requires learning and adaptation	New technology creates episodic processes of adaptation, thus generating "windows of opportunity" for technological change: call for "uneven adaptation"
WOODWARD	Unit, batch, process	Nature of production system serves to categorize different organizations
LEONARD-BARTON	Technology as core capabilities	Paradox of managing core capacities and core rigidities: structural rigidity may hinder technological change

No one theory can attempt to explain the entire spectrum of technology as an organizational dimension. What we know thus far is that technology is a highly complex, dynamic, uncertain and diffused phenomenon in the life and the structure of the organization. Now we turn our attention to the theories on how technology can or should be evaluated.

SOME THEORIES OF TECHNOLOGY IMPACTS

The literature on the impacts of science and technology is varied and ebullient. In a mix of economics, history, and sociology, researchers from these disciplines have attempted to show the actual and potential contributions from science and, in particular, from technology. I have selected what I believe to be the more influential theories, but also illustrative theories, of the discipline in which they were formulated.

Roughly, we can divide these theories into two main groups: (1) economic theories, and (2) social and other theories. In many of these theories the terms "innovation" and "technology" are used interchangeably. This seeming confusion in applying the key concepts is partially explained by the emphasis of most of these theories. They concentrate on the *impacts* side of the equation, so that a careful definition of what constitutes technology is not their main concern. Considering that technology and innovation are highly correlated, even intertwined concepts, such a mix is understandable, albeit perhaps not excusable—as we shall see in the next chapter.

ECONOMIC THEORIES

Perhaps the most celebrated, if not the most cited, economist who linked technology with economic growth was Joseph Schumpeter.[20] Over 50 years ago he described the central role of innovative and creative activities that, through the work of entrepreneurs, contributes to radical and sustained economic growth. Schumpeter's foundational work combined economics and managerial frameworks of reasoning, but was primarily anecdotal. About a generation later, economists have extended their research to consider more empirical descriptions of the role of technology and innovation.

Robert Solow concentrated on the effect of new technology on productivity in manufacturing companies.[21] He then expanded his search to include the impact of productivity on economic growth, hence the benefits of innovation on the economy. Similarly, Moses Abramovitz[22] and later Edward Denison[23] explored economic growth and attributed it in part to the effect of technology. The logic behind this body of work was the celebrated "Solow Residuals," which meant that whatever growth in output that could not be attributed to other inputs (e.g., labor and capital accumulation) would be then attributed to technological change.

This research has explored the phenomena commonly described as "technological diffusion" or the "diffusion of innovations." On the other side of the equation, economists have devoted considerable attention to measurement of economic growth through accounting of traditional output factors in industrial economics.

A seminal work in a particular set of circumstances was published by Zvi Grilliches, who studied the impacts from the introduction and diffusion of hybrid corn.[24] He showed that the rate of diffusion of the new type of seeds can be satisfactorily explained by the expectations of potential profits by both producers of the new seeds and farmers who would use them. This study was facilitated by the fact that it dealt with a simple and well-defined innovation, and a well-defined and limited set of producers-users.[25]

But, in exploring more aggregate economic phenomena and their ties to technology, Griliches[26] and more recent economists, such as Manuel Trajtenberg[27] and F. M. Scherer,[28] have criticized this theoretical link. They argued very convincingly that there are disturbing problems in the logic and methodology of aggregate studies. Among them are the discontinuity attribute of technology, long periods of adoption and diffusion of a new technology, and the relation between the rate of diffusion of a new technology and its effects on increased productivity and overall growth.

These were not the only problems. There were also those issues that relate to the methodology of growth accounting. For example, price indexes are considered to underestimate the impacts accrued from innovations in products and services in the economy. Another issue is the reliance of growth accounting on the assumption of perfect competition. So, if privately generated technology is being developed, it will lead to less than competitive rents to the innovator.[29] Finally, there is the issue of the lag between the generation and application of technology by economic entities and, in parallel, the issue of imputing an underlying causal effect of growth.[30]

SUMMARY OF ECONOMIC THEORIES

In general, for the mainline economists, technology and innovation have always been some kind of illegitimate children in the development of economic theories. Perhaps because technology and innovation could not be easily measured or manipulated as capital and labor. Perhaps also because technology is such a complex and intractable phenomenon. In econometric studies (Griliches and Scherer, for example) when the private rate of return from research and development was estimated at 30 percent, the estimated contribution of R&D to industrial productivity growth hovered below 0.5 percent (0.2 percent in 1970 and 0.4 percent annual contributions in the period 1948-1988).

Compare these figures with Denison's belief that contributions from technology accounted for about 20-25 percent of the productivity growth in nonfarm industries. How can we then reconcile such different conclusions (by a factor of ten)? Clearly, methodology differences alone may not be sufficient to account for this, unless we place the burden on definitions and the different boundaries of the concepts under study. Another explanation brings us back to the idiosyncratic attributes of R&D, science, and technology.

Consider, for example, that technology is a very special and unusual type of economic commodity. It is at once a nonrival good and, to an extent, also a nonexcludable good. Despite its ability to offer the firm strategic advantages (noncompetitive), technology (particularly in the form of knowledge) is imitable. What makes it even more exasperating is the fact that technology is embedded in both capital equipment and labor (again, primarily in the form of knowledge). So, if we consider only direct investments in R&D, we neglect the substantial portion of technological impacts across firms and industries, and across other economic commodities such as capital equipment and labor. Finally, technology also "spills over" to social entities and activities, which have their own economic value, with cumulation properties.[31]

SOCIAL IMPACTS AND OTHER THEORIES

Economic theories of the impacts of science and technology have generally ignored the impacts on the social aspects of human enterprise. Some economists, in particular economic historians, have attempted to incorporate S&T into their models that explain social and economic progress. Altogether there are three principal streams of studies that have attempted to measure the impacts of S&T on social entities.

Spillover Effects

The first stream included studies of *spillover effects* from science and technology, measured primarily by linking investments in R&D and the social returns from these investments. The pioneering work of Edwin Mansfield has contributed to our understanding of the diffusion of technology, from R&D to industrial applications, and from there to social benefits.[32] Mansfield concluded that the speed of adoption varies with the type of technology, and that imitation of a given technology by other industrial firms is directly related to its profitability, and negatively related to the level of investment needed for imitation.

But Mansfield also estimated *social* returns from R&D, and concluded that they are more than twice the private returns.[33] In his later studies of the impacts of academic research, Mansfield estimated that academic research contributed about 20 percent to industrial innovation.[34] This figure is similar to Denison's estimation of 20-25 percent of improved industrial productivity that can be attributed to impacts of technology.

Mansfield's methodology in the studies of the impacts from academic research considered the value of such research to industrial companies, if they had to invest in such effort themselves. This rationale is also a justification for outsourcing of R&D—a practice that has gained in popularity among industrial firms in the 1990s.

I agree with Nathan Rosenberg[35] who has commented on the paucity of our understanding of the "social determinants of a society's capacity for generating technical progress" (p. 29). In part, I believe that the difficulties lie in the complexity and diversity of social impacts of S&T, and correspondingly, the insistence of economists to study the phenomenon in the broadest of terms.

A partial solution to the diversity of impacts was offered in the seminal work of Albert Rubenstein and his students at POMRAD (Program on the Management of Research and Development) at Northwestern University.[36] Their pioneering studies of the contributions from NASA's space explorations to industry and to specific social areas generated a methodological answer to the predicament of economists. By concentrating on a single agency or on a single discipline or area, Rubenstein and his students advanced the exploration of some socially relevant impacts.[37] Thus, there arises a possibility to study specific spillovers or spin-offs from a well-defined S&T program. The method they used traced the transfer or diffusion of the innovation, technique, method, or even a product.[38]

Process Approaches

Despite attempts to study the impact of specific agencies or innovations, much of the investigative effort has been confined to the individual social area. For example, in the area of healthcare and medicine, technology and innovation were addressed in the specialized disciplinary literatures. Much of this effort has been transacted at the level of a specific piece of equipment (e.g., MRI, or the computerized Patient Record), or a set of technologies, such as those employed in telemedicine.[39]

Some studies did address the impacts of technology by employing a process approach. Two kinds of such studies are salient. The first are *retrospective* studies, most notably in the 1960s and early 1970s. They included such research effort as projects Hindsight and TRACES.[40] The method used in this research was a choice of an innovation, such as the contraceptive pill or magnetic tape, and a careful retrospective analysis of the contributions of basic and applied research to the innovation. This line of investigation was abandoned in favor of discipline-based *prospective* methodologies.

In the field of healthcare and medical technology, for example, the emphasis was on the evaluation of specific technologies and their impacts on patient care.[41] Health economists also studied the effect of using selected medical technologies on measures of quality of life, morbidity, and mortality.

A more comprehensive and generic approach was introduced by Eliezer Geisler and Albert Rubinstein.[42] This approach consisted of looking forward, downstream the innovation process: from research to the ultimate impacts of the resultant technology as it is applied in social and economic entities. In short, the approach identified the process of diffusion and adoption of the outputs from R&D, by concentrating on the main categories of the "impacts" or adopters/recipients of the technology that emerges from the R&D activity. In all, four categories of outputs and three groups of impacts were identified in the generic model. In addition, Geisler and Rubinstein also explored the transformation processes in which the technology is adopted and transformed as it moves downstream the innovation process.[43]

Historical Linkages: Technology and Wealth

Whether retrospective or forward looking, process approaches have enabled researchers to more precisely assess the transformation of science and technology downstream the innovation continuum. By expanding on the effort conducted by economists such as Griliches and Mansfield to evaluate selected innovations or fields of study, some economic historians have endowed technology with a key role in their theories of the accumulation of national wealth.

David Landes has published two seminal books with 30 years in between.[44] His first book, published in 1969, attempted to explain the technological superiority of European countries, and in particular England, beginning with the industrial revolution. On a very large historical canvas, Landes essentially described the factors that facilitated the generation and adoption of technology, in a mode similar to the factors that Geisler and Rubinstein had used in describing the transformations of the outputs from science/R&D by economic and social subsystems.

In his second book, published in 1998, Landes extended his line of reasoning to credit these factors (and some additional ones) for the wide differences in national levels of economic wealth. The book is not about better usages of technology, but about the social, economic, psychological, and religious conditions and circumstances that allowed some countries to become rich. In his summary chapter Landes commented that the spirit of enterprise, self-esteem, and the ability to learn and transfer knowledge are among these factors.

Yet, although Landes provides a comprehensive tapestry of factors that may have led to technological sophistication, he fails to explain how the *utilization* (or commercialization) and adoption of technology (in addition to its generation) have contributed to greater economic prowess.

Joel Mokyr, another historian of technology, has also considered the role that technological progress and diffusion have on economic prosperity of nations.[45] He argues that "technological inventiveness" has been the dynamo that propelled economic prosperity in the United States and in other Western countries. Mokyr also emphasized Schumpeter's view that social factors are the main reason for barriers to technological progress, not necessarily the lack of ideas or the paucity of technical inventiveness. Mokyr's analysis relied simultaneously on the historical progress of technology over selected time periods and on selected industries and disciplines.

Nathan Rosenberg criticized these broad-brush attempts to link technological development with economic progress.[46] Rosenberg concludes that the gap between technology and economics might be further and methodically investigated, so that "to assess the economic significance of an innovation, we need to know not only that it reduces costs, which is fairly obvious, but the magnitude of the cost reduction" (p. 28). To this end he explored the effects of learning, commercialization, market factors, and technology transfer.

Donald Stokes argued that the "compact" between science and government in the United States has essentially collapsed at the closing of the 20th century.[47] He proposed a renewal of this arrangement, thereby strengthening the case for basic research. The modified paradigm calls for a stronger integration of science with societal goals and with user-driven technological innovation.

Although merely an argument proposed to facilitate deliberations of science policy-makers, Stokes' idea is nevertheless anchored in theoretical foundations. Scientists are simply asked to look beyond their narrow aspiration at discovery and invention toward the greater goal of uses of technology and societal goals. The value from this shift in paradigm may be explained by theories of knowledge and information.[48] If one considers scientific outcomes to be knowledge that is diffused in society and the economy, then knowledge that contributes to technological innovation and real-life uses would be more attractive to investors. Basic research whose outcome is knowledge without such visible applications would be disjointed from the mainstream of the S&T-innovation process. This is particularly true for "big" science, at the industrial and national levels.

S&T and the Theory of Evolution

There are two major approaches to the view of science and technology in light of the theory of evolution. The first considers technological progress as an evolutionary process. The second approach views science and technology as "knowledge," hence subjected to theories of evaluation of knowledge (Evolutionary Epistemology).

Gary Cziko, for example, discussed cultural evolution, and within it, considered technology as an aspect of culture.[49] Since technology is viewed as a crucial ingredient in society's survival, Cziko argued that the evaluation of technology (defined primarily as tools and instruments) is similar to that of biological systems. The key argument in this approach seems to be based on the "continuity" of technological innovations, coupled with the "diversity" of tools and artifacts in human societies.[50] To the casual analyst, there appears to be a process by which technological innovations are contingent upon previous discoveries, and these seem to appear in various societies.

These theoretical arguments have merely suggested that there are similarities between the emergence and progression of technological innovations and the evolution of biological systems. Proponents of these comparisons have not examined (in detail) the processes of science and technology diffusion and transfer, including S&T adoption and utilization. At best the historical anecdotes have served as the main components for the theoretical comparison with the very engaging and comprehensive theory of evolution and its process of natural selection.

Technology as knowledge and its development by means of the evolutionary process have been the topic of the "evolutionary epistemology" framework of analysis of the progress of knowledge. In Chapter 7 a more comprehensive discussion of these theories will be presented.

THE QUEST FOR A UNIFIED THEORY

What have the theories or models of economic and social impacts contributed to our understanding of the benefits and other impacts accrued from technology? With the exception of process theories, the remainder of the theories or models simply considered technology as an economic commodity (like capital or labor) and linked it to economic prosperity. All this was accomplished by the researchers largely without being able or willing to measure technological progress. True, some outcomes had been measured, particularly patents and actual inventions, but the merit of this approach is doubtful. The lag between the production of patents and economic progress has remained largely unexplored.[51]

Even Rosenberg has shown dissatisfaction with this state of affairs and has consequently argued that "science" should not be considered an exogenous variable in the economic analysis of technology. By stressing the strong link and mutual influences between science and technology, Rosenberg in effect argues for a systematic exploration of the *process* of innovation, although his focus had been the knowledge that emerges from science and technology.

Perhaps the paucity of achievements of these theories lies in the complexity of the technological innovation phenomenon, thus making it somewhat unrealistic to pursue a unified theory. Hence also the need to trace this phenomenon even further in microanalyses of generation and diffusion processes within organizations. Finally, another crucial issue seems to be the variety of terms and definitions, used haphazardly, to describe different components of the phenomenon. This issue is discussed in Chapter 8.

NOTES

1. Woodward, J., *Industrial Organization: Theory and Practice* (Oxford: Oxford University Press, 1965).

2. Woodward's methodology has been criticized for ignoring such dimensions as size of the firm, which may explain some of the variability. However, as later studies have shown, a positive relationship between size and other structural variables, Woodward's findings, insofar as they characterize technology, seem valid.

3. Perrow, C., *Organizational Analysis: A Sociological View* (Belmont, CA: Wadsworth, 1970). In particular, see Chapter 3.

4. Perrow's scheme stopped short of positing a dynamic model whereby one type of technology can be transformed into another. He also marginally referred to the relationship between types of technology and structural variables. However, Perrow acknowledged that units *within* organizations may employ different types of technology.

5. Thompson, J., *Organizations in Action* (New York: McGraw-Hill, 1967).

6. Prahalad, C., and G. Hamel, "The Core Competence of the Corporation," *Harvard Business Review*, 68(3), 1990, 79-91.

7. More recently, the strategic management literature has adopted Thompson's concepts in the form of the resource-based theory. The harder it is for competitors to imitate such core technologies, the more advantageous is the strategic competitive portion of the firm. See, for example, Wernerfelt, B., "A Resource-Based View of the Firm," *Strategic Management Journal*, 52(2), 1984, 171-180.

8. Hickson, D., D. Pugh, and D. Phesey, "Operations Technology and Organization Structure: An Empirical Reappraisal," *Administrative Science Quarterly*, 14(3), 1969, 378-398.

9. Scott, R., *Organizations: Rational, Natural, and Open Systems* (Englewood Cliffs, NJ: Prentice-Hall, 1992). This is a well-written and insightful book that effectively summarizes theories of organizations, and offers a cohesive model of organizational technology.

10. See, for example, Trist, E., and K. Bamforth, "Some Social and Psychological Consequences of the Longwall Method of Coal Mining," *Human Relations*, 4(1), 1951, 3-38. This construct is also discussed in Chapter 5.

11. Orlikowski, W., "The Quality of Technology: Rethinking the Concept of Technology in Organizations," *Organization Science*, 3(4), 1992, 398-427. Also see Tyre, M., and W. Orlikowski, "Exploiting Opportunities for Technological Improvement in Organizations," *Sloan Management Review*, 34(4), 1993, 13-26.

12. Schumpeter, J., *Capitalism, Socialism, and Democracy* (New York: Harper & Brothers, 1942).

13. Tushman, M., and P. Anderson, "Technological Discontinuities and Organizational Environments," *Administrative Science Quarterly*, 31(4), 1986, 439-465.

14. Geisler, E., and O. Heller, *Management of Medical Technology: Theory, Practice, and Cases* (Boston: Kluwer Academic Publishers, 1997) 107-110.

15. See, for example, Kogut, B., and U. Zanger, "Knowledge of the Firm, Combinative Capabilities and the Replication of Technology," *Organization Science*, 18(6), 1997, 973-996. Also see Nonaka, I., "A Dynamic Theory of Organizational Knowledge Creation," *Organization Science*, 5(1), 1994, 14-37.

16. See Blackler, F., "Knowledge, Knowledge Work, and Organizations," *Organization Studies*, 16(6), 1995, 1021-1046.

17. Geisler, E., *Methodology, Theory, and Knowledge. Actions and Consequences in the Managerial and Organizational Sciences*.(Westport, CT: Quorum Books, 1999).

18. See, for example, Hedlund, G., "A Model of Knowledge Management and the N-Form Corporation," *Strategic Management Journal*, 15(2), 1994, 73-90. Another aspect of this approach concerns knowledge and learning. See, for example, Huber, G., "Organizational Learning: The Contributing Processes and the Literatures," *Organization Sciences*, 2(1), 1991, 88-115.

19. Leonard-Barton, D., "Implementation as Mutual Adaptation of Technology and Organization," *Research Policy*, 17(3), 1988, 251-267.

20. Schumpeter, 1942, *op. cit.*

21. See, for example, Solow, R., "Technical Change and the Aggregate Production Function," *Review of Economics and Statistics*, 39(2), 1957, 312-320.

22. Abramovitz, M., "Resource and Output Trends in the United States Since 1870," *American Economic Review*, 46 (papers and proceedings), 1956, 5-23.

23. Denison, E., *Why Growth Rates Differ* (Washington, DC: Brookings Institution, 1967).

24. Griliches, Z., "Research Costs and Social Returns: Hybrid Corn and Related Innovations," *Journal of Political Economics*, 66(5), 1958, 419-431.

25. Griliches estimated the rate of return on all investments (both private and public) in the generation and diffusion/implementation of hybrid corn at over 700 percent—in the period 1910-1955.

26. Griliches, Z., "Research Expenditures and Growth Accounting," in B. R. Williams (Ed.), *Science and Technology in Economic Growth* (London: Macmillan, 1973). Also see Griliches, Z., "Issues in Assessing the Contribution of Research and Development in Productivity Growth," *Bell Journal of Economics*, 10(1), 1979,

92-116. In these two papers Griliches refers to "research" and "research and development" as more measurable substitutes to technology and innovation.

27. Trajtenberg, M., "Product Innovations, Price Indices, and the (Mis)Measurement of Economic Performance," NBER Working Paper, No. 3261, Cambridge, MA, 1990.

28. Scherer, F. M., "Inter-Industry Technology Flows and Productivity Growth," *The Review of Economics and Statistics*, 64(4), 1982, 627-634. Also see Scherer, F. M., "R&D and Declining Productivity Growth," *The American Economic Review*, 73(2), 1983, 215-218.

29. This issue is similar to the concept of "core competencies" of the firm and the "resource-based" view of the firm. Technology may be considered a strategic core resource, thus enhancing the firm's competitive advantage in the marketplace, providing that the technology is difficult to imitate. See, Wernerfelt, B., "A Resource-Based View of the Firm," *Strategic Management Journal*, 5(2), 1984, 171-180.

30. Some attempts were made to add to the growth accounting procedure the "knowledge" variable, measured as the accumulated investments in R&D minus depreciation.

31. Consider, for example, the impacts of the Internet as a technology, with all its ramifications and "spillover" effects. See, for example, Geisler, E., "Information and Telecommunication Technology in the 1990s: Trends and Managerial Challenges," *International Journal of Technology Management*, 7(6/7/8), 1992, 381-389. Also see Townsend, A., S. DeMarie, and A. Hendrickson, "Virtual Teams: Technology and the Workplace of the Future," *The Academy of Management Executive*, 12(3), 1998, 17-29.

32. Mansfield, E., *The Economics of Technological Change* (New York: W. W. Norton, & Company, 1968). Also see Mansfield, E., A. Romeo, M. Schwartz, D. Teece, S. Wagner, and P. Brach, *Technology Transfer, Productivity, and Economic Policy* (New York: W. W. Norton & Company, 1982) in particular, Chapter 7, 132-153.

33. Mansfield, E., J. Rapoport, A. Romeo, S. Wagner, and G. Beardsley, "Social and Private Rates of Return from Industrial Innovation," *Quarterly Journal of Economics*, 91(3), 1977, 221-240.

34. Mansfield, E., "Academic Research and Industrial Innovation," *Research Policy*, 20(1), 1991, 1-12. Also see Mansfield, E., "Academic Research and Industrial Innovation: A further Note," *Research Policy*, 21(3), 1992, 295-296; and Mansfield, E., "Academic Research Underlying Industrial Innovations: Sources and Characteristics," Working Paper, University of Pennsylvania, 1993.

35. Rosenberg, N., *Inside the Black Box: Technology and Economics* (Cambridge: Cambridge University Press, 1984).

36. Rubinstein, A., *Managing Technology in the Decentralized Firm* (New York: John Wiley & Sons, 1989).

37. See, for example, Chakrabarti, A., "The Effects of Techno-Economic and Organizational Factors on the Adoption of NASA-Innovations by Commercial Firms in the US," Ph.D. Dissertation Northwestern University, 1972. Also see Ettlie, J., "The Impact of New Technologies: Organizational and Individual Learning," Ph.D. Dissertation, Northwestern University, 1972. Similarly see National Aeronautics and

Space Administration, *Useful Technology from Space Research*, Technology Utilization Program, Washington, DC, 1968.

38. Rubinstein and his students followed this rationale by addressing issues such as the link between R&D and marketing, and similar studies of the diffusion and transfer of innovation and technology in industrial companies, service companies, and government agencies.

39. See, for example, Darkins, A., and M. Cary, *Telemedicine and Telehealth: Principles, Policies, Performance, and Pitfalls* (New York: Springer Publishing Company, 2000). Also see Bauer, J., and M. Ringer, *Telemedicine and the Reinvention of Healthcare: The Seventh Revolution in Medicine* (New York: McGraw-Hill, 1999), and see, for example, Davis, M., *Computerizing Healthcare Information: Developing Electronic Patient Information Systems* (New York: McGraw-Hill, 1997).

40. Department of Defense, *Project Hindsight*, Office of the Director of Defense Research and Engineering, Washington, DC, DTIC No. AD495905, 1969, and Illinois Institute of Technology, *Technology in Retrospect and Critical Events in Science (TRACES)*, Report to the National Science Foundation, 1968.

41. For a summary of this research see Geisler, E., and O. Heller, *Management of Medical Technology: Theory, Practice, and Cases* (Boston: Kluwer Academic Publishers, 1998) particularly pages 91-117.

42. See, for example, Geisler, E., and A. Rubenstein, "Methodology Issues in Conducting Evaluation Studies of R&D/Innovation," *Proceedings of the Symposium on Management of Technological Innovation*, Worcester Polytechnic Institute, Washington, DC, 1983. Also see Rubinstein, A., and E. Geisler, "The Use of Indicators and Measures of the R&D Process in Evaluating Science and Technology Programs," in D. Roessner (Ed.), *Government Innovation Policy* (New York: St. Martin's Press, 1988) 185-204; and Geisler, E., "Key Output Indicators in Performance Evaluation of Research and Development Organizations," *Technological Forecasting and Social Change*, 47(2), 1994, 189-203.

43. This model is both a process and a content model.

44. Landes, D., *The Unbound Prometheus* (Cambridge: Cambridge University Press, 1969); and Landes, D., *The Wealth and Poverty of Nations: Why Are Some So Rich and Some So Poor* (New York: W. W. Norton & Company, 1998).

45. Mokyr, J., *The Lever of Riches: Technological Creativity and Economic Progress* (New York: Oxford University Press, 1990).

46. See, in particular, Rosenberg, 1989, *op. cit.*

47. Stokes, D., Pasteur's Quadrant: Basic Science and Technological Innovation (Washington, DC: Brookings Institution Press, 1997).

48. This is further discussed in Chapter 7.

49. Cziko, G., *Without Miracles: Universal Selection Theory and the Second Darwinian Revolution* (Camhridge, MA: MIT Press, 1995).

50. See, for example, Basalla, G., *The Evolution of Technology* (Cambridge: Cambridge University Press, 1988). Also see Vincenti, W., *What Engineers Know and How They Know It* (Baltimore: Johns Hopkins University Press, 1990).

51. See, for example, Griliches, Z., *R&D, Patents, and Productivity* (Chicago: University of Chicago Press, 1984). Also see Pfetsch, F., "The Measurement of

Technical Change: Toward a Taxonomy and a Theory," *Research Policy*, 13(4), 1984, 343-373.

7

THEORIES OF KNOWLEDGE AND THE KNOWLEDGE-DRIVEN SOCIETY

The link between S&T and knowledge is of two types. One is the nature of knowledge *in* S&T, which roughly translates into the definition of S&T *as* knowledge. The other type is the contributions of S&T *to* knowledge. Can S&T be considered a precursor or generator of knowledge, independent of its institutional characteristics? Moreover, can S&T be equated with information and knowledge so that its evaluation would focus on the latter as surrogates for the S&T effort?

This chapter examines the various theories of knowledge and the relationship between S&T and the knowledge-driven economy and society. There is a constantly expanding literature on knowledge and its uses, so this chapter will offer what I believe to be the more relevant aspects of this body of work.[1]

SCIENCE, TECHNOLOGY, AND INFORMATION

One of the outcomes from science, perhaps a major outcome, is in the form of information. Proximal outputs from the scientific effort include bibliometrics—that is, publications, books, reports, and citations thereof. All have as content the information generated by the scientific effort. When we confine outcomes to such items loaded with information, we thus define science in terms of the information it generates.

Theory of Knowledge-Creation (Nonaka and Takeuchi)

But technology also has embedded information, which is the scientific effort that has led to its creation. In their seminal book, Nonaka and Takeuchi have traced the philosophical development of the notion of "knowledge" in Western and Japanese philosophies.[2] They argue that the Western intellectual tradition has been influenced by the Cartesian duality of subject and object, mind and matter. In the Japanese tradition, however, there is a belief in a continuous flow between observer and his reality. The authors distinguish between the Western approach of seeking some eternal truths from the viewpoint of an objective observer—and the Japanese view that mind and matter are complementary.

Nonaka and Takeuchi then proceed to outline their synthesis of the two divergent perspectives. They suggest that economic and organizational theorists—from Schumpeter to Simon and Drucker—have discussed the "acquisition, accumulation, and utilization of *existing* knowledge; they lack the perspective of 'creating new knowledge' ... the subjective, bodily, and tacit aspects of knowledge are still largely neglected" (p. 49). However, Western scholars have considered information processing in organizations as means to adaptation to environmental pressures. Nonaka and Takeuchi thus argue that this approach fails to explain *innovation* in organizations, because the process of innovation also creates new knowledge, in addition to merely processing existing knowledge.

Their theory of organizational knowledge creation is anchored in the belief that much of the creation of new knowledge depends on the processes that capture, transform, and utilize tacit knowledge.[3] They also base their theory on the interplay among individuals, groups, and the entire organization. Such interplay leads to what Nonaka and Takeuchi describe as "spiraling," so that tacit and explicit modes of knowledge interact and are diffused throughout the organization.

Thus, they proposed five stages that describe the process of knowledge creation: (1) sharing tacit knowledge, (2) creating concepts, (3) justifying concepts, (4) building an archetype, and (5) cross-leveling knowledge. These stages and the theory in general may explain the dynamics of knowledge dissemination in organizations. They may also contribute to our understanding of the processes by which scientific outputs (in the form of knowledge) are transferred, diffused, and disseminated.[4] As items of information and knowledge, scientific outputs are absorbed and internalized by individuals, groups, and, finally, by the organization. As such, these outputs are added to the existing body of knowledge, in the form of explicit knowledge embedded in patents, products, and services.[5]

Social Construction of Knowledge

Mizruchi and Fein[6] have argued that "the interpretation and uses of knowledge have a socially constructed character and that this can lead organizational researchers, as well as scholars in general, toward misleading representations of phenomena" (p. 654). The authors reviewed 26 citations of an article by DiMaggio and Powell in which these authors had suggested three possible mechanisms for institutional isomorphism: (1) coercive (pressures from other organizations), (2) mimetic (decision by managers to imitate other organizations), and (3) normative (socialization due to similar professional training).[7]

Mizruchi and Fein have found that the mode of mimetics, one of the mechanisms identified by DiMaggio and Powell in their study of isomorphism, has been by far the mode of explanation preferred by scholars who studied isomorphism in organizations. Mizruhi and Fein conclude that this specific form of isomorphism is preferred because it is "consistent with the dominantly held view among leading North American organizational researchers that emphasizes cognitive decision-making processes at the expense of interorganizational power and coercion" (p. 677).

This tendency of researchers to prefer those constructs that coincide with their dominant and current wisdom has also been described by Kuhn in his notion of the paradigmatic structure of scientific progress.[8] Knowledge progresses through the selective interpretation by other scholars, who tend to remain within the confines of their "paradigm." This conclusion may contribute to our understanding of both the trajectory of the flow of scientific outputs, and the barriers to its progress.

When scientific outcomes in the form of knowledge (e.g., bibliometrics) flow downstream the innovation continuum, they will be selectively filtered and interpreted in accordance with dominant perspectives held by key scholars in the disciplinary area.[9] A similar process may be occurring in the flow of scientific knowledge toward its incorporation in technological achievements. Diffusion of scientific knowledge is thus biased by socially influenced preferences and selective filtering of what constitutes "relevant" knowledge.[10]

Knowledge and Theories of the Firm

Several well-established economic theories of the firm have more recently been shown to be structured responses to knowledge-based problems. Fransman provides a description of the various theories of the firm and their relation to information-processing and to knowledge acquisition and usage.[11] Behavioral approaches such as those of March, Simon, and Cyert contributed the notions of "bounded rationality" and the human-organizational processes of information-seeking behavior. Fransman argues that the firm is a "repository of knowledge" which emerges as a result of the historical nature of the individual firm's articulation of information-related problems.[12] Fransman has considered the theory of the firm proposed by Nelson and Winter.[13] These authors argued that the evolution of the firm's behavior is based on routine, search, and selection.

Fransman's main argument is centered around the notion that, due to behavioral constraints such as bounded rationality and the existence of uncertainty, information-processing and useful knowledge are divergent outcomes in the large modern firm. He argues that the distinction between information and knowledge is primarily that "information is a closed set, knowledge is essentially open-ended. Information and knowledge as thus defined, therefore, are loosely coupled" (p. 189).

In this framework, knowledge encompasses, in addition to information, the vision or image of the firm, hence its set of beliefs. Knowledge cannot be analyzed independently of the processor, so that behavioral strengths as well as limitations are at play. Identical sets of information processed by different firms may lead to different knowledge outcomes.

Fransman refers to the "IBM paradox," in which the company had sufficient information to the contrary, yet continued nurturing the "knowledge" that mainframes are the means for the company's growth and continued competitiveness.

Knowledge as Competence

The analyses by the aforementioned theorists of the firm lead to the conclusion that for the firm to maintain its competitive position and to grow and prosper, it relies on its ability to create useful knowledge. The existence of resources and the acquisition of information are not sufficient for sustained growth.

Geisler has provided an example of the disjointed flow of information and subsequent knowledge in the "Ritchie Incident."[14] In 1942, the British general Sir Neil Ritchie was facing Field-Marshall Rommel in the North African desert. Ritchie was in possession of vast and accurate information about Rommel's battle plan, yet he ignored the information and fell into Rommel's trap.

Knowledge-as-competence can be of two types. First, knowledge generated through information processing in the firm may lead to the creation or strengthening of the firm's competencies. These are generally defined as the skills, resources, and routines that allow the firm to successfully compete in its environment. Thus, knowledge contributes to the "competitive attributes" of these core capabilities. The contribution is primarily in providing the framework and tools for the articulation of the capabilities (competencies) toward the goals of the firm.

Another type of competence is the use of knowledge *as* the core capability. In this case the firm utilizes knowledge itself as the competitive weapon. The more the firm is engaged in knowledge-intensive business, the more its knowledge can and will be used as a competence in the firm's competitive environment.

Knowledge-as-competence may be illustrated by the relationship between information technology (IT) and strategy. In many firms IT is viewed as an ancillary resource that contributes to the main functions of the firm as a support activity. Other firms view IT as a competitive weapon, by moving it from the back-room operations to the provision of capabilities in direct contact with customers.

Assuming that knowledge is a key component of IT, then the knowledge generated by IT is in itself a core capability of the firm. The strategic importance of such capability is thus established and IT is considered to be much more than a cost center or an ancillary effort.

Embedded Knowledge

In order to contribute to the firm's core competencies or to serve as such, knowledge is embedded in almost every aspect of the firm's activities. Prahalad and Hamel, for example, define core competencies as they are manifested in the firm's products and technology.[15] Other scholars extend the notion to the value chain of the firm, in which marketing activities are also included.[16]

In the first instance, knowledge is embedded in the products and is primarily *technological* knowledge that provides the firm with a competitive edge. As the model of core competencies is extended to include other parts of the value chain, the embedded knowledge now includes technological, managerial, administrative, and even tacit knowledge of the people involved with these activities.[17]

Such embedded knowledge pervades all the attributes and activities of the firm, hence the difficulties in extracting and identifying it. Knowledge always existed in the firm, but only recently have we begun to systematically study its existence and its value in the firm's success.

The Firm as Institutionalized Knowledge

If we extend the rationale of the firm as a repository of knowledge, then the ability and pattern of each firm to process and utilize such knowledge would explain the different structures and performances of firms. Moreover, the firm may be viewed as the institutionalization of knowledge about the particular business. The firm is created in order to institutionalize the processing of the mix of tacit and explicit knowledge. The complexity and uncertainty of the environment require a formal manner of information and knowledge processing, ultimately resulting in the mode of the firm.

For example, in the late 1990s, Xerox Corporation made the transition from a hardware company to a document or knowledge company. As Dan Halfhouse, corporate strategy director for Xerox, described the transition, the company began by understanding the knowledge phenomenon and how knowledge workers perform their tasks. It was an effort to identify the "embeddedness" of knowledge in what Xerox was doing and how it was doing it."[18] To an extent, Xerox has restructured itself along the lines of what constitutes knowledge in its business and where it plays a role in the firm's effort.

Role of Science and Technology

Within the confines of the firm, science and technology may be viewed as producers of knowledge. In addition to generating innovative products and processes, S&T also adds to the historical pool of skills and capabilities.

Teece and Pisano have proposed a useful framework for the incorporation of S&T and its outcomes.[19] They argue that "dynamic capabilities" are a notion that better explains the sustained competitive advantage of firms. Dynamic capabilities "integrate existing conceptual and empirical knowledge, and facilitate prescription" (p. 193). They are the competencies of the firm to utilize all of its skills and resources (including knowledge) in adapting to the ever-changing environment.[20]

Some key concepts in this framework include *integration* of the various capabilities in a coherent manner. Along these lines, knowledge generated by S&T in the firm is integrated with other knowledge, imported from outside, and that which is already embedded in routines and processes within the firm's value chain. Such total knowledge is systematically applied in providing the firm with the dynamic capability to compete.[21]

Hence, the technical and administrative knowledge produced within the firm is embedded in products and processes, and is also integrated in routines that lead to an improved competitive position. Moreover, such knowledge is accumulated to form and strengthen the historical capacity of the firm through learning and diffusion of the knowledge among its members.

S&T, Knowledge, and Society

When we extend the concept of the role of S&T in the firm's competitiveness to the social context, there are two possible outcomes. The first implies that S&T creates knowledge that propels economic progress. If we bring together the framework of dynamic capabilities and the knowledge-economic progress relationship, the following scenario will emerge. Knowledge produced by firms and other organizations (e.g., government and universities) is diffused in the economy to the extent that it will be absorbed by firms and contribute to their success, thus propelling economic progress. By adding to the firms' dynamic capabilities, the knowledge that is generated and transferred to participants in the economy and society can be credited with economic development. As discussed earlier in Chapter 6, S&T may be viewed as key levers of economic progress and the accumulation of wealth.[22]

But how this process works is a matter of fascination to organization scientists and those scholars who study strategic management. Industrial firms, for example, produce knowledge and at the same time utilize it to enhance their competitiveness, to stay in business and grow. By so doing they generate wealth and economic progress. S&T is not only a generator of *new* knowledge, but also offers the means for the firm to adopt and utilize knowledge within the formation of its dynamic capabilities.

Diffusion of knowledge and the progression of S&T outcomes are therefore two areas of research that intertwine and empirically lead to similar conclusions. The diffusion of knowledge from S&T in the form of biblio-metrics, for example, contributes to the firm's capability to compete and to create wealth.[23]

The second possible outcome is knowledge produced by S&T that contributes to social events and activities, thus adding to the betterment of humankind. The process by which such knowledge is diffused to social entities is intimately linked to the diffusion of S&T in society, as well as through other means, such as education, training, and socialization.[24]

Knowledge generated by S&T is transformed through various mechanisms that depend on the social institution into which such knowledge is imported. Thus new knowledge produced in one discipline or area of inquiry may be adopted by a different area and added to the knowledge base in that area. For example, knowledge developed in biology and genetics on DNA is imported into law enforcement and utilized by the criminal justice institutions to determine guilt or innocence. Similarly, knowledge generated in materials science on wear and tear may be utilized by the aeronautics industry to test the wear of materials used in the construction of airplanes.

S&T and the Knowledge-Driven Society

As we move toward an economy driven by knowledge and knowledge workers, the role of science and technology becomes even more crucial. S&T is the source for *new* knowledge that is injected into the economy, and that fuels developments in social organizations such as education, healthcare, and communications. New knowledge is thus a critical driver of human progress.

In a special issue on the nature of the enterprise of the 21st century, the editors of the magazine *Knowledge Management* have concluded that "the organizations that are best able to employ KM technologies and practices to align their activities with these seven trends will be those that flourish in the unpredictable business environment of the emerging knowledge age."[25] The seven trends are: (1) the extended enterprise, (2) value creation through new customer relations, (3) customized sales models for on-going relations with customers, (4) the dynamic organization, (5) strategic information technology architecture, (6) empowered employees, and (7) flexible design of the workplace.

But these trends may not only be the result of the knowledge economy as they also foster and encourage added usages of knowledge. Where will this *new* knowledge come from? How will it be diffused, transferred, and adopted in these forthcoming organizations? Much of the vision of the knowledge society relates to the added speed, new frontiers, and new organizational and social formats. There is less emphasis among scholars and business managers on the source of new knowledge. In the early years of the 21st century, there seems to be an agreement as to the future trends and their impacts, yet little meaningful and systematic discussion on the sources of knowledge.[26]

The issue of generating new knowledge to propel social and economic progress will certainly be a fundamental issue in the coming years. There are three crucial elements to this issue: source, adoption, and synchronism. These are shown in Figure 7.1.

Source of New Knowledge. New knowledge is generated, to a large extent, by science and technology. The more knowledge-driven the society, the more it relies on new knowledge to maintain its institutions. At the same time, there will probably be a shift in the *type* of knowledge that S&T will be required to generate, so that it can be more relevant to the needs of the knowledge-driven society. Such a transformation will impact the nature of S&T and the processes by which it is produced.

This potential trend goes beyond the need for relevancy which had been at the core of industry S&T management.[27] The issue extends to the production of S&T that can be easily transformed into usable *new knowledge*, or that is already in the form of usable knowledge. In a vein similar to the trend to reduce "time to market" which was popular in the 1980s and 1990s, this trend will encourage behavior that reduces the path from the outputs of S&T to their incorporation as usable new knowledge.

Perhaps the more radical issue would be the changes that the knowledge-driven economy and society will impose on the S&T-producing organizations. New knowledge may thus be required, with the idea that it would be tailored

Figure 7.1
Diffusion and Adoption of Knowledge Generated by Science and Technology

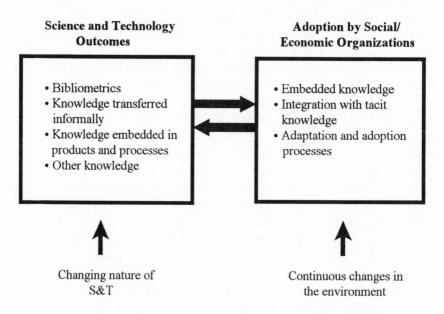

to the evolving institutions.   Such a trend leads to the second element: adoption.

Adoption of New Knowledge.   Institutions in the knowledge-driven society would have to be able to adopt and utilize the new knowledge they import and acquire. Even if S&T (academic, industrial, and governmental) is capable of producing potentially useful new knowledge, organizations would have to create and sustain mechanisms that would provide them with capabilities to absorb and adopt new knowledge.

Van den Bosch, Volberda, and de Boer argue that knowledge environments coevolve with the emergence of new organizational forms that are capable of better absorbing such new knowledge.[28] They also contend that changing knowledge environments will thus have significant impact on the adoption processes of new knowledge.[29]

But one would expect that the process of adoption in this case would not substantially differ from adoption of other types of S&T outputs. Human, organizational, and other barriers to adoption and diffusion will continue to exist and exercise their hindering effects. The composition of the set of barriers may vary, but the adoption process will be subjected to such basic factors as difficulties in sharing knowledge, transforming and diffusion of S&T outcomes, and the adaptation of knowledge procured elsewhere to fit within the existing framework of the institution.

Synchronism of New Knowledge. New knowledge that is produced by S&T and incorporated into economic and social organizations needs to be in harmony with these institutions, so as to reduce the difficulties of adoption, diffusion, and utilization. The more synchronous the knowledge, the smoother the adoption process will be. However, new knowledge may be similar to "revolutionary" innovations, in that it fosters "creative destruction" to the extent that it brings about radical transformations in the way the adopting organizations function and are structured.

In order to increase synchronism of the new knowledge with the existing knowledge base and other processes, there should be dynamic cooperation between knowledge producers and consumers. This phenomenon is similar to the notion of co-evolution.[29] But synchronism also implies convergence and adequacy which are dependent not only on the organization's absoprtive capacity, but also on the degree to which S&T institutions produce adequate knowledge. That is, for effective diffusion and adoption there is a need to have a systemic convergence of objectives and criteria (for the knowledge being produced) between producers and consumers. Our experience with traditional diffusion processes of S&T points to a host of difficulties along the way.[30]

SUMMARY

Traditional theories of knowledge have emphasized the attributes of knowledge and some of its processes within organizations. These theories are preliminary explorations of the phenomenon, offering little more than taxonomic descriptions and major paths in the progress of knowledge.

However we define and describe knowledge and knowledge-driven institutions, S&T is the principal activity that generates new knowledge per se (e.g., in the form of bibliometrics) and knowledge embedded in innovations and new products and processes.

Ultimately, S&T would be evaluated by criteria that would include its contributions to the knowledge-driven society. A possible trend may be that it may no longer be sufficient to produce innovations in the form of products and processes, but to generate—in a systematic fashion—knowledge that is new, implementable, and usable. This may be a revised role for S&T. It may also bring to renewed preeminence the role of bibliometrics in the total set of S&T outcomes, and to emphasize the role of knowledge embedded in technology and technological innovations.[31]

NOTES

1. See, for example, Greenberg, G., and E. Tobach (Eds.), *Theories of the Evolution of Knowledge* (New York: Lawrence Erlbaum Associates, 1990). Also see

Hill, T., *Contemporary Theories of Knowledge* (New York: Books on Demand, 1995); and Nonaka, I., "A Dynamic Theory of Organizational Knowledge Creation," *Organization Science*, 5(1), 1994, 14-37. More recently, see, for example, Pollock, J., and J. Cruz, *Contemporary Theories of Knowledge* (Savage, MD: Rowman & Littlefield, 1999). These are merely examples of the growing literatures on this topic in philosophy, social sciences, and management.

2. Nonaka, I., and H. Takeuchi, *The Knowledge-Creating Company: How Japanese Companies Create the Dynamics of Innovation* (New York: Oxford University Press, 1995).

3. See, for example, Geisler, E., "Harnessing the Value of Experience in the Knowledge-Driven Firm," *Business Horizons*, 42(3), 1999, 18-26 Geisler describes the role of tacit knowledge embedded in managerial experience, and proposed some ways to elicit and to utilize this knowledge as part of the organization's knowledge management system (KMS). Also see Leonard, D., *Wellsprings of Knowledge: Building and Sustaining the Sources of Innovation* (Boston: Harvard Business School Press, 1998). And see Sveiby, K., *The New Organizational Wealth: Managing and Measuring Knowledge-Based Assets* (New York: Berrett-Koettler, 1997).

4. Geisler describes several mechanisms for the transfer and diffusion of tacit knowledge in work organizations. A key mechanism is "debriefing" of executives. See Geisler, 1999, *op. cit.*

5. See Nonaka and Takeuchi, 1995, *op. cit.*, Figure 3-9, p. 84.

6. Mizruchi, M., and L. Fein, "The Social Construction of Organizational Knowledge: A Study of the Uses of Coercive, Mimetic, and Normative Isomorphism," *Administrative Science Quarterly*, 1999, 44(4), 653-683.

7. DiMaggio, P., and W. Powell, "The Iron Cage Revisited: Institutional Isomorphism and Collective Rationalizing in Organizational Fields," *American Sociological Review*, 48(2), 1983, 147-160.

8. Kuhn, T., *The Structure of Scientific Revolutions*, 2nd ed. (Chicago: University of Chicago Press, 1970).

9. See, for example, similar discussions of this topic in Hamilton, R., *The Social Misconstruction of Reality* (New Haven, CT: Yale University Press, 1996). Also see Strang, D., and S. Soule, "Diffusion in Organizations and Social Movements: From Hybrid Corn to Poison Pills," *Annual Review of Sociology*, 24(3), 1998, 265-290. And Powell, W., and P. DiMaggio, *The New Institutionalism in Organizational Analysis* (Chicago: University of Chicago Press, 1991).

10. When compared with the organizational model advanced by Nonaka and Takeuchi, the spiraling phenomenon of the creation and diffusion of knowledge will be hampered by social constraints and selective construction of reality. See, for example, Cole, S., *Making Science* (Cambridge, MA: Harvard University Press, 1992).

11. Fransman, M., "Information, Knowledge, Vision, and Theories of the Firm," in Dosi, G., D. Teece, and J. Chytry (Eds.), *Technology, Organization, and Competitiveness: Perspectives on Industrial and Corporate Change* (New York: Oxford University Press, 1998), pp. 147-191.

12. Fransman, *op. cit.*, p. 149.

13. Nelson, R., and G. Winter, *An Evolutionary Theory of Economic Change* (Cambridge, MA: Harvard University Press, 1982).

14. Geisler, E., *Managing the Aftermath of Radical Corporate Change: Reengineering, Restructuring, and Reinvention* (Westport, CT: Quorum Books, 1997).

15. Prahalad, C., and G. Hamel, "The Core Competence of the Corporation," *Harvard Business Reviews*, 68(3), 1990, 79-91.

16. See, for example, Hedlund, G., "A Model of Knowledge Management and the N-Form Corporation," *Strategic Management Journal*, 15(2), 1994, 73-90. Also see Kogut, B., and U. Zanger, "Knowledge of the Firm, Combinative Capabilities and the Replication of Technology," *Organization Science*, 18(6), 1997, 973-996. And see Stalk, G., P. Evans, and L. Schulman, "Competing on Capabilities: The New Role of Corporate Strategy," *Harvard Business Review*, 70(2), 1992, 57-69.

17. Here I close the circle, as this argument brings to mind Nonaka and Takeuchi who discussed the merging of tacit and explicit knowledge in all aspects of the corporation.

18. See the story of Xerox in Barth, S., "Knowledge as a Function of X," *Knowledge Management*, 3(2), 2000, 31-38.

19. Teece, D., and G. Pisano, "The Dynamic Capabilities of Firms: An Introduction," in Dosi, Teece, and Chytry (Eds.), 1998, *op. cit.*, pp. 193-214.

20. Also see, for example, Henderson, R., "The Evolution of Integrative Capability: Innovation in Cardiovascular Drug Discovery," *Industrial and Corporate Change*, 3(2), 1995, 607-630; and see Teece, D., R. Rumelt, G. Dosi, and S. Winter, "Understanding Corporate Coherence: Theory and Evidence," *Journal of Economic Behavior and Organization*, 23(1), 1994, 1-30.

21. Clearly the knowledge required to *integrate* and utilize the knowledge base of the firm is in itself knowledge that creates capabilities. Such knowledge may be embedded in the skills of managers, and in their tacit knowledge on how to manage the firm in a turbulent environment. See, for example, Lazonick, W., "Learning and the Dynamics of International Competitive Advantage," in R. Thompson (Ed.), *Learning and Technological Changes* (New York: Macmillan, 1993, pp. 172-197).

22. See, for example, Mokyr, J., *The Lever of Riches: Technological Creativity and Economic Progress* (New York: Oxford University Press, 1990).

23. See, for example, Montigny, P., "From Technological Advance to Economic Progress," *The OECD Observer*, 170(2), 1991, 9-14. Also see von Tunzelman, G., *Technology and Industrial Progress: The Foundations of Economic Growth* (New York: Edward Elgar, 1995).

24. See, for example, the case of S&T contributions to health care: Golub, E., *The Limits of Medicine: How Science Shapes Our Hope for the Cure* (Chicago: University of Chicago Press, 1997). Also see Rothman, D., *Beginnings Count: The Technological Imperative in American Health Care* (New York: Oxford University Press, 1997), and Wyke, A., *21ˢᵗ Century Miracle Medicine: Robosurgery, Wonder Cures, and the Quest for Immortality* (New York: Plenum Press, 1997).

25. Ruby, D., and J. Bartlett, "The Enterprise of the 21ˢᵗ Century," *Knowledge Management*, 3(1), 2000, p. 28.

26. See, for example, Bontis, N., N. Dragonetti, K. Jacobsen, and G. Roos, "The Knowledge Toolbox: A Review of the Tools Available to Measure and Manage Intangible Resources," *European Management Journal*, 17(4), 1999, 391-402. Also see McKenney, J., R. Mason, and D. Copeland, *Waves of Change: Business Evolution Through Information Technology* (Boston: Harvard Business School Press, 1995). And see Dijksterhuis, M., F. van den Bosch, and H. Volberda, "Where Do New Organization Forms Come From? Management Logics as a Source of Coevolution," *Organization Science*, 10(5), 1999, 569-582. Also see Inkpen, A., and A. Dinur, "Knowledge Management Processes and International Joint Ventures," *Organization Science*, 9(4), 1998, 454-468. And see, for example, Conceicão, P., D. Gibson, M. Heitor, and S. Shariq (Eds.), *Science, Technology, and Innovation Policy: Opportunities and Challenges for the Knowledge Economy* (Westport, CT: Quorum Books, 2000).

27. See, for example, Ganguly, A., *Business-Driven Research and Development: Managing Knowledge to Create Wealth* (West Lafayette, IN: Purdue University Press, 1999). The author discusses the role that R&D plays in corporate strategy and the need to make R&D responsive to business objectives.

28. Van den Bosch, F., H. Volberda, and M. de Boer, "Coevolution of Firm Absorptive Capacity and Knowledge Environment: Organizational Forms and Combinative Capabilities," *Organization Science*, 10(5), 1999, 551-568.

29. *Ibid.*

30. See, for example, O'Dell, C., C. Jackson Grayson, and N. Essaides, *If Only We Knew What We Know: The Transfer of Internal Knowledge and Best Practice* (New York: Simon & Schuster Trade, 1999). Also see Cross, R., and S. Israelit, *Strategic Learning in a Knowledge Economy: Individual, Collective, and Organizational Learning Processes* (London: Butterworth-Heinemann, 1999).

31. See, for example, Messick, D., J. Levine, and L. Thompson, *Shared Cognition in Organizations: The Management of Knowledge* (New York: Lawrence Erlbaum Associates, 1999). In particular see Chapter 3, pp. 49-59.

8

DEFINITIONS OF CONCEPTS

What is the universe of science and technology? Which are the concepts that compose it, the elements that make it happen, and the components and dimensions that allow us to study it? Traditionally, the definitions and resultant taxonomy have described the activity or selected characteristics of a slice of that which for now will be described by the generic term: the *innovation* phenomenon.

Thus, the terminology is abundant with such terms as basic research, applied research, development, engineering, technology, invention, and innovation. There are several definitions for each of these concepts, largely related to the interests of the entity that provides the definition. By and large, however, the U.S. National Science Foundation (NSF) has proposed an objective set of definitions for several concepts.

DEFINITIONS OF RESEARCH AND DEVELOPMENT

Basic research is defined by the NSF as an activity that "has as its objective a fuller knowledge or understanding of the subject under study, rather than a practical application thereof."[1] To accommodate the industrial experience, NSF has provided the following definition: "In industry, basic research is defined as research that advances scientific knowledge but does not have specific immediate commercial objectives, although it may be in fields of present or potential interest to the company."[2]

Applied research is defined by NSF as "research aimed at gaining knowledge or understanding to determine the means by which a specific, recognized need may be met. In industry, applied research includes investigations oriented to discovering new scientific knowledge that has specific commercial objectives with respect to products, processes, or services."[3]

Development is defined by NSF as "the systematic use of the knowledge or understanding gained from research toward the production of useful materials, devices, systems, or methods, including the design and development of prototypes and processes."[4]

By comparison, the National Academy of Sciences has offered somewhat more concise definitions. In the Research, Development, and Engineering spectrum, *research* is defined as "applied research, which is directed toward practical applications of scientific knowledge—in contrast to basic research directed toward increasing scientific knowledge."[5]

Development is defined as "the systematic use of knowledge gained from research for the production of useful materials, devices, systems, methods, or processes, exclusive of design or production engineering."[6] *Engineering* is "concerned with actual construction, assembly, layout, and testing of models for pilot processes and procedures—to produce a system that will work."[7]

Technology was defined as "the application of knowledge to new ways of doing things. It is distinguishable from science, which produces new knowledge, although science and technology form part of a single system interacting with other systems."[8] Finally, *innovation* was defined by the Academy as "the act or process of giving a new idea or an invention an economic impact."[9]

The U.S. Department of Defense[10] (DOD) has established its own set of definitions in specifically coded categories so that:

6.1 = *Research*: directed to the development of fundamental knowledge.

6.2 = *Exploratory Development*: directed to the development of new techniques, methodologies, and criteria.

6.3 = *Advanced Development*: concerned with design and development and hardware (material) items for experimentation.

6.4 = *Engineering Development*: Directed to testing, and demonstration of new techniques or methodologies, and to technical systems development.

6.5 = *Management and Support*: Directed to the support of installations for their operations and maintenance and for the procurement of special purpose equipment.

Another yet similar definition of research and development activities was provided by the Organization for Economic Cooperation and Development (OECD).[11] *Basic research* was defined as "experimental or theoretical work undertaken primarily to acquire new knowledge of the underlying foundations of phenomena and observable facts, without any particular application or use in view." *Pure basic research* was defined as being "carried out for the advancement of knowledge, without working for long-term economic or social benefits and with no positive effort being made to apply the results to practical problems or to transfer the results to sectors responsible for its applications." Another category was *oriented basic research*, which was defined as "carried out with the expectation that it will produce a broad base of knowledge likely to form the background to the solution of recognized or expected current or future problems or possibilities."

Similarly the OECD defined *Applied Research* as "also original investigation, undertaken in order to acquire new knowledge . . . directed primarily toward a specific practical aim or objective . . . develops ideas into operational form."

DEFINING TECHNOLOGY AND INNOVATION

Some authors in the field of Management of Technology (MOT) have attempted to define technology. Nino Levy, for example, defined the concept as the "assembly of hardware and software means and tools used by human beings to achieve socioeconomic goals."[12] Dale Compton defined technology as "the body of engineering and scientific knowledge and methods concerned with the design, development, production, distribution, support, and disposal of products and services."[13]

Innovation has been defined with and without the technological component. Alan Afuah, for example, defined innovation as "the use of new technological and market knowledge to offer a new product or service to customers."[14] Nelson and Rosenberg defined innovation as "the processes by which firms master and get into practice product designs and manufacturing processes that are new to them, if not to the universe or even to the nation."[15]

Peter Drucker defined innovation in economic and social terms, rather than simply technological. He offered a concise definition, that innovation is an activity that changes the yield from economic resources, so that it would ultimately change "the value and satisfaction obtained from resources by the consumer."[16] Similarly, Edosomwan defines the term as "the introduction of a new product, process, or service into the marketplace."[17]

WHY ARE THE DEFINITIONS CONCEPTUALLY INADEQUATE?

Confusing as these definitions may be, they offer a broad-brush idea of the conceptual foundations and temporal occurrence of each term. Clearly, innovation extends to the marketplace whereas research and even development are restricted to exploration and experimentation. Technology is defined largely in a catchall fashion, but mostly in a format that is both descriptive and instrumental: what is the activity and why are people and institutions engaged in it?

Figure 8.1 shows the interaction of the components of the phenomenon of research-technology-innovation—with the aspects or characteristics used in their definition.

These intersects do answer our questions: Who conducts these activities? How are they conducted? Why are we doing this? and Who benefits? If, however, we continue this analysis and decompose the activities into the stages of their existence, and intersect these with the tangible and intangible elements that constitute them—we end up with a much more revealing scheme, portrayed in Figure 8.2.

Tangible components are the knowledge, methods, techniques, devices, applications, and solutions that emerge from science and technology. Intangibles are, for example, the satisfaction and achievement of needs by clients, customers, and impactees. Of interest is how this intersection depicted in Figure 8.2 works, so we ask: How fast? How much or how many (knowledge, methods, etc.)? How costly were these outcomes at each stage? and How effectively has this system worked?

Figure 8.1
Intersect of Components of the Phenomenon of Technical Change and Aspects of its Definition

Compounds	Description Of Activity	Instrumentality (For What Purpose?)	From Whose Viewpoint?
Science	What	Why	Who
Research	is	are we	conducts the
Development	explored	doing this?	activity?
Innovation	and	For what	Who gains
Technology	How?	purpose?	from it?

Figure 8.2
Intersect of Stages of Progress of Science and Technology, and Elements That Compose Them

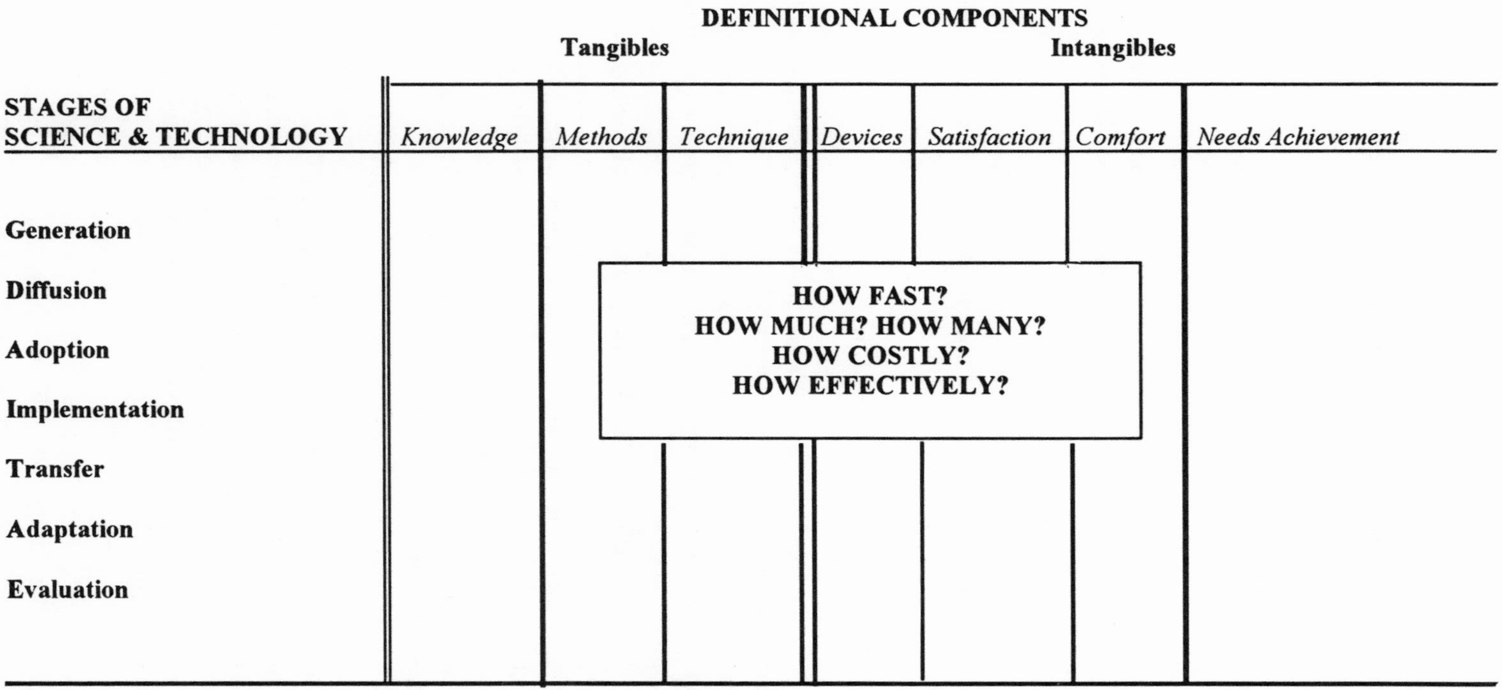

	DEFINITIONAL COMPONENTS						
	Tangibles				Intangibles		
STAGES OF SCIENCE & TECHNOLOGY	Knowledge	Methods	Technique	Devices	Satisfaction	Comfort	Needs Achievement
Generation							
Diffusion				HOW FAST? HOW MUCH? HOW MANY? HOW COSTLY? HOW EFFECTIVELY?			
Adoption							
Implementation							
Transfer							
Adaptation							
Evaluation							

Yet these definitions and their multiple components fail to reflect the *human experience* that is embedded in science, technology, and innovation. From the moment primitive *homo sapiens* ventured outside a cave to explore his surroundings, to believe in his future, and to visualize his ability to control his environment, science and technology were born.

Traditional definitions fail to describe the attributes and characteristics of the activity *itself.* Not what it does, for whom, or by which means—but what the activity *means*, what it *entails*, and what it *represents*. Moreover, what *value* it creates.

Science, technology, and innovation encompass very noble and unique characteristics of the human spirit. Figure 8.3 shows a list of some of these characteristics and a very preliminary attempt to tie them (by the use of generic terms) to the existing definitions.

Human attributes that so greatly contribute to the generation and progress of S&T also exist and flourish within states of nature, such as chance, serendipity, happenstance, and the random convergence of natural occurrences.

SO, WHAT IS THE UNIVERSE?

Conceptually, then, S&T and R&D are more than some focused activities that may contribute to increase our stock of knowledge and to fulfill our needs and desires with machines, devices, and other novelties. They are also the operational condensation of the human spirit and its surge beyond the existing reality.

In his brilliant prose, Bertrand Russell contemplated that in this brief and transitory life, and in this uncertain universe of ours, scientists happily advance their metes because, they say "it is monkish and futile . . . to dwell on such cold and unpractical thoughts. Let us get on with the job of fertilizing the desert, melting arctic ice, and killing each other with perpetually improving technique. Some of our activities will do good, some harm, but all alike will show our power."[18]

The universe of S&T extends beyond the activities themselves, thus the measure of S&T is also the measure of the human spirit and of human achievements and failures. The evaluation of S&T, as expressed in this book, is the assessment of the processes of S&T, *and* the outputs from S&T, as they progress to accomplish the utmost of human enterprise. Schumpeter and Drucker were correct when both linked technical and other innovations to entrepreneurship, as the latter encompasses many of the human characteristics listed in Figure 8.3.[19]

Investments in S&T or the range of activities themselves are but a portion of the overall picture. There is a conceptual as well as a temporal link between S&T and the overall innovation process. This process extends from the most fundamental research to the application of technology in commercial products, services, and engineering.[20] But, even beyond this process, the universe of S&T extends to the benefits, harmful effects, and otherwise all the contributions and impacts of S&T and its outputs on society and on the economy. Thus it encompasses all aspects of human endeavors, from curiosity-driven exploration of the physical world to the effects on how we live our lives.[21] This comprehensive view seems to be the true representation of the process of human enterprise, as it is reflected in science, technology, and innovation—at the levels of the individual, the institution, and even the nation.

Figure 8.3
Science, Technology, and Innovation: Characteristics and Definitions

CHARACTERISTICS	SOME LINKS TO TERMS IN DEFINITIONS
Imagination	Creating scenarios and analyses of the physical university.
Newness/Novelty	Creation and diffusion of novel ideas and their outcomes.
Extension of Capability	Moving beyond constraints of human physical and mental limitations.
Risk Taking	Operating within an inherently risky activity.
Defying the Odds	Knowingly carrying on even though the odds are clearly unfavorable.
Conquering Uncertainty	Although success is doubtful, S&T proceeds without fear or retreat.
Curiosity	Driving force of human inquiry that precedes the rush to glory and fortune.
Mastering Natural Forces	The will and ability to deal with and to master the forces of nature.
Ability and Will to Improve	Not being satisfied with current conditions—always looking to improve.
Looking Forward	Futuristic outlook, beyond nature's changing seasons.
Creativity	Ability to generate things that are new, that have not existed before.
Dreaming	Attempting to go beyond the possible

NOTES

1. National Science Board, *Science Indicators 1982* (Washington, DC: U.S. Government Printing Office, 1983) p. 237.

2. National Science Board, *Science & Engineering Indicators* (Washington, DC: U.S. Government Printing Office, 1993; NSB-93-1) p. 94. This definition from a more recent publication of the NSB is only slightly different from the 1982 version.

3. *Ibid.*.

4. *Ibid.*

5. National Academy of Sciences, *U.S. International Firms and R,D&E in Developing Countries* (Washington, DC, 1973) p. xv.

6. *Ibid.*

7. *Ibid.*

8. *Ibid.*

9. *Ibid.*

10. U.S. Army, *Army Research Information Systems and Reports—AR70-9* (Springfield, VA, May 1981).

11. Organization for Economic Cooperation and Development, *The Measurement of Scientific and Technical Activities* (Paris: OECD Press, 1993).

12. Levy, N.,*Managing High Technology and Innovation* (Upper Saddle River, NJ: Prentice-Hall, 1998) p. 9.

13. Compton, D., *Engineering Management: Creating and Managing World-Class Operations* (Upper Saddle River, NJ: Prentice-Hall, 1997) p. 409.

14. Afuah, A., *Innovation Management: Strategies, Implementation, and Profit* (New York: Oxford University Press, 1998) p. 4.

15. Nelson, R., and N. Rosenberg, "Technical Innovations and National Systems," in R. Nelson (Ed.), *National Innovation Systems: A Comparative Analysis* (New York: Oxford University Press, 1993) p. 4.

16. Drucker, P., *Innovation and Entrepreneurship: Practice and Principles* (New York: Harper & Row, 1985) p. 33.

17. Edosomwan, J., *Integrity, Innovation, and Technology Management* (New York: John Wiley & Sons, 1989) p. 3.

18. Russell, B., *The Impact of Science and Society* (New York: Simon and Schuster, 1953) p. 15.

19. Donald Stokes argued that basic science and technological innovation are inexorably intertwined. He also contended that the artificial distinction made between science and technology tends to establish a paradigm that has harmed the "compact" between science and the American government. See Stokes, D., *Pasteur's Quadrant: Basic Science and Technological Innovation* (Washington, DC: Brookings Institution Press, 1997). Stokes proposed a revised model based on "use-inspired basic research." He also proposed a quadrant model of scientific research whereby there is an intersection between the "quest for fundamental understanding," and the "considerations of use."

20. An illustration of such convergence is given by Andrew Grove in recounting his years with Intel. Grove argued that, in what he called "Strategic Inflection Points," there is a radical transformation in which science and engineering are combined with

unconventional business thinking that will redirect the company. This dramatic change requires leadership abilities not only to recognize the need for change, but also to marshal the various resources of the organization—science, engineering, and business—into a coordinated force. See Grove, A., *Only the Paranoid Survive: How To Exploit the Crisis Points that Challenge Every Company* (New York: Random House, 1999).

21. See the example in note 20.

PART III

EVALUATION OF SCIENCE AND TECHNOLOGY

The term Science should not be given to anything but the aggregate of the recipes that are always successful. All the rest is literature.

Paul Valery
(1871-1945)

9

WHAT IS EVALUATION? ESTABLISHING THE BOUNDARY

In this chapter I will introduce the key components of the process and functions of evaluation in general and, in particular, the evaluation of science and technology. There is a well-established literature and a coherent tradition in the field of social and economic evaluation of programs, institutions, and projects.[1] In this chapter the emphasis is on establishing the common ground for discussion of the issues and methods involved with the evaluation of science and technology. To this end, the following is a selective compilation of various concepts, findings, and arguments that exist in the current evaluation literatures.

The generic or dictionary definition of evaluation is an activity geared toward establishing or judging the value of something or some entity. A more precise definition is "to determine the significance or worth by careful appraisal and study."[2] Such an activity may be straightforward as we set the value of a simple event or entity. But, in most cases, the event or entity is very complex, as is the attempt to determine the value.

Any evaluation effort depends on at least three sets of factors or conditions. These are summarized in Figure 9.1.

EXISTING COMPONENTS

These are the conditions required for an evaluation to occur.[3] The first is the existence of the "object" for evaluation, that is, what or who is evaluated. Although common sense would dictate that this is a simple issue for determination, it is nevertheless sufficiently nontrivial to require further examination.

Figure 9.1
Factors or Conditions for Evaluation

SET OF CONDITIONS	FACTORS OR CONDITIONS	
Existing Components	(1)	Existence of some "object" for evaluation—what/who is evaluated.
	(2)	Existence of interested parties to evaluate.
	(3)	Existence or agreed-upon measures and procedures for evaluation.
Participants & Background	(1)	Why evaluate?
	(2)	Cui Bono (who benefits?)
	(3)	Who can and should evaluate?
Process & Outcomes	(1)	What are the origin and acceptance of measures/criteria for use in evaluation to determine value?
	(2)	What are the processes and procedures to be used in evaluation (how to do it?)?
	(3)	What is to be done with the results?

In cases where the event or entity (process, program, intervention, or institution) is multifaceted or multidimensional, it becomes a matter of convention as well as compromise to fully agree on what or who to evaluate. Even partial agreement on the event or entity to be evaluated may produce misconceptions and disagreements concerning the *exact* item or area to be evaluated within the more general framework on which there has been a measure of accord.

Second, there is a need to have parties that are both interested in being the target of evaluation and willing to conduct the evaluation. In some instances, such as program evaluation, this activity is the result of the rules by which the system operates—whether in the case of the evaluator or the evaluated, or both. Such mandatory activities are part of an existing functional prerogative of the parties. A different set of circumstances may arise when a different party is brought into the system for the purpose of conducting an evaluation. This may lead to reexamination of the rules and a rehauling of procedure.

The third component is the existence of both measures and procedures for evaluation that have been agreed upon by the parties. This refers to *criteria* for evaluation and to the *process* (how to evaluate) that the parties have concurred to its implementation. Since some portion of determining value is based on judgment, the name of the game in this instance is to achieve a balance between formalized procedures and preestablished criteria and measures—and informal, judgmental, and even *ad hoc* procedures and measures. There is seldom an optimal formula for successful design, as much depends on the parties and their level of agreement and compromise.[4]

It is very easy to see that these needed components will generate a situation of contention in the evaluation of science and technology. In order to determine the object of the evaluation, there is a need to clearly define those elements of science and technology that will partake in the evaluation. As shown in the previous chapters, there are many issues associated with unambiguously defining these activities and those who participate in them.

PARTICIPANTS AND BACKGROUND

Why Evaluate?

Any person who has ever been involved with evaluation of an individual, project, or organization will certainly appreciate the struggle to ascertain the motives and reasons for evaluation. Why do institutions conduct evaluations? Figure 9.2 summarizes the commonly used motives and reasons for evaluation. These are generic reasons that may be applicable to different levels of entities being evaluated.

Figure 9.2
Reasons for Undertaking Evaluation Efforts

Why Evaluate?
• Assess, measure, determine, and elicit outcomes or outputs from an activity and efforts of individuals and units.
• Provide data for organizational and strategic processes, databases, and decision-making mechanisms.
• Provide feedback and induce awareness of those evaluated as to expectations, standards, and the value of their effort.
• Establish the value of the activity or effort, for use by the evaluators themselves and by other interested parties.
• Provide inputs in the resources allocation effort.
• Utilize the results of the evaluation as a mechanism for changes, redirection, and termination of the effort under evaluation.
• Utilize the results of the evaluation to change or redesign evaluation criteria, measures, and objectives/motives/reasons.

In addition to the desire to add information to selected databases, evaluation efforts are conducted to establish the value of the activity, individual, entity, or effort. Such value is then translated into strategic and operational processes, and ultimately leads to decisions on whether the activity should be modified or terminated.[5] Clearly, the value of the effort and ancillary outcomes are also incorporated as inputs to a resource allocation process.

Who Benefits?

An evaluation effort links the outcomes from that which is being evaluated with the ultimate goals and objectives of the evaluation. Figure 9.3 shows this process. But the link to goals and objectives becomes valuable and even useful to the evaluators only if there are some benefits to the evaluators from undertaking this effort. In some instances the benefits are to the evaluators as well as to other interested parties. So the evaluation will be worthwhile when such benefits are identified. Moreover, knowing who benefits from the evaluation will greatly help to clarify why the evaluation is undertaken at all, and why some criteria and measures have been chosen for use in the evaluation.[6]

Figure 9.3
Linking Outcomes from Evalution to Ultimate Goals

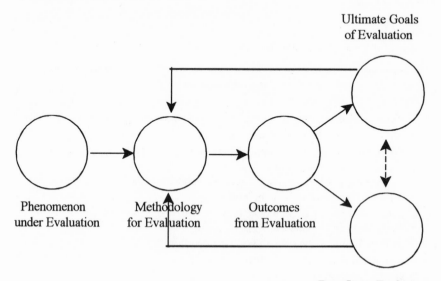

Ultimate Goals
of Evaluation

Phenomenon
under Evaluation

Methodology
for Evaluation

Outcomes
from Evaluation

Benefits to Evaluators
and Others

Consider, for example, the case of technoeconomic networks and their use to evaluate programs of the French Agency for Energy Management (AFME).[7] These tools helped managers of AFME to restructure programs and redesign resources allocation. Beneficiaries from the evaluation included not only the programs themselves, but also the managers of the agency, industrial companies involved with energy research and technology, and the public in general.

Benefits may also accrue to external parties (such as the public in the example of the AFME). In the case of public laboratories, for example, the public is an interested party since it funds these laboratories. But, in the interdependency of so many actors that are interconnected to the entity being evaluated or to the evaluators, chances are that several parties will receive benefits from the evaluation. Sometimes such benefits are long-term, as the beneficiaries, for example, would benefit from the database supplied by the said evaluation.[8]

Who Can and Should Evaluate?

These are two very distinct questions, which are artificially lumped together. Who can evaluate is an organizational issue that requires at least two prerequisites. First, that the evaluator has the legitimate claim or right to evaluate, hence the authority, resources, and ability to enter the domain of whoever is evaluated and so conduct the evaluation.[9]

In cases where there is a specific function assigned to conduct evaluations, the issue may be partially resolved. Although certain units are in charge of evaluation (for example, auditors, legal and financial departments, and task forces assigned for specific evaluations), many other entities and units would conduct their own, *ad hoc* evaluation activities. Confusion, overlapping efforts, and duplication of efforts are common occurrences in such instances.[10]

The importance of determining who can evaluate is primarily reflected in the objects, measures, and usages of the evaluation. The more the evaluators have institutional legitimacy, the more the evaluation would be carried out in harmony, with cogent participation and more truthful data generated. Another potential benefit would be increased standardization of criteria, measures, and procedures—hence leading to a more consistent database and a more useful and trustworthy tool for assessment and for comparisons across units and over time.

The second prerequisite is that the evaluator (including self-evaluator) is capable of carrying out the evaluation effort. This means that the evaluator has the necessary tools to conduct a worthwhile and comprehensive evaluation.

Tools include the arsenal of procedures, criteria, and measures, as well as the preestablished process for analysis and for the transfer of evaluation results.[11]

Clearly, not all who evaluate are also capable of doing so and should evaluate. Problems usually arise when task forces are composed to provide assessment, and generally with any *ad hoc* evaluation efforts. There is usually lack of experience, of a track-record, and of the level of understanding of the unit being evaluated. Such understanding comes as a result of trials and errors, and the resolution of problems that have plagued prior evaluation efforts. With experience and understanding one gains fewer conflicts and a smoother conduct of the evaluation effort.

The issue of who *should* evaluate is thorny at best, since it is a pregnant question. The normative assignment of evaluators is based on selective objectives for the evaluation, and on complex political and organizational considerations. An illustrative example can be found in the evaluation of R&D laboratories in industry. Divisional laboratories are evaluated at the division's level, but corporate managers also conduct their own evaluation effort.[12] The issue of who should evaluate is not only a formal issue, but also a question of who would be best suited to conduct this effort.[13]

PROCESSES AND OUTCOMES

Origins of Measures and Criteria

This is the question of where do the criteria and measures for evaluation come from and how are they accepted by the parties involved in the evaluation effort. The origins of the criteria for evaluation are in the objectives of the evaluation, combined with the specific criteria generated by the evaluators and those being evaluated.

The measures have their origin in the state of the art, namely, in what we know about measuring the phenomenon to be evaluated. They are also subjected to a process of filtering and selection, as shown in Figure 9.4.

Yet both the criteria and the measures that are finally selected reflect the principles and underlying beliefs of the evaluators. Final acceptance is a result of compromise, thus introducing inherent bias—in addition to the biases imposed by adherence to values and beliefs of the evaluators.[14] Such biases account for much of the subjectivity factor in evaluation efforts, but it should not be overemphasized. Subjectivity due to biases in selection of criteria and measures complements the agreement on objectives and procedures for the evaluation—both of which reflect biases of evaluators and of those being evaluated.[15]

Figure 9.4
Reducing Potential Measures to a Workable Set

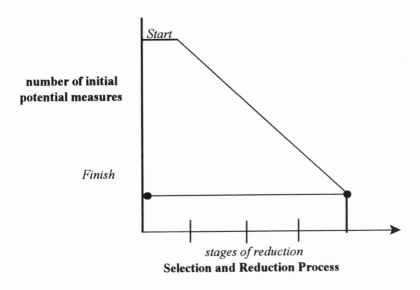

stages of reduction
Selection and Reduction Process

How To Do It?

An integral part of processes in the evaluation effort is the determination of the procedures to be used. There are two major approaches or types of procedures. The first is *ex post facto*, in which the entity or activity under evaluation are evaluated after the fact. Generally the procedure involves analysis of data generated by the object of the evaluation, followed by conclusions being drawn on how well, how efficiently (or any other measure) the entity or activity had performed.[16]

If the first approach is a passive assessment after the fact, the second is *ex ante*, more active and involves experimentation, designed to empirically assess the progress or the accomplishments of an entity or activity being evaluated.[17]

Both are methods that utilize data from measures that had been pre-selected for the evaluation. In most instances, data for these measures are being or have been collected by those evaluated as part of their routine data generation. This is an effective approach in cases where there has been an agreement (between evaluators and evaluated) on the purposes of the evaluation and the procedures and measures to be used.[18] However, in cases in which the evaluation effort is imposed on the evaluated, and where a clear agreement on criteria and measures is lacking, active evaluation would be a more acceptable option.[19]

In all cases there are outcomes from the evaluation effort. These outcomes are sometimes left in the form of raw data, but usually there is an analysis, and conclusions are drawn. The question that evaluators now face is: where to go from here?

What To Do With The Results?

Once the data from the evaluations are collected, there are usually two methods to initially deal with them. The first is when the evaluators (those who conducted the evaluation) are also the analyzers and the decision-makers as to what the next steps are. A second method is based on different actors, in that the collectors of the evaluation data transfer the data (in raw format or after an analysis) to a separate person or entity who will decide on subsequent steps.[20]

For example, the evaluation of federal technology laboratories in the United States is conducted by the parent agencies, with parallel evaluation and analyses performed by congressional staffs. Although direct impacts on the laboratories are from decision-makers in the parent agency, funding and the ultimate survival of the laboratories depend on Congress.[21]

Armed with the results of the evaluation, conclusions are drawn and consequences are charted. Here also there are two possible avenues of action. The first includes a simple feedback loop to the evaluated, in which the results are transferred and explained. The objective is to provide the person or entity evaluated with analytical results of their assessment, so that measures can be undertaken for corrective action.

The second avenue is based on inclusion of the results from the evaluation into the policy or decision-making processes of the evaluators. Decisions are then made which may affect the evaluated, but may also serve as inputs to decisions involving others. For example, in the healthcare delivery environment, evaluation of delivery of services in hospitals may be used as inputs to policy decisions by government agencies, regulators, and other third-party payers such as insurance companies.[22]

In the case of science and technology, due perhaps to its complexity and ramifications into so many areas of human endeavor, both avenues are utilized. Feedback results are provided to the people and units who generate S&T, and results are also provided to external bodies who decide on such issues as funding of research, for both programs and entire disciplinary areas.

LEVELS OF EVALUATION

Evaluation in general and S&T in particular is conducted at different levels of those being evaluated. Figure 9.5 displays the eight levels in the case of science and technology.

Figure 9.5
Levels of Evaluation Efforts and Programs in Science and Technology

- Individual Researcher
- Group or Team of Researchers
- Project
- Area Thrust
- Program
- Institution (R&D Department, University, Federal Laboratory)
- Discipline
- State or Country

Levels range from the individual researcher, through project and program, to an entire scientific discipline and the evaluation of a state or a country. Generally, evaluation efforts are designed for organizationally viable activities of S&T. Thus, the evaluation of projects, programs, and institutions are the most common forms. Perhaps the main reason for this is the ability of such entities to be subjected to processes of allocation of resources, hence the power of the evaluation to contribute to decisions on resources.[23]

Levels and Measures

Although there are some core measures that apply to S&T evaluation at all levels, there are nevertheless different measures for each level. Individual researchers, for example, are evaluated by measures of their performance, such as contributions to the state of the art in their respective discipline. Publications, citations, and patents are most commonly used as measures of scientific performance.[24]

Project and program evaluations are more comprehensive, as they also include the assessment of organizational performance and capabilities. Generally such evaluations consist of a combined value of the sum of individual and group performance, with the addition of an *overall* measure of the organization's performance. The nuances of organizational workings are thus captured in the evaluation of processes and procedures of the unit being assessed—in addition to the regular and obligatory outcomes evaluation.[25]

At the discipline level, evaluations of S&T include the usual outcomes measures, but they also heavily rely on peer review. Bibliometric measures are thus coupled with judgmental assessment on the progress in a discipline and the state of the art.

Institutional and Country Evaluations

Perhaps the most prevalent evaluations of S&T that serve as inputs to policy decisions are those at the levels of the institutions conducting S&T and states or countries. In the former, institutions are evaluated by specific assessment over time and in comparison with similar organizations.

It is, however, at the national level that evaluators of S&T acquire a life of their own and are conducted to the beat of different drummers.[26] Why are these evaluations different from those at other levels? Primarily because they are based on massive statistical data of the usual measures (bibliometric, patents, and investments), and analyses of inputs, outputs, and cost-efficiencies. Such evaluations serve at least two crucial purposes. First, they assist in establishing empirical support and justification for investments in S&T at the national level. Second, they provide a valuable (although not necessarily accurate) tool for comparisons across countries and regions, thus furnishing an element of national pride. Another use of these evaluations is by supplying empirical data of S&T productivity at the national level for the effort to explain economic and social progress (both within countries and in cross-comparisons).[27]

Comparisons among countries utilize performance indicators (e.g., bibliometrics) and counts of patents. A study of 32 countries made use of such bibliometric indicators to arrive at international comparisons. As expected, countries with massive investments in S&T and a large and prolific body of scientists scored higher on the scales of these indicators.[28] The basis for such studies is the development of *science indicators*.

THE CONCEPT OF VALUATION

In his book on marketing technology, Geoffrey Moore has described a model of the "value triad," composed of the customer, the product, and its application.[29] The triad thus consists of the value proposition that ties the three elements together, so that a change in any of them creates subsequent changes in the proposition.

Similarly, valuation has also been suggested for determining the value of a company. Moore's model refers to the inherent qualities of the dimensions of the value proposition, whereas the valuation of a company is a combination of its inherent dimensions and external parameters.[30] In essence, the value of a company is an economic/financial assessment of its assets (equity) and its earnings. According to the accounting approach, the value is computed as the earnings of the company times the price-to-earning (P/E) ratio. Another approach utilizes the discounted cash flow (DCF) and computes the value as the expected cash flow in future years, discounted to its present value by a discount rate.[31]

"Continuing value" is an approach similar to DCF, with the provision that its time horizon extends way into the future, beyond the company's

Figure 9.6
Basic Assumptions Underlying the Concept of Valuation

- Well-defined activity and its organizational framework.
- Future flows are clearly identified.
- Quantification in economic and financial terms is feasible.
- There is an acceptable rate of discount for present value computations.
- Different methods yield similar (not necessarily identical) results.

planning and forecasting time frame.[32] Other non-DCF methods for valuation include the liquidation-value method and market-to-book ratio.

Basic Assumptions

The concept of valuation thus constitutes an effort to compute a single quantity that provides a unique descriptor of the *total* value of a given unit. However, the concept and method used to arrive at this quantity depend on several assumptions, summarized in Figure 9.6.

Conceivably, different evaluators utilizing different methods would arrive at similar results. The value of a company computed by using the DCF method would not drastically differ from the market-to-book value.[33] In all these methods there is a clear and identifiable flow of future earnings from a well-defined activity.

What About Science and Technology?

The idea that one quantity can adequately (or at least consensually) describe the value of an entire activity or organization is not easily transferred to the realm of science and technology. Few, if any, of the basic assumptions for such valuation can be made in the case of S&T. The financial assessment of outcomes from S&T usually yields only a limited appraisal of *some* of the outputs from science, and a limited assessment of the impacts from technology. S&T is a nebulous set of activities that may be satisfactorily quantified only insofar as the investments in them. Even in the case of investments, there are many "holes" in the costs of development, engineering, and commercialization of downstream S&T.

In addition there are limitations in our ability to unequivocally identify and quantify the outcomes from *all* the stages of the S&T continuum.[34] The value of individual outputs (such as publications, citations, or even patents) cannot be precisely determined, let alone be the total value of the S&T organization. Outcomes from the scientific activities are diffused downstream the innovation continuum, hence very difficult to identify and to accurately measure.

How much is a S&T organization worth? Familiar techniques such as DCF or production function are wholly inadequate. In recent years there have been attempts to quantify large-scale S&T efforts within the framework of public investments. In the United States, such efforts included, for example, the case of the preservation of the nation's environment.[35] A proposed approach considered the environment as inputs to the national production function.[36] Comparisons with transportation have concluded that its value lies with its usage, hence proportionate taxation may be in order.

But this illustration still leaves unresolved the value of environmental S&T as a component of the value to society of the preservation of the nation's environment. Even as a portion of the total value of the environment, there is not one value that can determine the worth of S&T in this area. The complexity of the S&T phenomenon thus calls for more than a simple quantity. It is a matter of measurement by indicators and the use of several other methods that are described in the next chapter.

Discounted Value of Technology?

Is it possible to think of technology in terms that value it by the present value of its future flow of some economic returns? Evidently these returns would be much different from the income that flows to the company being valued. In the case of technology, the returns (or impacts) occur in *other* organizations, so that any benefit (including economic payoffs) accrue to the impactees. This condition alone seriously complicates the application of any present-value method to technological outcomes.[37]

Even economic studies of R&D outcomes and impacts that are described later in this book have merely linked investments in research to the benefits accrued to institutions downstream the R&D continuum. Similarly, unsatisfactory attempts have focused on specific technologies, with the hope of isolating any flows of returns. Lacking adequate means of measuring the process by which S&T progresses has been a critical factor in the puny results of valuation of technology using the methods that were employed in the case of business companies.[38]

NOTES

1. See, for example, Caro, F. (Ed.), *Readings in Evaluation Research* (New York: Russell Sage Foundation, 1971). Also see Schuman, E., *Evaluative Research* (New York: Russell Sage Foundation, 1967); Cronbach, L., *Designing Evaluations of Educational and Social Programs* (San Francisco, Jossey-Bass, 1982); and Struening, E., and M. Guttentag (Eds.), *Handbook of Evaluation Research* (Beverly

Hills, CA: Sage Publications, 1975). In addition, there are countless studies and publications in the evaluation of specific fields and programs. For example, Ihilevich, D., and G. Gleser, *Evaluating Mental-Health Programs: The Progress Evaluation Scales* (Lexington, MA: Lexington Books, 1982). Also see, Berk, R., and P. Rossi, *Thinking About Program Evaluation, 2nd ed.* (Thousand Oaks, CA: Sage Publications, 1998), and Sonnichsen, R., *High Impact Internal Evaluation* (Thousand Oaks, CA: Sage Publications, 1999).

2. *Webster's New Collegiate Dictionary* (Springfield, MA: G&C Merriam Company, 1977).

3. For an insightful model, see Thompson, C., "A Framework Model of Evaluation," paper presented at the National Conference on Criminal Justice Evaluation, Washington, DC, February 1977; and Morell, J., "Follow-up Research as an Evaluation Strategy: Theory and Methodologies," in T. Abramson, K. Tittle, and L. Cohen (Eds.), *Handbook of Vocational Education Evaluation* (Beverly Hills: Sage Publications, 1979) pp. 217-248.

4. See, for example, Thompson, C., "Design and Procurement of Evaluation Systems," *Proceedings of the 1976 International Conference on Procurement and Grants Management*, University of Virginia, Charlottesville, April 1976, pp. 169-188. Also see Rossi, P., and H. Freeman, *Evaluation: A Systematic Approach*, 3rd ed. (Beverly Hills, CA: Sage Publications, 1985).

5. See, for example, Weiss, C., *Evaluation: Methods for Studying Programs and Policies* (Upper River Saddle, NJ: Prentice-Hall, 1997); and Alkin, M., *Costs of Evaluation: Concept and Theory* (Beverly Hills, CA: Sage Publications, 1983).

6. For example, see the seminal book, first published in 1979 by Rossi and Freeman, *op. cit.* Also see Isaac, S., and W. Michael, *Handbook in Research and Evaluation* (San Diego, CA: Edits Publishers, 1977). Also see Preskill, H., and R. Torres, *Evaluative Inquiry for Learning in Organizations* (Thousand Oaks, CA: Sage Publications, 1998).

7. Callon, M., P. Laredo, and V. Rabecharisoa, "The Management and Evaluation of Technological Programs and the Dynamics of Techno-Economic Networks: The Case of AFME," *Research Policy*, 21(2), 1992, 215-236.

8. See an excellent description of this phenomenon whereby extraneous entities benefit from data collected for reasons and objectives different from those of the ultimate beneficiary, in Webb, E., D. Campbell, R. Schwartz, and L. Sechrest, *Unobtrusive Measures: Nonreactive Research in the Social Sciences* (Chicago: Rand McNally, 1966), in particular, pp. 53-110.

9. See discussions of these issues in Chelinsky, E., and W. Shadish (Eds.), *Evaluation for the 21ˢᵗ Century* (Beverly Hills, CA: Sage Publications, 1997).

10. See St. Pierre, R. (Ed.), *Management and Organization of Program Evaluation* (San Francisco: Jossey-Bass, 1983).

11. See Glass, E., "Methods of Evaluating R&D Organizations," *IEEE Transactions on Engineering Management* 19(1), 1972, 2-11; and Gold, B., "Some Key Problems in Evaluating R&D Performance," *Journal of Engineering and Technology Management*, 6(1), 1989, 59-70.

12. For example, see Posavac, E., and R. Carey (Eds.), *Program Evaluation: Methods and Case Studies* (Upper River Saddle, NJ: Prentice-Hall, 1996).

13. See Rubenstein, A. H., *Managing Technology in the Decentralized Firm* (New York: John Wiley & Sons, 1989), in particular, Chapter 7 (Evaluation of Projects and Programs).

14. See, for example, Pawson, R., and N. Tilley, *Realistic Evaluation* (Beverly Hills, CA: Sage Publications, 1997), particularly Chapters 6-8, pp. 153-213.

15. For example, Patton, M., *Utilization-Focused Evaluation: The New Century Text* (Beverly Hills, CA: Sage Publications, 1996). See, in particular, Chapter 3, pp. 39-62, in which the author discusses making decisions on methods and the biases involved in such decisions.

16. See, for example, Martin, L., and P. Kettner, *Measuring the Performance of Human Service Programs* (Beverly Hills, CA: Sage Publications, 1996). See especially the comprehensive case study of an evaluation of a social program.

17. Boruch, R., *Randomized Experiments for Planning and Evaluation: A Practical Guide* (Beverly Hills, CA: Sage Publications, 1996). Professor Boruch has written extensively on evaluation of social programs in general and on experimentation in particular. See Chapter 2 (Experiments in the Context of Evaluation), pp. 19-37, for an illuminating discussion of such an empirical approach. Also see Greenberg, D., and M. Shoder, *Digest of Social Experiments* (Washington, DC: Urban Institute Press, 1997).

18. The discussion here is not a comprehensive nor an exhaustive review of evaluation procedures. Only key points are described, inasmuch as they are useful in subsequent Chapters 10 and 11 in the discussion of the evaluation of research and technology. For additional readings, see, for example, Weiss, 1997, *op. cit.*; and Bloom, M., *Evaluating Practice: Guidelines for the Accountable Professional* (New York: Allyn & Bacon, 1998). Also see Guba, E., and Y. Lincoln, *Effective Evaluation: Improving the Usefulness of Evaluation Results Through Responsive and Naturalistic Approaches* (San Francisco: Jossey-Bass, 1992). The authors have criticized evaluation efforts based on statistical analyses. Based on episodic research and such disciplinary methodologies as those employed by anthropologists, the authors have argued for a practical orientation toward specific situations under evaluation, rather than a pre-selected generic method. Also see LeCompte, M., J. Preissle, and R. Tesch, *Ethnography and Qualitative Design in Educational Research* (New York: Academic Press, 1993). See especially Chapter 9, pp. 315-356, where the authors list criteria for evaluation. A similar approach has been considered in Geisler, E., *Methodology, Theory, and Knowledge in the Managerial and Organizational Sciences: Actions and Consequences* (Westport, CT: Quorum Books, 1999). In particular see Chapter 6, pp. 127-142.

19. See, for example, Struening, E., and M. Guttentag (Eds.), *Handbook of Evaluation Research* (New York: Books on Demand, 1975). Also see Heider, F., and M. Benesh-Weiner, *Attributional and Interpersonal Evaluation* (New York: Springer-Verlag, 1988); and Bingham, R., and C. Felbinger, *Evaluation in Practice: A Methodological Approach* (New York: Longman, 1989).

20. See, for example, Patton, 1996, *op. cit.*, Chapters 4 and 5, pp. 63-114.

21. See Walsh, R., and J. Heilman (Eds.), *Energizing the Energy Policy Process: The Impact of Evaluation* (Westport, CT: Quorum Books, 1994). The authors

detailed the role that evaluation outcomes and analyses play in decisions regarding energy programs at the level of the federal government.

22. There is a vast literature in this topic. See, for example, Wan, T., *Analysis and Evaluation of Health Care Systems: An Integrated Approach to Managerial Decision Making* (New York: Health Professionals, 1995), in particular, Chapters 9 and 10, pp. 167-202. Also see Jenkinson, C., *Assessment and Evaluation of Health and Medical Care: A Methods Text* (London: Taylor, 1997), especially Chapter 10, pp. 171-179, in which the contributing authors discuss meta analyses of healthcare delivery.

23. For illustrations of an extensive body of literature on project and program evaluation, see Gallimore, R., and G. Boggio (Eds.), *Evaluation of Research & Development* (Boston: Kluwer Academic Publishers, 1982); and Mohr, L., *Impact Analysis for Program Evaluation* (Beverly Hills: Sage Publications, 1995). Also see Owen, J., *Program Evaluation: Forms and Approaches* (New York: Paul and Company, 1994), especially Chapter 2 (Forms of Evaluation) and Chapter 6 (Impact Evaluation).

24. For a general perspective, see Van Raan, A. (Ed.), *Handbook of Quantitative Studies of Science and Technology* (New York: Elsevier Science, 1988); and the seminal study of Keller, R., and W. Holland, "The Measurement of Performance Among Research and Development Professional Employees: A Longitudinal Analysis," *IEEE Transactions in Engineering Management*, 29(2), 1982, 54-58.

25. See Owen, 1999, *op. cit.*, Chapter 8, pp. 129-143. Also see an interesting description of different approaches to process and outcome evaluations in Albrecht, G., and H. Otto, *Social Prevention and the Social Sciences: Theoretical Controversies, Research Problems, and Evaluation Strategies* (New York: Walter de Gruyter, 1991).

26. See, for example, Nelson, R. (Ed.), *National Innovation Systems: A Comparative Analysis* (New York: Oxford University Press, 1993).

27. See, for example, Andrews, F. (Ed.), *Scientific Productivity: The Effectiveness of Research Groups in Six Countries* (New York: Cambridge University Press, 1979). Also see Anderson, J., P. Collins, J. Frune, P. Israel, B. Martin, F. Marin, and S. Kimberley, "On-Line Approaches to Measuring National Scientific Output: A Cautionary Tale," *Science and Public Policy*, 15(3), 1988, 153-161; and Frame, J., "Modeling National Technological Capacity with Patent Indicators," *Scientometrics* 22(3), 1991, 327-339.

28. Braun, T., W. Glanzel, and A. Schubert, *Scientometric Indicators: A 32-Country Comparative Evaluation of Publishing Performance and Citation Impact* (Singapore: World Scientific, 1985).

29. Moore, G., *Crossing the Chasm* (New York: Harper-Business, 1991) pp. 99-102.

30. See, for example, the foundational book by a team of consultants with McKinsey & Company: Copeland, T., T. Koller, and J. Murrin, *Valuation: Measuring and Managing the Value of Companies* (New York: John Wiley & Sons, 1990).

31. For example, see Palepu, K., V. Bernard, and P. Healy, *Business Analysis and Valuation: Using Financial Statements* (Dallas: South-Western Publishing,

1996); and Yegge, W., *A Basic Guide for Valuing a Company* (New York: John Wiley & Sons, 1996).

32. See Pratt, S., R. Reilly, and R. Schweihs, *Valuing a Business: Analysis and Appraisal of Closely Held Companies*, 3rd ed. (New York: McGraw-Hill, 1995) pp. 253-297.

33. For example, see the comprehensive text by Damodaran, A., *Investment Valuation: Tools and Techniques to Determining the Value of Any Asset* (New York: John Wiley & Sons, 1995). Also see the practical summary of tools and methods for evaluation of securities, Hooke, J., *Security Analysis on Wall Street: A Comprehensive Guide to Today's Valuation Methods* (New York: John Wiley & Sons, 1998).

34. See related works in Guba, E., and Y. Lincoln, *Fourth Generation Evaluation* (Beverly Hills: Sage Publication, 1989); and Schalock, R., *Outcome-Based Evaluation* (New York: Plenum Press, 1995).

35. National Academy of Sciences, *Linking Science and Technology to Society's Environmental Goals* (Washington, DC: National Academy Press, 1997).

36. Accutt, M., and P. Mason (Eds.), *Environmental Valuation; Economic Policy and Sustainability: Recent Advances in Environmental Economics* (New York: Edward Elgar, 1998) pp. 51-98.

37. This issue will not be resolved even if we consider the impactees to be "customers" of the R&D producing organization.

38. See Chapters 10 and 11 for detailed discussions of the evaluation of research and technology, respectively.

10

EVALUATION OF RESEARCH

Science and technology and the phenomenon of innovation have been defined earlier in Chapter 8 as a continuum of interlocked activities. Such is the traditional definition of the continuum. Recently, however, there have been attempts to describe the innovation process and science and technology in nonlinear terms.

If we consider science and technology to be a succession of events that are interconnected temporally and logically, then the terms "research," "development," or "technology" become descriptors of more complex activities. These terms thus describe broader events than those defined in Chapter 8. They are not only interconnected, linked, and stages in a process, but also overlapping and interwoven. The degree to which such links are materialized is the glue that holds together this virtual process. The weaker the links, the less actualized the process.

This chapter describes the evaluation of the *research activity* within the continuum of innovation. Later in the book, I will discuss applications of evaluation and measurement of science and technology and the innovation continuum within the framework of *organizational units* and specific *organizational arrangements*.

The current chapter considers the research activity in broad terms as an operational configuration of science and of scientific endeavor. The chapter starts with descriptions and some analysis of the process of basic and applied research, and ends with the question: what can and should we measure in the evaluation of this configuration of scientific effort?

THE PROCESS OF BASIC AND APPLIED RESEARCH

Robert Teitelman, a senior editor at *Institutional Investor* magazine, wrote an intriguing book in 1994 in which he explored the gap between science and technology.[1] His main concern was to provide an analysis of how scientific outcomes are transformed by industry into marketable and profitable products and services. Teitelman argued that available and inexpensive capital, used to exploit the outcomes from science, helps to narrow the gap between science and technology, and may serve as a lubricant for technological revolutions in the economy.

Teitelman described science as a precursor to technology, but failed to establish its operational boundaries. Earlier, Vannevar Bush, who advised President Franklin D. Roosevelt, had written a report, later transformed into a best-selling book, *Science, The Endless Frontier*,[2] which reported the plan of the agency he was managing. Even in this much-publicized agenda for science and science policy, there is no clear and precise definition of what constitutes science.[3]

Bush introduced *basic* research in a positive light, as the activity that pushes the frontiers of science. He called for government support of research-as-science, conducted with the sole purpose of gaining understanding of the phenomenon. Thus, Bush distinguished between basic and applied research where, in the case of the latter, the impetus for ideas comes from the potential application of the outcomes.

Broadly then, science encompasses the entire spectrum of the research universe: exploratory, basic, applied, and directed basic research. These are activities that generate knowledge and scientific outcomes that are different from technology. These outcomes include publications, citations, and any other form of knowledge, or in a more recent terminology: intellectual capital.[4]

An interesting approach to distinguish science from technology has been advanced by Stokes.[5] He explored the attributes of "understanding" and "use" as indicators of the way science is performed. Stokes reexamines the "linear model" of science from basic research to applied research, to development, and so on, to the useful innovation. Figure 10.1 shows a generic "linear model" of the research continuum.

Stokes challenged this model by advancing a more interactive perspective, in which research moves closer to technology, and technology becomes more oriented toward science. The outcome is a narrower gap between the concepts.[6]

Notwithstanding such distinctions, they seem to be a conceptually artificial slicing of the same unique phenomenon. The terms "science" and "research" both seem to describe the phenomenon of the generation of new

Figure 10.1
A Generic Linear Model of Research and Its Aftermath

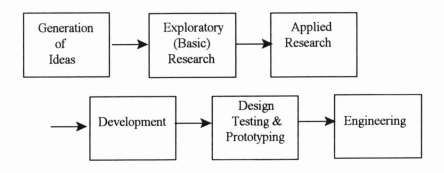

Figure 10.2
Intersect and Overlapping of Science, Research, and Technology

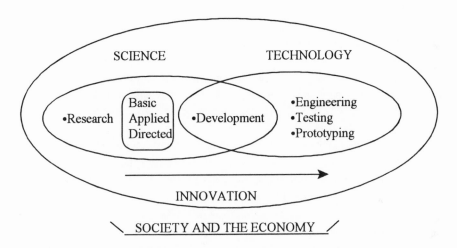

knowledge and understanding of our world, with or without potential applications or usage down the line. Figure 10.2 shows the intersections as well as the overlapping conceptual components of science, research, and technology.[7]

In particular, the intersect of science and research is largely seamless. Whereas science describes a very generalized conceptual framework, research is the systematic pursuit of scientific activity and the *organizational* manifestation of this framework—hence the artificial division into the components of the flow of research, shown in Figure 10.1. In order to accommodate organizational realities, the research flow is categorized by its implications and those of its outcomes to the organizations that support it. Thus, applied research may be classified by its potential contributions to an outcome that may be used by the supporting organization, or even defined by the needs and criteria imported from other units in the organization.

There may be very little difference between the nature of the activity in what we would thus classify as "basic" and "applied" research. There is a seamless flow throughout the process described in Figure 10.1. This assertion leads to an analysis of the different models of research.

MODELS OF RESEARCH

The linear model of research activity, shown in Figure 10.1, has been criticized and alternative models have been proposed.[8] Strict definitions of what constitutes basic, exploratory, or directed research have ceased to apply. To suggest nowadays that exploratory research is carried out by academia and government laboratories and directed research by industry disregards the realities of the seamless flow of research.

Since the late 1970s, two major factors have contributed to the emergence of an alternative, nonlinear, feedback-based model of research. First, competitive environments in the economy have led to the compression of the innovation process from the laboratory to the commercialized product. Researchers are increasingly pressured to be "relevant" and to work more closely with marketers and product developers.[9] Such pressures and the following trend to make research more "applicable" have also generated a backlash of protests. Many scholars and researchers (including the author of this book) recognized a certain danger in what they perceived to be the dismantling of a magnificent basic (blue-sky) research system that the United States had built and nurtured for half a century.[10]

The second factor was a combination of shifting strategies and a revised outlook on research and technology by both industrial companies and the federal government. Due to international competition and the trends to reorganize and reengineer, units and processes—including R&D—were targets for restructuring and careful economic examination. Scarcity of resources and the desire to introduce efficiency in operations led to sharp cuts in many central industrial laboratories, coupled with outsourcing of research activities.

The result was a model of research in which a seamless flow of activities and transfer of knowledge is influenced by the ultimate usage of the outcomes in the form of new and improved products, processes, methods, and techniques. Figure 10.3 shows the advantages and attributes of the linear versus the nonlinear models.

Figure 10.3
Linear and Nonlinear Models of Research: Key Attributes and Advantages

LINEAR MODEL	NONLINEAR MODELS
Key Attributes	**Key Attributes**
• Ideas come mainly from scientific curiosity • High-risk work without a practical end • Investigation at the exploratory level is independent of down-stream • Objective is fundamental under-standing: "ivory tower" • Time and cost are secondary con-cerns • Slow progression to downstream stages	• Ideas come mainly from future applications • Short-term low-risk work with potential applications • Seamless flow and continuous feedbacks • Objective is to provide scientific basis for innovations and new products and processes • Economic and efficiency considerations are applied
Advantages	**Advantages**
• Provides advanced scientific and technical training to employees • Provides longer-term capabilities and competitiveness • Knowledge of basic phenomenon helps to push scientific frontiers and scientific breakthroughs • Long-term work provides cross-disciplinary fertilization and shared advances across sciences	• Ability to outsource research activities • Closer relations with the commercial side of the organization • Helps to shorten the time-to-market • Allows research to be conducted concurrently with design and manufacturing • Ability to work with flexible manufacturing

The transformation of research in the industrial context to a more relevant and less exploratory mode has left the universities with the burden to advance the frontiers of science. Hence the concerted effort in the late 1990s by Nobel Prize winners and other notable scientists and university administrators to persuade American policymakers to strengthen their support for fundamental research.[11]

But, besides the structural changes that occurred in the organization of the research function in industry, the nonlinear model has had minimal influence on the conduct of the research itself. The advantages of the nonlinear model can be achieved only if there is indeed a continuous flow between researchers and developers, and between researcher and production people, and all of these with marketers. Studies of the interface between research and these other functions have identified many problems, such as difficulties in communication, lack of ability to cooperate, and the handing-over of research results without continuing support.[12]

Despite the problems, the reality today is a much more flexible form of research (basic and applied) with strong links to potential uses and downstream applications. This revised system may not be wholly effective, but it has been adopted by industrial firms and even federal laboratories. Accountability and efficiency are the new concepts that are creating concern among researchers. At the same time, the stronger ties of research to downstream applications have also contributed to a change in the way we consider and even measure the value of research.

VALUE OF RESEARCH

In the previous chapter the concept of *valuation* was discussed. The value of research is a form of valuation of an activity, within the institutional and organizational boundaries in which it is practiced. The value of the research function is not an independent quantity, rather it depends on the nature of the evaluation as described in Chapter 9. In this way, the value of research depends on who evaluates, which questions are being asked, who benefits from the evaluation, and the metrics used.[13]

However, the value of research is also influenced by the model used to conceptually describe this function. In the case of the linear model of research, the value is computed solely within the boundaries of the research activity itself. Thus, outputs are defined as the *immediate* and *observable* (hence measurable) products of the research activity, to include publications, citations, and students who graduate from the educational side of this activity.

Additional outputs may be in the form of information and knowledge. The value of research will thus be computed to reflect the knowledge generated from the activity. Although theoretically attractive, this approach has severe methodological difficulties.

Consider the case of corporate research laboratories (CRL) working under the linear model. In this category were Bell Laboratories in New Jersey (renamed Lucent after the breakup of the telephone giant) and Xerox Palo Alto Research Center Laboratories in California (PARC).[14] As shown in the study of methods used to evaluate corporate research described later in this chapter, the most prevalent method was committee evaluation (judgment or peer review). Little emphasis was given to the impact of this research on new products, process improvements, or compliance with regulations.

Under the revised model of integration of research and downstream functions, central corporate laboratories have been transformed from bastions of advances in science and research to increasingly performing scientific support to the commercial side of the organization. As the study of methods shows below, this transformation not only terminated some of these historically distinguished laboratories (for example PARC), but has also led to the preeminence of such criteria for research evaluation as impact on new products and processes.

WHAT TO MEASURE?

So, what do we measure in the evaluation of research? In the linear model the evaluation calls for measures of proximal outputs, whereas in the nonlinear model it calls for an extended measure of downstream impacts. Figure 10.4 summarizes the criteria of evaluation effort for each of the models and the type of measures applicable in each case.

The distinct measures shown in Figure 10.4 can be best illustrated with the results from a longitudinal study of corporate research laboratories.[15] This study investigated the methods and criteria used by large American manufacturing companies in their evaluation of their in-house research programs. The original study was conducted in 1983-1984, and the follow-up study was conducted over a decade later, in 1995-1996. In both studies the respondents were managers of research, vice-presidents of R&D, or similar title, but all in charge of the research activity in the firm. In the original study, the sample was 31 companies, representing five industries: materials, machinery, petroleum, transportation, and chemicals. All but three of the sample companies ranked in the Fortune 100 category.

In the follow-up study, 23 of the original companies have been included in the sample. Eleven new companies were added to a total sample of 34 companies. Respondents were asked to list criteria and methods used by their firms to evaluate their research, and to characterize these methods by such attributes as frequency of use, satisfaction with the method, and a brief history of its use.[16]

Figure 10.5 shows the results from the studies, for the case of economic and financial methods. The figure shows only the 23 companies that had participated in *both* studies.

Similar findings are shown in Figure 10.6 for the original and the follow-up studies of 23 companies, and for the noneconomic or financial methods used in evaluation of research. The figure also shows the differences in frequencies of use.

Figure 10.4
Criteria and Measures for Evaluation of Research

CRITERIA	MEASURES	
	Linear Model	**Nonlinear Model**

Why evaluate?
•to prove value
•to improve flow
•to reexamine
   objectives
	•immediate outputs
	•measures of internal flow
	•accomplishments in
	   scientific terms
		•intermediate and other
		   downstream outputs
		•efficiency measures
		•contributions to the
		   downstream process

Level of evaluation
•project
•thrust area
•entire program
	•immediate outputs (e.g.,
	   publications)
	•immediate outputs
	•immediate outputs
		•immediate *and*
		   intermediate outputs
		•contributions to products
		•impacts on new products

Who evaluates?
•research managers
•scientific peers
•general managers
	•scientific achievements
	   and on-time, on-cost
	•contribution to SOA
	•reputation of research
	   unit
		•transfer of outputs
		   downstream
		•scientific achievements
		•ROI, "dollarization"

**Source of
evaluation criteria**
•scientific discipline
•strategic plan
•business units
	•standards of scientific
	   outputs
	•prestige of organization
	•technical advice
		•relevancy to organization
		•business value and
		   competitiveness
		•transfer of outputs

**Who benefits from
evaluation?**
•research unit
•state of the art
•marketing and
   production
•the entire organiza-
   tion
	•maintain or increase
	   scientific reputation
	•scientific breakthroughs
	•scientific and technical
	   advice
	•prestige and reputation
	   as
	   technology-based
	   organization
		•relevant partner to
		   business units
		•technique support,
		   exchange, and transfer to
		   business units
		•viable contributions to
		   new products and
		   processes
		•assistance in competitive
		   stance

The findings show a dramatic increase in the use of economic and financial methods in the evaluation of research for the same 23 companies who participated in *both* studies. Figure 10.5 shows a doubling in the use of the measure of return on investment or assets, and a tripling in the number of companies using cost savings. A more acute change is seen in other financial methods, such as research-return ratio, and payback of investment (from 1 company to 8). In all of these methods the trend has clearly been in the direction of increased use of economic and financial methods for research evaluation.

Figure 10.5
Economic and Financial Methods for Evaluation of Research Used by Large Manufacturing Firms in the U.S. (N=23)

METHOD	No. of Firms Using[1]		Frequency of Use[2]	
	Original Study	Follow-Up	Original Study	Follow-Up
Return on Investment or Return on Assets	6 26%	11 48%	Annual	Annual
Cost-Savings	3 13%	8 35%	Annual	Semi-annual
Research-Return Ratio	1 4%	4 16%	Annual	Annual
Payback of Investment	1 4%	8 35%	Annual	Annual
Research Expenditures/Unit Sold	1 4%	3 12%	Semi-annual	Semi-annual
"Dollarization": Profit/ Cost of Research Employees	1 4%	4 16%	Annual	Annual
Match of Research Expenditures and Sales	3 13%	12 52%	Annual	Annual

(1)   *Number of companies differs from sample, because of the use of multiple methods by some firms.*
(2)   *Average.*

Figure 10.6
Noneconomic Methods for Evaluation of Research Used by Large Manufacturing Firms in the U.S. (N = 23)

METHOD	No. of Firms Using[1]		Frequency of Use[2]	
	Original Study	Follow-Up	Original Study	Follow-Up
Committee Evaluation	21 91%	20 87%	Varies	Varies
On Time and On Budget	20 87%	22 95%	Periodical	Periodical
Goal Achievement	10 43%	12 52%	Periodical	Periodical
New Products and Processes	5 22%	11 48%	Annually	Annually
Improvements in Products and Processes	5 22%	18 78%	Annually	Annually
Innovation Break-throughs	13 56%	12 52%	Annually	Annually
Regulatory Compliance	4 17%	6 26%	Quarterly	Quarterly
Business Customer Satisfaction	1 4%	8 35%	Semi-annually	Quarterly
Contribution to Business Strategic Objectives	1 4%	14 61%	Annually	Annually

(1)   *Number of companies differ from sample, due to use of multiple methods by some firms.*
(2)   *Average.*

SHIFTING MODELS AND METHODS

The shift in models, from the linear model of research to nonlinear models, has also produced a shift in methods used by industrial companies to evaluate their research activities and research performance. As Figure 10.5 and 10.6 show, the shift involved the enormous rise in the number of companies that decided to use economic and financial methods, such as return on investments (ROI), cost savings, payback on investment, and "dollarization."[17]

Simultaneously, many companies in our sample have shifted their focus (in the period 1984-1996) to methods that measure the contribution of their research to new products, business customers' satisfaction, and business strategic objectives. As Figure 10.6 shows, only one company in 1984 considered satisfaction and strategic objectives in their evaluation of research, whereas 12 years later the numbers (on average) had jumped to 8 and 14, respectively.

This shift in both the frame of mind for evaluation of research and the methods utilized have contributed to a higher level of involvement of the research function with the business aspects of the company. Developments in managerial trends in the 1990s have also accelerated these shifts. Five such trends or factors have emerged: quality, conversion, time to market, cost cutting, and reengineering and the evolution of outsourcing and cooperative arrangements.

Quality concern was a remnant of the trend in the 1980s by which American industry had made vast improvements in the quality of its products and services. It had also evolved into a frame of mind for industrial executives that quality products and services lead to customer satisfaction, profitability, and higher competitiveness. The research function had become subordinated to this trend, thus moving toward the provision of its skills and knowledge in the service of developing and maintaining quality products and services.

As Figure 10.6 shows, there has been a sharp increase in companies using the method of "improvements in products and processes." A substantial component of these improvements was the need to support the quality function of the firm.

Conversion from military to civilian uses of some parts of the American industry after the end of the cold war has been the hallmark of many companies in such industries as aerospace, electronics, and machinery.[18] *Time to market* was another factor, as was *cost cutting* and reengineering. Finally, the evaluation of *outsourcing* and *cooperation* among companies in the 1990s have all contributed to the shift in both models and methods.

The shift in methods was due to the convergence of all of these factors so that the emphasis was moved toward including downstream components in the evaluation of research. Cost cutting, reengineering, and outsourcing have combined to create practices by American companies where the emphasis refocused on efficient processes and profitable results. Research, as a function in the company, was swept in this trendy watershed of becoming "lean and mean" companies in an aggressive and uncompromising marketplace.

But, most important, the shift manifested itself in a process by which the methods of research evaluation (and substantially the bulk of the evaluation effort) were taken away from the researchers and *their* managers, and handed over to the general managers in charge of the business side of the company. Research was now evaluated not by what the researchers themselves suggested to management, but by what general management concluded, based on its own criteria and methods.

This shift has practically stripped the research function in the firm of its uniqueness, and has made it into just another support function. It has also stripped the research unit of its long-cherished privilege and ability to self-assessment. In all, the shift was a radical departure from established practices.

Thus, to use the terms introduced in the previous chapter, the modified climate for evaluation of industrial research in American companies had, to an extent, changed the parameters of the evaluation effort. Questions such as: what to evaluate? who benefits? who evaluates? why evaluate? and which metrics to use? have now been subjected to a structural overhaul.

What to evaluate, for example, has been shifted from the immediate outcomes to the downstream impacts on business indicators. Hence, different metrics had to be applied. Why evaluate has changed from the purpose of value of the research activity itself—to the value of the activity as a contributor to the strategic and commercial concerns of the organization. Similarly, who evaluates has shifted to the business or general managers.

Some Illustrative Cases

With current and future reductions in military research and federal support of exploratory and basic research, U.S. industrial companies are not only reducing the level of their investment in research, but also converting much of it into "responsive" and "interactive" effort, directed toward the business of the corporation. For example, Exxon Research and Engineering shifted its emphasis in the 1990s from research for the sake of scientific accomplishments to an activity guided by specific business needs of the parent company.[19] The key to the change was developing not only a different climate of commercial relevancy in the research laboratories, but also specific mechanisms for communication and coordination between the research unit and downstream entities. These mechanisms included cross-functional teams, task forces, personnel exchange, and other such traditional techniques. Managers at Exxon have conceded that the modifications introduced in the 1990s have contributed to improvements in commercially viable products and services, but have also considered that it may be too early to tell (after only 4-6 years) whether there has been any damage to the company's knowledge pool or from the shrinking base of its exploratory research.

However, the issue goes beyond what is expressed by Exxon's managers. Clearly, when research scientists and engineers—as a collectivity of industrious and highly skilled professionals—are put to work in conjunction with commercial concerns of the company, some visible improvements are bound to be achieved. But, in such a business-driven environment, how can or should companies *measure* the performance and the outputs from their research?

In one such case, a large manufacturer of industrial machinery shifted the focus of its research laboratory from exploratory to business-directed activity. When I visited the company in the late 1990s, there were rumors that the central laboratory would be entirely dismantled, and that its remnants would be divided among the much smaller and more specialized divisional laboratories. In addition, the director of the central laboratory concluded that:

> We really cannot measure the degree to which we are succeeding. If you ask me today: are we better off? I don't know. Is the company better off? I don't know. We are different than, say, ten years ago. The problem is not to work with our products people, but to be able to remain scientists and to be able to justify our existence as something more than a workshop for repairs, or even an exchange that connects our divisions to university professors who are expert in this or that.

The chief operations officer disagreed. In his view the research function of the company was best served by a combination of divisional laboratories that are highly focused on the products manufactured by each division, and a modified central laboratory that *supports* these laboratories.

> The time for the central lab to run free and to really indulge in whatever they want to do is over. We are paying for it and we want results that are relevant and that will bring, at the end of the day, profits and sales. The point is that we, the chairman, the president and I know what this company needs and where the future lies. I don't need some scientist to tell me where the next generation products will be or come from. But I need them to tell my production people why our material fails, or how to make our products stronger.

The *redefinition* of research and its role in the industrial company has an excellent example (albeit due to regulation) in the transformation of Bell Laboratories into Lucent Technologies. In early 1999, Richard McGinn, chief executive officer of Lucent, declared that his company is "the clear leader in communications networking. We will be the architects and builders of the next generation networks."[20] With this in mind, Lucent acquired Kenan Systems (a billing and customer services software) for over $1 billion, and Ascend Communications (maker of switches) for $20 billion. In the 15 years since deregulation of the telephone industry, the research arm of the industry gave way to an aggressive technology company. Scientific breakthroughs which were common at Bell Laboratories had been substituted by relevant development of commercial products and network applications.

ISSUES IN EVALUATION OF RESEARCH

Even with a revised model and new methods, most industrial companies are struggling with their need to adequately measure the contributions of research to business objectives and their commercial success.

Figure 10.7 summarizes the issues in the effort to evaluate research. The Senior Vice President for R&D in a major chemical company expressed his frustration by commenting that:

> It's easy to ask us to come up with measures of ROI, but the data is not there. My main problem is not to generate good research or to deliver good outputs, but to measure all this and to justify what we are doing in terms that can be quantified.

Source of Evaluation Criteria

Deriving evaluation criteria for research is an activity that depends, among other factors, on the model of research discussed earlier. Whether criteria are generated by the business managers or the R&D managers, the tension between the two sets of criteria is a permanent fixture in research organizations.[21] The more criteria are derived from the strategic plan and its objectives (as commonly advocated), the more difficult it is for the research function to measure such criteria.[22]

In most industrial companies in the U.S., there is an effort to arrive at a compromise between business and technical (research) criteria. Much

Figure 10.7
Issues in the Evaluation of Research

• Source of evaluation criteria
• Acceptance of evaluation criteria
• Source and acceptance of measures
• Identification of the process
• Data nonexistent, sparse, or difficult to obtain
• Interpretation and drawing conclusions (judgment mechanisms)
• Use of "co-variation" method for data analysis
• Link with other evaluation efforts

depends on the power exercised by the research managers, the nature of the industry, and similar factors.[23]

Acceptance of Evaluation Criteria

It's hardly enough to select the criteria for evaluation of research. The tension between the technical and the commercial sides of the firm lead to a need for both sides to accept the criteria. As already mentioned, *compromise* is the operational term. But, compromises are political, seldom reflecting actual problems with such practical issues as measurement.

Consider the case of a large pharmaceutical company, with operations in over a dozen countries. The chief technology officer (CTO) described the process by which criteria are established and accepted as a "Machiavellian race, fraught with misunderstandings and bad attitudes." When tied to project selection and allocation of resources, these criteria help to determine the termination of projects as well as those projects which will and will not be funded.[24] In many instances, therefore, good science is sacrificed in favor of poor commercial choices. But, over the long run, such politically-generated compromises help to strengthen the much-needed link between research and the commercial side of the firm.

Source and Acceptance of Measures

Selection and acceptance of the measures to be used in research evaluation are also thorny issues in industrial R&D organizations and research organizations in general. Each of the methods and corresponding measures listed in figures 10.4, 10.5, and 10.6 required a process of acceptance and compromise. Some measures have their genesis in the commercial side of the company or, in the case of federal laboratories, in the congressional arsenal of goals and performance measures. Other measures, such as scientific achievements, publications, and patents, reflect the research side of the organization.

The director of research at a successful division of a large manufacturer of consumer products described his organization's selection of evaluation measures:

We use a set of measures, and some are product oriented and division oriented. But my problem is to make sense of a measure of a ratio of my expenditures to sales or to profits—and measures of what my research people have done *technically*. It's a matter of the right translation of very different—almost diametrically different—terms.

Decisions on the composition of the set of measures will ultimately determine the data to be collected and fed into the organization's control and evaluation processes.[25] This in turn determines any ability of the organization to take corrective action. The director of research quoted earlier had this to say:

> If we pack the evaluation with business-type measures, we get a database that satisfies some managers, but we lose touch with our research capabilities. If *vice-versa*, our credibility in the division is shot. Besides, we must support our product line, so data on business benefits can be obtained from our daily activities. I'm concerned about keeping a "right" mix of measures.

Identification of the Process

Using measures in evaluation of research carries with it the inherent assumption that the evaluators know how research interacts with the business areas of the organization and with its strategic objectives. Inasmuch as this may be far from true, measures of immediate outcomes of research (which are generally descriptors of the scientific activity) and measures of the business end of the organization are linked across a gap. This gap is the process by which research interacts with commercial entities.

So, if one mixes a measure of an immediate output, such as number of publications, with a measure of return on investments, the assumption is that publications interact with some measures of return or performance. The gap between the outcomes from the research activity and those of the commercial end of the firm is not necessarily filled simply by executing such measurements.[26]

Data Nonexistent, Sparse, or Difficult to Obtain

As measures selected approach the downstream area of the innovation continuum, and are thus generated by the business or strategic sides of the organization, the data necessary for an appropriate evaluation may be lacking. Such data may not exist, or be sparsely found in the organization, or difficult and costly to obtain. Mansfield, who pioneered many of the studies of contributions of research, listed some problems in studies on the relationship between R&D and productivity.[27] He also commented: "Some of these problems are inadequacies of the output measures used, poor specification of the relationship among inputs, and difficulties in measuring impacts" (p. 479).

Key problems in such data acquisition are inherent in the need to develop quantitative measures with data that are not routinely collected. Compounded by a process that is poorly understood and inadequately documented, specialized data are hard to come by and too costly to standardize.

For example, the director of a national research and technology institute established criteria to link the scientific activity of the institute to the overall objectives of its parent agency. To his painful surprise, the director soon discovered that there were very few data items, reliable and accessible, that could be assembled and used in the evaluation. The objectives of the parent agency made reference to social phenomena, whereas the institute was barely able to quantify its very immediate outputs.

Interpretation and Drawing Conclusions (Judgment Mechanisms)

With as much data as it is possible to process, the evaluation must proceed. Armed with whatever measures one can muster, data need to be interpreted and conclusions regarding the evaluation must be drawn. Mansfield recognized early on that this was a very difficult task. He noted that "it is clear that the current state of the art in this area is not strong enough to permit very accurate estimates of the contribution of R&D. . . . At best, the available estimates are rough guidelines."[28]

Similarly, Rubenstein and Geisler have also argued that "the difficulties and uncertainties of detection and measurement are compounded by points of view reflecting different attitudes . . . . Improved, credible, and organizationally/ politically acceptable methods of evaluation of ROI are urgently needed."[29]

Interpretation of the available data for the purpose of evaluation of research also includes the use of a judgment mechanism. Therefore, in order to make an evaluative judgment there is a need for at least two things: (1) a set of rules on how the evaluation will be judged, including the underlying model and the criteria, and (2) standards and benchmarks.

Every measure in use is the result of convention. In the case of research evaluation the measures are agreed upon corresponding indicators. Yet, to make the evaluation meaningful, there is a need for standards and benchmarks. These are measurement readings that the parties to the evaluation have agreed would serve as anchors that allow for comparisons. Thus, once such benchmarks are established, comparisons can be made between the research being evaluated and a standard, or other comparable research efforts and organizations.

The result is an evaluation that judges individual researchers, laboratories, thrust areas, or even countries. Evaluation judgments, such as "leading," "average," or "outstanding" are common outcomes. Another outcome is the concept of "best practices" which also relies on benchmarks.

What are the standards and benchmarks for research? Most are generated by peer review and judgment by other researchers. For example, a study of subfields (areas of thrust) of information science and technology has generated a list of what experts consider the "leading" research organizations.[30] Researchers in these fields had been asked to rank some 20 universities and industrial and national laboratories for each thrust area. Ranking was done along five possibilities: outstanding, important, "me too," not really doing research in this area, and new or unknown. The benchmarks were not provided, but interviews with the evaluators have shown that the standard consisted of at least two annual scientific publications per researcher in a given institution. Any performance below this benchmark was less than "important."

Lists and rankings abound within research organizations and among them. However, it should be remembered that even the process of setting up benchmarks is a judgment call. In the case of standards that are preestablished (such as rates of return on investment and discounted cash flow) and ignore the judgment of researchers, the result is usually a gap between desired and measurable performance.[31]

Use of "Co-Variation" Method for Data Analysis

Because of the gap in the link between research results and business objectives, evaluators of research tend to utilize "co-variation" methods to measure a desired relationship. The outcome is invariably some statistical correlations that may not produce substantially credible knowledge about the link.[32]

Co-variation describes the method by which independent events are studied and a relationship is established due to a statistical correlation of their variation. Two events separated by time, geography, or logical construct may thus be linked and a relationship between them pronounced. As one event varies, and the other event also varies, the correlation is presumably beyond a random occurrence. In most cases of co-variation, the link, although statistically significant, lacks the necessary theoretical, conceptual, and logical connection between the events or variables.

For example, increases in investments in research may be correlated with technological breakthroughs. Such a link is established over time and across organizational actors and stages in the innovation process. The link is therefore at best tenuous, yet considered to be the basis for such notions as "research intensity." Expenditures for research are only the beginning of a complex process that includes new product development, engineering, design, manufacturing, and, of course, marketing, distribution, and sales. The extremity of the value chain in a business organization and its complexity make such a link across the wide temporal and logical gap an inadequate convention.

Ralph Gomory, who was IBM's senior vice president for science and technology, expressed this gap in his 1987 Scientist of the Year lecture.[33] He argued that "understanding the manufacturing-development process is the key to industrial leadership," and that "we need to recognize the difference between the more spectacular ladder style of innovation and the more-common cycles of product development" (p. 74). Clearly, understanding this gap and measuring the link as it progresses in this gap remains a challenge.

Link with Other Evaluation Efforts

Earlier in this chapter I discussed the link between research evaluation and the strategic evaluation of corporate or organizational performance. Similar evaluation efforts are carried out—routinely and *ad hoc*—in various quarters and levels of the organization. These efforts produce benchmarks, criteria, and evaluation results. They influence the overall culture of the organization, so that the effort to evaluate research should not only be cognizant of these other activities, but to systematically link with them. How to do so is an issue that needs to be resolved.

A senior manager in a large pharmaceutical company commented that the evaluation of research in his organization is done independently of the evaluation of the performance of personnel.

> We have the human resources component where people are assessed and merit is assigned. I understand the concept of matrix, but we don't really operate this way. We have the scientific merit and the human resources merit, and the two are not somehow merging. So you end up with a brilliant researcher with a poor evaluation as a company employee."

The pharmaceutical company has managed to correct this problem by creating a bridge between the different evaluation systems.

STAGES OF THE RESEARCH PROCESS: GENESIS AND FLOW OF IDEAS

Regardless of the model of research employed by research organizations, a key parameter in the initiation of the research process is the stage of generation, evolution, and flow of ideas. In a comprehensive review of the sources and flow of ideas in industrial organizations, Rubenstein defined the notion of *idea* in terms of an organizational event.[34] Ideas are the product of the creative mind of researchers that are translated into descriptions in the form of proposed work, and that, if approved, would employ resources, and may be transformed into a project or program. That is, ideas are only worthwhile as objects for discussion and measurement when they are converted into identifiable organizational occurrences.

However, some ideas are transformed into actual work and commitment of resources in the organization without having been proposed or approved. For example, long after the supersonic transport (SST) program had been officially terminated by Boeing Corporation, research in the corporation continued and ideas germinated *outside* the normal channels of corporate resources allocation and project selection.

Sources of Ideas

All innovations start with an idea. In research organizations, ideas originate from two main sources: (1) within the organization and (2) outside the organization. Similarly, ideas may also emerge from researchers or from the business side of the house, or the marketplace. Figure 10.8 shows the sources of ideas for research, and their interface with the models of research.

This is a rough classification of research ideas generated by four potential sources. The difference in the nonlinear model is the preponderance of market-generated ideas that would impact the final selection of projects to be funded

Figure 10.8
Sources of Ideas for Research and Models of Research

MODEL OF RESEARCH	INTERNALLY		EXTERNALLY	
	Research (Academic)	Business (Commercial)	Research Marketplace	(Academic)
Linear	(a)	(c)	(e)	(g)
Nonlinear	(b)	(d)	(f)	(h)

(a)   *Ideas for exploratory investigations.*
(b)   *Ideas for exploratory investigation with potential applications.*
(c)   *Ideas for potential applications of research already undertaken.*
(d)   *Ideas for products and other applications that would inspire or motivate research.*
(e)   *Ideas for exploratory/basic research from disciplinary state of the art.*
(f)   *Ideas for research to complement and supplement existing projects.*
(g)   *Ideas on potential uses of research when they are ultimately transformed by other units in the organization.*
(h)   *Ideas on market trends and generation of potential applications.*

within the research unit. So, assuming that the quality of ideas is similar in all instances, the source of the ideas finally approved and converted to viable projects may determine, to a large extent, the nature of the portfolio of research projects in a given research organization.[35]

The director of research in a medical devices manufacturing division of a large company has commented on the link between sources of ideas and the selection of projects:

> Nowadays we keep our eyes and ears to the ground to find out what is happening in the market. To run an R&D department is not enough to just do good research. We are doing the other fellow's job. We have to know what the new generation of products looks like in the market, and we extract ideas from this knowledge.

Flow of Ideas

In recent years, as management scholars have increasingly turned their attention to knowledge systems in organizations, it has become even more important to understand the flow of ideas. Knowledge and skills in the organization are partially based on the accumulation of ideas and the results from projects that would end up in an "inventory" of ideas.

Figure 10.9 is the first of three figures that depict the three stages of the generation, flow, and development of ideas in research.[36]

In the research environment of the linear model, ideas are generated by individuals within the research area, then discussed with colleagues and submitted for support and for allocation of resources. This is the traditional flow of academic research ideas and initial proposals. The source is usually external to the organization, most probably originating within the academic community and the state of the art (SOA). However, in the nonlinear model, the idea, although generated by the individual researcher, probably had its origin within the organization, at the commercial or product-related activities.[37]

The processes of screening and evaluation are usually similar in both models of research. Figure 10.10 shows the stages generally involved with screening and evaluation of research ideas and proposals. It would be presumptuous to assume that even in the linear model of research most or all research proposal approved as projects had been generated by individual researchers whose objective was solely to expand the scientific horizons in their discipline. The true situation is more prosaic, as such ideas, proposals, and resultant projects are set within the framework of organizations. In the era of "big science," where ideas for research usually require commitments of relatively large resources and organizational support, even ideas that spring in

Figure 10.9
Generation and Preproposal Flow of Ideas

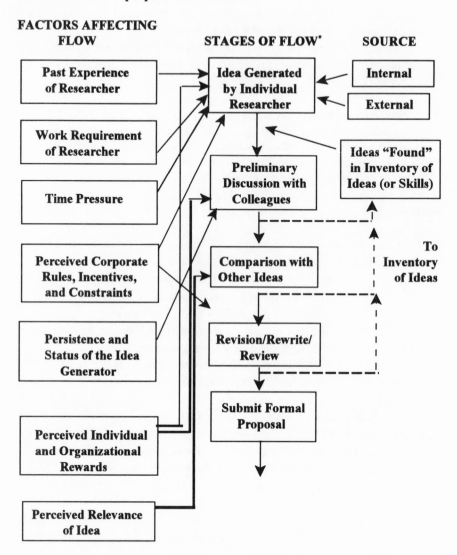

*Not all stages occur for all ideas, and not all stages occur in the same sequence,
although a formal procedure would tend to maintain an established sequence.*

Figure 10.10
Screening and Evaluation of Ideas

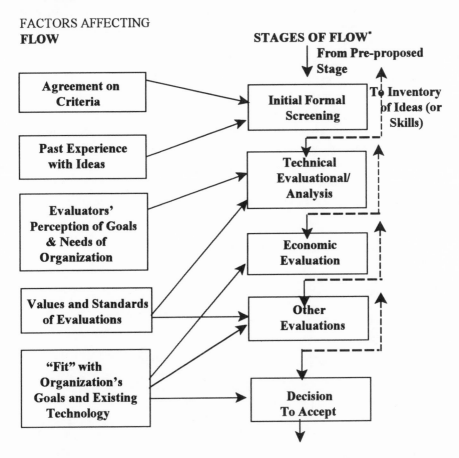

FACTORS AFFECTING
FLOW

STAGES OF FLOW*

Not all stages occur for all ideas, and not all stages occur in the same sequence, although a formal procedure would tend to maintain an established sequence.

the minds of eager individual scientists are routinely imputed by factors and conditions external to the researcher.

If such external parameters are not factored into the ideas and resultant proposals, the screening process may reject them within the criteria of "fit" with organizational goals, or perception of need. In the 1970s, for example, the regulatory climate was credited with the generation of much of the industrial R&D in the United States. Among the primary criteria for evaluation of projects, the degree to which the research would address regulatory pressures had become paramount in the mind-set of many companies.[38]

Finally, proposals usually undergo a process of review and implementation. Figure 10.11 shows some of the key stages in the flow of such a process.

As proposals are accepted and resources allocated, projects come into being and the research work begins within the organizational framework of execution. How do we measure the outcomes and value of projects, and how do organizations decide when to terminate a project? These issues are further discussed elsewhere in this book. It is sufficient to add at this point that in our attempts to evaluate research we should consider the following emerging facts. First, that science, the organization in which it is explored, and the market are deeply intertwined. This is the essence of what "big science" really means. Second, that although individual researchers are the progenitors of most of the exciting and forward-looking ideas for research, the "purity" of such scientific genesis is conditioned by the processes of screening and preliminary evaluation for the purpose of funding and resources allocation.

Figure 10.11
Review and Implementation of Ideas-Proposals

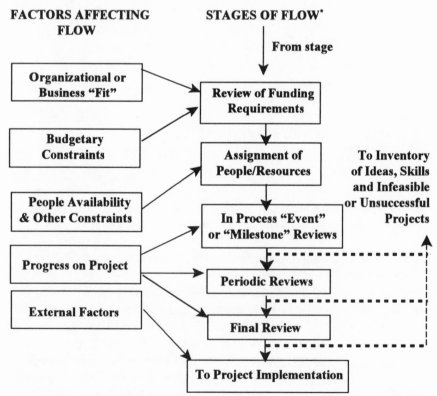

Not all stages occur for all ideas, and not all stages occur in the same sequence, although a formal procedure would tend to maintain an established sequence.

Part of the difficulties in evaluating research stems from the link between science and technology, as between the "scientific" ideas of individual researchers and the market influences on the relevance of such ideas. Pavitt, for example, has argued that because of the complexity of the link between science and technology, the empirical evidence of the impact of science is, to date, inconclusive, ambiguous, and incomplete.[39] He has also argued that scientific skills and unplanned applications are crucial factors in the impact of science on technology. Pavitt's analysis leads to the conclusion that the pressures to make research more relevant and responsive to the market are unwarranted and may produce undesirable consequences. The reason is the role that science plays in generating crucial skills which may also generate unplanned applications.

Pavitt's arguments have far-reaching implications to the processes of idea generation and their evaluation. From a policy viewpoint, the nonlinear model of research may be insufficiently productive inasmuch as it will tend to decrease the value of scientific ideas that may encourage development of training and skills acquisition, as well as lead to unforeseen discoveries and applications.

In commenting on such topics, the vice-president for R&D of a large manufacturing company had this to say:

> It's absolutely not true that our scientists do not understand what this company does. We know exactly what we sell, and how our products fare in the market. We have our own capabilities in the internal team of scientists that no other group has outside—because we work shoulder-to-shoulder with others in the company. We talk to them, we teach them, and we learn from them. It's a symbiotic relationship and it adds strength to our organization.

SUMMARY

Both as a concept and as an activity, evaluation of research is a difficult and challenging task. It combines the peculiar nature of the research activity with the traditional issues of any evaluation. Individual researchers and their organizations are aware of the difficulties as well as the sensitivity of all involved in any evaluation determinations. Much of the challenge is in the metrics—measuring the activity and its outcomes. But a better understanding of what constitutes evaluation of research can only be achieved by also considering the evaluation of technology and the innovation process.

This chapter illustrated the concepts, approaches, and methods used in the evaluation of research. It also underlined the difficulties in linking research outcomes to downstream activities. These difficulties will become apparent later in this book when I discuss the contributions of S&T to the economy and society in Chapters 14 and 15.

NOTES

1. Teitelman, R., *Profits of Science: The American Marriage of Business and Technology* (New York: Basic Books, 1994).

2. Office of Scientific Research and Development (ORSD), *Science: The Endless Frontier* (Washington, DC, July 19, 1945).

3. For an insightful biography of Vannevar Bush, see Zachary, P., *Endless Frontier: Vannevar Bush, Engineer of the American Century* (New York: Free Press, 1997). Also see Bush, V., "Of Inventions and Inventors," *Research Management*, 14(4), 1971, 27-36. Other publications that belong to the science policy literature and that fail to adequately define the essence of the scientific endeavor are, for example, Teich, A., and R. Thornton (Eds.), *Science, Technology, and the Issues of the Eighties: Policy Outlook* (Boulder, CO: Westview Press, 1982).

4. See, for example, Brooks, H., "Can Science Survive in the Modern Age? A Revisit After Twenty Years," *National Forum*, 70, September 1990, 31-32. Also see Isaacs, E., and J. Tang, "So Much Research So Few Good Products," *Communications of the ACM*, 39(9), 1996, 23-25.

5. Stokes, D., *Pasteur's Quadrant: Basic Science and Technological Innovation* (Washington, DC: Brookings Institution, 1997).

6. Stokes also argued that in this mode there is a more productive way of expending public funds for science, since the scientific activity (basic research) will be much more responsive to public needs.

7. See, for example, Johnson, J., "R-D, not R&D," *Communications of the ACM*, 39(9), 1996, 32-34. Also see the story of Steelcase Corporation, in which the R&D function redefined the role that corporate research plays in the innovation process, Miller, W., and L. Morris, *Fourth Generation R&D: Managing Knowledge, Technology, and Innovation* (New York: John Wiley & Sons, 1998).

8. For example, see Frankel, M. and J. Cave (Eds.), *Evaluating Science and Scientists: An East-West Dialogue on Research Evaluation in Post-Communist Europe* (London: Central European University Press, 1997). Also see, Swinbanks, D., "Basic Research Fighting for Survival," *Nature*, 379, January 11, 1996, 112; and Robb, W., "How Good is Our Research?" *Research-Technology Management*, 34(2), 1991, 16-21.

9. See, for example, Iansiti, M., "Real World R&D: Jumping the Product Generation Gap," *Harvard Business Review*, 71(3),1993, 138-147, and Geppert, L., "Industrial R&D: The New Priorities," *IEEE Spectrum*, September, 1994, 30-41. Also see Alston, J., G. Norton, and P. Pardley (Eds.), *Science Under Scarcity: Principles and Practice for Agricultural Research Evaluation and Priority Setting* (New York: CAB International, 1998).

10. See Geisler, E., "When Whales Are Cast Ashore: The Conversion to Relevancy of American Universities and Basic Science," *IEEE Transactions on Engineering Management*, 42(1), 1995, 3-8. In this article I decried the decline of

federal support for academic research as the main supplier of basic science. Also see Lederman, L., "The Value of Fundamental Science," *Scientific American*, 251(5), 1984, 34-41.

11. See Benowitz, S., "New Nobel Laureates Speak Out for Increased Research Finding," *The Scientist*, 10(22), 1996, 35-37.

12. For studies of research and marketing interface, see Souder, W., and A. Chakrabarti, "The R&D/Marketing Interface: Results from an Empirical Study of Innovation Projects, *IEEE Transactions on Engineering Management*, 25(4), 1978, 88-93. For the research-production interface, see Sagal, M., "Effective Technology Transfer: From Laboratory to Production," *Mechanical Engineering*, 100(4), 1978, 32-35.

13. From the vast literature on evaluation of research and R&D, see, for example, Jones, P., "Cost-Benefit and Public Policy Issues," *R&D Management*, 19(2), 1989, 127-134. Also see Kostoff, R., "Research Impact Quantification," *R&D Management*, 24(3), 1994, 207-218; and Evered, D., and S. Harnett (Eds.), *The Evaluation of Scientific Research* (Chichester, U.K.: John Wiley & Sons, 1989).

14. The case of Xerox Corporation and its corporate research laboratory is a fascinating case in corporate transformation, including transformation of its research and technology. See Harris, C., *In Search of Innovation: The Xerox PARC Pair Experiment* (Cambridge, MA: MIT Press, 1999). Also see Kearns, D., and D. Nadler, *Prophets in the Dark* (New York: HarperCollins, 1992). This book is an insightful account of Xerox and its reemergence as a powerful competitor. For another perspective, see Palermo, R., *A World of Quality: Business Transformation at Xerox* (Burr Ridge, IL: Irwin, 1996). This book contains a model used by Xerox to dramatically improve the quality of its products, and a description of internal company documents and its strategic plans. Also see, for example, Salasin, J. *et al.*, "The Evaluation of Federal Research Programs," *MITRE Technical Report*, MTR-80W123, June 1980. Also see Gibbons, M., and L. Georghiou, *Evaluation of Research: A Selection of Current Practices* (Paris: OECD Press, 1987).

15. Geisler, E., "Metrics of Industry-University Interactions," *TIMS/ORSA Joint National Meeting*, San-Francisco, CA, November 1-4, 1992. Also see Geisler, E., "Quantitative Methods in Evaluating R&D: Some Cases from Large Industrial Firms," Working Paper, University of Wisconsin-Whitewater, 1989.

16. The original study was conducted by International Applied Science and Technology Associates, Inc. The follow-up study, which was more comprehensive, was partially supported by the College of Business and Economics, University of Wisconsin-Whitewater, during my sabbatical leave.

17. See other studies and books on this topic, for example, Rosenbloom, R., and W. Spencer (Eds.), *Engines of Innovation: U.S. Industrial Research at the End of an Era* (Boston: Harvard Business School Press, 1996). Also see Brockhoff, K., *Industrial Research for Future Competitiveness* (Berlin: Springer-Verlag, 1997).

18. This was briefly discussed earlier in this chapter. See, for example, Geisler, E., 1995, *op. cit.*; and Chakrabarti, A., and C. Anyanwul, "Defense R&D, Technology, and Economic Performance: A Longitudinal Analysis of U.S. Experience," *IEEE Transactions on Engineering Management*, 40(3), 1993, 136-148.

19. See, for example, Lord, N., *Darkened Waters: A Review of History, Science & Technology Associated with the Exxon Valdez Oil Spill & Clean-Up* (New York: Homer Society of Natural History, 1997). Also see Peyton, K., *Nalco/Exxon Fuel Field Manual: Sources and Solutions to Performance Problems* (New York: McGraw-Hill, 1997). In particular, see the Introduction and Chapter 1.

20. Wilson, C., "Ascend to Wear Lucent's Ring," *Interactive Week*, 6(3), January 18, 1999, 46-47.

21. See, for example, Frame, J., "Quantitative Indicators for Evaluation of Basic Research Programs/Projects," *IEEE Transactions on Engineering Management*, 30(3), 1983, 106-111; and Bisio, A., and L. Gastwirt, *Turning Research and Development into Profits: A Systematic Approach* (New York: Amacom, 1979). Also see, in particular, Mechlin, G., and D. Berg, "Evaluating Research—ROI Is Not Enough," *Harvard Business Review*, 58(5), 1980, 93-99.

22. For example, see Mansfield, E., and S. Wagner, "Organizational and Strategic Factors Associated with Probabilities of Success in Industrial R&D," *Journal of Business*, 48(2), 1975,179-198. Also see Moser, M., and M. Plante, "Linking R&D with the Strategic Management Process of the Firm," *Engineering Management International*, 492, 1987, 127-132; and Roussell, P., K. Saad, and T. Erickson, *Third Generation R&D: Managing the Link to Corporate Strategy* (Boston: Harvard Business School Press, 1991). More recently, see, for example, Grupp, H., and S. Maital, "Perceived Innovation of Israel's Largest Firms: An Empirical Study," *Technovation*, 20(3), 2000, 129-137. Also see Pallett, D., J. Garofolo, and J. Fiscus, "Measurements in Support of Research Accomplishments," *Communications of the ACM*, 43(2), 2000, 75-79. And see Mitchell, G., "Industrial R&D Strategy for the Early 21st Century," *Research-Technology Management*, 43(1), 2000, 31-35. Mitchell discusses the shift toward information and health research, and the increase in the role of the Internet. He also suggests that corporate executives view technology and innovation more favorably as critical assets in the future of their companies.

23. See an excellent discussion of internal corporate power distribution in Rubenstein, A. H., *Managing Technology in the Decentralized Firms* (New York: John Wiley & Sons, 1989). In particular, see Chapters 3.9 (Power and Influence of the Chief Technical Offices) and 3.10 (Who Champions and Protects Technology in the Firm?), pp. 98 and 112, respectively.

24. There is a vast literature on this subject. See, for example, Gaver, D., and V. Srinavasan, "Allocating Resources Between Research and Development: A Macro Analysis," *Management Science*, 18(9), 1972, 492-501. Also see Joglekar, P., and M. Hamburg, "Industry Resource Allocation to Basic Research Under Normally Distributed Benefits," *Decision Sciences*, 18(1), 1987, 1-24; and Van Dyk, E., and D. Smith, "R&D Portfolio Selection by Using Qualitative Pairwise Comparisons," *OMEGA*, 18(6), 1990, 583-594; and for a summary of existing models, see a seminal paper, Souder, W., and T. Mandakovic, "R&D Project Selection Models," *Research Management*, 29(4), 1986, 36-42. Also see Meyer-Krahmer, F., and G. Reger, "New Perspectives on the Innovation Strategies of Multinational Enterprises: Lessons for Technology Policy in Europe," *Research Policy*, 28(7), 1999, 751-776.

25. See, for example, some early studies such as: Baker, N., J. Siegman, and A. Rubenstein, "The Effects of Perceived Needs and Means on the Generation of Ideas for Industrial Research and Development," *IEEE Transactions on Engineering Management*, 14(4), 1967, 156-163; and Souder, W., *Project Selection and Economic Appraisal* (New York: Van Nostrand, 1983). Also see an example from the health care industry in Showstack, J., S. Schroeder, and H. Steinberg, "Evaluating the Costs and Benefits of a Diagnostic Technology," *Medical Care*, 19(5), 1996, 498-509.

26. See, for example, Rubenstein, A., and E. Geisler, "Methodology Issues in Conducting Evaluation of R&D/Innovation," Paper presented at the NSF/Worcester Polytechnic Institute Conference on Management of Technological Innovation, Washington, DC, May 1983. Also see Mansfield, E., "Contribution of R&D to Economic Growth in the United States," *Science*, 175 (4021), 4 February 1972, 477-486.

27. Mansfield, 1972, *op. cit.*, p. 479.

28. *Ibid.*, p. 478.

29. Rubenstein, A. H., and E. Geisler, "Evaluating the Outputs and Impacts of R&D/Innovation," *International Journal of Technology Management*, Special Publication in the Role of Technology in Corporate Policy, 1991, p. 182.

30. Rubenstein, A., and E. Geisler, *Some Trends and Initial Listing of Leading Research Organizations in Selected Sub-Fields of Information Science and Technology* (Evanston, IL, IASTA, Inc., 1987).

31. See, for example, Cooper, A, "Research Findings in Strategic Management with Implications for R&D Management," *R&D Management*, 19(2), 1989, 115-125. The author relates R&D intensity and other attributes to performance measures such as return on investment, cash flow/investment, and pretax/profits to sales. Also see Ulhoi, J., "Toward a Theoretical and Methodological Corporate Technology Management Framework: The Strategic Perspective," *International Journal of Technology Management*, 12(2), 1996, 199-208.

32. For a thorough discussion of the threats from use of "co-variation" design in the generation of knowledge in organizational and managerial sciences, see Geisler, E., *Methodology, Theory, and Knowledge: Actions and Consequences in the Organizational and Managerial Sciences* (Westport, CT: Quorum Books, 1999).

33. Gomory, R., "Dominant Science Does Not Mean Dominant Product," *Research & Development*, 14(4), 1987, 72-74.

34. Rubenstein, 1989, *op. cit.*, pp. 221-245.

35. See, for example, Bar, J., "A Systematic Technique to New Product Idea Generation: The External Brain," *R&D Management*, 19(1), 1989, 69-78. Also see Conway, H., and N. McGuiness, "Idea Generation in Technology-Based Firms," *Journal of Product Innovation Management*, 3(4), 1986, 276-291; and for a viewpoint from the business perspective see Gagliano, C., "How to Mine and Refine New Product Ideas," *Business Marketing*, 70(11), 1985, 102-112.

36. The model used in Figures 10.9, 10.10, and 10.11 is a composite of several models. See Baker, Siegman, and Rubenstein, 1967, *op. cit.*, and Baker, N., S. Green, and A. Bean, "How Management Can Influence the Generation of Ideas," *Research Management*, 28(6), 1985, 35-42; and Pound, W., "Research Project Selection:

Testing a Model in the Field," *IEEE Transactions on Engineering Management*, 11(1), 1964, 16-22.

37. Some early work on this topic includes, for example, Schoman, C., D. Dick, and T. McKnight, "Relating Organization Goals and Technological Forecasting for Research and Development Resource Allocation," *IEEE Transactions on Engineering Management*, 16(4), 1969, 148-160. In this paper the authors described allocation of resources for projects by the U.S. Navy, by using a method of Navy Exploratory Development Goals (EDG). In a manner similar to industrial screening, a utility matrix is developed relating the value of projects to the worth of military objectives. Also see Rock, A., "Eureka! But What Do You Do Next?", *Money*, 6(2), 1984, 136-143.

38. This was particularly noticeable in the chemical industry. See, for example, Foster, R., and F. Gluck, "Impact of Antitrust and Regulatory Actions on Progress of Technology," *Research Management*, 18(4), 1975, 7-10. Also see Gerstenfeld, A., and H. Nason, "The Effect of Government Regulation on Innovation in the Chemical Industry," in Hill, C. (Ed.), *Federal Regulations and Chemical Innovation* (Washington, DC: American Chemical Society, 1978). The main argument was that regulations are forcing the industry to channel its research toward meeting the challenges of the regulators, rather than generate research toward new products and processes. In the case of the pharmaceutical industry see, for example, Schnee, J., "Regulation and Innovation: U.S. Pharmaceutical Industry," *California Management Review*, 22(4), 1979, 23-32. Also, in the biotechnology industry, see Huber, P., "Biotechnology and the Regulation Hydra," *Technology Review* 90(8), 1987, 57-65. The arguments for all these industries were similar in their criticism of regulatory processes.

More recently, see Williams, D., "Food Enzyme Producers Face Pressures to Innovate," *Chemical Market Reporter*, 253(25), 1998, F16-F17; and see Schoening, N., W. Souder, J. Lee, and R. Cooper, "The Influence of Government Science and Technology Policies on New Product Development in the USA, UK, South Korea, and Taiwan," *International Journal of Technology Management*, 15(8), 1998, 821-835.

39. See Pavitt, K., "What Makes Basic Research Economically Useful?", *Research Policy*, 20(2), 1991, 109-119.

11

EVALUATION OF TECHNOLOGY

Early in the 20th century, the German writer Oswald Spengler lamented the decline of the Western European civilization.[1] He called for the new generation to embrace "the technical instead of the lyrical, shipping instead of painting, politics instead of epistemology" (p. 57). Toward the end of the century, there were different voices that forcefully criticized the dependence on technology and called for a more humanized approach to whatever is "technical."[2]

REITERATING THE THESIS OF THIS BOOK

The overarching thesis of this book is that the evaluation of science and technology is based on a theoretical and conceptual framework that extends the reach and impacts of S&T well beyond the boundaries of the activities themselves. Thus science, and particularly technology, are viewed and measured by their impacts (both positive and negative) on the economy and society. Science is evaluated through research as an activity but also by its contributions to progress in the economy and society.

Technology can and must be evaluated and measured within the context of its social and economic environments, inasmuch as it is an extension and a dimension of human enterprise. To paraphrase the saying "if you build it they'll come" is true only insofar as social and economic entities make use of technology as an extension of their own needs, values, and cultural dictates.

In this regard, the truism expressed by Mary Ash Kay contributes to our respect for the downstream flow of innovation. The American businesswoman who revolutionized the marketing of cosmetics suggested that "a mediocre idea that generates enthusiasm will go further than a great idea that inspires no one." Thus, the actualized value of ideas rests with their further acceptance and application by others.

In 1872, the American essayist Ralph Waldo Emerson remarked in one of his lectures: "If a man can write a better book, preach a better sermon, or make a better mousetrap than his neighbor, though he build his house in the woods, the world will make a beaten path to his door."[3] Although it has become a much-quoted and popular statement in praise of inventors and inventions, Emerson's statement reflects only half of the conditions for use of a new technology. The mere possession of the technology is not a guarantee that it will be utilized and that the "world" will perforce "make a beaten path" to the inventor's door. Technology is not judged by its existence alone, nor is its mere existence a sufficient condition for its successful usage.

We cannot evaluate technology unless and until we put it in the context of social and economic phenomena. Namely, until and unless we put a *human* dimension upon it. A better mousetrap, by itself, is useless, until and unless it is used and assessed by its users. So technology is evaluated as a tool, subjected to human needs, desires, preferences, and emotional as well as material parameters of existence.

Therefore, love or hate of technology *per se* is an empty concept. Since science is universal, hence shared and almost impossible to isolate or conceal, the technology that it generates will come into fruition regardless of any barriers imposed on its formation. For example, technological advances in genetics and bioengineering will emerge regardless of the debate concerning their ethical viability.

Such sentiments were best expressed by the futurologist Alvin Toffler who once commented that "technology feeds on itself—technology makes more technology possible." In reference to such a process of technological progress, Andrew Grove, the founder of Intel Corporation, argued that "what can be done, will be done." These statements reflect a strong belief that technology may be viewed as a watershed which, when accepted by or useful to individuals and their organizations, becomes a social and economic reality.[4]

To reiterate, this book is about the evaluation of science and technology, as it impacts human life and enterprise. How we define technology will take us to a frame of reference whose main criterion for viability is its distance from the human target. How close we are to assessing technology as a human dimension will determine the feasibility as well as worthiness of our definition of what technology is and what it means.

SETTING THE BOUNDARIES

In this chapter the term "technology" is defined for practical purposes as that portion of the innovation process beyond research. Thus, technology includes new product development (NPD), development in general, engineering, testing, prototyping, and altogether the conversion of knowledge into commercialized or useful products, systems, and processes. These portions or steps which lead to an innovation may or may not have to become commercially applicable "things" (such as products), but by going beyond the framework of research in this chapter, they come under the terminology of technology.

Another way of defining technology in this context is by considering the concept itself. Terminology aside, technology can be viewed as the outcomes from research that have found a use. So that, as soon as a use is identified, the term technology is introduced.

A conceptual interpretation suggests that one key difference between research and technology is that research can (and is) evaluated *per se* on the merit of its addition to the state of knowledge with, or more likely without, potential applications. Technology, on the other hand, is normally evaluated only in terms of its uses by others. Its value is not determined by its mere existence, nor by its immediate outcomes. Rather, its value is manifested by how its users assess it and decide on its merit.

TECHNOLOGY AND ITS CONTEXT

The concept of "technology," as defined in this chapter, is uniquely approached and understood within the context of the social and economic environment within which it is utilized. Technology evaluation can be credibly executed only when its criteria and measures are selected from beyond its immediate domain.

What are we evaluating? We evaluate the process of moving down-stream along the innovation continuum, from the research component to the final destination of a *useful* outcome and its impacts and benefits. As already stated, the mere possession or existence of technology is not a guarantee for its actual use. We cannot understand technology by its existence alone, but only within the context of the users: people, organizations, and society.

In its actual manifestation, technology ranges from just a piece of knowledge, a method or a technique, all the way to a complex system of machinery and its inherent intelligence. The key is that technology is not defined and evaluated by what it is, but by criteria *outside* itself—by its actual and potential users. This attribute creates a wide range of possible definitions and multiple interpretations of what constitutes technology and what its impacts, outcomes, benefits, or harmful effects are.

Another consequence of this attribute is the fact that evaluation of technology thus depends on the characteristics of the users—their ability to make assessments, to utilize the technology, and to minimize their preferences, predilections and subjectivity. Clearly, potential users generally cannot entirely distance themselves from subjectivity and idiosyncratic preferences—hence the multiple approaches to the evaluation of technology.

In the context of *organizations* we encounter such constructs as "absorptive capacity" and "core competencies." They refer to the organization's limited ability to absorb and utilize technology.[5] Similarly, the concept of "bounded rationality" refers in part to the individual's limited ability to absorb and utilize information, and technology in general.[6]

Consequently, technology is evaluated by users who are themselves limited in their capacity to fully integrate and utilize technology, and who are inherently biased due to their culture, unique needs, and a host of other factors, including even the mere understanding of the technology itself.

The writer Kenneth Grahame once commented that "the strongest human instinct is to impart information—the second strongest is to resist it."[7] Biases are reflected in resistance to the progress and utilization of technology and to the flow of information and knowledge connected with it.

PARADOX OF TECHNOLOGY EVALUATION

A commonly discussed paradox of technology refers to the reality of technology diffusion and maturation. Once adopted, every technology is bound to be replaced. But the difficulties and the complexity of technological development and adoption/integration make replacement an activity mired in frustration, failure, and chance.

But the other less obvious paradox is that of technology evaluation. It concerns the gap between producers and users of technology. The more technology producers attempt to bridge the gap and to apply users' criteria and measures to their own reasoning and processes, the less likely they are to produce technology that will replace the existing technology.

To clarify, the more researchers, for example, attempt to subordinate their thinking to the commercial reasoning of the ultimate users of the technology, the less innovative the technology may thus become. Since the criteria for evaluation are generated by the users, producers of technology find themselves in a position where they must act in accordance with these criteria in order to survive. By doing so they may lose their distinctive edge of inventiveness, creativity, and novelty.[8] Hence, in order to be successful (by the criteria of the users), producers of technology have to conform to the "rules of the game" of users. But conformity is an antidote to inventiveness, exploration, and risk taking—all of which are necessary conditions for humans to innovate.

PUSH-PULL APPROACHES

The basic relationship in the evaluation of technology is its link to commercialization or, otherwise, its ultimate use by social and economic actors. The link from generation to utilization may be viewed in the "pull" or "push" approaches.

The "pull" approach is also sometimes known as "demand-pull," in which the impetus for the technology comes from the user. The "push" approach describes the case where the generators of the technology put their effort into bringing the technology to the users.[9]

These approaches and the distinction between them are important because of the criteria for evaluation that each approach seems to encompass. The "push" approach would be guided by the values and attitudes of the generators of the technology, whereas in the case of "pull," the criteria would be those of the users.

Who decides on the flow of technology? This question is at the heart of the push-pull framework for analysis of technological change, transfer, and utilization. In studies of the process of innovation, it has long been known that when the research activity simply "throws" its outputs "over the wall" to development, engineering, and other product-related functions in the company, the chances for successful transfer are diminished. When there is, however, a reciprocal wish to accept these outputs and the awareness on the part of the recipients that there is a need and potential uses for them, the chances for successful transfer are thus enhanced.

"Push" or "pull" alone cannot necessarily make the technology flow successfully toward utilization. As stated before, the mere existence of the technology will not always lead to successful usage. The graveyards of corporate technology laboratories are burgeoning with technological achievements that never made it to usable commercial applications.

So evaluation of technology in terms of its ultimate usefulness to the economy and society depends, in part, on the source of the flow, or the motivation to make it happen. Both sides of this equation must be committed if successful utilization is to be achieved. Total push may bear fruit in the short run, but without reciprocity from users it will ultimately fail. For example, Henry Ford's insistence on pushing his cars in one color, black, finally succumbed to the users' demand for a variety of colors. The need for reciprocity is magnified in the case of technology, as sometimes superior technologies in certain products are not preferred by customers.[10]

EMBEDDED TECHNOLOGIES

Until now this chapter approached technology as a self-contained entity that appears in the form of, for example, a product, technique, or system. But technology also appears in the form of components or capabilities that are *embedded* in everyday products and services. The most common household devices and tools may contain embedded technologies that provide them with unique capabilities. For instance, even microwave ovens and toaster-ovens may have embedded in them such technologies as heat-sensoring devices. Automobiles contain a variety of embedded technologies, in the form of sensors, regulators, and data analysis and transmission devices.

Rubenstein has pioneered the discussion on what constitutes embedded technology.[11] He defined the term "imbedded technology" by using the notions that such technology is knowledge embedded in products, procedures, systems, materials, and processes, as well as technical skills that individuals and organizations possess on how to make things work, how to improve them, and how to make *new* things that will work better.

This broad definition suggests that embedded technology constitutes the backbone of products, processes, and services. It is the *cumulative* knowledge and skills, in a way similar to the overall definition of technology stated earlier in the chapter and to the definitions offered in the section on technology analysis below. Moreover, embedded technology that appears as technical skills and know-how (in individuals as well as organizations) is an indicator of assets that are imbued in organizations.

As we take the viewpoint of such embedded technology as assets to the individual and the organization, the evaluation perspective would call for some attributes of embeddedness. Figure 11.1 lists some of these attributes.

The last characteristic in this list refers to a very difficult issue. How far do we go to establish the embedded technology in a product, system, procedure, or process? The technological infrastructure that serves as background to any embedded "piece" of technology may be traced as far back as we so wish. This is the issue that was central to tracing the role that basic research played in technical innovations and how much it contributed to them. For example, sensoring devices in an automobile may have benefitted from heat-transfer and heat-measurement technologies, which themselves may have benefitted from research in physics, chemistry, and ancillary fields of knowledge.

The Case of the Bullpup Weapon System

Perhaps the earliest systematic attempt to assess the role of research and technology in a product or system was the trial study conducted by the U.S.

Figure 11.1
Attributes or Characteristics of Embedded Technologies

CHARACTERISTICS OF EMBEDDED TECHNOLOGIES
• *Cycle* or *timeline* (How old is the technology?) • *Usefulness* (to the user of the product, system, procedure, etc. in which technology is embedded) • *Replaceability* (How difficult is it to replace the technology?) • *Imitability* (How difficult is it to imitate the technology?) • *Functionality* (How much does the technology contribute to the function of the unit where it is embedded?) • *Cost* (How much does the embedded technology add to the cost of the unit in which it is embedded?) • *Substitutability* (How close are we to having another technology substitute this embedded technology?) • *Cumulative History* (How much technology has been accumulated to this point?)

Department of Defense in the case of the Bullpup air-to-surface guided missile.[12] The study was directed by The Research and Exploratory Development Management Steering Group, which included Colonel Isenson, who later also participated in project Hindsight.

The Bullpup missile was selected for this study because it was a guided missile system, hence represented an entire range of similar systems, and also because it was a relatively simple weapon system used by Navy and Air Force airplanes. The larger version B was 13.6 feet in length, weighed 1,785 pounds, had a range of 3-9 miles, and carried a warhead of 1,000 pounds of conventional explosives, with capability for a nuclear load.

The methodology in this study consisted of identification of *critical events* of research and exploratory development that led to essential inputs to the system, subsystems, and the interface of the subsystems in the final creation of this weapon. The study defined such events as "corresponding to a period of technical activity with a well-defined end point....Typically a creative or innovative act is involved" (p. 11). As such, 43 events were identified, insofar as their inclusion was based on judgment calls by the task group. For example, the propulsion subsystem had 18 events credited with its development—among them the 1949 development of the hydrazine-derivative family of propellants, and even before that, the 1942 conception of propellant injector-mixes, developed by a U.S. Navy laboratory.

Since the cut-off point was arbitrary, the earliest event was dated to 1940. Yet almost half of the events that led to this weapon system were in the areas of innovations in *materials*. Nevertheless, the issue of how much "technology" had accumulated in some basic sciences remained largely unanswered.[13]

Duality of Attributes of Embedded Technology

The notion of embeddedness of technology in other entities carries with it a duality of attributes. On the one hand, there are the attributes or characteristics of the technology itself: capacity, efficiency, accuracy, power, and similar attributes that make the technology a desirable input into products, systems, procedures, and processes.

But there are also economic and social attributes that play a very important part in the embeddedness of the technology. These parameters are different from the economic and social values of the organizations that implement and apply the technology, and the entities in which technologies are embedded. Rather, they are the values that emanate from overall societal values, yet are part of the technology itself.

For example, a technology embedded in a given product or system may be influenced by such values or parameters as safety and health considerations—in addition to such technical attributes as power, accuracy, or efficiency. Figure 11.2 shows the matrix of embeddedness of technology and social values.

The matrix shows five social attributes. *Safety* refers to the value society attaches to the prevention of hazards from a technology embedded in a product, process, or system. *Health* refers to medical hazards of a technology. For example, signs above roads and highways could be painted with radioactive isotopes that would glow in the dark and would save large electrical bills, but they would also pose medical risks to the general population. Hence this technology is restricted to, for example, medical diagnostics. *Ecology* refers to environmental threats from a technology, such as pollution, destruction of the ozone layer, and adding to global warming. *Cost* is the cost of the technology when all other attributes remain constant. For example, in the debate over the cost of medical technology, some argue that the technology is needed and useful but economically destructive to the healthcare delivery system. Finally, cost of opportunity is the cost society would incur if the technology is not embedded in a product or system. Similarly, the attributes of the technology provide a picture of what the technology can do and, by extension, what the characteristics of the product or system in which it is embedded are.[14]

The power of this matrix is in the manipulations of the cells. In the intersect, which appears in each cell, a quantity may be assigned for the level of benefit, damage, or constraints. For example, the level of power (energy) given by a technology to a product may have safety threats intersect

Figure 11.2
Matrix of Embeddedness of Technology and Society

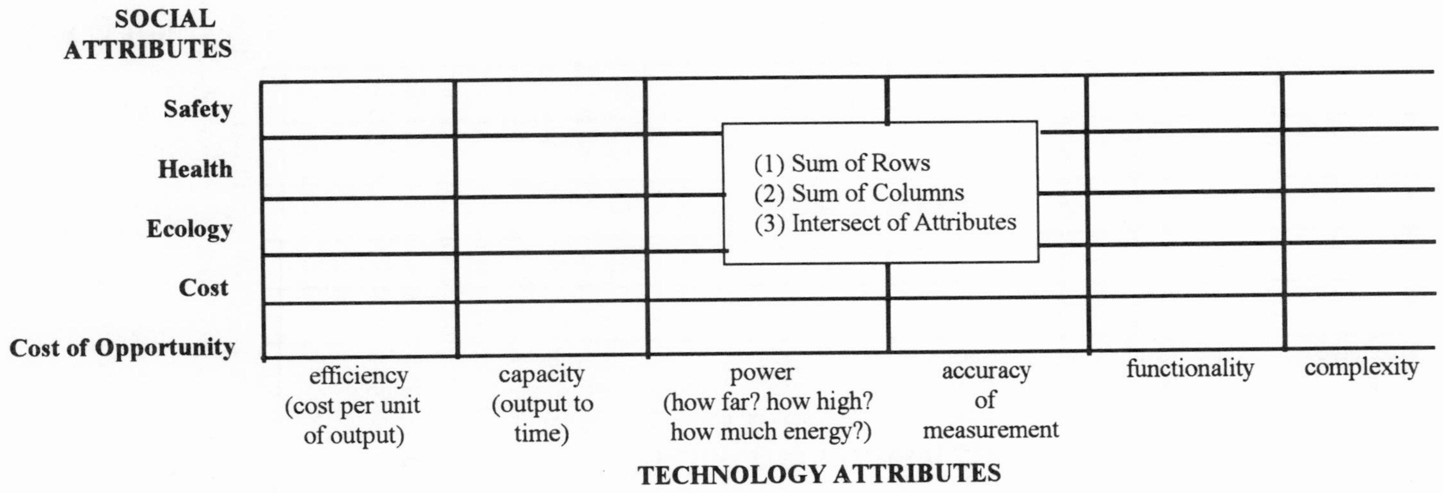

SOCIAL
ATTRIBUTES

Safety

Health

Ecology

Cost

Cost of Opportunity

(1) Sum of Rows
(2) Sum of Columns
(3) Intersect of Attributes

efficiency (cost per unit of output) | capacity (output to time) | power (how far? how high? how much energy?) | accuracy of measurement | functionality | complexity

TECHNOLOGY ATTRIBUTES

(1) *Sum of Rows: Along each social attribute, the sum of benefits or damage from the technology attributes.*
(2) *Sum of Columns: Summation of social values impinging on each technology attribute.*
(3) *Intersect: Each cell is the view of individual attributes in matrix.*

power and safety. Thus, the sum of the safety will now add the potential safety hazards from this technology, measured by its sum or all of efficiency, capacity, power, accuracy, functionality, and complexity. The sum of columns would compute the constraints that societal values impose on the technology so that its power, for instance, would be limited by such concerns as health, ecology, safety, and cost.

Thus, the inclusion of a technology into a product, process, or system would be the result of merging of technological and social attributes and values. The higher the "content" of technology in a product, process, or system, the more such merging would occur. Hence, a product, process, or system can be evaluated on its embedded technology by utilizing the matrix in Figure 11.2 as a useful tool for analysis.

TECHNOLOGY ANALYSIS

Any evaluation of technology needs a framework of the analysis of the concept, its boundaries, and its structure. The pioneering work of such scholars as Rias Van Wyk and his colleagues has led to advances in this area.[15] Van Wyk systematically framed the notions of technology and technology change in a taxonomical structure. This effort gave impetus to the modeling of the complex phenomenon of technology and technological change.

Classification Schemes

Taxonomic schemes for technology have generally been based on attributes of the technology itself and the roles or functions it performs. In line with the definition provided earlier in this book, some classifications suggest technological types that are encountered in the areas of shelter, health, communication, tools, packaging, raw materials, and transportation.[16] Other schemes are built on the characteristics of the technology, the scientific laws and knowledge embedded in it, and the type of processing or transformation it creates.[17]

The lesson learned from such classification schemes is that the complexity of the technology phenomenon makes it very difficult to arrive at a standard taxonomy that will satisfy all concerned. The more attractive schemes are those that focus on the changes that technology brings about and on its impacts.

For example, an early and much-cited scheme of the development and evolution of technology has focused on seven trends, such as increased capabilities (human and social) in energy, transportation, materials, sensory and communication skills, and mechanization (automation) of physical and intellectual functions.[18]

It seems that regardless of how we attempt to classify technology, the emphasis tends to eventually shift toward the analysis of impacts on individuals and society. Hence the importance attached in this chapter to the notion of embeddedness of technological and societal attributes in any product, process, system, or activity where technology is a component and does or may impact the "host" framework in which it is embedded.

VALUATION OF TECHNOLOGY

So, what then is the value of a given technology, and can we arrive at a unique measure or quantity that would satisfactorily assess technology? In Chapter 9, I suggested that since technology is evaluated by its impacts on other entities, hence by criteria developed by such extraneous entities, we are therefore severely limited in generating a single measure of value.

But if we link the embeddedness matrix in Figure 11.2 with extant theories of the firm, we may be able to arrive at a framework for analysis of the total value of technology to the firm. Each of the extant theories of the firm would be a unique perspective on the value of the technology to the firm.

Transaction Cost Theory

Transaction cost economics (TCE) suggests that the existence of the firm is due to its ability to avoid costs of market transactions.[19] Within the framework of this theory, TCE helps to explain the cost to a firm of meeting the embedded attributes. As an issue of "make or buy" of technology, organizations need to assess the technological *and* the social attributes of their acquisitions, or in their decision to "make" the necessary technology. Valuation of a technology is thus contingent upon the process by which an organization decides on its choice of boundary by deciding on "make" or "buy" of a given technology.[20]

In general terms, the matrix in Figure 11.2 helps to mediate the TCE and knowledge-based theory of the firm.

Knowledge-Based Theory

Poppo and Zenger, for example, have asserted that knowledge is codified in the organization in a way that contributes to its efficient governance.[21] Thus the more the organization is able to assess the content of technology and social attributes in its planned acquisition of resources, the more it will be able to make performance-enhancing decisions on make-or-buy of these resources.

Similar analyses may be used in the evaluation of technology and its effects on the performance of organizations. Technology provides not only assets (thus subject to analyses of TCE or knowledge base), but also plays a distinct role as facilitator and enabler of the processes of transformations of resources.

In another view of the firm, the *resources-based approach* suggests that the competitive strength of the firm will benefit from resources or assets that are difficult to imitate. In this view, internalizing specific assets and activities would add to the organization's comparative advantage and its market competitiveness.[22]

By gaining knowledge about the technology as an asset, and technological and social contents of other assets and activities, the organization can assess its market competitiveness and its potential for enhanced and sustained performance. The matrix in Figure 11.2 provides an effective tool that can be used in analyses that employ extant theories of the firm.[23]

BEST PRACTICES: A REVIEW

How do successful companies evaluate their technology? In this section I provide two illustrations of different companies and their unique ways of assessing the impacts and benefits of technology. In general, the "best practices" in the examples below are all based on very few chosen methods and measures. Perhaps it is not the method or measure used, but *how* it is counted and assessed that makes all the difference.

General Electric

Walter Robb, who was GE's senior vice-president for corporate research and development, points out that his company has used a mix of subjective and more objective measures.[24] An overall assessment is based on the subjective view of the company and its successes, *without* the existence of the R&D laboratory and the technology it has generated over the years. Robb calls this the "Jimmy Stewart Test," based on the actor's role as Mr. Bailey in Frank Capra's *It's a Wonderful Life*. In this movie Mr. Bailey is shown how different and less valuable his town and the life of its inhabitants would have been if he hadn't lived.

In the area of more precise and objective measures, GE has resorted to a count of patents and various attributes of patents, such as cost per patent, comparisons with other companies, and income from licensing. Another measure was the amount of royalty payments the company saves by having a specific patent.

GE also used a discounted rate-of-return applied to the transfer of a technology from the laboratory to a commercial use. To insure objectivity, GE asked a consulting company, Booz, Allen & Hamilton, to calculate the return on investments. By using a methodology similar to that of historical description of key events used in the Bullpup and TRACES studies, the consultants conducted interviews with key informants in both the technology center and the business units. They then proceeded to assess the level of credit of the benefits that the technology center can be assigned from each of the 190 technology transfer projects they had analyzed.

Finally, based on the level of credit, the part played by the technology/R&D center in the returns from each project/product was determined. Compared with the expenditures for the R&D center, a rate of return was thus computed.

Robb emphasized that the methodology described also helped to alert GE to the fact that a very small number of products (technologies) generated by the center and transferred to commercial applications had accounted for much of the payback. This knowledge, according to Robb, was instrumental in redesigning the company's allocation of resources for R&D.

Eastman Kodak

At Eastman Kodak, the preferred methodology for evaluating technology was a modified risk analysis described by the company as an "R&D Portfolio Analysis."[25] The methodology is driven by the business aspects of desired products. Two main flow diagrams are constructed. The first starts with the features of the product and contains the other factors that will influence the net-present-value of the product once it is marketed. The second flow diagram (described by the company as an "influence diagram") shows the various R&D tasks or activities needed to accomplish specific features.

What follows is the application of probabilities (in the form of a decision tree) of the potential performance of the R&D tasks. How probable is it that specific tasks will generate the R&D outputs (technology) necessary for the achievement of product features (such as sharpness, speed, and grain)?

In essence, the methodology compares what a certain product, with proposed features, will gain in the marketplace with the potential of the R&D function in the firm to generate technology that would help form such a product. Thus, when dividing such a value of R&D by the projected cost of this R&D effort, what emerges is an indication of how well R&D performs.

Inherent in this methodology and the "influence diagrams" are the assumptions that the risks are fairly well understood and that all the critical stages and tasks have been included in the analysis. The methodology starts with the product itself and its projected successful commercialization in the marketplace. It then looks back to "What can R&D do for us in this specific case?"[26]

This method also contributed to reallocation of resources at Eastman Kodak in favor of those activities that showed higher commercial promise. Such bias is consonant with the more stringent non-linear models of research and technology evaluation.

EVALUATION AND METRICS: THE UNHOLY ALLIANCE

As this chapter clearly shows, technology has to be evaluated in conjunction with the scientific activity that generated it, on the one hand, and the impacts it produces, on the other hand. Technology as a stand-alone entity loses much of its power as the object for evaluation. There is always the need for the context of where technology has originated and where it is going.

In addition to this imperative, the seamless flow of the innovation process—from research to development to engineering and commercialization—creates even more powerful barriers to a strictly isolated identification and evaluation of self-contained stages and activities in this process. In what I would call "balkanization" of the process of innovation, the available methods for evaluation are few, thus providing only a partial picture of the true phenomenon.

By using decision trees and interviews with 43 managers of technology, Hauser summarized the practices in American companies of using metrics for Research, Development, and Engineering (RD&E).[27] He identified three tiers in describing the process: basic research, development programs, and applied engineering. Hauser also distinguished between what he called "market-outcome" metrics and "research-driven" metrics that are standard and more direct. Thus, different types of metrics are applied differently to activities within each tier. Moreover, a given type of metrics would result in a predicted type of behavior, such as "not invented here" or empire building.

Although approaches such as Hauser's do consider the balance between the market and research metrics, they do not effectively deal with the flow of the innovation process. A key deficiency seems to be the compartmentalization of the process into self-contained activities, such as research, development, and engineering. The interconnectedness and the seamless flow of activities—hence of metrics—are not well incorporated into the operational measurements of these approaches.

For example, bibliometric measures, such as counts of publications and citations, may not be viewed as "direct" measures of a research activity. These measures are, for all practical purposes, "market" measures, since they contain peer review, which is the result of evaluations by people *outside* the organization.[28] Only the internal evaluation of researchers, scientists, and engineers by the organization, and when considered employees of the organization, may be entitled to be called "direct" or activity-related.

The Technovalue Framework of Analysis

Geisler has proposed a somewhat different approach to evaluation of technology and to the identification of values it produces.[29] The approach is based on two complementary frameworks of analysis. One considers the embeddedness of technology in the processes and value chain of the organization. The other framework considers technology in its relation with the key phenomena and stakeholders of the organization. The resultant analysis contains six principles for technology energizing of the innovative organization.

Figure 11.3 shows the four relationships that characterize technology in the organization and possible avenues for its monitoring and evaluation. These relationships are categories of technology in the organization.

For each of the four categories, the *technovalue* approach utilizes the embeddedness matrix shown in Figure 11.2. By doing so, the analysis extends to include the social and organizational values that impinge on the technology phenomenon.

There are several benefits to using these categories. Chief among them is the reference to technology beyond the usual compartmentation of organizational activities or stages of the innovation process. Such a "meta" approach is similar to considering technology to be the linking-pin among stakeholders and phenomena at the various activities of the organization and regardless of the stage of the innovation process. Needless to say, such an approach also has another benefit, which is the improved conceptual link of any impacts of technology generated by the organization on the social and economic environment.[30]

The Unholy Alliance

There is a conflicting discrepancy between the effort to evaluate science and technology and the metrics available for the task. The objectives and expectations from the evaluation effort have by far outreached the pool of measures. So any attempt to match existing metrics to the evaluation scheme would almost always encounter gaps, challenges, and unanswered questions.

For example, technology cannot be evaluated without regard, on the one hand, to its generation in science and, on the other hand, its impacts on the market. Yet, as measures tend to follow a "balkanization effect" in which compartments are formed in the process, the effort to employ metrics is insufficient.[31]

Much of what science and technology provide are an integral part of their evaluation, yet remain intangibles and very difficult to measure, other than by surrogates and similar techniques. The exhilaration of flying that pilots experience is an example of what we gain from technology. Similarly, the

Figure 11.3
Categorization of Technology as It Is Related to Organizational Phenomena

CHARACTERISTIC OR TYPE OF RELATION	POTENTIAL AVENUES FOR EVALUATION
T2T (Technology-to-Technology)	• System-to-system connection • Connectivity and embeddedness issues of concern • Knowledge about needs for change and updating
T2C (Technology-to-Customers)	• Role of technology in satisfying customers' needs • Benefits and shortcomings of technology used to provide customers' needs • Knowledge about need to change or update
T2E (Technology-to-Employees)	• Uses of technology by managers and employees in general to carry out their tasks • Knowledge about gaps in skills and other aptitudes needed for effective use of technology
T2O (Technology-to-Organizations)	• Role of technology in the strategic competitiveness of the organization • Role of technology in the "value chain" of process and activities

"eureka" feeling of extreme accomplishment in discovery and invention remains beyond the reach of common metrics. If science is our exploration for understanding, technology is the extension of what we can do.

Such achievements are sometimes as subjective as they are objective, and as long term as they are immediate. Science and technology are embedded in our senses, in humanity's affinity for work as well as entertainment, for mastering the challenging environment, as well as for amusement and pleasure. For instance, many breakthrough innovations in computers and software in the 1990s were an almost direct outcome from games for children invented in the 1980s. The game called "Pac-Man" was the direct progenitor of the sophisticated computer graphics of the 1990s. So many of the inventors who were the driving force behind computer graphics and the Internet throughout the 1990s were young, sometimes *very* young. Playing with this technology was *fun*, pure and simple.

Science and technology are not a luxury, to be applied only by people, organizations, and countries who have enough slack resources to exploit this expensive "pastime." Although science is no longer a preferred leisurely activity of inquisitive gentlemen and has become "big science" with its own dynamics—the exhilaration of creation and exploration is nevertheless very much alive in the scientific community.

Thus, the count of a publication or a patent, or a system that emerges from the flow of innovation, is barely enough of a metric to express all that S&T can do.[32] There is always the human element of risk versus pleasure, failure versus fun, and the balancing of a calculated feeling of discovery with the convulsion of energy and pleasure people feel when they ride the technological achievements of their doing.

NOTES

1. Spengler, O., *The Decline of the West*, translated by Charles Atkinson (New York: Oxford University Press, 1990). This is a reprint of the original book which was first published in 1917.

2. See, for example, Pool, R., *Beyond Engineering: How Society Shapes Technology* (New York: Oxford University Press, 1997). Also see Buckley, J., and J. Moynihan, *Going For Growth: Realizing the Value of Technology* (New York: McGraw-Hill, 1998). There is also a considerable body of studies and publications regarding ethical considerations of technology in general, and specific issues and topics in particular. See, for example, Ermann, D., M. Williams, and M. Shauf (Eds.), *Computers, Ethics, and Society* (New York: Oxford University Press, 1997). In particular, see Chapter 31 (People Are Responsible, Computers Are Not) and Chapter 32 (The Ten Commandments of Computer Ethics). Also see Birsch, D., and J. Fiedler (Eds.), *The Ford Pinto Case: A Study in Applied Ethics, Business, and Technology* (New York: SUNY Press, 1994); and Barbour, I., *Ethics in an Age of Technology* (San Francisco: Harper, 1992). Barbour has criticized modern technology for routinely and systematically impacting not only the environment but also such human conditions as justice, freedom, and economic development in a negative fashion. Also see Jonas, H., *Imperative of Responsibility: In Search of an Ethics for the Technological Age* (Chicago: University of Chicago Press, 1985).

3. This is a quote that Sarah Yule and Mary Keene attributed to Emerson, in notes they had taken during a lecture Emerson supposedly gave in 1871. See Yule, S., and M. Keene, *More Borrowings* (San Francisco: Dodge Book & Stationery Co., 1891).

4. See Toffler, A., *The Third Wave: The Classic Study of Tomorrow* (New York: Doubleday Dell, 1981), and Grove, A., *Only the Parnoid Survive: How To Exploit the Crisis Points That Challenge Every Company* (New York: Random House, 1999). Also see Steele, L., *Managing Technology: The Strategic View* (New York: McGraw-Hill, 1989). In particular, see page 59, where Steele addresses his

misconception number 5, that technological advances have no intrinsic value, but their value is determined by the customer (i.e., user of the technology).

5. For example, see Teece, D., and G. Pisano, "The Dynamic Capabilities of Firms: An Introduction," *Industrial and Corporate Change*, 3(3), 1994, 537-556; and Cohen, W., and D. Levinthal, "Absorptive Capacity: A New Learning Perspective on Learning and Innovation," *Administrative Science Quarterly* 35(2), 1990, 128-152.

6. See, Simon, H., R. Lapthorn Marris, and M. Egidi, *Economics, Bounded Rationality, and The Cognitive Revolution* (New York: Elgar, 1992).

7. Grahame, K., *The Wind in the Willows* (New York: St. Martin's Press, 1995).

8. A similar argument is constantly borne by those who criticize cuts in exploratory or basic research. See Geisler, E., "When Whales Are Cast Ashore: The Conversion to Relevancy of American Universities and Basic Science," *IEEE Transactions on Engineering Management* 42(1), 1995, 3-8.

9. See, for example, Bisia, A., and L. Gastwirt, *Turning Research and Development Into Profits* (New York: Amacom, 1979). There is a fertile literature, some of it concentrated in the area of new product development (NPD) and technology commercialization and transfer. Illustrative studies are Garud, R., and A. Van de Ven, "Technological Innovation and Industry Emergence: The Case of Cochlear Implants," in A. Van de Ven, S. Angle, and M. Poole (Eds.), *Research on the Management of Innovation* (New York: Harper Collins, 1989). Also, Alange, S., S. Jacobson, and A. Jarnehammar, "Some Aspects of an Analytical Framework for Studying the Diffusion of Organizational Innovations," *Technology Analysis and Strategic Management*, 10(1), 1998, 3-21; and Autio, E., and T. Laamanen, "Measurement and Evaluation of Technology Transfer: Review of Technology Transfer Mechanisms and Indicators," *International Journal of Technology Management*, 10(7/8), 1995, 643-664. More recently, see Hsi-cheng, L., and S. Mirmirani, "Global Transfer of Arms Technology and Its Impact on Economic Growth," *Contemporary Economic Policy*, 16(4), 1998, 486-498; and Hoppe, H., "Second-Mover Advantages in the Strategic Adoption of New Technology under Uncertainty," *International Journal of Industrial Organization*, 18(2), 2000, 315-338.

10. For example, Sony's beta technology in video cassette recording and the Macintosh personal computer illustrate cases of products that failed to gain a large market share, despite their technological advantages.

11. Rubenstein, A., *Managing Technology in the Decentralized Firm* (New York: John Wiley & Sons, 1989), 362-387.

12. Department of Defense, *A Trial Study of the Research and Exploratory Development Origins of a Weapon System—BULLPUP*, Washington, DC: Office of the Director of Defense Research and Engineering, 15 December 1964.

13. Project Hindsight (in 1967) was designed to provide some answers to this question.

14. See, for example, DeVulpian, A., *New Directions for Innovation in Products and Services* (Paris: COFREMCA, 1984); and Van Wyk, R., "Management of Technology: New Frameworks, *Technovation*, 7(3), 1988, 341-351. Also see Van Aken, J., and M. Waggeman, "Managing Learning in Informal Innovation Networks: Overcoming the Daphne-Dilemma," *R&D Management*, 30(2), 2000, 139-149; and

see Cooper, R., "Product Innovation and Technology Strategy," *Research-Technology Management*, 43(1), 2000, 38-41.

15. Van Wyk, R., G. Hadur, and S. Japp, "Permanent Magnets: A Technological Analysis," *R&D Management*, 21(4), 1991, 301-308. Also see Van Wyk, R., "Technological Advance: Unraveling the Strands," in Tisdel, C., and P. Maitra (Eds.), *Technological Change, Development, and the Environment* (London: Routledge, 1988), 322-340.

16. See Farrell, C., "A Theory of Technological Progress," *Technological Forecasting and Social Change*, 44(2), 1993, 161-178. Also see Horner, D., "Frameworks for Technology Analysis and Classification," *Journal of Information Science*, 18(1), 1992, 57-68.

17. This taxonomic structure will be later cited in the discussion of the process approach to outputs from science and technology. Technology is thus classified not only by the notion of its own transformation but by the conversions/processes it impacts and facilitates.

18. See Bright, J., "Opportunity and Threat in Technological Change," *Harvard Business Review*, 41(6), 1963, 76-86.

19. See, for example, Williamson, O., *Markets and Hierarchies* (Englewood Cliffs, NJ: Prentice-Hall, 1975); and Ghoshal, S., and P. Moran, "Bad for Practice: A Critique of Transaction Cost Theory," *Academy of Management Review*, 21(1), 1996, 13-47.

20. Poppo, L. and T. Zenger, "Testing Alternative Theories of the Firm: Transaction Cost, Knowledge-Based and Measurement Explanations for Make-or-Buy Decisions in Information Services," *Strategic Management Journal*, 19(9), 1998, 853-877.

21. *Op. cit.*, pp. 860-861. Also see Kogut, B, and U. Zander, "Knowledge of the Firm, Combinative Capabilities, and the Replication of Technology," *Organization Science*, 3(4), 1992, 383-397.

22. See, for example, Wernerfelt, B., "A Resource-Based View of the Firm," *Strategic Management Journal*, 5(2), 1984, 171-180.

23. This discussion is illustrative and is not an exhaustive review of the relevant literatures. Its objective was to acquaint the reader with the possibilities and the advantages potentially inherent in matching technology valuation with organizational and strategic theories of the firm.

24. Robb, W., "How Good Is Our Research?" *Research-Technology Management*, 34(2), 1991, 16-21.

25. See, for example, Rzasa, P., T. Faulkner, and N. Sousa, "Analyzing R&D Portfolios at Eastman Kodak," *Research-Technology Management*, 33(1), 1990, 27-32.

26. This method is an excellent illustration of the nonlinear model of research discussed earlier in the book.

27. Hauser, J., "Research, Development, and Engineering Metrics," *Management Science*, 44(12), 1998, 1670-1689.

28. Assuming, of course, that an academic discipline may be viewed as a segment of the market. See, for example, Wade, N., "Citation Analysis: A New Tool for

Science Administrators," *Science*, 188, 1978, 429-432; and Small, H., and B. Griffith, "The Structure of Scientific Literatures," *Science Studies*, 4(1), 1974, 17-40.

29. Geisler, E., "Energizing the Organization with *Technovalue*: A Framework for Monitoring Value from Technology," Working Paper, Stuart Graduate School of Business, Illinois Institute of Technology, 2000.

30. When compared with the model suggested by Hauser (1998, *op. cit.*), the "technovalue" approach extends the analysis beyond the three stages to the participants and impactees in technology throughout the organization and within its environment.

31. This topic is further explored in Chapter 12.

32. See, for example, Matheson, J., and D. Matheson, *The Smart Organization: Creating Value Through Strategic R&D* (Boston: Harvard Business School Press, 1998).

12

THE INNOVATION CONTINUUM

In the previous chapters I approached science and technology within the framework of the activities that generate, transform, or utilize this effort. Moreover, the classification schemes used in the various modes of analysis considered organizations and their units as the structural foundations for the study of S&T.

As the book progresses toward a discussion of the link among S&T, the economy, and society, it is necessary also to provide a different outlook. Rather than concentrate on the organizational framework, we may now consider S&T as a phenomenon reflected in the innovation continuum.

Assume, for the purpose of the analysis below, that S&T is operationalized via the innovation continuum, and that we classify this continuum by the different phenomena it contains, rather than by the organizational units in which it occurs. Such an outlook that we may name "mode 2" encompasses distinct phenomena *across organizational boundaries*. Figure 12.1 shows these phenomena as they are identified within the context of the innovation continuum.

CURIOSITY AND APPLICATION DRIVEN PHENOMENA

For the purpose of nomenclature, we shall name the phenomena: "Curiosity-Driven Research" and "Application-Driven Research." The first encompasses research, exploration, and all effort that arises from the curiosity of the investigator. Clearly, the motivation (or sources) for such curiosity may

Figure 12.1
Mode 2: Phenomena-Based Outlook of Innovation

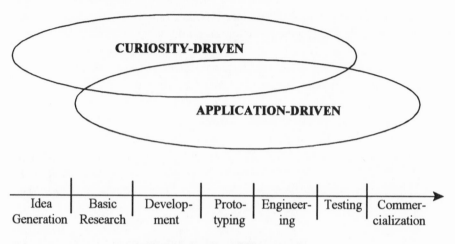

| Idea | Basic | Develop- | Proto- | Engineer- | Testing | Commer- |
| Generation | Research | ment | typing | ing | | cialization |

INNOVATION CONTINUUM

be traced to simple scientific curiosity or to a more complex web of motives, including the "hidden agenda" of some potential usages of the knowledge thus generated.

Curiosity-driven research is an effort that expands throughout the innovation continuum. It may be simply defined as the scientific investigation of a phenomenon for the purpose of generating knowledge—learning and understanding. As the innovation continuum progresses downstream, such curiosity-driven effort does not cease to exist. Researchers who work on the development of new products have long recognized the fact that questions of "pure science" emerge at any point of the new product development process. In one such instance, industrial researchers were baffled by the breakdown of some parts in a machine. Tribological tests of the dynamics of the crack propagation failed to yield the desired knowledge.[1] The issue was "basic science" of the nature of materials used to build the machine.

Curiosity-driven research not only generates ideas and provides the basic understanding of a phenomenon, but also continues to follow the progress of the research throughout the innovation process. In this sense, the *generation* of the subject under investigation and the actual *research and development* of it are mixed. The effort is thus defined as the search for answers, insofar as this search is continually driven by curiosity: Why is this happening? How is this happening? The questions are not: How can we make it better? or, What is the use of this?, but more fundamental and related to the curiosity of the researcher.

Hence, the curiosity-driven research effort is much more generalized. In the case of the material breakdown, curiosity-driven research will explore the behavior of materials in general, as a phenomenon in nature. This means that the effort is not necessarily looking at the specific product or application. We hope that by learning more about how and why materials tend to break, we will be able to understand what happened to our specific product.[2]

APPLICATION-DRIVEN RESEARCH

The research effort that relates to the ultimate application of the knowledge thus gained (in the form of a product, process, or system) may be gathered under the name "Application-Driven Research." As shown in Figure 12.1, such an effort extends throughout the innovation process. Ideas for research may be influenced by the marketplace, other products, or any of the participants in the innovation continuum (e.g., developers, testers, and marketers).

Application-driven research differs from curiosity-driven research because its origins are in the potential usage of the outcomes of the research. It should be clearly emphasized that this distinction is not necessarily the criterion that distinguishes between science and technology. Rather, in the process of innovation, from idea to market, application-driven research may extend all the way to the idea-generation stage, whereas curiosity-driven research may be found at the commercialization stage of the innovation continuum.[3]

Moreover, the two phenomena of curiosity and application research may exist contemporaneously, regardless of which of the two initiated the innovation process. For example, at some point innovations that began as application-driven research may require curiosity-driven research to complement the sustained advantages of the innovation in the marketplace. Recent innovations in engine technology for automobiles are a good illustration. Automakers have introduced engine parts made of composite materials. The performance of such composites, under conditions of combustion and stress, require curiosity-driven research that will establish meaningful criteria of the strengths and limitations of such materials.[4]

The distinction between curiosity and application research is similar to Hauser's categories of "research" and "market" type metrics. However, the argument for mode 2 is the interconnectedness and seamlessness of the phenomenon. Hence, although different metrics are needed to measure each of the perspectives or outlooks on innovation, they nevertheless should be combined to form a cohesive evaluation of the *innovation process*.

That is, regardless of how we approach the phenomenon of innovation, it is ultimately a process by which research is transformed into useful and marketable innovations. We therefore need to measure not only the individual components and perspectives of this process, but find a way to identify and evaluate its relevant flow into marketable innovations. This is partially achieved by evaluation at different levels as well as by evaluation of stages of the process.

LEVELS OF EVALUATION EFFORT

Figure 12.2 shows the intersect between the two phenomena and the levels at which they are evaluated. The importance of such intersects is in the choices of metrics for the evaluation.

The figure shows a hypothesized distribution of type of phenomenon and level of evaluation (as well as level of effort at which the research is conducted). It would stand to reason that curiosity-driven research would be more prevalent in individual and, perhaps, groups of researchers, and less prevalent with the more structured units. At the project, area thrust, and program levels, it would be logical to assume that application-driven research would be more prevalent. However, we may also assume that at the institution, discipline, and country levels, curiosity-driven research will again be more prevalent.

As discussed in Chapter 9, the different levels would require different metrics in the evaluation of S&T. Similarly, when different phenomena of research are evaluated at each level, they may influence the choice of adequate metrics. Thus, the intersect of program and application-driven research would call for the use of different metrics than the same level intersecting with curiosity-driven. To a large extent, the type of phenomenon (curiosity and application) should become one of the key determinants of the metrics to be adequately used for each level of evaluation. This may help to explain the failure of certain measures to adequately assess research activity, particularly when the type of phenomenon is not taken into consideration.

Thus, a level of evaluation *per se* would not be a sufficient criterion for the use of metrics. There is a need to determine, for each level, the type of research effort that is preponderant in this instance.[5]

SUSTAINABILITY AND DISCONTINUITY

Levels of effort in development innovative technologies have been widely discussed in the literature.[6] Technological innovations reach maturation and are replaced by other innovations when the returns on the effort expended in their development begin to decline. Figure 12.3 shows the growth of the innovation and its eventual replacement. The figure is based on Foster's "S" curve.[7]

Replacement of a current technology by a new technological innovation may be due to: (1) reaching the physical limits of technological advance, hence decline in what the technology can offer (e.g., increased efficiency, increased

Figure 12.2
Curiosity- and Application-Driven Research and Levels of Evaluation

	Individual	Group	Project	Area Thrust	Program	Institution	Discipline	State or Country
CURIOSITY-DRIVEN								
APPLICATION-DRIVEN								

Also see Figure 9.5.

Figure 12.3
Progression and Replacement of Technological Innovations

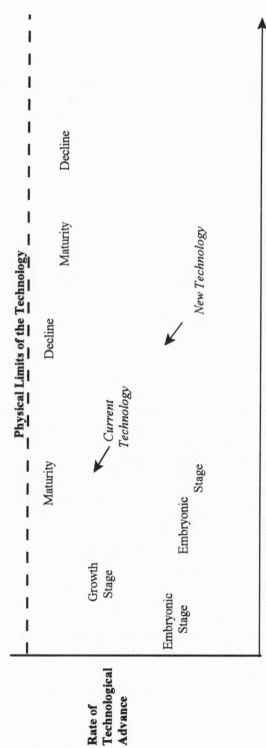

power), and (2) reaching commercial (application) limits of the contributors of the technology to a product, process, or other economic activity of the commercial unit or organization.

Physical Limits

There are some instances in which replacement technological innovations may progress beyond established physical limits, as shown in Figure 12.4. In this case, the breakthrough may be based on a totally new approach. Jet propulsion as the replacement for propellor-based technology is an example of a leap in the state of current limits.

In the case where the progression and replacement curves (shown in Figures 12.3 and 12.4) are "pushing the envelope" by leaping beyond physical limits, the *dominant type* of effort would tend to be curiosity-based. The basic nature of the explorations of phenomenon that is the hallmark of curiosity-based research may be the driving force behind leaps in technology. By exploring foundational questions about nature, and by pushing the discipline to its limits, curiosity-based research challenges the existing standards, knowledge, and practices.[8]

Application Limits

Replacement and discontinuities in technologies also occur because of limits in applications. Perhaps we may refer to them in general as "commercial limits," since they are imposed by the barriers and inherent bounds

Figure 12.4
Replacement of Technological Innovations and
Advancing Beyond the Physical Limits

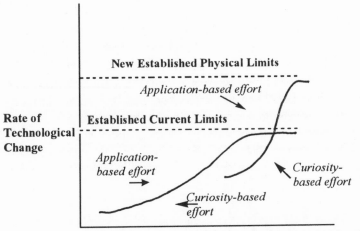

Level of Effort Expended in Developing the Innovation

of the targeted market. Several reasons may account for the existence of such limits.

First, the market may lack the absorptive capacity to integrate the technology because of its newness, sophistication, need for elaborate training, and similar factors. Second, the market may perceive the technology to have only marginal benefits. For example, some diagnostic medical technologies fall into this category. Although they are "breaking" the disciplinary limitations, their targeted market fails to recognize their adequate benefits. Third, the technology fails to adequately fit within products, systems, or processes. For example, some forms of data compression may be superior technologies but lack the facility to be installed in existing telecommunication devices. Fourth, the cost of the technology and its adoption may be prohibitive and, finally, the need for an extensive learning curve during the adoption process.

Application-based research tends to be the *dominant type* of effort expended in "pushing the commercial envelope." Clearly, the earlier such barriers are considered by the developers of the technology, the better the chance of breaking through these barriers.

The case of High Definition TV (HDTV) applies to several of the factors that influence the limits to application. A concerted effort by European governments and telecommunication firms in the early 1990s to introduce an HDTV system (HD-MAC) was unsuccessful. Similar difficulties in penetrating the market were also found in the introduction of HDTV in the United States.[9]

CLASSIFYING TECHNOLOGICAL INNOVATIONS

Technological innovations were classified into a variety of taxonomies: source, rate of progress, and their impacts. For example, technological innovations were classified as radical versus incremental, familiar versus unfamiliar, available versus tightly held, and enhancing versus destructive.[10] The matrix in Figure 12.5 offers a classification of technological innovations according to the dominant factor that facilitated their development and ultimately their commercial application.

"Leap innovations" are technological discontinuities that have not yet led to successful commercial applications. Examples include neural mechanisms for data storage and manipulation, and artificial blood. Another term that fits this type of innovation is "emerging technologies," in a pre-commercial stage.

"Replacement innovations" are technological changes that have not gone beyond the established physical limits. They are additive or incremental, and have successfully challenged the commercial barriers to application. Examples include the applications of information technology in manufacturing and medicine (telemedicine). These may also be called "lateral applications" across industries, yet, for the specific host industry, such innovations are discontinuities as they may replace existing practices and technologies.[11]

Breakthrough innovations" enjoy the codominance of challenging physical limits and commercial barriers. These are radical, destructive, and highly different technologies. They provide entirely new capabilities, translated into commercial applications. These are next-generation technologies that are also applied commercially. They represent the dream of inventors and technology companies. Examples are solid state materials, lasers, and optical transmission of information.

The typology in Figure 12.5 may be useful for a more explanatory approach to the different metrics for the evaluation of technology. Thus, different types of innovations may require different metrics. So measures that evaluate market penetration of an innovation whose key feature is the technical breakthrough may be premature or even misleading. Similarly, innovations that excel in challenging commercial boundaries should be evaluated with metrics appropriate to their key features.

Figure 12.5
Classification of Technological Innovation
by Type of Replacement or Discontinuity

Types of Technological Communication	REPLACEMENT/DISCONTINUITY BY OVERCOMING:	
	Physical Limits	Commercial Limits
"Leap Innovation" (primarily radical innovation, destructive, may generate new industry)	Dominant Factor	
"Replacement Innovation" (primarily incremental innovation, changes the face of an industry)		Dominant Factor
"Breakthrough Innovation" (radical, destructive, and "new-generation," creates new industries, and has far-reaching socioeconomic effects)	Dominant Factor	Codominant Factor

Family of Technologies (Technology Mix)

By contributing a more lucid approach to evaluation, the typology of innovations also projects its benefits to another issue of concern. The discussion thus far may have suggested that an innovation is composed of a single technology if, indeed, such a distinction is at all possible. However we define it, a technological innovation consists of more than a single technical capability. In much of the literature and even in parochial exchanges, the notion of "innovation" and "technological innovation" are used without resorting to a precise definition. The dictionary defines innovation as "the introduction of something new," or "a new idea, method, or device."[12] Edward Roberts, for example, in his studies of S&T has used the definition provided by the Industrial Research Institute at one of its roundtables, that innovation is composed of "the generation of an idea or invention" and "the conversion of that invention into a business or other useful application."[13] Moreover, this definition also suggested that since it is very broad and includes all the stages from idea to market, therefore "the technical contribution does not have a dominant position."[14] Hence, Roberts concluded that the innovation process is defined by the sum of the invention activity and the exploitation effort.

Considering the broad definition that includes the exploitation of an invention, technological innovation contains not one technology, but a family of technologies. At any given time, there are two phases in the continuum of innovation. The first is the invention itself, prior to its adoption into a useful application. As shown in Figure 12.5, the invention may or may not have challenged the physical limits of technological progress. This invention contains the key technology and other (supporting) technologies. As the invention is exploited in the form of a product, technique, process, device, or system, the convergence of the set of technologies that make up the innovation is more pronounced.

Every technological innovation contains a family of technologies that gives it unique capability and features. Figure 12.6 shows the intersect of the set of technologies. There are three categories of technologies in the family: (1) *embedded*, (2) *current*, and (3) *emerging*.

Embedded technologies are those that have become integrated into the innovation. At some earlier point they may have been new inventions, since made into the basic capabilities of the given device, system, technique, process, or product.[15] *Current* technology is key for innovation. Its newness may be expressed in the increments to existing capabilities. Finally, *emerging* technology is another key for innovation. Its newness is by breaking through the physical limits of the existing technological capabilities.

Figure 12.6
Family of Technologies (Technology Mix) in Technological Innovation

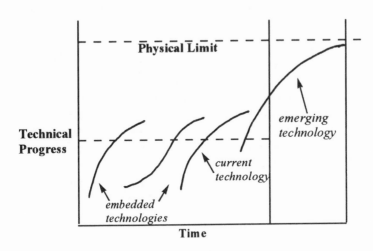

Hence, even "leap" or "breakthrough" innovations contain as their "engines" of new capabilities not one but several technologies. For example, the integrated circuit, instant photography, or radical therapeutic products such as gene therapy are all innovations that are based on a mix of embedded, current, and emerging technologies. Dominance of a given category in the mix will impact the degree of radicalness and newness of the innovation.[16]

Finally, the emphasis within the mix will also impact the *metrics* for evaluation of the innovation. Measuring for evaluation is important for prospective approaches (outcomes and benefits), and also for retrospective evaluation that explores the role that previous S&T effort has played in the innovation being evaluated.

SUMMARY

Innovations are the combined effect of a family of technologies and their exploitation. Key technologies play a dominant role in constituting the unique attributes and capabilities of the innovation. So it is important to recall that the evaluation and measurement of S&T and innovation will be conditioned upon the nature and composition of the phenomena under study. Innovations such as the personal computer (PC) or Interferon are complex phenomena, created and made workable by a combination of efforts and actors over time and across different types and levels of achievements, failures, laughs, tears, and other human emotions—all wrapped in a not-so-neat package of the exploration and exploitation of nature.

NOTES

1. "Tribology" is a disciplinary area within materials sciences and mechanical engineering that is concerned with the wear and tear of materials and moving parts. The origin of the word "tribology" is from the Greek word "to rub."

2. See, for example, Jolly, V., *Commercializing New Technologies: Getting From Mind to Market* (Boston: Harvard Business School Press, 1997). Jolly had argued that technology may be viewed as a capability within a product, hence he recommended the creation of small R&D units that will follow the product as it progresses "from mind to market." In the terms used in Figure 12.1, Jolly has argued for curiosity-driven research effort to continue throughout the innovation process.

3. See, for example, Christensen, C., *The Innovator's Dilemma: When New Technologies Cause Great Firms to Fail* (Boston: Harvard Business School Press, 1997). One of Christensen's theses in this book is the failure of well-managed companies because of displacement by inferior, yet disruptive technologies. So even when the company "listens" to its customers, it may be defeated in the marketplace by innovations that appeal to a restricted segment. A similar example could be made with application and curiosity-driven efforts.

4. A similar example is that of the airplane engine RB211 by Rolls-Royce. The company experimented with graphite-based blades that crumbled from stresses of common operational impacts. Rolls-Royce had to "go back to the drawing board" and the redesign effort largely contributed to its financial difficulties, as well to the difficulties experienced by its customers, such as Lockheed Corporation. See, for example, Boyne, W., *Beyond the Horizon: The Lockheed Story* (New York: St. Martin's Press, 1998). Also see, Rich, B., and L. Janas, *Skunk Works: A Personal Memoir of My Years at Lockheed* (New York: Little Brown & Co., 1996).

5. Although, for example, a given innovation may be primarily guided by application-driven research, at a certain level there may be a preponderance of curiosity-driven research. Hence the original source of the innovation effort must be considered also in light of the subsequent distribution of types of phenomena at each level of evaluation. See, for example, Litterback, J., M. Meyer, T. Tuff, and L. Richardson, "When Speeding Concepts to Market Can Be a Mistake," *Interfaces*, 22(4), 1992, 24-37.

6. For example, see Foster, R., *Innovation: The Attacker's Advantage* (New York: Summit Books, 1986). Also see Wheelwright, S., and K. Clark, *Revolutionizing Product Development* (New York: The Free Press, 1990).

7. See Foster, 1986, *op. cit.*

8. See, for example, Rosenberg, N., "Why Do Firms Do Basic Research?", *Research Policy*, 19(3), 1990, 165-174. Also see Buratti, N., A. Gambardella, and L. Orsenigo, "Scientific Gateleapers and Industrial Development in Biotechnology," *International Journal of Technology Management, Biotechnology Review*, No. 1, 8(1), 1993, 59-75.

9. See, for example, Fox, B., "Digital TV Comes Down to Earth," *IEEE Spectrum*, 35(10), 1998, 23-29. Also see Parthasarathy, M., and A. Bhattacherje, "Understanding Post-Adoption Behavior in the Context of On-Line Services," *Information Systems Research*, 9(4), 1998, 362-379.

10. There is a vast literature in which classification schemes for technological innovations are proposed. See, for example, the seminal studies by John Ettlie and his colleagues in Ettlie, J., W. Bridges, and R. O'Keefe, "Organization Strategy and Standard Differences for Radical Versus Incremental Innovation," *Management Science*, 30(4), 1984, 682-695. Also see, Abernathy, W., and K. Clark, "Mapping the Winds of Creative Destruction," *Research Policy*, 14(1), 1985, 3-22; and, Afua, A., and N. Bahram, "The Hypercube of Innovation," *Research Policy*, 24(2), 1995, 51-76.

11. For example, see Slack, W., *Cybermedicine: How Computing Empowers Doctors and Patients for Better Health Care* (San Francisco: Jossey-Bass, 1997). In particular, see Chapter 10, pages 147-164, in which the author lists these barriers to clinical computing: (1) age and computer phobia, (2) computer literacy, (3) administration, (4) politics, (5) territorialism, and (6) cost. Thus it is a superb achievement to overcome such barriers. Another example is Intelligent Transportation Systems (ITS) that have begun to penetrate the global market in the late 1990s. See Kujawa, M., "Navigating the Market for ITS," *Telecommunications*, 33(2), 1999, 51-56.

12. *Webster's New Collegiate Dictionary* (Springfield, MA: G&C Merriam Company, 1977), p. 595.

13. Roberts, E., "Managing Invention and Innovation: What We Have Learned," *Research-Technology Management*, 31(1), 1988, p. 11.

14. *Ibid.*, pp. 11-12.

15. See Chapter 11 above.

16. See, for example, Kanter, R., F. Wieserma, J. Kas, and T. Peters (Eds.), *Innovation: Breakthrough Thinking at 3M, DuPont, GE, Pfizer, and Rubbermaid* (New York: HarperBusiness, 1997). Also see Tidd, J., K. Pavitt, and J. Bessant, *Managing Innovation: Integrating Technological, Market, and Organization Change* (New York: John Wiley & Sons, 1997).

PART IV

SCIENCE AND TECHNOLOGY, THE ECONOMY, AND SOCIETY

Technology . . . is a queer thing. It brings you great gifts with one hand, and it stabs you in the back with the other.

Charles Percy Snow
(1905-1980)

13

SCIENCE, TECHNOLOGY, AND MODELS OF INNOVATION

The impacts of science and technology on the economy and society are of various types, levels of contribution, and the resultant outcomes. In the previous chapter I described some attributes of the innovation continuum, including a classification scheme for technological innovations.

The fourth part of this book is aimed at a comprehensive discussion of the role that science and technology plays in the economy and society. Basic questions will be examined in the following chapters, such as: Why, how, and to what extent does S&T contribute to the economy and society? What are the mechanisms by which S&T's contributions are made? Also, what are the ethical aspects of the impacts of S&T on the economy and society?

A key element in this book's theme has been to examine and describe the link between S&T and the entities that it impacts and influences. The evaluation of S&T relies heavily on the existence of such a link. In some instances, such as in the case of direct outputs from science, the link is imputed or assumed to exist by means of a leap of faith and, perhaps, even in logic. Yet for the broader range of outcomes from S&T effort, the establishment of this link is a critical foundation for the relationship between S&T and the economy and society.[1]

Why Should S&T Contribute to the Economy and Society?

In evaluating S&T, the question that seems to continually arise is the degree to which S&T contributes to the economy and society.[2] But the question that precedes it is: Why should S&T contribute at all? From the viewpoint of the individual, as an average citizen who is not directly involved with S&T generation and diffusion, this activity is enveloped in a thin tunic of magic. The average individual *expects* S&T to produce continuing outcomes that are breakthroughs in combating the effects of nature and that offer marvelous improvements in the human condition.[3]

Americans, in particular, are confident in the powers of S&T and keep expressing their satisfaction with its accomplishments. Positive reactions to S&T have been consistent in various surveys of public opinion conducted over the years by the National Science Foundation. Some very specific public concerns have nevertheless arisen from time to time, such as the proliferation of Internet-based medical sites where patients receive medical advice and where confidentiality has been a major issue.[4] In the view of the individual citizen, S&T has an "obligation" to provide the initiative, perhaps even the foundation, for a better life. S&T has been doing so for over a century, so there seems to be no impediment for the continuation of this trend.

Industrial companies are engaged in the production of S&T and have traditionally paid for about half of its expenditures. They behave in a dual mode. As generators of S&T, companies are primarily concerned with its contribution to their commercial success. On the other hand, companies and their owners and members are also civic-minded participants in the body politic, the economy, and society. Therefore, they also view S&T by its role as contributor to the common good. The main issue in this perspective is the allocation of national resources toward S&T that benefits commerce versus that which benefits societal objectives. In many instances, such as defense, healthcare, and space certification, the government assumes the leading role by investing in S&T that is targeted toward public benefits.

As long as the S&T activity is sponsored by a certain constituency, there will be expectations for a payoff from the activity. The benefits may be immediate or forthcoming, measurable or elusive, and specific to a given entity or shared by the public. Regardless of the nature of the actual benefits from S&T, individuals, organizations, and the nation in general expect some measure of contributions from S&T. In the minds of potential beneficiaries, outcomes from S&T may not always be in line with inputs to the activity. Breakthroughs in technology are expected to occur at any time, whatever the effort already expended in a specific area of inquiry. This phenomenon is clearly manifested in medical S&T.[5] Here the expectations are for continuous improvements and discoveries, coupled with frustration over the inability of S&T to uncover cures for specific diseases.[6] Overall there seems to be in the public view a set of "promises" of S&T that need to be kept. As discoveries are made and breakthroughs revealed, the limits are then continually expanded, and the promises refurbished.

A Parsimonious Model of S&T Impacts

Science and technology contributes to the economy and society in two distinct, yet highly converging formats. First, S&T contributes by means of the impacts of technologies and knowledge that are *embedded* in products and processes. Second, S&T contributes via the introduction of *new* products and processes. A parsimonious model of such impacts is shown in Figure 13.1. The figure shows the movement of outcomes from S&T toward new and existing targets for contributions. This movement is impinged upon by a set of factors in the economy and society, such as political, organizational, and commercial variables.

These intervening variables create powerful constraints that influence the direction and degree to which S&T contributions are received and adopted by economic and social institutions. Moreover, there is continuous feedback from the contributors to the intervening variables and from those to S&T. For example, impacts of S&T on such areas as transportation or healthcare will trigger responses in the economic and political arenas, so that policies regarding their respective S&T may be reformulated. This, in turn, will impact the allocation of resources to S&T and then the distribution and the nature of S&T outputs.[7]

The missing construct in the model depicted in Figure 13.1 is the means by which outputs from S&T impact their contributions to economic and social entities. This construct is the *technological innovation*.

SOME MODELS OF S&T INNOVATION

What is S&T innovation? In Chapter 12 I examined the innovation *continuum* as a chain of events that starts with exploratory research and converges into new products, processes, and similar inventions and innovations. I also classified technological innovations as "leaps" or radical innovations, "replacements" or incremental innovations, and "breakthroughs" or radical innovations. In addition, I also suggested that innovations are the combined effect of a family of technologies and their exploitation.

But what exactly is the construct of a S&T innovation? How does it conjure the impacts of S&T on economic and social entities? A related question is why we need such a construct to explain the contributions of S&T.

Defining S&T Innovation

The dictionary defines innovation as "the introduction of something new," or a new idea, method, or device or a novelty.[8] Other synonyms or descriptors include cutting edge, leading edge, change, and newness.

Figure 13.1
A Generalized Model of Impacts of Science and Technology

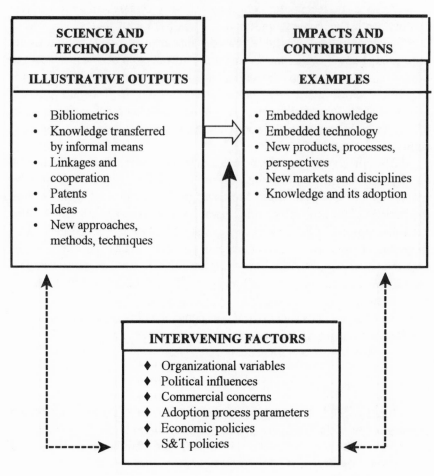

Invention is defined as the process of producing new devices, objects, ideas, or procedures that may be of use "in accomplishing human objectives in ways that were formerly difficult or impossible."[9]

The business literature has had a fair share of conceptual and empirical definitions of what constitutes innovation in general, and "technological innovation" in particular. For example, Windrum suggested that "innovation is concerned with the generation of new solutions to new or established problems."[10] He also argued that "innovation alters the existing set of possible events, introducing new options that were previously unattainable and that could not be precisely forecast" (p. 1533). Daly defined innovation as "the process of transforming ideas into commercial implementation through rapid knowledge sharing." Dertouzos, director of MIT's laboratory for Computer Science, identified four basic ingredients that drive or generate technological innovation: risk-aware capital, high-tech infrastructure, creative idea, and entrepreneurial culture.[11]

These definitions and those listed in Chapter 12 provide a perspective on innovation that emphasizes three key attributes: (1) S&T innovation is a process with distinguishable stages; (2) S&T innovation can best be understood in the context of its implementation or exploitation; and (3) S&T innovation encompasses a whole range of activities, from invention to usage. Thus, different models of S&T innovation consider different stages of the process, and emphasize distinct activities and transformations within this process. For example, researchers who are interested in the social diffusion of technological innovations would focus on the downstream stages.[12] Those who are more interested in understanding the sources of technological innovation would consider the movement from science to technology.[13]

There is no single and acceptable definition, nor agreement, on what constitutes S&T innovation. Ettlie, for instance, suggested that innovation is the sum total of invention plus its exploitation or application.[14] He also commented that "there continues to be great confusion on what technology *is*" (p. 40). So the effort to define S&T innovation tends to concentrate on the various perspectives from which scholars depart, and on the selected components of innovation they choose to study. We thus end up with a literature that offers a vast array of explorations, such as S&T strategies, management of R&D (the upstream or front-end of the precommercial stages), and the process of new product development and its commercial adoption and other applications.[15]

The complexity of the notion of S&T innovation and its extension to various phenomena (such as commercial applications, secondary impacts on society and the economy, and the process of invention and creativity) requires the confluence of these distinct dimensions to even exist as a conceptual construct. Figure 13.2 lists some models of innovation discussed in the extant literature.

Models of the Performer-Innovator

Scholars who study the phenomenon of S&T innovation tend to adapt their models in a Procrustean manner.[16] They usually start out with a preferred approach, then force the innovation concept to fit this approach. Good examples are the attempts to explore S&T innovation by considering the performer, whether individual, group, or organization.

Figure 13.2
Some Models of Science and Technology Innovation

MODEL	MAIN DESCRIPTORS*
A. Performer-Innovator • *individuals* • *groups* • *organizations* • *states and nations*	• Who creates, processes, and utilizes innovation? • What are their attributes? • What drives these performers?
B. Process and Stages • *process models* • *stages and outputs*	• How does S&T innovation progress in a process mode? • What are the stages and the mechanisms by which S&T innovation progresses? • What are the outputs at each stage?
C. Models of Change and Evolution • *breakthroughs and punctuated equilibrium* • *"forceful" evolution model*	• How does S&T innovation contribute to the survival of companies and industries? • How are organizations made to innovate by forces in their environment?
D. Economic, Social & Organizational Benefits & Constraints	• How do benefits and constraints help to generate S&T innovation?

This list is not exhaustive. It is shown for illustrative purposes.
*Refers to what the model attempts to describe or explain.

Individuals are viewed as basic performers-innovators. Studies of the individual innovator include explorations into the psychological attributes (such as risk strategies, motivation, curiosity, and creative genius), and the behavioral dimensions (such as entrepreneurial activities, professional zeal, modes of information seeking, mobility, leadership styles, and approaches to decision-making). Scholars have asked the questions: How do individuals innovate? What drives them to pursue S&T innovations? And how do they behave in such pursuit that distinguish them from noninnovators?[17]

A different view of the performer-innovator is to focus on the *group* or the *unit* in which the S&T innovation is generated, and the groups charged with its commercial exploitation. This approach yielded studies of R&D-marketing and R&D-production interfaces, intergroup cooperation and rivalry, and sociotechnical systems.[18]

These studies addressed the issues of innovation resulting from the combined effect of social and technical variables in work groups. There was an emphasis on the role that group dynamics and social relations play in the productivity of technological work groups. These studies concluded that innovative behavior and its effectiveness in work groups should be explained by considering not only the technical aspects of work, but also the social ties inherent in group dynamics.

Similarly, studies of R&D-marketing and R&D-production interfaces generated a literature that identified these phenomena and their effect on the effectiveness of the innovation process. The overall conclusions reiterated the complex nature of these interfaces, and the difficulties in moving the S&T innovation from the R&D environment to the commercial side of the organization.[19]

Finally, performers-innovators were studied at the levels of the entire organization and that of states or even nations. *Organizations* are viewed as innovators in the sense that they are not only conducive to innovative behavior by individuals and groups, but they also generate S&T innovation, measured by such outputs as patents, bibliometrics, and new products. The research questions posed by scholars in the case of the organization-as-innovator are similar, perhaps identical, to those directed at individuals.[20]

In the case of states-as-innovators, studies tend to focus on state-supported policies to encourage innovation, and on the formation of networks and cooperative arrangements to foster innovations. Similar studies are conducted at the national level.[21]

These models describe the performers of innovation at the different levels of aggregation. The findings indicate that certain patterns of behavior (by individuals, groups, organizations, states, and nations) may be more conducive to effective innovation. This applies to both the generation of S&T innovation (at the level of invention), and to the exploitation, by means of commercial utilization. The key question is: What should one do to generate, foster, support, and improve S&T innovation?

Models of Process and Stages

In the search for a better understanding of how S&T innovation is generated and flows from invention to the marketplace, models of process have been of great use. Such models generally describe the stages in the progression of S&T innovations and their transformation along the way.[22]

Process-Outcomes Model. There are two basic models that employ process modes as descriptors of the progression of S&T innovation. The first is a model of process-outcomes. This model was developed to serve as a framework for the evaluation of the outputs from S&T. The model was proposed by Rubenstein and Geisler[23] and Geisler.[24] Six basic assumptions underlie the model.

1. There are identifiable stages in the innovation process.
2. These stages may serve as the building-blocks of the process and flow of S&T.
3. S&T flows through the stages, from research, development, new products, to the final stage of technology that is commercialized and used.
4. There are distinct outputs at each stage that can be measured and compared across stages.
5. The S&T process is composed of transformation and diffusion activities, in which the outputs from the various stages flow toward the downstream of the innovation continuum.
6. There are social and economic organizations that compose the various subsystems in which the transformation and diffusion activities occur.

The process described by this model contains several stages of the progression of S&T, the outputs that they generate, and the social and economic entities that transform, use, and benefit from them. Figure 13.3 shows the stages, outputs, and these entities.

There are several advantages to this process model. It identifies the conceptual and temporal stages in the life of S&T innovation, from the point of generation to its utilization in society and the economy.[25] Second, this process identifies the transformations that S&T innovations go through as they progress from invention to the marketplace. By concentrating on the specific output at each stage and their subsequent incorporation by downstream entities, the process model allows for focused measurements over the life of the innovation, hence allowing for better managerial intervention at appropriate time and place.[26]

Tracking Dynamic Processes. Another process model is the descriptive review of the development of a S&T innovation. An excellent example of this model is the Minnesota Innovation Research Program, in which a large group of scholars studied the progress and development of 14 innovations as they unfolded in their original organizational settings.[27] In a mode similar to the tracking of innovations in project TRACES (Technology in Retrospect and Critical Events in Science),[28] the researchers mapped what they called "the innovation journey" of such innovations as the 3M Cochlear Implant.[29]

In project TRACES, conducted by researchers at the Illinois Institute of Technology, the model focused on tracking-in-hindsight five innovations. Looking back ten years, the researchers identified critical events in the life of the innovation. By combining an analysis of the sequence of these critical events and their duration, the study concluded that there were different rates

Figure 13.3
The Process-Outcomes Model of the Linkages Between the S&T Process and Social and Economic Systems

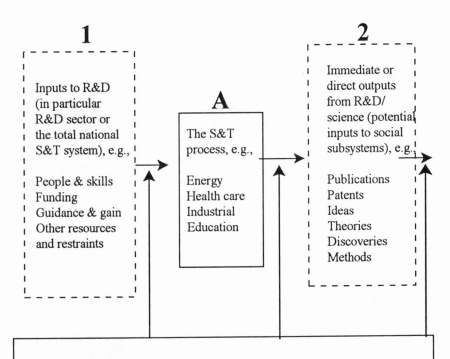

Other factors in the specific situation (e.g., the S&T) sector or the social subsystem) which affect the transition, transportation, adoption, usefulness, cost or economic benefit from transfers between adjacent and more distant stages. Such factors may include economic, cultural, organizational, technical, personal, or political ones. Some are particular to a given stage (e.g., the barriers and difficulties involved in designing economical and socially acceptable energy or safety devices and systems or the diffusion problems in curing a disease); others may apply to several stages in the overall process (e.g., capital shortages or regulations); and still others are pervasive across the whole process (e.g., organizational barriers to innovation, individual risk preferences, diffuse decision-making responsibility).

Figure 13.3 Continued.
The Process-Outcomes Model of the Linkages Between the S&T Process and Social and Economic Systems

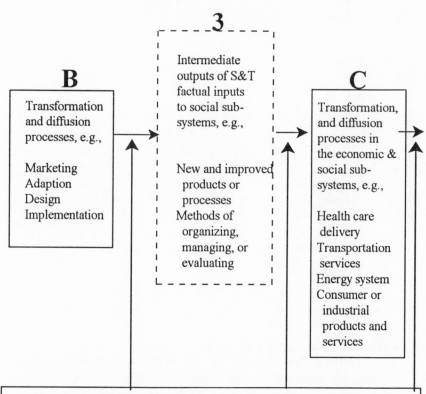

Other factors in the specific situation (e.g., the S&T) sector or the social subsystem) which affect the transition, transportation, adoption, usefulness, cost or economic benefit from transfers between adjacent and more distant stages. Such factors may include economic, cultural, organizational, technical, personal, or political ones. Some are particular to a given stage (e.g., the barriers and difficulties involved in designing economical and socially acceptable energy or safety devices and systems or the diffusion problems in curing a disease); others may apply to several stages in the overall process (e.g., capital shortages or regulations); and still others are pervasive across the whole process (e.g., organizational barriers to innovation, individual risk preferences, diffuse decision-making responsibility).

Figure 13.3 Continued.
The Process-Outcomes Model of the Linkages Between the S&T Process and
Social and Economic System

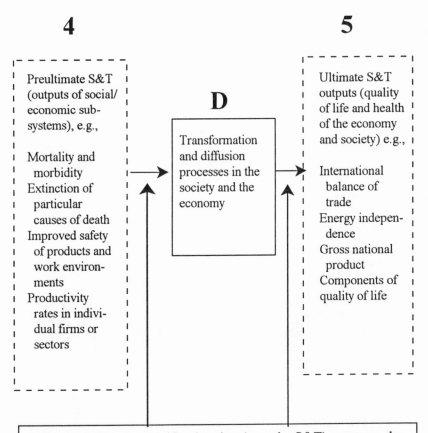

4		5
Preultimate S&T (outputs of social/ economic sub-systems), e.g.,	**D**	Ultimate S&T outputs (quality of life and health of the economy and society) e.g.,
Mortality and morbidity	Transformation and diffusion processes in the society and the economy	International balance of trade
Extinction of particular causes of death		Energy independence
Improved safety of products and work environ-ments		Gross national product
Productivity rates in indivi-dual firms or sectors		Components of quality of life

Other factors in the specific situation (e.g., the S&T) sector or the social subsystem) which affect the transition, transportation, adoption, usefulness, cost or economic benefit from transfers between adjacent and more distant stages. Such factors may include economic, cultural, organizational, technical, personal, or political ones. Some are particular to a given stage (e.g., the barriers and difficulties involved in designing economical and socially acceptable energy or safety devices and systems or the diffusion problems in curing a disease); others may apply to several stages in the overall process (e.g., capital shortages or regulations); and still others are pervasive across the whole process (e.g., organizational barriers to innovation, individual risk preferences, diffuse decision-making responsibility).

of absorption in the early events (10-30 years) and the development of technology into marketable products (1-9 years).[30] Although focused on the contributions of basic research to the innovations under study, project TRACES delineated the components of the process by which innovations progress, from idea to market.

By contrast, the scholars who tracked the "journey" of S&T innovation had done so in "real time," as the innovations were under way. They concluded that the process is nonlinear and dynamic, and that it lacks sequence and order. The process is thus imbued with congruent and even conflicting cyclical subprocesses that include technical as well as social components.[31]

Whether using identifiable and distinct stages, critical events in the life of the innovation, or dynamic description of cyclical progress, this type of model allows for a longitudinal view of the S&T-innovation phenomenon. Performers can thus be "plugged into" the stages or events, or serve as background to the actions and activities of the performers-innovators. In any case, the process models are more powerful for research on S&T innovation and for explaining crucial aspects of this phenomenon.

Models of Change and Evolution

Among the more salient approaches to the question of how S&T innovation is generated and progresses, models of change and evolution attempt to explain how firms innovate through incremental changes.[32] For example, Tushman and Anderson[33] borrowed the concept of "punctuated equilibrium" from evolutionary biologists such as Stephen Jay Gould.[34] They introduced the similar concept of "technological discontinuities" and related them to environmental characteristics and dynamics.

Models of evolution and change attempt to explain why and how innovation contributes to the survival of companies. The generation, adoption, and strategic adaptation of technological innovation is seen as crucial factors that may determine the entry, performance, success, and failure of firms in their respective markets.[35]

"Forceful evolution" is a related model that attempts to explain how organizations are made to innovate by forces in their environment. Threats (real or perceived) from the external environment seem to be conducive to technological innovation—as a strategic response by the affected organization. The guiding assumption in this trend is that technological innovation can counter environmental threats.[36]

In summary, models of evolution and change do seem to offer some explanation regarding the behavior of innovative organizations. The models assume that technological innovations are created and adopted by organizations in a process that has some attributes similar to that of biological evolution. Proponents of such models argue that in a mode similar to that of the impact of certain evolutionary traits on the survival of species, organizations that adapt certain technological innovations are more likely to succeed, hence survive and avoid extinction.

To an extent, technological innovation is viewed as an evolutionary tool that acts to differentiate between "winners" and "losers" in the competitive industrial environment. Natural selection is replaced by the ability of organizations to adopt and strategically utilize technological innovations. By incorporating them into core competencies, these organizations have the competitive edge that may be crucial to their survival.

Like any model that has been "borrowed" from a different context, evolutionary models of innovation fail to address the issues of process and measurement of other variables that impinge on adoption of innovation and strategic survival. The processing of adoption and utilization of technological innovations is much more complex in its various stages than evolutionists are willing to accept. Measurement difficulties also contribute to their use of the simplistic relationship between technological innovation and strategic survival.[37]

It's impractical to simply connect technological innovation to organizational survival. Even when individual innovations are monitored and their effects are measured, the outcomes are tenuous. The main difficulty is to isolate the effect of the innovation from a host of other, nontechnology variables. The problem is thus magnified when a broad assessment is made, linking in a covariation mode technological innovation as a general phenomenon with the overall survival of the "fittest" organization.[38]

Economic and Social Benefits

As much as we try to assess the benefits from S&T, we are bound to relate to economic and social activities and their outcomes. There are two types of models of technological innovation that consider the impacts or feedback from society and the economy on the generation and process of S&T innovation. One such model is based on a theory of technology, discussed earlier in the Preface and in Chapter 5. The traditional theory of technology portrays the S&T process as a force that impacts society and the economy with some feedback and adjustments that occur in S&T policies. In this approach there is a learning process by which the organizations that generate S&T are impacted by social and economic entities, so that these impacts are incorporated into the preferences and allocation of resources for S&T projects.[39]

Another model rejects the notion that S&T has an autonomous existence. Rather, this model advocates the existence of technology only within the limited context of social interaction. Contrary to the technology-centered theorists, the proponents of this model argue that technology can be described and understood only as a function of social and political preferences, actions, and relationships.[40]

Proponents of the two distinct models congregate along lines of political preferences so that their beliefs in one or another political end of the spectrum and in who has socioeconomic power influence their view of technology in light of "who controls" it. However we view the relation between S&T and society and the economy, there is clearly a two-way stream of impacts, feedback, and consequences—both intended and unintended.[41] These impacts cannot be entirely devoid of social and economic ramifications and influences. So, whether S&T is a tool used by political powers for their own advantage, or a force that propels itself through a complex process—the realities of its impacts are present in almost all human activities and should be assessed, as humanly possible, with a minimum of preconceived, politically-construed notions and theories.

SUMMARY

What does it all mean? Why are these models of S&T innovation important? For one they provide a framework that tries to explain how S&T creates value for the impacted organizations. Only when S&T innovations are adopted by social and economic entities can value be extracted from these innovations and made available for exploitation and usage. The key issues are not sociological views of ownership and utilization of S&T outcomes, but rather the more trivial yet crucial means to identify and measure the impacts of S&T and the value thus created. I argued earlier in the Preface and in Chapter 5 that the thesis of this book focuses on the more mundane exploration of "how value is created by S&T innovations for the economy and society," regardless of any overarching perspectives of ownership and utility of select groups, oligarchies, and other power holders and seekers. This view doesn't negate the need to view S&T innovations within the context of social and economic impacts and activities. S&T innovations are not a "stand-alone" entity, nor should they be viewed as mere instruments of political and economic struggle.

The variety of models described above attest to the complexity of the phenomenon. S&T progresses by means of innovations and their diffusion within social and economic entities. Hence, there are multiple perspectives to this phenomenon, describing different stages, activities, and actors. Due to the complexity of S&T, no one model is sufficient nor comprehensive enough to offer a resolute description. Each model describes certain aspects of the ways in which value is created from S&T, how the value is created, by whom, for whom, and to what end. These issues are further elaborated in Chapters 14 and 15.

NOTES

1. There is an extensive literature on this relationship that will be listed in the notes to this chapter. For some introductory publications, see, for example, Ciciatti, E., N. Alderman, and A. Thwaites, *Technological Change in a Spatial Context: Theory, Empirical Evidence, and Policy* (New York: Springer-Verlag, 1990). Also see Saviotti, P., *Technological Evaluation, Variety, and the Economy* (New York: Edward Elgar, 1996); and see Roycroft, R., and D. Kash, *The Complexity Challenge: Technological Innovation for the 21st Century* (Boston: CRC Press, 1999).

2. See, for example, Canton, J., *Technofutures: How Leading-Edge Technology Will Transform Business in the 21st Century* (New York: Hay House, Inc., 1999). Also see Stoneman, P., *The Economic Analysis of Technology Policy* (New York: Oxford University Press, 1990).

3. See, for example, Olshansky, J., B. Carnes, and C. Cassel, "In Search of Methuselah," *Science*, 250 (November 2) 1990, 634-640, and Schwartz, W., "In the Pipeline: A Wave of Valuable Technology," *Health Affairs*, 13(3), 1994, 70-79.

4. See, for example, Wyke, A., *21st Century Miracle Medicine: Robosurgery, Wonder Cures, and the Quest for Immortality* (New York: Plenum Press, 1997), p. 280-281. Also see Callahan, D., *What Kind of Life: The Limits of Medical Progress* (New York: Simon & Schuster, 1998).

5. See, for example, Bailor, J., and H. Gornick, "Cancer Undefeated," *The New England Journal of Medicine*, 336 (May 29), 1997, 1569-1574. Also see White, K., and S. Preston, "How Many Americans are Alive Because of Twentieth-Century Improvements in Mortality?" *Population and Development Review*, 22(3), 1996, 419-430.

6. See, for example, the use of HIV/AIDS research and the frustration over the inability to discover a cure. See Epstein, S., *Impure Science: AIDS, Activism, and the Politics of Knowledge* (Berkeley: University of California Press, 1998). Also see Shenton, J., *Positively False: Exposing the Myths Around HIV and AIDS* (New York: St. Martin's Press, 1998). Joan Shenton described in this book the controversy between the traditional AIDS researchers and those who contend that the mainstream scientific community and the pharmaceutical industry have "wasted" precious time and resources in their quest for the cure. Also see Grady, C., *The Search for an AIDS Vaccine: Ethical Issues in the Development and Testing of a Preventive HIV Vaccine* (Bloomington: Indiana University Press, 1995).

7. The generalized, yet parsimonious model of how S&T contributes to the economy and society is anchored in a vast literature on the impacts of S&T. See, for example, Wilson, A., K. Ramamurthy, and P. Nystrom, "A Multi-Attribute Measure for Innovation Adoption: The Context of Imaging Technology," *IEEE Transactions on Engineering Management*, 46(3), 1999, 311-321. Also see Henderson, A., "Information Science and Information Policy: The Use of Constant Dollars and Other Indicators to Manage Research Investments," *Journal of the American Society for Information Science*, 50(4), 1999, 366-379; and see Winner, L., "A New Social

Contract for Science," *Technology Review*, 96(4), 1993, 65-67; and Cope, G., *Diffusion of Innovations in the Public Sector: Proceedings of a Conference* (Austin, TX: LBJ School of Public Affairs, 1992).

8. *Webster's New Collegiate Dictionary* (Springfield, MA: G&C Company, 1996).

9. *Funk and Wagnalls New Encyclopedia* (New York: Softkey Multimedia Inc., 1996) (Infopedia).

10. Windrum, P., "Simulation Models of Technological Innovation," *The American Behavioral Scientist*, 42(10), 1999, 1531-1550.

11. Daly, D., "The Value of Innovation," *Management Accounting*, 80(3), 1998, 57-58; Dertouzos, M., *What Will Be: How the New World of Information Will Change Our Lives* (New York: Harper Collins Publishers, 1998).

12. See, for example, studies of diffusion of technological innovations seen on innovative products, such as computers and medical devices. See Valente, T., and G. Barnett (Eds.), *Network Models of the Diffusion of Innovations* (New York: Hampton Press, 1995). Also see Mahajan, U., and Y. Wind (Eds.), *Innovation Diffusion Models of New Product Acceptance* (New York: HarperBusiness, 1986); and Auerswald, P., S. Kauffman, J. Lobo, and K. Shell, "The Production Recipe Approach to Modeling Technological Innovation: An Application to Learning by Doing," *Journal of Economic Dynamics & Control*, 24(3), 2000, 389-450.

13. See the seminal book, Rogers, E., *Diffusion of Innovations*, 4th ed. (New York: Simon & Schuster, 1996), particularly Ch. 3, pp 131-160.

14. Ettlie, J., *Managing Technological Innovation* (New York: John Wiley & Sons, 2000), pp. 38-40.

15. See, for example, Feenberg, A., *Questioning Technology* (London: Routledge, 1999). Also see Douglas, J., D. Garets, M. Ball, and D. Garets (Eds.), *Strategies and Technologies for Health Care Information: Theory into Practice* (New York: Springer-Verlag, 1999); and Kennedy, W., *Diffusion of Innovation: A Select Bibliography* (Westport, CT: Quorum Books, 1989). Also see Ziman, J. (Ed.), *Technological Innovation as an Evolutionary Process* (New York: Cambridge University Press, 2000).

16. Based on the Greek mythological figure of Procrustes, who used to cut and stretch people to fit a bed of unique size.

17. See, for example, Stafford, H., "Innovative Behavior in Space and Time," *Journal of Regional Science*, 38(4), 1998, 694-696. Also see Anthony, A., and A. Robben, *A Study of Innovative Behavior in High Technology Product Development Organizations* (New York: Garland, 1999); and see Scott, S., and R. Bruce, "Following the Leader in R&D: The Joint Effect of Subordinate Problem-Solving Style and Leader-Member Relations on Innovative Behavior," *IEEE Transactions on Engineering Management*, 45(1), 1998, 3-10.

18. See, for example, Jacobs, D., A. Fernandez, and C. Keating, "Analyzing Complex Processes with a Socio-Technical Systems Tool," *Research-Technology Management*, 43(2), 2000, 8-14. Also see Adler, N., "Bringing Business into Sociotechnical Theory and Practice," *Human Relations*, 51(3), 1998, 319-322.

19. See, for example, Vanconcellos, E., "Improving the R&D-Production Interface in Industrial Companies," *IEEE Transactions on Engineering Management*, 41(3),

1994, 315-323. Also see Moenaert, R., "Context and Antecedents of Information Utility at the R&D-Marketing Interface," *Management Science*, 42(11), 1996, 1592-1608.

20. See, McBride, R., "Implementation of Organizational Innovation: Studies of Academic and Research Libraries," *Journal of Academic Librarianship*, 25(4), 1999, 338-343. Also see Gerybadze, A., "Globalization of R&D: Recent Changes in the Management of Innovation in Transactional Corporations," *Research Policy*, 28(2-3), 1999, 251-275.

21. See, for example, Swan, J., "National Differences in the Diffusion and Design of Technological Innovation: The Role of Interorganizational Networks," *British Journal of Management*, 10(2), 1999, 45-60. Also see Vertova, G., "Technological Similarity in National Styles of Innovation in a Historical Perspective," *Technology Analysis and Strategic Management*, 10(4), 1998, 437-451.

22. See, for example, Haggerdon, J., *The Dynamic Analysis of Innovation and Diffusion* (New York: St. Martin's Press, 1989). Also see David, P., K. Arrow, and R. Solow, *Behind the Diffusion Curve: Theoretical and Applied Contributions to the Microeconomics of Technology Adoption* (Boulder, CO: Westview Press, 1997). This book compiles contributions by noted economists on the technological aspects of microeconomics. Although this reference belongs to the section on models of economic, social, and organizational benefits and constraints, it nevertheless provides illustrations of the process development of technology in economic systems. Also see Fischer, L. L. Suarez-Villa, and M. Steiner (Eds.), *Innovation, Networks, and Localities* (New York: Springer-Verlag, 1999).

23. Rubenstein, A., and E. Geisler, "Evaluating the Outputs and Impacts of R&D/Innovation," *International Journal of Technology Management*, Special Publication on the Role of Technology in Corporate Policy, 1991, 181-204.

24. Geisler, E., "An Integrated Cost-Performance Model of Research and Development Evaluation," *Omega*, 23(3), 1995, 281-294.

25. See Geisler, E., "Integrated Figure of Merit of Public-Sector Research Evaluation," *Scientometrics*, 36(3), 1996, 379-395.

26. See Geisler, E., and A. Rubinstein, "Methodology Issues in Conducting Evaluation Studies of R&D/Innovation," *Proceedings of the Symposium on Management of Technological Innovation* (Worcester Polytechnic Institute, Washington, DC, 1989).

27. See the enlightening review in Van de Ven, A., R. Gharud, W. Polley, and S. Venkataraman, *The Innovation Journey* (New York: Oxford University Press, 1999).

28. See, for example, Thompson, P., "TRACES: Basic Research Links to Technology Appraisal," *Science*, January 24, 1969, 374-375.

29. See, for example, the description of the cochlear implant case in: Garud, R., and M. Rappa, "A Socio-Cognitive Model of Technology Evolution: The Case of Cochlear Implants," *Organization Science*, 5(3), 1994, 344-353.

30. Among the innovations studied were the input-output analysis, the birth control pill, and the magnetic tape.

31. See, for example, Auerswald, P., S. Kauffman, J. Lobo, and K. Shell, "The Production Recipes Approach to Modeling Technological Innovation: An Application

to Learning by Doing," *Journal of Economic Dynamics & Control*, 24(3), 2000, 389-450. Also see Deeds, D., D. DeCarolis, and J. Coombs, "Dynamic Capabilities and New Product Development in High Technology Ventures: An Empirical Analysis of New Biotechnology Firms," *Journal of Business Venturing*, 15(3), 2000, 211-229.

32.   See, for example, the original book, Nelson, R., and S. Winter, *An Evolutionary Theory of Economic Change* (Cambridge, MA: Belknap Press, 1982); and more recently, see Kwasnicki, W., *Knowledge, Innovation, and Economy: An Evolutionary Exploration* (New York: Edward Elgar, 1996).

33.   Tushman, M., and P. Anderson, "Technological Discontinuities and Organizational Environments," *Administrative Science Quarterly*, 31(3), 1986, 439-465.

34.   Gould, S., *The Flamingo's Smile: Reflections in Natural History* (New York: W. W. Norton & Company, 1987); also see Gould S., and R. Lewontin, "The Spandrels of San Marco and the Panglassian Paradigm: A Critique of the Adaptation of Programs," *Proceedings of the Royal Society*, B-25, 1979, 581-598.

35.   See, for example, Cooper, C., *Technology and Innovation in the International Economy* (New York: Edward Elgar, 1994). Also see Audretsch, D., and R. Thurik (Eds.), *Innovation, Industry Evolution, and Employment* (New York: Cambridge University Press, 1999).

36.   See, for example, Sciulli, L., and S. Bruchey (Eds.), *Innovations in the Retail Banking Industry: The Impact of Organizational Structure and Environment on the Adoption Process* (New York: Garland, 1998). Also see Aghion, P., C. Harris, and J. Vickers, "Competition and Growth with Step-by-Step Innovation: An Example," *European Economic Review*, 41(3-5), 1997, 771-782; and see Klepper, S., and K. Simons, "Innovation and Industry Shakeouts," *Business and Economic History*, 25(1), 1996, 81-90. The authors explored the cases of automobiles, penicillin, tires, and television, as illustrations of technological innovation. They concluded that such innovations led to industrial shakeouts and were a component in an evolutionary process by which certain companies dominate their respective markets.

37.   This phenomenon is similar to the approach taken by some economists in relating technological innovations to economic growth and to industrial productivity. See, for example, Lay, G., P. Shapira, and J. Wengel (Eds.), *Innovation in Production: The Adoption and Impacts of New Manufacturing Concepts in German Industry* (New York: Springer-Verlag, 1999). Also see Adas, W., *Technology and European Overseas Enterprise: Diffusion, Adaption, and Adoption* (New York: Ashgate Publishing Company, 1996). In this book the author argued that technological innovation had been the critical factor in the global expansion of European nations. In particular the author focuses on military technology and its far-reaching impacts. See also part 2, pp. 135-296 in which the author discusses technology transfer and economic exchange.

38.   This methodological issue is discussed in Geisler, E., *Methodology, Theory, and Knowledge in the Organizational and Managerial Sciences* (Westport, CT: Quorum Books, 1999).

39.   See, for example, Wiebe, B., T. Hughes, and T. Pinch (Eds.), *The Social Construction of Technological Systems: New Directions in the Sociology and History of Technology* (Cambridge, MA: MIT Press, 1987). Also see MacKenzie,

D., and J. Wajcman (Eds.), *The Social Shaping of Technology* (Philadelphia: Open University Press, 1985).

40. See, for example, Feenberg, A., *Questioning Technology* (London: Routledge Kegan, 1999). Also see a critique of this model in Veak, T., "Whose Technology? Whose Modernity? Questioning Feenberg's Questioning Technology," *Science, Technology and Human Values*, 25(2), 2000, 226-237.

41. See, for example, the case of HIV/AIDS, discussed in the form of different models: Cullen, J., "The Needle and the Damage Done: Research, Action Research, and the Organizational and Social Construction of Health in the Information Society," *Human Relations*, 51(12), 1998, 1543-1564. Also see Epstein, S., *Impure Science: AIDS, Activism, and the Politics of Knowledge* (Berkeley: University of California Press, 1996).

14

SCIENCE & TECHNOLOGY AND ECONOMIC PROGRESS

In a speech given in November 1999, Peter Drucker suggested that the most important economic change of the 20th century had been the rapid emergence of vocational choices for all levels of society.[1] Young adults today do not necessarily need to follow in their parents' footsteps and are free and able to enter the vocation of their choice. I disagree with Drucker, as I consider this change to be one of several outcomes of a much more influential change.[2] This change has been the public acceptance of science and technology as a national patrimony, and as an indispensable asset for economic progress and social welfare. As such, the new public awareness has resulted in massive funding (both public and private) for S&T in almost all areas of the economy and of social endeavors. This is why I started this book with the historical background of how S&T has evolved and how it has been increasingly funded by industry and government.

As a result of this change in the public perception and awareness of S&T (including trust, hope, even heightened expectations), the 20th century witnessed radical improvements in education at all levels, and the emergence of a myriad of careers in the new economy that is driven by S&T. In 1900 S&T was not considered a national asset. Rather, it was regarded as an interesting occupation with mysterious procedures and consequences, perhaps better reserved for the well-to-do and the universities.

In Chapter 6 I discussed economic theories of S&T. I especially explored the link between technology and wealth, and the role of technology as an economic quantity. In this chapter I examine S&T as a force in promoting economic progress, with the discussion confined to the role of S&T in creating *economic* value.

HOW S&T CREATES ECONOMIC VALUE

This chapter focuses on the ways and means by which S&T creates economic value or at least contributes to the creation of economic value. Chapter 6 described salient theories that attempted to explain the link between S&T and economic progress. These theories considered the economic impacts of S&T in two general categories. The first was through the effects of technical change and its measurable impacts on selected economic variables. The second category considered the effects of S&T via statistical links between outputs of S&T (such as patents) and macro-economic variables.[3]

The current state of knowledge can be summarized as composed of theories that explore impacts via a mediatinxg effect such as knowledge, technical change, and patents, and those theories that consider broad statistical connections. In both cases there are empirical problems that range from issues inherent in the S&T phenomenon, and issues inherent in the choice of the economic variables that are purported to be imparted by S&T (such as productivity, profitability, and the genesis of new companies).

Modes of Economic Impacts

To put this in context, I propose here two broadly defined modes of the impacts of S&T on economic variables. They are based on the assumptions that (1) S&T is a process, extending over several time periods and carried out by a variety of organizations and institutions, and (2) modes of impact will depend not only on the choice of the economic variable of concern, but also on how the impact will be measured and evaluated.

Focused or Targeted Mode. The first mode is the *focused* or *targeted* mode of impact. The impacts of S&T are assessed via the effects of specific technological innovations that create technical change, which, in turn, impacts selected targets in economic organizations, such as employment, industry structure, profitability, or productivity. A schematic view of the *focused mode* is shown in Figure 14.1.

In the focused mode, S&T is evaluated by means of its impacts on selected economic variables. This mode considers outcomes from S&T, such as technical change, and measures their effects on growth, productivity, and similar variables. Whether utilizing a process approach or statistical analyses, this mode produces findings that credit positive increments in the economic variables to the effects from technological change.

Figure 14.1
Focused or Targeted Mode of S&T Impacts on Economic Variables

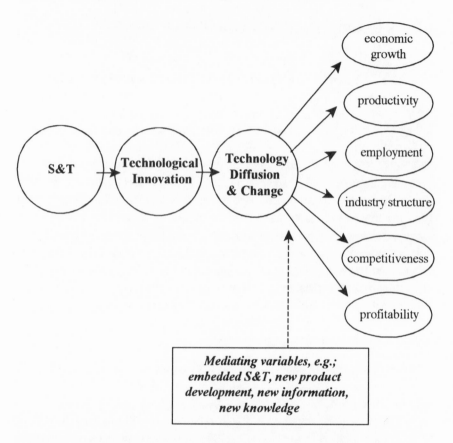

For reasons of simplicity and to accentuate the nature of the impacts, the figure shows a unidirectional flow from S&T to economic variables. Clearly, there are feedback loops associated with every link in the figure.

Thus, the value created via improvements in key economic variables can be attributable, in part, to the adoption and subsequent diffusion and utilization of the outcomes from S&T in the industrial firm.[4]

Wide-dispersion Mode. This mode considers the effects of S&T on economic entities in the form of a diffused set of impacts that are subsequently immersed in the structure and processes of these entities. Figure 14.2 shows a schematic representation of this wide-dispersion mode

In the wide-dispersion mode, the outcomes from S&T are diffused throughout the economic entity (e.g., the industrial firm), and are embedded in the various economic activities of the entity. There is what I may call the

Figure 14.2
Wide-Dispersion Mode of S&T Impacts on Economic Variables

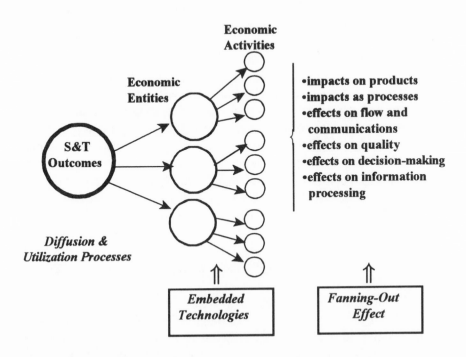

"Fanning-Out Effect," in which a phenomenon similar to a *Dispersoid* takes effect. This phenomenon is defined as "finely divided particles of one substance dispersed in another." In a sense, this is what happens to technological change in economic organizations. The impacts are embedded in processes and structure, and have impacts present throughout the organization and over time.[5]

In such a context, in order to determine the value created by S&T and its outcome of technical change in economic organizations, one may embark on either a specific process approach or the diffusion approach. The process approach calls for the evaluation of the impacts of S&T on a specific and detectable process. In Figure 14.2 this will be to follow up the flow of S&T outcomes within the organization, to a given economic activity, and from there to specific impacts on a product, process, quality, and the like. Examples of this approach are evaluations of S&T on manufacturing, new product development, and e-commerce.[6]

The two modes differ in at least two characteristics. They differ by the direction from which we initiate the evaluation of possible impacts. In the focused mode we identify selected economic variables that we wish to examine, then proceed to assess the impacts that S&T had on them via outcomes such as patents, and the effects of the resultant technical change. However, in the wide-dispersion mode, we do not select specific variables that have been impacted. Rather, the effects are "fanned-out" and may have impacted *any* of the economic activities, processes, and phenomena within and between organizations. As the impacts are considered more diffused, the assessment becomes more difficult, in large part because of the added problem of isolating the relevant impacts and those entities that had been thus affected.

Another distinction is the emphasis in the wide-dispersion mode on the embeddedness of technology in economic processes and activities. Some, if not much, of the effects of S&T, innovation, and technical change occur at the level of the embedded technology. For instance, impacts on flow and communications may be due to technologies embedded in the communication instruments and devices. These technologies allow for communication among people and units to flow faster, with more precision, and perhaps with the ability to transfer more relevant information. Yet the technological changes are not easily identifiable, because they are "hidden" in the capabilities of instruments and devices—hence much more difficult to assess and to quantify.[7]

So, how is economic value actually created with S&T? Both approaches are empirically valid. Value is created through embedded technologies, as well as in relatively direct impacts of the outcomes of S&T on selected variables (productivity, growth, and profitability, among others). The phenomenon of economic value creation is complex and multifaceted, hence different approaches are able to yield some positive findings of value creation.

The evaluation of this phenomenon depends on the method we select. If we choose to assess the impacts and contributions of a technological innovation, we would probably engage the focused mode. So we would assess the impacts of the innovation on specific variables such as productivity. In this context we may be able to "map" the flow of the innovation and its contributions to the economic variable.[8] Industrial companies use a similar method to assess the benefits from their technology and new products.

If, however, we choose to go beyond individual innovations, we would embark on the case of "Cascading Effects." S&T would impact a variety of economic variables, in a continuous manner, and through the embeddedness of its outcomes in a host of organizations, processes, and devices.

The Case of "Cascading Effects"

When we describe the phenomenon of the economic impacts of S&T, the reality of its complexity tends to direct us toward the case of "Cascading

Effects." Rather than offer a more elegant and simple flow of the impacts of individual innovations, there is a more pervasive yet disorganized form by which S&T is more likely to influence economic organizations.

"Cascading Effects" occur as technological innovations are diffused in organizations. They become embedded in almost all aspects of the organization and influence processes, structures, and interactions. Value is thus created sometimes in subtle ways, and almost always in a cumulative form.

For instance, consider the case of computer-integrated-manufacturing (CIM) technology.[9] This technological innovation may be assessed by its impacts on productivity, new products developed, and the profitability of the business. Yet it can (and should) also be assessed by its "Cascading Effects" on a variety of other processes and activities in the company. The technology in CIM allows for improvement in quality assurance, materials handling and planning, as well as improved communications, establishing standards, and overall process planning.[10] This technology contributes to the notion of value in the form of better and cheaper products, improved processes, and the emergence of *other processes* in the company (beyond manufacturing) that will continue to generate benefits.

The reality seems to be that whenever we attempt to "freeze" this phenomenon and to measure the flow and benefits created, we are able to capture only a small portion of the "Cascading Effects."

The Economy Without Science and Technology

Another approach to measuring the impacts of S&T on economic organizations would be to imagine economic activities and growth *without* S&T. Economists have long argued that technological progress is responsible for much of the *economic* progress. They have also suggested that technological progress is disembodied, so its impact on all factors of production is considered to be equal.[11] Economists thus concluded that technological change will have equal effects on capital and labor.

When, however, measurements are made for specific investments, the role of technology appears to be substantial. Some economists have concluded that technological change in equipment may account for 37 percent of economic growth, and structures may account for an additional 15 percent. Thus technological change may explain more than half of what constitutes economic growth.[12]

If, indeed, this is the case, consider economic activity and economic growth without the contributions from science and technology. By closing the spigot of innovations, an economic system would be traumatized because its growth would be halted, or at least severely crippled. Applications of innovations in specific areas such as agriculture and transportation have shown a tremendous growth in productivity and in the overall growth of these activities as part of the larger economic picture.

Consider the possibility that without the technological progress of the 20th century in agricultural production and transportation, it would have been impossible in the days of the dawn of the 21st century to produce and transport emergency grain and other foods to victims of famine in countries half a world away. The Malthusian nightmare would have been omnipresent as an unsolvable reality.

DERIVING VALUE FROM SCIENCE AND TECHNOLOGY

So in what ways does S&T contribute to economic welfare and to creating economic value? Figure 14.3 lists the eight categories of value that can be derived from S&T. Each category is then described and illustrated below.

Figure 14.3
Categories of Economic Value Created by S&T

CATEGORY	ILLUSTRATIVE VALUE CREATED BY S&T
LABOR	• increased employment • skills acquisition
CAPITAL	• improved flow • more rational allocation
LAND	• improved use • improved conservation
EQUIPMENT	• new machines & devices • new processes
GROWTH & EXPANSION	• new products • new industries
COMMERCE & EXCHANGE	• cross-national commerce • improved exchanges in transportation & information
ORGANIZATIONAL EFFICIENCIES	• improved organizational efficiencies • reengineering & restructuring
INFORMATION PROCESSING & UTILIZATION	• improved processing • reduced costs

Labor

The impacts of S&T on the labor force in the economy are various and highly complementary. At the outset, S&T contributes to increased employment through the creation of new ventures, new industries, and new markets for innovations. Second, S&T contributes to the training and skills development of workers. For example, the Internet and personal computers have generated a host of training programs and opportunities, linking experts and workers across distances.

Third, S&T contributes to the health of the workforce in two key ways. Advances to medical S&T have contributed to increased longevity of productive workers, hence allowing for a higher output per worker over the person's lifetime. Another benefit has been the contribution toward a heathier workforce, hence lowering the rate of morbidity and accidents due to poor health. The result is a more productive workforce and, overall, a lower cost of labor.

The resulting benefits accrued from S&T add up to a labor force with improved skills, much more mobile, better adept at absorbing continuous technological changes, healthier, and with a longer work-life. This means that the "technology-laden" workforce is not only more flexible, but is also more versatile and adaptive, making it an economic asset of a much higher magnitude than, for example, the workers of the early 20th century.[13]

Capital

S&T generates value by affecting several attributes of capital. First, S&T contributes to a more efficient flow and movement of capital. Technological innovations in the financial services sector have greatly contributed to the electronic revolution in the processing, flow, and accounting of capital throughout the world.

Second, major improvements in communication networks and usage of information by banks, investment firms, accounting and insurance firms, and by securities exchanges in major industrial countries have allowed for much more flexible and dynamic capital markets. Such dynamics largely account for ubiquitous funding of new ventures and new ideas, across geographical distances, hence contributing to an increased stream of new businesses.

But the contributions of S&T to the new face of capital are also manifested in improved utilization and processing of financial information. This, in turn, allows for marked improvements in rational allocation of financial resources across industries. Moreover, such improvements in the flow and processing of information also make it possible for financial markets to be aware of early signs of problems, thus being able to correct costly mistakes with a higher probability of success.[14]

Land

There are three main types of value that S&T adds to this factor of production. First, S&T contributes to better use of the land for agriculture, construction and transportation. Better use impacts regional planning, so that rational and much more efficient allocation of this resource can be applied.[15] Better use of land is also reflected in efficient distribution of land resources such as water, and in the design and construction of transportation resources, such as roads, railroads, maritime ports, and airports.

A second type of value is the improved use of land resources through construction technologies. Efficient utilization of space has been the focus of the construction of skyscrapers in large cities, as well as densely populated commercial and industrial centers. These technologically inspired construction projects have facilitated economic activity and growth.[16]

A third type of value created by S&T is in conservation and environmental protection of land and its resources. This includes S&T applied in soil conservation, as well as technological innovations used to preserve and save, for example, highly valued seaside and beach properties from erosion and other natural threats.

S&T also contributes to conservation of water supplies and to resources such as fisheries.[17] Another element of conservation and protection that is supported by S&T is improved extraction of petroleum and other underground resources such as minerals, coal, and gas. Technological innovations have contributed to the ability of mining companies to restore the land to its original scope after the mines have dried out.

S&T therefore creates value for the various uses and resources that exist in the land. In addition to agriculture, other economic usages of land are enhanced and protected. They include residences, use for tourism, use for industrial production, transportation, and for extraction of raw materials. In all these activities S&T performs a vital role of a major contributor to preserving and improving the land.

Equipment

In this category, we find contributions of S&T to new products, new devices, new machinery, and the knowledge required to build, install, and operate them. These machines and devices have contributed to marked increased in production and in the productivity of agriculture, manufacturing, and services.[18]

Another contribution of S&T to equipment has been in new processes that utilize equipment in manufacturing as well as services. S&T increased the stock of knowledge needed to improve processes, partly by allowing for a more efficient interface between processes and the equipment used in them.

Flexible manufacturing and computer-aided production have greatly increased the total output from these processes, and have added to their efficient utilization.[19]

New machines and devices have consistently contributed to improved economic activities. For instance, new and innovative drilling equipment has allowed for more effective exploration of oil in locations hitherto difficult to reach, such as maritime sites and deeper in the Earth's crust. New and innovative equipment has contributed to improved navigation, microsurgery, and the exploration of solar energy—to list just a few such impacts.

Growth and Expansion

S&T has also greatly contributed to growth and expansion of economic activities, at the levels of the company, state, and nation. In the case of companies, S&T has been a crucial factor in creating new products and processes, hence opening new markets, creating new marketing niches, and overall expanding the economic impact of corporations to include additional categories of customers and consumers.

Consider the Internet as an illustration of growth and expansion. This technological development has not only created new industries and new ways of conducting business, but has also given many consumers who, up to that point, did not participate in some economic activities, the opportunity and ability to do so. Consumers are now bidding on goods and services, purchasing goods and services, even gambling—all from the secure environment of their homes— worldwide.

New and innovative products and services expand the reach of corporations and also help to create new industries, while making some existing industries obsolete. Such "creative destruction" of technological innovation has established new rules of the game, by which winners are not always determined according to how efficiently they manage their organizations. As much as companies that made carriages pulled by horses continually improved their operations, they were nevertheless replaced by the automobile industry.[20]

Commerce and Exchange

Perhaps a more subtle impact of S&T, but nonetheless as powerful as more visible contributions to the economy, has been the effects on commerce and the exchange of products, services, and information. S&T has dramatically contributed to cross-national commerce. Such impacts were made possible because of two key developments. The first was in the area of transportation. S&T has contributed to improvements in maritime and air transport, as well as developments in ports, airports, and road construction.

The second key development has been improvements in computing, communications, telecommunications, and archiving. These allowed for a revolutionized banking and monetary system that transcended national boundaries. Capital is now free and able to instantaneously flow to and from attractive or unpromising markets. The instability of Asian economics in the late 1990s has been a phenomenon triggered by such capital mobility.

But improvements in monetary flow were not enough to foster increases in international commerce. S&T has also contributed to the exchange and processing of commercial information across national boundaries. The economist's dream of "complete information" of a given transaction came closer to being achieved, as developments in computer and telecommunications technologies have made possible the continuous and inexpensive exchange of information among trading partners around the globe.

Organization and Resources Efficiency

S&T has contributed to the implementation of various mechanisms to improve the efficiency of private and public organizations. In their original suggestions for corporate reengineering in the early 1990s, Hammer and Champy argued that reengineering became possible because of developments in information technology.[21] Exact numbers are hard to come by, but my estimate, based on the published cases of successful restructuring of American companies in the 1990s, the overall improvement in efficiency has been in the range of 10-20 percent. These are improvements in the *internal* workings of organizational units, their activities, and stages in their value chain.

In addition to increased efficiencies, the contributions of S&T were in making the allocation of scarce organizational resources a more efficient endeavor. Such resources are thus channeled to those activities and units that have a higher promise to deliver results where the resources will be better utilized, that is, more efficiently. Overall, then, economic resources are put to better use in those activities when they can be of higher utility.[22]

Yet these improvements come with a price. In my comments on reengineering, I have concluded that the practice of implementing efficiencies may lead to the "Efficiency Trap."[23] When efficiencies are achieved,

> everybody is impressed, and the cases keep coming and we continue to report them and to wonder at their contribution to the bottom line. Managers at all levels were also impressed. They feel that this is a winner, this is the way to go, so they want more of the same. Over time the savings are less and less dramatic, until they are not more than a trickle. But the *frame of mind* is still there: efficiency is the key to success (personal as well as that of the firm). This frame of mind creates a climate

of retrenchment, as managers distance themselves from risky undertakings, and from a more strategic view of their activities and their corporation (p. 101).

S&T was also a contributor to corporate and organizational efficiency by facilitating mergers, acquisitions, and cooperative management. Improvements in information processing, retrieval, and storage have allowed for much more efficient transitions and for the merging of information and databases among organizations. Issues such as confidentiality and access to information, that used to plague and to threaten cooperative effort, have been partially resolved by the impacts of S&T.

Information Processing and Utilization

Intertwined with the previously discussed categories, this class of contributions of S&T includes such economic benefits as reduced costs and improved processing in terms of time and effort expended on them. S&T has contributed to the ability of economic entities to process and utilize massive amounts of information, and to do so cheaper, quicker, and with many more applications hitherto impossible to exercise.

As the cost of processing declines and the range of applications increases ("Moore's Law"), there are many avenues for economic activities that now become available and feasible. For example, improved and cheaper manipulation of massive databases allow for more efficient studies and assessment of marketing segmentation and the targeting of market opportunities that had been previously obscure or unapproachable.[24]

Overall, improvements in the processing and utilization of information seem to permeate and influence other economic activities of both individuals and organizations, across industrial sectors. Improved ability to manipulate large amounts of data and very large databases may also foster the creation of new economic efforts, new enterprises, and even new industries. A salient example is in biotechnology and energy research, where large-scale computer simulations allow for reduced time to market, by greatly reducing the time needed for actual testing.

PROPOSED FRAMEWORKS FOR ANALYSIS

So what does the evidence show? Overall, there is a preponderance of documented evidence to support the claims that S&T indeed generates economic value. Such value is made up of several and distinct categories, and is diffused in many aspects of economic activities.

Following the conceptual framework suggested by Dosi[25] and Rosenbloom and Christensen,[26] a summary picture emerges in which the effects of S&T and the nature of the value created can be better described by the relation between type of innovation and market disposition. This is shown in Figure 14.4.

Figure 14.4 combines the notions of incremental versus radical innovation with the degree to which the marketplace in the given industry was predisposed toward low or high embeddedness of the technology. The concept of embeddedness was discussed in Chapter 11, and its attributes include "functionality," "imitability," and "replaceability." The more the industry is dependent upon the technology for such aspects as functionality and usefulness, the more it will be predisposed to "cutting-edge" technologies. That is, if the technological innovation is a major contributor to what makes a product or service competitive, its embeddedness would be high, since it represents the core of the marketable or competitive characteristics of the product or service. This leads to the dependency of the industry on the technological innovation, hence to the need for a stream of such innovations, hence to "cutting-edge" and "cut-throat" scenarios.[27]

Four possible scenarios are depicted in Figure 14.4: stable, cumulative, dynamic, and hypercompetitive. These are descriptions of the environments in which industries and individual companies utilize S&T and exploit its value— within the specific conditions of their markets.

Stability-in-Motion Scenario

Incremental innovations are created in a market environment that is relatively stable and in which technological change is not crucial to economic activity nor to competitiveness. Examples include the energy industry, electric power companies, and the oil and gas companies.[28] In this scenario, value from S&T is continuous, yet delayed. This means that although value is added to

Figure 14.4
Technological Innovation and Market Disposition for S&T

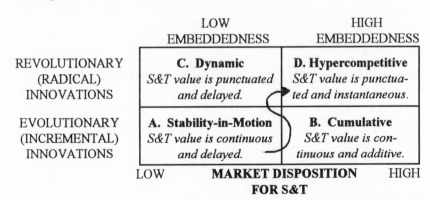

	LOW EMBEDDEDNESS	HIGH EMBEDDEDNESS
REVOLUTIONARY (RADICAL) INNOVATIONS	**C. Dynamic** *S&T value is punctuated and delayed.*	**D. Hypercompetitive** *S&T value is punctuated and instantaneous.*
EVOLUTIONARY (INCREMENTAL) INNOVATIONS	**A. Stability-in-Motion** *S&T value is continuous and delayed.*	**B. Cumulative** *S&T value is continuous and additive.*

LOW   **MARKET DISPOSITION**   HIGH
FOR S&T

the corporate stock, such value will not be visible for each innovation that is incorporated in the company's routine operations. Rather, incremental innovations will add value by small improvements in the company's operations, customer relations, billing, vendor relations, and similar activities. Over time these improvements represent substantial (and measurable) added value.

Cumulative Scenario

When incremental innovations are created in a market environment in which embeddedness of technology is high, S&T value is cumulative and continuous. In this scenario, technological innovations may be crucial to competitiveness in specific areas of competition in the industry. For example, certain medical technologies for clinical use add value to their organization by the additive nature of their benefits, while these benefits are considered critical components of the organization's arsenal of competitive tools. Hospitals employing CAT scans or similar technologies have a distinct competitive advantage.

Similarly, some areas of office automation may also be included as an example of the cumulative nature of S&T value. Companies that employ technological innovations in office automation will add competitive value via the cumulative benefits accrued to them from these technologies.

The key difference between the cumulative and stability-in-motion scenarios is the *competitive* nature of the value from S&T in the cumulative scenarios. In the stability-in-motion case, the value is added to operations rather than by directly benefitting the competitive stance of the company.[29]

Dynamic Scenario

This is a peculiar state of affairs. Revolutionary or radical innovations are incorporated by companies in a punctuation format, but the environment favors low embeddedness. Hence, although technological innovations are thrust upon the company, they do not form a crucial element of competitiveness in the marketplace. For example, adoption of computers by physicians and the introduction of telecommunication technology in automobiles are examples of a dynamic scenario. These innovations create value by contributing to the overall comparative advantage of the company, but are not crucial to its survival or competitive stance.[30]

Hypercompetitive Scenario

Radical innovations that occur in a punctuated manner and are highly embedded in products or processes provide immediate benefits that contribute to the competitive position of the company. The case of the hard disk drive in the computer industry is an example of this cutting-edge technology.[31]

Value is added by the "creative destruction" of the punctuated emergence and adoption of radical innovations. Because of the high embeddedness of the market disposition to technology, such innovations displace existing products, thus changing the structure of the marketplace. These disrupting innovations possess *technological* attributes that create such upheaval, dislodging existing leaders and catapulting other players (sometimes new entrants) into positions of market dominance.[32]

Value from S&T, Competition Redefined, and Creative Destruction

In Joseph Schumpeter's terminology, "creative destruction" is the dynamics by which new entrants in an industry, armed with radical technological innovations, dislodge incumbent firms. The value accrued to these companies from their technological innovations is primarily the strategic ability to compete with established firms and to gain a foothold in the marketplace.[33]

But the battlefield between incumbents and "destructors" is not necessarily a scene of unmitigated competition and chaotic destruction in mortal combat. Unlike popular video games, there are increasing episodes of cooperation, collaboration, and symbiotic relations between new entrants and incumbents.[34]

The value added to the individual entrant is mitigated by the value to the industry, influenced by the disadvantages of the chaotic disarray of hyper-competition and disruptive innovations. Figure 14.5 lists some advantages and disadvantages of unrestrained competition driven by radical technological innovations.[35]

The overall picture that emerges from Figure 14.5 is that although creative destruction leads to revolutions in market and industry structure, there are some mitigating factors that may help control this phenomenon. Entrants do not completely dislodge and replace the established companies in every case. Often the net result is some form of cooperation, where incumbents learn to be more dynamic and current, as well as resigned to giving up some of its share in the market. Total replacement (or destruction) of incumbents may not provide the most value to the industry or the economy.

When entrants capitalize on the attributes of existing companies, there is a redefinition of competition, and a more enduring value is created in the industry. These attributes may have been one factor leading to the ossification and obsolescence of established firms. Their strong presence in the market, hitherto unchallenged, may have led to complacency and lack of energy and innovation.

Figure 14.5
Advantages and Disadvantages to Industries from Radical
Technological Innovations and Hypercompetition

ADVANTAGES FOR VALUE CREATION	DISADVANTAGES FOR VALUE CREATION
• Industry is rejuvenated by entrepreneurial effort driven by radical innovations. • Incumbents are "forced" to become more dynamic and more current. • Outdated products and activities are replaced by those driven by and made of the radical innovations. • Jobs are created and new skills are introduced, leading to additional jobs and subindustries. • Total value created in the industry compensates for cost and time of adoption and learning curve of the radical technologies. • "Cascading effects" of additional energy awakened by revitalized industry.	• Incumbents possess knowledge about processes, business acumen, and experience. • Incumbents possess market presence, portals, exposure, and networks. • Incumbents have imbued trust and stability to conduct commerce. • Chaos and uncertainty diminish market stability and hinders adaptation to new realities. • Without adequate support (e.g., financial backing), entrants lack skills and experience to educate market to new realities. • Entrants may become "tired" and exhaust resources in hypercompetition, hence unable to materialize their "victory." • Unless value is overwhelmingly created, entire industry may exhaust resources in competition.

Yet these same qualities are also essential for small, innovative, and untried entrants, whose main (perhaps only) advantage is their revolutionary technological innovation. Hence, some form of cooperation and symbiosis may increase the total value created in the industry, and the rate at which it is being generated.[36]

The "Snake Curve" in Evolution of S&T Value

The framework for analysis shown in Figure 14.4 allows for a progressive view of the scenarios of value creation from S&T. Companies progress from the scenarios where value is generated from incremental innovations to the cases of revolutionary innovations.

Historically, transformations in certain industries have been a move from the *stability-in-motion* and *cumulative* scenarios to the *dynamic* and *hypercompetitive* scenarios. Established industries, in which technology incrementally contributed to improvements and continuous progress, found themselves in the midst of a revolution. This was brought about by new entrants on the path of "creative destruction," where the technology embedded in the product or service had become the crucial component for competition and survival.

The Typewriter Industry

Consider the case of the typewriter industry. This industry emerged in the 1870s when practical typewriters that were easy to use were introduced. Three American inventors, Sholes, Glidden, and Soule patented a workable typewriter in 1868, and in 1873 they made an agreement with the Remington Company to manufacture their invention. In September 1873 the first Remington typewriter was produced and marketed. This machine had many of the basic features of contemporary typewriters. Moreover, it started an industry of components and accessories—such as ribbons, carbon paper, white outs, and similar items—for use in the office and the home, where typewriters became ubiquitous in the 20th century.

Several technological innovations were introduced and adopted by this industry. They included the key and lever that allowed for typing lower and upper cases, addition of numbers, and touch-typing. In the 1920s, electric typewriters appeared in the marketplace, followed in the 1960s with interchangeable type spheres.

Following the model shown in Figure 14.5, these innovations may be considered incremental and cumulative. In the 1990s there was a radical transformation in the industry. Personal computers replaced typewriters as the machines of choice for office productivity. In the period 1986-1988 about 1.4 million typewriters were sold in the United States, whereas in 1992-1993 the numbers dropped to less than half.[37] In 1999 only avid consumers or technophobes still purchase and use typewriters. The price of these machines, such as the IBM's Wheelwriter 1000 and 7000, exceed that of very powerful personal computers.[38]

With the proliferation of computer technology, the industry moved into a different phase in the model of Figure 14.5. This was a radical innovation, and one that credited the *technology* itself as the key aspect for the market's willingness to purchase these machines. The typewriter industry, for all practical reasons, simply ceased to exist as a force in office productivity.

The advantages of personal computers over typewriters are many, but the advantages of typewriters were defined in 1986 (the year before the main switch in the marketplace) as: (1) cost, (2) portability, and (3) ability to perform small jobs quickly.[39] In the following decade personal computers became portable, much less expensive, and able to perform all types of jobs.

In addition, the advantages of personal computers now included graphics, connectivity to the Internet, networking, and a ubiquitous presence in the office and the home.

The Qwerty Keyboard and Path Dependence

Christopher Latham Sholes (1819-1890), the coinventor of the typewriter, also developed the standard keyboard (which he patented in 1868 and sold in 1873). Known as the Qwerty keyboard, because of the first six letters in the top row of the keyboard, this original design of the keyboard layout has persisted since its introduction in 1873, despite the fact that several technological innovations have been adopted by the industry in its almost 130 years.

Some economists have used this example of the persistence of this design to argue that it illustrates how markets make mistakes. The awkward layout of the keyboard was originally designed to solve the problem of keys being jammed when the typist reached a certain speed. Sholes' design alleviated the problem by placing the most-often-used keys on the opposite sides of the board. So, although jamming ceased to be a problem when typewriters became electrical and when personal computers were produced, the awkward design was maintained, even though it slowed typing and other, perhaps better, designs appeared over the years.[40]

In particular, economists point to the keyboard invented by August Dvorak in the 1930s as superior to the Qwerty in speed of typing. Yet in 1983 there were about 5,000 Dvorak keyboards in the United States and over 30 million Qwerty keyboards. In 1999, with the proliferation of personal computers, the number of Qwerty keyboards almost doubled, whereas the number of Dvorak keyboards remained insignificant.[41]

Economists argued that the Qwerty design illustrates the theory of path-dependent technology choice. The theory assumes that positive feedbacks follow the choice of a technological path, thus locking the users and the industry into the chosen technology.[42] This feedback may include economics of scale, increased consumer acceptance of the selected technology, learning by actually using it, and ancillary industries that emerge with this technology. Thus, even when competing technologies are superior in some respect to the chosen technology, they will not gain wide acceptance.[43] Unless the competing technology can provide—within a reasonable time—increasing returns that will compensate for the large investments in the industry, it will be economically imprudent to switch to the competing technology.[44]

Debunking the Qwerty Myth

The "myth" of the Qwerty design as an example of market failure was challenged in the 1990s by Stanley Leibowitz and Stephen Margolis.[45] They argued that the competing designs, such as the Dvorak layout, offered only marginal superiority, if any. Thus the cost of retraining and overall costs of adoption of the new design to supplant the Qwerty layout would be prohibitive. Hence, the existing technology is sufficiently efficient and there is no reason to believe that this exemplifies market failure.

They concluded that economic models of technology choice and replacement should include such variables as entrepreneurship, mergers and acquisitions, loss leader pricing, and similar events. In short, they argued that economic analysis should reflect the social and organizational forces that lead consumers onto a given path, and tend to keep them with the standard selected.[46] In a similar vein, these authors also examined the resiliency of Microsoft in the personal computer industry, and the ubiquitous Windows applications and operating systems.[47]

Path Dependence, Technological Innovations, and Embeddedness

Staying the course is a preferred action when a standard technology is established. It will be maintained by externalities or infrastructure variables, plus the benefits from competitors that are not enough to warrant a change. In terms of the scenarios shown in Figure 14.5, the role of such externalities or infrastructure variables may be explained by the movement among cells. When the technology is not crucial to competition, evolutionary improvements will continue to generate value. In the absence of radical innovations, cumulative benefits will accrue even when the marketplace is disposed to regard the technology as highly embedded, hence competitive.

Simply put, unless the competing technology is radical *and* highly embedded in the product or service, there will be no incentives to adopt it, in lieu of the existing technology. Add to this the proposition that in the absence of such compelling embedded technology, the product or service hypercompetes with *other* attributes than the said technology. Hence, competitiveness, or the possibility of threats to survival, is absent in this instance, and does not favor change.[48]

There have been cases where an alternative technology was highly embedded in the product or service and was critical to the strategic survival of the company. Yet the adoption of the technology by the marketplace was not successful, because of infrastructure variables (externalities). It may have been too difficult to use, too costly to learn, incompatible with ancillary products and services, and much too different in design and operation. Examples include the market failure of "zap mail" by Federal Express in the early 1990s, and the overall failure of robotics in the 1980s and 1990s to produce usable and marketable robots (for nonmanufacturing purposes).

So a technological innovation may be embedded in the product and provide it with competitive advantage, yet still be rejected by the marketplace. Displacement of an existing product with a competing technology must also be considered from the perspective of market disparities and the variables of adoption and diffusion.

The Notion of "Linking Familiarity"

When radical technologies are introduced in the marketplace and adopted by consumers, their success also depends on whether they possess a crucial link to previous technology. This is the essence of the notion of "linking familiarity." As described above, radical innovations require retooling, adaptation, learning, and substantial economic and psychological investments in the new technology. "Linking familiarity" is a powerful facilitator that softens the transition from the incumbent to the new technology.[49]

Initial users of computer keyboards needed a familiar link to established machines, namely typewriters. Hence the resilience of the Qwerty design. This need to "hold on" to "tried and true" artifacts, components, designs, or even terminology seems to manifest itself whenever a radical technology replaces the incumbent. Some technical terms continue to be used with the new technology, even though they have completely lost their original meaning. How else can we refer to "horsepower" as a measure of the output from engines? Similarly, some products in which radical technologies are embedded will take a familiar shape. This explains creating robots that resemble people and have bipedal locomotion (which is an awkward and inefficient mode for machines to move around).

Summary

How then do we derive value form S&T? In the special case of radical or revolutionary technological innovations, value is created in both a punctuated and cumulative manner (increasing returns). The choice of one technological path over other competitors may indeed lock the industry into a seemingly inferior scenario. However, the overall value derived from this choice will be contingent on the degree to which the adoption and adaptation processes are eased into, so that more intensive exploitation of the technology thus becomes possible. The total value is not only economic, but a combination of means and ends, where the means are influenced by externalities. As Redmond put it: "One intriguing aspect of nonlinear market processes is a propensity for small, outside influences to exercise a powerful and long-term influence on market response."[50] Finally, Arthur concluded that "the prediction of market shares may become impossible, according to the degree that this technological evolution depends on small events beneath the resolution of the observer's mode."[51]

NOTES

1. Cited in Mattox, W., "The Able-Bodied Retiree Doesn't Need Our Help," *USA Today*, May 8, 2000, 19A.
2. Peter Drucker is correct in pointing out that in centuries past young men followed in their fathers' footsteps. However, salient historical exceptions abound. In the Middle Ages, Hildebrand of Tuscany was of a poor family and became Pope Gregory VII (1020-1085), the pontiff who challenged the German Emperor Henry IV at Canossa. Although in the era of mercantilism the emergence of guilds and trade organizations fostered the family traditions of specific trades, there were many exceptions fueled by such factors as the discovery of new lands, and the industrial revolution. Even today, however, there are incentives inherent in college admission procedures that give preference to sons and daughters of alumni or members of a profession (e.g., medicine). Overall, however, Drucker identified a relevant phenomenon. In my view this phenomenon is an outcome of the evolving predominance of S&T in our lives.
3. See, for example, some recent studies and reviews of the extant literature in Mowery, D., and N. Rosenberg, *Paths of Innovation: Technological Change in 20th Century America* (New York: Cambridge University Press, 2000). Also see Griliches, Z. (Ed.), *R&D and Productivity: The Economic Evidence* (Chicago: University of Chicago Press, 1998); Larson, C., "New National Innovation System Seen as Key to Transforming China into a Market Economy," *Research-Technology Management*, 43(2), 2000, 2-4; and Sallstrom, S., "Technological Progress and the Chamberlin Effect," *The Journal of Industrial Economics*, 47(4), 1999, 427-449.
4. For example, in the literature, see Nelson, R., *The Sources of Economic Growth* (Cambridge, MA: Harvard University Press, 2000). Nelson argued that technological change has been the main force that fueled economic progress. See, in particular, Chapters 1 and 2, and Chapters 6-8 which discuss science and technical advance. Also see Antonelli, C., *The Economics of Localized Technological Change and Industrial Dynamics* (Boston: Kluwer Academic Publishers, 1995). See Chapters 5 and 6 on diffusion and on productivity growth. And see Welfens, P., *Globalization of the Economy, Unemployment, and Innovation* (New York: Springer-Verlag, 1999).
5. In this regard see the discussion on the recent explorations of the notions of General Purpose Technologies (GPT) and Gross Technology Outcomes (GTO) in Chapter 15.
6. See, for example, Liv, J., *Manufacturing Innovations and Technological Operations: Theory and Application* (New York: World Scientific Publishing, 2000). Also see Torrisi, S., *Industrial Organization and Innovation: An International Study of the Software Industry* (London: Edward Elgar, 1998), and see Ohkawa, K., and K. Otsuka, *Technology Diffusion, Productivity, Employment, and Phase Shifts in Developing Economies* (New York: Columbia University Press, 1994). Here the

authors used the input-output ratio approach to show the effects of technology, as diffused, on productivity and employment. See in particular, pp. 3-112.

7. For example, see Tapscott, D., *Creating Value in the Network Economy* (Boston: Harvard Business School Press, 1999). Also see Parolini, C., *The Value Net* (New York: John Wiley & Sons, 1999). Also see Harvard Business Review, *HBR on the Business Value of IT* (Boston: Harvard Business School Press, 1999).

8. See, for example, Chapter 9 on technology maps in Geisler, E., *The Metrics of Science and Technology* (Westport, CT: Quorum Books, 2000).

9. See, for example, Usher, J., H. Parsaei, and R. Uptal (Eds.), *Integrated Product and Process Development: Methods, Tools, and Technologies* (New York: John Wiley & Sons, 1998).

10. Rembold, U., *Computer-Integrated-Manufacturing and Engineering* (New York: Longman, 1993). See, in particular, pp. 47-103.

11. See Gort, M., J. Greenwood, and P. Rupert, "How Much of Economic Growth is Fueled by Investment-Specific Technological Progress?", *Federal Reserve Bank of Cleveland—Economic Commentary*, March 1, 1995, pp. 1-4.

12. See, Gort, M., J. Greenwood, and P. Rupert, "Measuring the Rate of Technological Progress in Structures," *Review of Economic Dynamics*, 2(1), 1999, 207-230. Also see Verspagen, B., G. van Tunzelmann, and J. Fagenberg (Eds.), *The Dynamics of Technology, Trade, and Growth* (New York: Edward Elgar, 1995); and see Scherer, F., *New Perspectives on Economic Growth and Technological Innovation* (Washington, DC: Brookings Institution Press, 1999).

13. See, for example, Caselli, F., "Technological Revolutions," *American Economic Review*, 89(1), 1999, 78-102. Also see Chen, B., and K. Schimomura, "Self-Fulfilling Expectations and Economic Growth: A Model of Technology Adoption and Industrialization," *International Economic Review*, 39(1), 1998, 151-170.

14. See, for example, Von Tunzelmann, *Technology and Industrial Progress: The Foundation of Economic Growth* (New York: Edward Elgar, 1995). Also see Greenspan, A., "Technology and the Economy: Monetary and Fiscal Policies," *Vital Speeches of the Day*, 66(8), 2000, 228-230; and see, especially, Yam, J., "The Impact of Technology on Financial Development in East Asia," *Journal of International Affairs*, 51(2), 1998, 539-553.

15. See, for example, Grodvahl, D., and E. Hill, "Regional Planning and Intelligent Transportation Systems: Effects on Land Use and Society," *Institute of Transportation Engineers Journal*, 70(3), 2000, 34-38. Also see Nagaraja, G., S. Subramanian, and V. Venkataram, "Empirical Study of Technological Innovations and Productivity Change to Ground Nut Production in the Karnataka State of India, " *Journal of Financial Management Analysis*, 12(2), 1999, 85-87.

16. See, for example, Majidzadeh, M., "Web-Based System Aids Construction," *The American City & County*, 115(5), 2000, 8-10. Also see Bowels, L., "Using Technology to Drive Value," *Professional Builder*, 65(1), 2000, 161-166. Bowels argued that construction technology may enable the industry to "build and remodel higher performance houses over the next decade that will be 20% less expensive to own and operate" (p. 161).

17. See, for example, the case of the salmon in North America, Schwindt, R., A. Vining, and S. Globerman, "Net Loss: A Cost-Benefit Analysis of the Canadian Pacific Salmon Fishery," *Journal of Policy Analysis and Management*, 19(1), 2000, 23-45.

18. See, for example, Jasinowski, J., "Technology and Economic Success," *Vital Speeches of the Day*, 65(23), 1999, 716-718. Also see Nadiri, I., and B. Nandi, "Technical Change, Markup, Divestiture, and Productivity Growth in the U.S. Telecommunications Industry," *The Review of Economics and Statistics*, 81(3), 1999, 488-498.

19. For example, see: Perreto, P., "Industrial Development, Technological Change, and Long-Run Growth," *Journal of Development Economics*, 59(2), 1999, 389-419. Also see Papaconstantinou, G., "Technical Change and Economic Growth," *Economic Systems Research*, 10(4), 1998, 369-371; and Gaponenko, N., "Innovations and Innovation Policy at the Stage of Transition to a New Technological Order," *Problems of Economic Transition*, 40(10), 1998, 43-58.

20. See Tysen, L., "Old Economic Logic in the New Economy," *California Management Review*, 41(4), 1999, 8-16. Also see Fingleton, E., *In Praise of Hard Industries: Why Manufacturing, Not the Information Economy, is the Key to Future Prosperity* (Boston: Houghton-Mifflin, 1999).

21. Hammer, M., and J. Champy, *Reengineering the Corporation: A Manifesto for Business Revolution* (New York: HarperBusiness, 1993).

22. See, for example, Mansfield, E., "Intellectual Property Protection, Direct Investment, and Technology Transfer: Germany, Japan, and the United States," *International Journal of Technology Management*, 19(1/2), 2000, 3-21.

23. See Geisler, E., *Managing the Aftermath of Radical Corporate Change* (Westport, CT: Quorum Books, 1997), pp. 101-102.

24. See Greenspan, A., "Is There a New Economy?", *California Management Review*, 41(1), 1998, 74-85. Also see *The Economist*, "Science and Technology: Drowning in Data," 351(8125), June 26, 1999, 93-94. In this article, the author argued that as "biologists are confronted by a tidal wave of information" (p. 93), the discipline's main challenge is increasingly in the limited capabilities of computing technology.

25. Dosi, G., "Technological Paradigms and Technological Trajectories," *Research Policy*, 11(1), 1982, 147-162.

26. Rosenbloom, R., and C. Christensen, "Technological Discontinuities, Organizational Capabilities, and Strategic Commitments," in Dose, G., D. Teece, and J. Chytry (Eds.), *Technology, Organization, and Competitiveness* (New York: Oxford University Press, 1998), pp. 215-245.

27. Clayton Christensen convincingly described this phenomenon in the case of the hard disk drive. See Christensen, C., *The Innovator's Dilemma* (New York: HarperBusiness, 2000), pp. 120-141.

28. See, for example, Barrell, R., and N. Pain (Eds.), *Innovation, Investment, and the Diffusion of Technology in Europe* (New York: Cambridge University Press, 1999), in particular, pages 89-119. Also see Scherer, F., *New Perspectives on Economic Growth and Technological Innovation* (Washington, DC: Brookings Institution Press, 1999).

29. See Norberg-Baum, V., and M. Rossi, "The Power of Incrementalism: Environmental Regulation and Technological Change in Pulp and Paper Bleaching in the US," *Technology Analysis & Strategic Management*, 10(2), 1998, 225-245. Also see Howells, J., and J. Michie (Eds.), *Technology, Innovation, and Competitiveness* (New York: Edward Elgar, 1997).

30. See, for example, the case of rail transportation which is similar to that of automotives, in Churella, A., "Market Imperatives and Innovation Cycles: The Effects of Technological Discontinuities on the Twentieth Century Locomotive Industry," *Business and Economic History*, 27(2), 1998, 378-389. The author argued that companies who were able to time their movement in the market with the cycles of technological changes in the industry tended to be more competitive, hence successful.

31. Christensen, 2000, *op cit.*

32. See, for example, Nolan, R., and D. Croson, *Creative Destruction: A Six-Stage Process for Transforming the Organization* (Boston: Harvard Business School Press, 1994). Also see Panth, S., *Technological Innovation, Industrial Evolution, and Economic Growth* (New York: Garland, 1997).

33. See the case of "Silicon Valley" and the story of such firms as Silicon Graphics, Netscape, and Healtheon, in Roush, W., "Creative Destruction," *Technology Review*, 103(2), 2000, 108-110. Also see Kessler, A., "Market Mayhem: Creative Destruction Can be Lucrative," *Wall Street Journal*, April 18, 2000, p. A18. See Schumpeter, J., *History of Economic Analysis* (New York: Oxford University Press, 1996).

34. See, in particular: Rothaermel, F., "Technological Discontinuities and the Nature of Competition," *Technology Analysis & Strategic Management*, 12(2), 2000, 149-160.

35. See, for example, Becker, G., "Make the World Safe for Creative Destruction," *Business Week*, February 23, 1998, 20-21.

36. See, Hart, S., and M. Milstein, "Global Sustainability and the Creative Destruction of Industries," *Sloan Management Review*, 41(1), 1999, 23-33

37. See Cosgrove, N., "Typewriters Adopt: They're Here to Stay," *The Office*, 117(1), 1993, 87-89.

38. Hershey, R., "Out of the Past, the Click and Clack of Low Technology," *New York Times*, December 20, 1999, C, 20-24.

39. Stevenson, J., "Typewriters and Word Processors," *Modern Office*, 25(3), 1986, 25-32.

40. See David P., "Clio and the Economics of Qwerty," *The American Economic Review*, 75(2), 1985, 332-338.

41. See Cary, L., "Qwerty Forever!" *Across the Board*, 20(4), 1983, 6-8. Also see Adler, M., *Antique Typewriters: From Creed to Qwerty* (New York: Schiffer Publishing, 1997).

42. See, for example, Goodstein, E., "The Economic Roots of Environmental Decline: Property Rights or Path Dependence?" *Journal of Economic Issues*, 29(4), 1995, 1029-1040. Also see Habermeier, K., "Competing Technologies, the Learning Curve, and Rational Expectations," *European Economic Review*, 33(7), 1989, 1293-1312; and Arthur, B., *Increasing Returns and Path Dependence in the Economy* (Ann Arbor: University of Michigan Press, 1994). See, in particular, Chapter 2:

"Competing Feedbacks in the Economy," and Chapter 3: "Path-Dependent Processes and the Emergence of Macrostructures."

43. See, for example, Atkinson, G., "Evolutionary Economics and Path Dependence," *Journal of Economic Issues*, 32(3), 1998, 885-887. Also see Arthur, B., "Competing Technologies, Increasing Returns, and Lock-In by Historical Events," *The Economic Journal*, 99(394), 1989, 116-133.

44. The path-dependence theory has contributed to evolutionary economics. As economic institutions lock themselves into a chosen technology, proponents of this approach have argued that competition will be in the form of evolutionary or incremental changes, rather than radical change to a competing technology. See, for example, Nelson, R., and S. Winter, *An Evolutionary Theory of Economic Change* (Cambridge, MA: Harvard University Press, 1982). Also see Atkinson, 1998, *op. cit.* and Hickson, C., "A Review of Evolutionary Economics," *Journal of Economic Dynamics & Control*, 22(5), 1998, 801-810.

45. In their seminal paper, Liebowitz, S., and S. Margolis, "The Fable of the Keys," *Journal of Law and Economics*, 33(2), 1990, 1-25. Also see Leibowitz, S., and S. Margolis, "Policy and Path Dependence: From Qwerty to Windows 95," *Regulation*, 18(3), 1995, 33-43. The advent of voice recognition may put the matter to rest, as it will soon replace the PC's keyboard.

46. See the application of a similar analysis to scientific progress in Sterman, J., and Wittenberg, J., "Path Dependence, Competition, and Succession in the Dynamics of Scientific Revolution," *Organization Science*, 10(3), 1999, 322-341.

47. Margolis, S., and S. Leibowitz, *Winners, Losers, and Microsoft: Competition and Antitrust in High Technology* (New York: Independent Institute, 1999).

48. See, for example, Redmond, W., "When Technologies Compete: The Role of Externalities in Nonlinear Market Response," *The Journal of Product Innovation Management*, 8(3), 1991, 170-184. Also see Lane, S., "The Determinants of Investment in New Technology," *The American Economic Review*, 81(2), 1991, 262-267.

49. The development of this notion greatly benefitted from discussions with Dr. Janet Goranson. See the more detailed description and the empirical study of this notion in Chapter 15, and in Geisler, E., "Path Dependency, Linking Familiarity, and the Adoption of Radical Innovation," Stuart Graduate School of Business, Illinois Institute of Technology, Working Paper, August, 2000.

50. Redmond, 1991, *op. cit.*, p. 170.

51. Arthur, 1989, *op. cit.*, p. 116.

15

HOW COMPANIES CREATE ECONOMIC VALUE WITH SCIENCE AND TECHNOLOGY

The previous chapter dealt with the broad issues of the process and types of economic value created by S&T. In this chapter the focus will be on how individual companies have successfully exploited innovation and created economic value with S&T.

To the individual company, S&T may generate several outcomes of value. These are summarized in Figure 15.1.

Usually companies gain economic value from both the S&T developed in-house (internal R&D) and outcomes transferred to them from other R&D producers. Mansfield studied the phenomenon of S&T diffusion in industry

Figure 15.1
Outcomes of Value to Industrial Companies Created by S&T

ECONOMIC VALUE CREATED BY S&T
• New and improved products and revenues from sales thereof
• Profits from sale of new products
• Cost savings due to new and improved processes in manufacturing
• Revenues from licensing patents
• Improved market share in existing market
• Opening up new "niches" and new markets
• Savings due to more efficient use of resources, better project selection
• Cost savings, sales, and profits due to shorter "time to market"

and concluded that new technologies tend to be diffused within an industry much more rapidly than generally believed.[1] Kenneth Arrow, in a paper in honor of the late Edwin Mansfield, called this finding "startling" and argued that it calls into question such issues as technological leadership and first-mover advantages.[2]

Outcomes from S&T are thus utilized by the industrial company and may generate items of value described in Figure 15.1. Some of these items are tangible values, such as improved profits and revenues. Other items are less tangible as they are embedded in processes, as for example, efficiency of resources allocations and decision-making.

Sales From New Products

Hewlett-Packard (HP) is a major player in a very competitive industry of computers and ancillary products such as printers and scanners. The company established its research laboratory in 1966, when its sales were around $170 million. In 1998 HP had sales of $47 billion, of which it spent 7.6 percent on research and development. Throughout its history, the founders and managers of HP insisted that its tremendous business success was due to innovations that emerged from its laboratories.

Such claims are difficult to substantiate across companies and industries. Although it is commonly assumed that new products lead to increased sales, profits, and other economic benefits, it is also known that almost half of all new products introduced by companies fail to achieve commercial penetration and success. Examples abound of well-publicized failures. In the case of RCA's Video Disc Player, the company lost almost a billion dollars, whereas Campbell's Soup failed in its attempt in 1997 to market the Intelligent Quisine, with losses over $500 million.[3]

Statistically, the link between new products and corporate success seems to be consistently strong. The consulting company of Booz, Allen, & Hamilton studied over half of the Fortune 1000 companies in the 1980s and concluded that sales from new products account for over one-third of their profits.[4] Strategy researchers concluded in the 1990s that companies that were first to introduce "important incremental product innovations" also enjoyed a larger market share in their industry.[5] Among companies marketing consumer products, the case of Gillette stands out in the 1990s. This company's return on sales was almost as high as Coca-Cola's, whereas over 40 percent of its sales could be credited to new products.[6]

Clayton Christenson has argued, however, that in most cases where technology contributes to market competitiveness, being the market leader or prime mover is not necessarily critical to sustained or increased market share.[7] He explained his opinion by considering the bases of the competition in the industry. In those cases where the basis for competition is technological attributes of the product or process (uniquely or principally), leadership in such technologies determines the firm's sustained and improved market position.

Yet the value that new products provide through sales and profits has also been occasionally attenuated by a different set of findings. A survey of Italian industry in the late 1990s revealed that in the manufacturing sector, only 1.2 percent of total sales could be credited solely to new products. The bulk of sales originated from existing, not innovative, products and processes. The authors claimed that these data are representative of the European union.[8]

Impact of New Products on Corporate Valuation

Sales of new products and the profits they generate impact the value of the company's stock. Even at the very early stage of announcing a discovery, the expectation that this will turn into a new product, hence generate sales and profits, is enough to boost the value of the stock. In some cases, the expectations lead to a drastic soaring of the stock, only to severely retreat when these expectations are not met.[9]

Guidelines for assessing potential "winning" companies with S&T innovations usually focus on corporate experience, nature of the product, and size of potential market for the innovation.[10] The nature of the product is defined in terms of enjoying the protection of a patent, and having technological attributes that are unique and not easily copied. Hence, financial analysts look more favorably upon companies that have new products in which the technology is unique and provides the product with competitive functionality.

Cost Savings

Another major category of economic value created by S&T is savings in the cost of activities, processes, and product in the corporation.[11] Savings and subsequent cost reductions lead to competitive advantages in dynamic markets. Similar value is also created when cost reductions allow the company to better allocate its resources and to apply means of restructuring hitherto impossible.

Following Christensen's logic, cost savings from incremental innovations (especially in processes) would facilitate competition and retention of market share even when the focal company is not a leader in the industry. By using proven technologies, entrepreneurial companies are able to gain market share with products that are cheaper to make. The Finnish telecommunication company, Nokia, is an illustration of such penetration and gain of market share for cellular telephones.[12]

In 1999 Nokia had a worldwide share of almost a third of the market for handsets. Sales and profits have continually increased by 30-40 percent annually. Although many analysts credit Nokia's success to its marketing and branding techniques, the company's strongest competitive asset has been the manufacture of products with an abundance of desired features, yet *at a very competitive price*. This the company was able to accomplish by implementing technological innovations in its manufacturing facilities, so as to attain a desired level of quality and cost that would remain highly competitive.[13]

Value from Incremental and Radical Innovations

Are there differences between economic value derived from incremental (evolutionary) technological innovations and those that may be considered radical or revolutionary? Figure 14.4 offered a framework for analysis. Following the "snake curve" in the figure, companies derive value from incremental innovations in two basic modes.

The first is by *increasing returns*, as the technological innovation is adapted and becomes established in the product or service. The second is by the cumulative addition of economic benefits, so that the innovation becomes entrenched and difficult to replace. Benefits accrue to the company as ancillary industries are created and also become entrenched.[14]

Radical innovations are somewhat different in the way they contribute value to the company. In cases of a hypercompetitive market, contributions from technological innovations are attenuated by the way the market reacts to and accepts such innovations. When a "linking familiarity" is inherent in the technological innovation, the market will be more prone to accept the product in which the innovation is embedded, hence to allow for a more durable existence in the market. This, in turn, translates into increasing returns over a longer period of time. Thus, as a revolutionary innovation displaces and replaces the established product or service, the company that introduced it has a better opportunity to exploit this introduction over time, if and when the company is able to "sell" it to the market so as to gain acceptance and subsequent continuous adoption.

Unlike incremental innovations, the radical innovation, in order for it to be adequately exploited by the company, must be amenable to the market's idiosyncratic demands. Some of these demands are psychological tendencies of consumers, such as fear of the unknown and anything radically new, and fads and fashion trends.[15]

This boils down to "management of change," as companies who wish to successfully introduce radical innovation into the marketplace have to master networking, the understanding of currents of resistance to change that underlie market trends, and the challenge of presenting the innovation in favorable terms.

After the fact, we tend to admire companies who launched a revolutionary technology and reaped handsome returns over long periods. We are amazed at how their radical innovation displaced the incumbent and how it established new standards. Besides simple luck, these companies succeeded because they had excelled in at least three aspects of their endeavor: timing, mode of introduction, and integration.

Timing

The first aspect is the fact that they correctly estimated the timing of introducing the innovation. Timing is closely tied to the market's absorptive capacity and its "readiness" to accept a radical departure from established practices. Such timing is almost impossible to accurately assess, but some companies evaluate their markets and instinctively conclude that "the time is right."

For example, when General Electric introduced its Computerized Axial Tomography (CAT scan) in 1975, there were several competing interests within the company.[16] The key executives at the time were Jack Welch, vice-president of the components and material group, in charge also of medical systems (he later became CEO), and Walter Robb, head of medical systems. The company opted for a new and largely untested technology (fan-beam), and in favor of developing and marketing a full-body scanner. Marketing estimates were at best fuzzy, and as Robb explained: "We came up with it off the top of our head."[17] To complicate matters, the consulting firm of Booz, Allen & Hamilton recommended that the fan-beam technology should not be applied, and that GE should use a more proven technology.

Jack Welch and Walter Robb made a decision to exploit—what they believed to be—a window of opportunity, and to introduce their system in a timely fashion to an uncertain market. The decision was based on a combination of trust in the technological competence of the company, strong "hunch," and support from senior GE management of the risk associated with their decision.[18]

Mode of Introduction

Successful exploitation of technological innovation also requires adequacy in the mode of introduction. This aspect involves such dimensions as functionality and design of the product or service within which the innovative technology is embedded.

Consider the functionality of the product and imagine implementing a radical technology in a format that falls short of performing to the extent promised, advertised, or expected by the market. In the specific case where functionality depends on the technological capabilities of the product, in the eyes of the market and potential consumers, the product and its embedded technology are one and the same.

Functionality usually relates to attributes: How well does the product work? How fast does it perform? How accurately? How simple to operate? How economical? In the case of a radical technological innovation, the superiority of performance that allowed for its replacing the incumbent would be based on the competency of the new technology to offer a total departure from established practice, or to break the physical limits of the established technology. However, in any of these cases, the radical technology must outperform the incumbent—at first—in at least one dimension.[19] Figure 15.2 shows the superiority of the radical innovation.

Figure 15.2
Radical Technological Innovation: Cases in Superiority
of Performance and Functionality

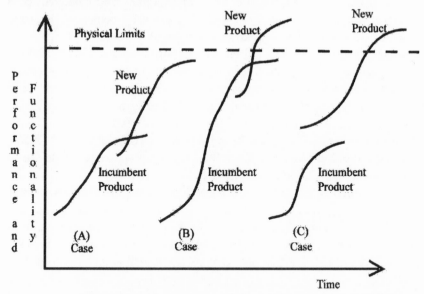

Case (A) =   New product is superior in *functionality* but has not gone beyond physical limits of the technology. This is a much better product but not revolutionary.

Case (B) =   New product is superior in its *technological* departure from established practice and limits on performance.

Case (C) =   New product is much superior in *both* functionality and in its revolutionary technology, at the very moment of its launch into the marketplace.

Although technological innovations that are disruptive will lead to new entrants' successful penetration, consumers will in the final analysis determine the *continuous* success of the new product.[20] Based on functionality and economics, consumers will redefine the competitive landscape and rearrange the order of leadership in the industry.[21] Hence, expectations of what the new product can do must be met and even excelled. Superiority in performance is crucial, but so is superiority in design.

Design, Robots, and "Flying Octopi"

Much of the successful introduction and continuous market presence of new products embedded with radical innovations depend on their design. If companies introduce products whose design is "unfriendly" to consumers, chances are that consumers will not accept these products, however high-performance they may be. Successful companies who enjoy long-standing winning services and products continually send employees (from various levels and departments) to explore and understand how the products are utilized by their customers, and how their design and utility can be improved. Honda, DuPont, Marriott, and Southwest Airlines are some of these companies.

But, in the case of revolutionary technology [such as case (C) in Figure 15.2], consumers will naturally be overwhelmed by the technological competence of the product—it's totally new, different, and threateningly high performance. Consumers feel the need to be comforted by elements of the design that allow for "linking familiarity." This notion, described in Chapter 14, suggests that the revolutionary product should retain one or more elements in its design that resemble established (incumbent) products.

Imagine, for instance, that we design a domestic robot, in charge of the chores of cleaning and serving. A revolutionary technology will allow the robot to be imbued with abilities of defiance of gravity and ultrasensorial attributes. This, by itself, is highly menacing and apprehensive to the user. Now, imagine that we build the robot to look, not as a person, but as an octopus, with several tentacles with suction ability, and capable of flying. Such a "flying octopus" will be totally unfamiliar to the potential user, because of its strange looks, and the difficulties of manipulating and working with the robot. Clearly, when a design of a product is familiar, consumers have an easier task of working with it, and the interface becomes much more manageable.[22]

Integration

The third aspect of successful and lasting introduction of revolutionary innovations is the adequacy of integration with established products and networks. For example, the introduction of scanning technology (MRI, PET) in hospitals was facilitated by its coherence with existing diagnostic products, and its integration with computer technology.

When a revolutionary technology is embedded in a new product, the adoption process will be much less difficult, lengthy, and costly when the new product is compatible with existing systems. Issues of connectivity and adaptability become paramount variables that may help to derail the successful path of utilization and acceptance by consumers.

This proposition was examined in the retail banking industry.[23] The study found that adopters of *radical innovations* had higher levels of organizational integration. Hence, stand-alone radical innovations have an additional hurdle to overcome, and a difficult time in "getting acclimated" or integrated into the existing systems. A similar case occurred with the introduction of new residential lighting technology in the 1980s. Although compact fluorescent lamps had a distinct superiority over incumbents, large-scale adoption was constrained by issues of lack of integration, compatibility, and familiarity.[24]

So for radical innovations to become successful introductions in the marketplace, consumers need to: (1) gain understanding of the superiority of the product, service, and technology; (2) perceive that their expectations are met; (3) be familiar with the product's features and feel at ease with its use; and (4) consider its integration with the existing system—even when the new product or service replaces an incumbent.[25] It is not enough for the company to develop and launch a technologically superior product. It must adjust and tailor it to the requirements of the consumers. If this were not the case, our homes would gladly welcome the "flying octopi!"

WHAT COMPANIES WANT AND WHAT S&T CAN DELIVER

The question: "What do companies want from S&T?" is different than "Why do companies innovate?" The answer to the former question may illuminate the latter but not answer it entirely. What companies want from S&T is a variety of goals, desires, and the fulfilment of needs. Usually these may vary across industries, and by such attributes as the size of the firm. Yet there are several basic and identifiable "things" that all companies want from S&T.

The "things" that business companies want from S&T can be divided into three categories, shown in Figure 15.3: (1) external needs and expectations, (2) internal needs and expectations, and (3) intangibles.

External Factors

Companies want, need, and expect their S&T to assist them in dealing with external factors that are inherent in keeping the organization competitive.

Figure 15.3
Needs, Goals, and Expectations of Companies from Their S&T

NEEDS, GOALS, EXPECTATIONS
A.   Related to *external* factors, such as: competitive position in the marketplace; survival; customer requirements; stakeholders' requirements and expectations; regulatory exigencies and compliance.
B.   Related to *internal* factors, such as: efficiency of operations; cost-savings and cost-cutting; improved utilization of scarce resources; effective managerial and organizational processes of control, communication, decision-making, and coordination.
C.   Related to *intangibles*, such as: prestige; pride; social responsibility; fads and fashion; and cultural factors.

The complexity of the company's external environment is such that there are many "stakeholders," each with its own needs, requirements, and expectations.[26] The proposition that S&T (or R&D) in the company can and should primarily lead to shareholder value and increased net worth may be in line with prevailing theories of the firm, but it grossly underestimates the complex array of stakeholders.[27]

Customers, regulators, cultural trends, and vendors exert their relative pressures on corporate management to satisfy these stakeholders' needs and to meet their expectations. Figure 15.4 shows the key actors who determine what the needs, wants, and expectations of the company are.

To a degree, all of the factors listed in Figure 15.4 and the inputs from the actors are filtered through the reasoning of senior management. In some companies, the result of such compilation of data and diverse interests may be translated into technology policy and planning. But, in most companies, the resulting outcome is an informal agreement on what to expect from S&T and what should be the needs and requirements from it. At best, such needs and expectations are spelled out to a certain degree in the tasks assigned to the R&D function in the company, and may form a source of reasoning in creating criteria for selection of S&T projects and allocation of resources for R&D.[28]

External factors account for the firm's overall need to maintain its competitive position in the marketplace, and to grow and expand. This is the link between S&T and strategy, advocated by many students of management of science and technology.[29] Briefly, the link is based on the question: What is the role of S&T in the sustained success, growth, and survival of the company? Proponents of the notion of "alignment" or "integration" of S&T and strategy in the firm start out with the conviction that S&T indeed crucially impacts success, growth, and survival.[30]

Figure 15.4
Key Actors and Other Factors Determining What Companies
Want, Need, and Expect from S&T

KEY ACTORS	
• Senior Management	• Regulators
• Stockholders	• Employees
• Customers	• Competitors
• Vendors	• S&T Professionals
	(scientists and engineers)
FACTORS, CONDITIONS, AND OTHER SOURCES	
◆ Corporate S&T policy (to the extent it exists)	
◆ State of the art in general management and in management of S&T	
◆ Quality and level of knowledge of senior management	
◆ Customs, culture, and traditions of the corporation	
◆ S&T state of the art	
◆ History of the industry in S&T and its management and utilization	
◆ Social factors, e.g., social responsibility	

But there is a difference between advocating the strategy—S&T alignment—and the reality of corporate behavior and structure. In the vast majority of companies, the link between external factors (condensed into the strategic plan) and the S&T planning, resources allocation, and project selection and prioritizing is, at best, tenuous, manifested in the form of inputs to deliberations of committees in charge of S&T policy. Alignment is seldom unambiguously defined, nor is it formally established.[31]

Why such discrepancy between theory and actual corporate behavior? The answer lies in the complex nature of both the strategy process and S&T evaluation. Gaps exist between strategy formulation—which considers external factors and demands—and its implementation into the different functions of the firm. Since precise evaluation of S&T impacts on survival and competitiveness is not a feasible and on-going practice in corporate assessments, a formal and continuous link between S&T (R&D) and strategy remains a desired state of affairs, rather than a plausible reality.[32] Companies will focus their S&T efforts as closely as possible on the external factors that are more visible and more "threatening," so that "the squeaky wheel gets the oil."

Paradox of S&T Evaluation and Disruptive Innovations

This state of affairs brings about a paradox, which can be described as follows:

The more S&T producers attempt to bridge the relevancy gap and to apply users' criteria and metrics to their own reasoning and processes, the less likely are they to produce technology that will replace the existing technology, and the less likely are they to recognize such radical and disruptive technologies.

Not only do such companies fail to generate S&T that can compete effectively with the advanced innovators in their industry, but they also lack the abilities to recognize such technologies. They also lack the intellectual tools to become aware of changing conditions, that invariably lead to disruptive innovations arriving and creating havoc in the industry.

As Christensen correctly explained, managers of these companies are not caught napping at the wheel, but they fail because they are diligently following the tenets of good, yet shortsighted management practices.[33] In essence, what companies want are incremental innovations that keep the enterprise going, with reasonable competitive power. Internally, S&T and these innovations assist the various functions of the company, and help to solve problems. These benefits from S&T are relatively easy to justify, demonstrate, and to measure.

Radical and disruptive technologies tend to create new businesses and new beginnings. They disrupt the existing relations with customers and suppliers, they are very hard to predict and to justify, and almost impossible to manage with the company's existing structure and processes. Companies end up "cannibalizing" their resources, thus creating havoc. Christensen proposed the creation of spin-off companies, similar to the practices of some companies in creating incubators and "skunk works," and in spinning off new businesses to their own fate, with their own resources.

The paradox has several implications. First, the obvious lesson for companies is that their focus on internal factors and being attuned to customers undermines their ability for long-term survival. Second, unless *external* factors (see Figure 15.3) are not only taken into account and S&T strategically evaluated, management will lack the means to avoid self-destruction.

However, self-destruction is not inevitable. Disruptive innovations are hypercompetition under a different name. Strategic implications of radical technological innovations can be understood and acted upon only if the company has the competencies to realize their significance. Such competencies are gained by being engaged in or extremely interested in strategic S&T: What's on the horizon, and how much does it matter to us?[34]

Internal Factors

As shown in Figure 15.3, companies expect their S&T to meet *internal* needs. Paramount among these are efficiency factors, savings and cutting of costs, and the assistance given to operating units in solving problems. These benefits from S&T provide actual value to the company that can be measured and assessed.

When costs are visibly reduced, problems are being solved in production or customer relations, and when the efficiency of operations is increased, S&T (corporate or divisional R&D) can be justified and positively evaluated. These are matters for the "here and now" that S&T is helping to resolve and manage. These are not concerns about "over the horizon" threats which may or may not crystallize in the near future. So when resources in the company are carefully allocated, whatever can support the current operations receives priority.[35]

With such cultural determinants, corporate R&D will first ensure its survival as a viable corporate unit. Hence its emphasis will be on the creation of outcomes whose benefits can be easily measured and assessed without delay. Justification for subsequent funding is the key. Clearly, internal factors will be at least as important as those external benefits that, although crucial to the firm's survival, are nevertheless difficult to measure and justify.[36]

What S&T Can Do (from the Company's Perspective)

The S&T function in the firm can deliver a variety of outcomes, which then are transformed into benefits to the organization. Figure 15.5 shows these outcomes, grouped by the category of corporate factors they may address.

But, although Figure 15.5 is a more elaborate list than appeared in Figure 15.1, it nevertheless depicts the "desired" or potential outcomes from S&T in the company. In reality, S&T (or R&D) produces outcomes in the form of knowledge (bibliometrics), prototypes, and information (in the form of advice, problem-solving, and altogether a technological database or warehouse). These outcomes are then transformed by other units of the company to generate desired and expected benefits. Much, therefore, depends on the process of S&T in the company, how well R&D works with the rest of the company, and how successfully the company transforms the outcomes into benefits.[37]

To illustrate this broader picture, Figure 15.6 shows the relationship between what companies want from S&T and what S&T can deliver. This figure combines the previous figures in this chapter to present a bird's-eye view of the complex phenomenon: how value is created from S&T.

Figure 15.6 shows that along the innovation continuum, and in the process of new product development, the delivery of S&T outcomes is not enough to produce and maintain value to the company. Economic value is

Figure 15.5
What S&T Can Do (from the Company's Perspective)

EXTERNALLY ORIENTED OUTCOMES*
• New products and services • Incremental improvements in products and services • S&T knowledge as marketable, intellectual property • Receiving, processing, warehousing, and diffusing S&T knowledge from outside the company • Technological solutions to problems of safety, environment, and similar regulations • Quality standards • Solving technological problems for customers
INTERNALLY ORIENTED OUTCOMES*
• Improvements in processes and operations • Contributions to increased efficiency in processes and operations • Replacing people with technology • Replacing antiquated technology • Knowledge on processes, methods, techniques, procedures • Cost cutting and cost savings

Not necessarily in order of priority or importance.

created when the company is able to overcome such factors as its ability to commercialize innovations and market response.

Key Issues: Meeting Expectations and Creating Value

As shown in Figure 15.6 there are two key issues: (1) how S&T outcomes meet the expectations and needs of the company, and (2) how S&T creates value, once these expectations are met. The first issue reflects the matter of how companies manage their S&T. The second focuses on the company's ability to transform S&T outcomes into value. This involves managing not only S&T but also other units and functions of the firm.[38]

So the main lesson from this complex phenomenon can be summarized as:

> A company that is able to adequately resolve *both* issues, namely, how S&T outcomes meet company needs and how they are commercialized to create economic value, will be successful in extracting meaningful and durable value from S&T.

This proposition explains the case of companies that generate S&T outcomes—even as "first movers"—but are unable to translate these outcomes

Figure 15.6
Summary of What Companies Want from S&T and What S&T Can Deliver

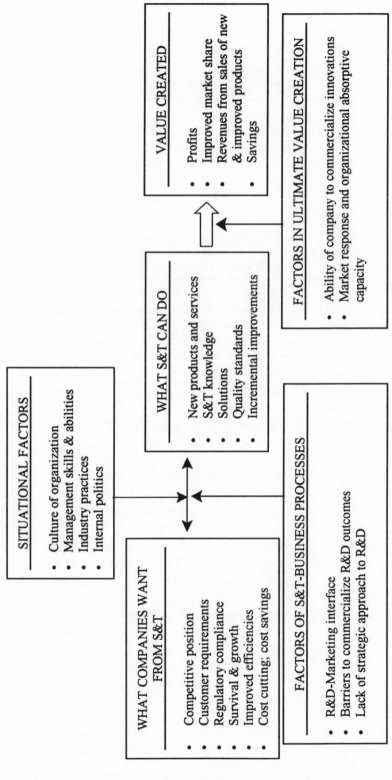

into durable value, such as Sony's Betamax videocassette recorder introduced in 1975. Although first in the market, Sony lost its market share to the Video Home System (VHS) introduced in 1976 by Japan Victor Corporation (JVC).[39] Sony was able to generate an innovative product, but failed to transform this achievement into economic value.

Similarly, there are many other examples of successful *technological* innovations that failed in the marketplace. CompuAd/NewsAd was a superior product that created advertising for the real estate industry, but failed to gain a foothold in the market.[40] Overall, rate of market failure of innovative products is around 30 percent, and this rate has been relatively constant across industries for several decades.[41]

Recently, some authors have been advocating for companies to accept the need for failure of their technological innovations as the reality of the new, fast-paced economy.[42] To the extent that new products are rushed into the market, some degree of market failure is almost inevitable, regardless of how successful the technology is embedded in the new product or service.

A corollary case is when companies fail to generate the S&T outcome. In 1982, Digital Equipment Corporation (DEC) introduced its Rainbow computer and in its PCs had installed DOS 8086 architecture. Yet in the decade that followed, DEC failed to introduce personal computers that would even compete with other vendors, hence it ceased to play a major role in the PC market.[43]

In summary, a company needs to manage both its S&T and new product development, and its commercialization and marketing processes. In many instances it is hardly enough to meet the needs and expectations of the company. Emphasizing some of these needs may lead to the phenomenon of creative destruction described earlier in this chapter. Durable value is created when there are both S&T and market successes.

SO, WHY DO COMPANIES INNOVATE AND WHAT VALUE DO THEY GAIN FROM S&T?

With at least 30 percent of new products failing in the marketplace, and at least half of corporate S&T projects never graduating to prototypes, why would companies engage in S&T at all? There are several reasons, some already mentioned in this book. None of these reasons, by itself, explains corporate S&T effort. But, taken together, the picture that emerges summarizes the dimension of this unique phenomenon.

Cultural Imperative

Since the middle of the 20th century, industrial companies have acquired and carefully cultivated a culture that promoted the role of R&D (S&T) in product as well as corporate success.[44] Embraced by "technologists" and managers alike, the tenets of the cultural framework became protective across industries. Thus, aided by increased academic studies, energetic management consultants, and heightened expectations from a public fascinated by S&T—companies increasingly based their growth, survival, and profitability on technological innovations.[45]

Much of the literature on S&T management focused on improving the process. Here the questions emphasize the entire company and *why* it practices S&T. When, in some "high technology" industries, companies invest up to 20 percent of sales in S&T, namely, developing next-generation products and services, there is ample reason to question such behavior. This is particularly logical in the current state of affairs where we are unable to unambiguously compute the value gained from S&T, or to *directly* and causally connect such value to the investments in S&T.

In the absence of a truly convincing economic justification for S&T, the answer to why companies engage in S&T may also be attributed to the cultural appreciation of how S&T contributes to corporate growth, success, and survival. Thus, the belief in the role of S&T in corporate life has continually grown over the past 50 years. Such belief grew in parallel to the strong favorable attitudes of the American public toward S&T as a dramatic force that shapes and reshapes almost every aspect of our lives—including corporate achievements. So corporate managers also exhibit cultural values that treat S&T as a key element in overall corporate success[46]

Relation to Sales

Companies innovate because one of the tenets of the relation between S&T and corporate success is the link between technological innovations and corporate sales. Consider the share of new products in the annual sales of the company. New products are generally defined as those products introduced in the previous three-year period. Exact figures for this share vary by industry, but overall, in the late 1990s the average was 30-40 percent of sales.[47]

This dependence on a stream of new products creates expectations not only within the company but also in the marketplace. Customers, suppliers, and competitors are "conditioned" to a continuous appearance of new products that are driven by technological innovations.

Market Competition

Propelled by individual companies who continuously innovate, markets become more competitive. As the share of new products generating sales and market share continues to grow, competition becomes increasingly dominant as a force that determines corporate behavior in the marketplace. Incumbents are heavily threatened by new technology innovators, hence many of the existing rules of coexistence are defined and redefined.

This pattern of events also generates continuous change, whose dynamics tends to create the condition Richard D'Aveni called "hypercompetition."[48] By engaging in such "cut-throat" competitive behavior—fueled by S&T and innovations—industries resemble battle fields, and competitors are exhausted combatants, unable to maintain sustained competitive advantages. Hence leaders in the industry tend to lose their edge to newcomers.[49]

Economists have also argued that companies with high market shares tend to innovate in a preemptive move, to deter competitors. Similarly, when product market competition in the industry increases, this tends to stimulate technological innovation.[50]

There is a consistent, positive correlation between technological innovation and product market competition. This relation presents the apparent problem of "the chicken and the egg"—who came first: increased innovations or the existence of competition? Companies are both creators of conditions and affected by such market conditions. From the individual company's viewpoint, there is hardly a way out. It doesn't matter who came first. Competitive markets require, in the view of the firm, continuous technological innovation in order to survive and to succeed. This becomes "the name of the game," thus played by all.

Technology Addiction

In the late 1990s, companies and management scholars have begun to study some addiction disorders among workers that could be attributed to the ubiquitous use of technology in the workplace.[51] Workers are discovering that technology may be as addictive as a powerful drug. Experts have named such dependencies "Netaholics" and "Internet Addiction Disorder."[52]

But such behavior may also be found at the level of the firm. In hypercompetitive markets, companies become addicted to technology. In order to effectively compete, companies need a steady flow of new products. The competitive effort is driven by technology. Therefore, companies are caught in the cycle of generating S&T and new products and services, and facing devastating transformations *vis-à-vis* competitive innovations. The "game" is fascinating, yet addictive, and the driving force is technology.[53]

The Concept and Reality of the Technology Race

Should we reconsider individual and corporate addiction to technology? Should the tantalizing pace of technological change be reduced or somehow attenuated? In the foreseeable future the pace may even increase, as technology will breed and encourage the generation of more technology.

Practically, corporations are in the midst of a "technology race," similar to the "arms race" of the cold war. The concept of a technology race is defined as the feverish and competitive pursuit and accumulation of technological innovations and technology-driven assets, without a specified final objective or time limitation in the minds of the competitors.[54] When companies continue to launch new products and services, and when the time to market is continually reduced, the race is out of control. Competition becomes the objective itself, rather than the means to achieving strategic objectives. "Success in competing" becomes the new war cry, substituting the traditional "competing *for* success."

Is there any value created for the company and for society from this maddening pursuit? Some value is derived from regular economic outcomes, while other forms of value are inherent in the transformations themselves, where companies and entire industries are replaced, redefined, and periodically reenergized. In a broader sense, this is the essence of the phenomenon of General Purpose Technologies, as described below.

The Notion of General Purpose Technologies

In recent years some economists have attempted to identify the notion of what they call General Purpose Technologies (GPTs). These are revolutionary technological innovations—such as the steam engine, electricity, internal combustion, and computers—that drastically change not only a company or an industry, but have sustained implications that reverberate throughout the economy.[55] Such technologies cast a vast shadow on a variety of social systems, and produce transformations in the behavior of individuals and organizations. The internal combustion engine produced the network of interstate highways, aviation, and a radical transformation in how people work, live, and spend their leisure time.

Models of economic growth thus allow for such radical technologies to be an explanatory variable for growth cycles. One such model proposed that economic growth is driven by both the radical displacement of key technologies (emerging GPT) and the incremental innovations in *components* for the new GPT.[56] By extension, as new components are being created, their impacts on vendors, customers, and social processes are also being felt.

General Purpose Technologies are different from other radical technological innovations (that generate disruptions and dissipation of comparative advantages in business firms) because their disruptive effects are felt beyond the boundaries of the firm. They impact social processes and individual behavior.[57]

How society exploits S&T is described in the next chapter. Social transformations due to S&T are a mix of positive and negative effects. With a combination of their "cascading effects" and disruptive power, GPTs change the world in which we live to such an extent that many other aspects of our existence (e.g., social intercourse, work traditions, and religious and ethical beliefs) are left behind, struggling to catch up.

COMPUTATIONAL NATURE OF S&T VALUE TO THE COMPANY

How much should the company invest in S&T (R&D) to obtain a certain level of economic growth and economic rents or returns? In some industries (such as pharmaceuticals and consumer electronics) companies invest in excess of 15 percent of their annual sales figures. On average, industrial companies invest about 2-4 percent of sales. Examples from the 20 top industrial S&T investors are given in Figure 15.7.

The simple average R&D expenditures of the top 20 companies in 1997 was 8.87 percent of sales. In the period 1998-2000, industrial companies increased their expenditures for R&D (in current dollars), but as a percent of sales the ratio may have remained the same as in 1997 or even lower, due to the prosperous U.S. economy in that period.[58] The average of about 9 percent for the top 20 companies is two to three times higher than the overall industrial norm.

A growing consensus among scholars is the belief that industrial companies underinvest in S&T. Some argue that it takes an *increase* of 4 percent per year in R&D expenditures to obtain a 3 percent rate of economic growth. Few companies invest enough in S&T to ensure future growth and prosperity.[59] But, as already discussed earlier in this chapter, S&T intensity is only one factor in the complex phenomenon of growth and market success.

To accrue value to the company, the computational nature of the phenomenon is the sum of the factors, as shown in the equation below:

$$\text{Value} = \sum_{i=1}^{5} (I + C_t + D + E + O)_{ij} W_j$$

and

$$\sum_{j=1}^{m} w_j = 1$$

where:

Figure 15.7
R&D Intensity of the Top American Companies in 1997:
R&D Expenditures as Percent of Sales

Company	R&D Expenditures (billions of current dollars)	Percent of 1997 Sales
General Motors	8.20	4.88%
Ford Motor Co.	6.32	4.10%
IBM	4.30	5.47%
Lucent Technologies	3.10	11.78%
Hewlett-Packard	3.07	7.15%
Motorola	2.74	9.19%
Intel	2.34	9.36%
Johnson & Johnson	2.14	9.46%
Pfizer Inc.	1.92	15.36%
Microsoft	1.92	16.90%
Boeing	1.92	4.19%
Chrysler	1.70	2.89%
Merck & Co.	1.68	7.10%
American Home Products	1.55	10.92%
General Electric	1.48	1.67%
Bristol-Myers Squibb	1.38	8.26%
Eli Lilly & Co.	1.38	16.20%
Abbott Labs.	1.30	10.94%
Procter & Gamble	1.28	3.57%
Pharmacia-Upjohn	1.21	18.03%

Source: National Science Foundation, *Science and Engineering Indicators 2000* (Washington, DC, 2000) Vol. 1, p. 2-26.

I = Immediate outputs from corporate R&D activities, such as patents, bibliometrics, and rents they produce.

C_t = Internal company benefits from R&D activities and immediate outputs, such as cost-cutting and cost-savings. (Question: how much of cost-cutting or saving can be attributed to S&T outputs?)

D = Downstream outcomes, such as sales, profits, market share, customer loyalty, and the monetary equivalent of these outcomes.

E = Externalities, such as prestige and good name, and economic rents they produce.

O = Overall benefits, such as survival and growth.

Value is computed as the economic rents accrued from all of these factors, attenuated by relative weights as measures of importance. For example, if a company considers downstream outputs more vital to its strategy than the gains from immediate outputs, it will assign a higher weight to this factor. Weights are indicative of the role of value from S&T in corporate thinking. Moreover, this computational framework will be reflected in resources allocation. The company will allocate more resources to those factors with higher weights, hence considered more important to its vital strategies.

To an extent, and with some degree of accuracy, all the factors in the equation may be expressed in economic terms to reflect the economic rents they generate for the firm.[60] The remaining issues are: (1) how to measure these economic rents? and (2) how to attribute them to S&T in the firm, in light of all the other variables that influence the firm's economic activity? Adequate answers and solutions are yet to be found.

SUMMARY

Regardless the actual quantity of value from S&T created by the company, the most crucial aspect of economic value from S&T is in the broader view of the company as it competes in its environment. S&T may generate a rate of return of 10, 20, or 50 percent, yet these are hardly a sufficient nor adequate measure of S&T value. Reliance on contributions to sales, profits, and market share leads to a myopic view of only a portion of what S&T delivers.

S&T delivers economic value by generating immediate producers of wealth (such as new products leading to sales, revenues, and profits) and downstream outcomes that benefit the company (such as development of new markets, customer satisfaction, customer loyalty, and meeting regulatory exigencies).[61]

There is a pervasive belief in today's companies that technological innovation is a key driver of competition and economic growth, and that this trend will continue in the foreseeable future. Value from S&T is therefore the sum of all the benefits accrued to the company from its internal R&D and S&T adopted from external sources.

How Companies Exploit S&T: Key Propositions

Industrial companies exploit S&T innovations by integrating them into their processes and activities. The outcomes from S&T are thus embedded in products, processes, market measures, and tactics and strategies. S&T innovations are similar to other resources the firm uses and transforms, such as human resources and facilities. When a company invests, for example, 10 percent of sales to generate S&T, it will also invest similar, perhaps larger amounts on adoption, adaptation, and utilization of S&T innovation from all sources.

Eight propositions listed below may summarize the key dimensions and factors that influence the firm's creation of value from S&T, as discussed throughout this book. The propositions are not an exhaustive set that summarizes the topic: how companies generate economic value from S&T. But they do provide a flavor, or an indication, of the key elements of an analytical framework of this phenomenon.

Proposition 1:   Companies exploit S&T and generate value from it by integrating S&T outcomes into their on-going and planned processes and activities.

Proposition 2:   Value extracted from S&T and innovations is diffused throughout the company, in a variety of activities and functional units.

Proposition 3:   Paradox of S&T evaluation states that the more S&T producers attempt to bridge the relevancy gap and to apply users' criteria and metrics to their own reasoning and processes, the less likely they are to produce technology that will replace the existing technology, and the less likely are they to recognize such radical and disruptive technologies.

Proposition 4:   A company that is able to adequately resolve the issues of how S&T outcomes meet company needs and how they are commercialized to create economic value will be successful in extracting meaningful and durable value from S&T.

Proposition 5:   The concept of "linking familiarity" states that for revolutionary products to be successfully introduced, adopted, and integrated into the company's processes and activities, their design should retain one or more elements that resemble established (incumbent) products or processes.

Proposition 6:   In the absence of a truly convincing economic justification for S&T, companies engage in S&T because of their cultural application of how S&T contributes to corporate growth, success, and survival.

Proposition 7:   The utilization of information technology in the creation of value nets and business-to-business networks based on the power of the Internet are illustrations of how S&T creates value beyond the immediate benefits to companies, such as using the Internet for communication purposes.[62]

Proposition 8: The diffusion of S&T innovations obeys the "law of preponderant diffusion." This law states that due to the existence of communities of science and their equivalent in technology, S&T innovations propagate, cross-fertilize, and create value—regardless of the disciplinary area or the targeted objectives of the S&T original effort (e.g., investments in social S&T objectives versus investments in military S&T).[63]

These propositions provide some key building-blocks of what constitutes the phenomenon of creating value from S&T. Companies indeed benefit from S&T in various ways, some of which we are able to identify and measure, others which we can only estimate and conjecture. But the overall picture is that the company does much better with than without S&T. Exploiting the benefits from S&T does not, by itself, guarantee commercial success, but it is certainly a key ingredient in the success and growth of those companies who are able to negotiate both S&T and the business aspects of their operations.

NOTES

1. See, for example, the early work of Edwin Mansfield in Mansfield, E., "Technical Change and the Rate of Imitation," *Econometrica*, 29(2), 1961, 741-766; and Mansfield, E., "Intrafirm Rates of Diffusion of an Innovation," *Review of Economics and Statistics*, 45(3), 1963, 348-359; and, more recently, Mansfield, E., "How Rapidly Does New Industrial Technology Leak Out?" *Journal of Industrial Economics*, 34(2), 1985, 217-223.

2. Arrow, K., "Preface: Edwin Mansfield's Research on Technology and Innovation," *International Journal of Technology Management*, 19(1/2), 2000, 1-3.

3. See, for example, Sivadas, E. and R. Dwyer, "An Examination of Organizational Factors Influencing New Product Success in Internal and Alliance-Based Processes," *Journal of Marketing*, 64(1), 2000, 31-49.

4. Booz, Allen & Hamilton, *New Product Development in the 1980s* (New York, 1982).

5. See, for example, Banbury, C., and W. Mitchell, "The Effect of Introducing Important Incremental Innovations on Market Share and Business Survival," *Strategic Management Journal*, 16 (Special Issue), 1995, 161-183.

6. Grant, L., "Gillette Knows Shaving—And How to Turn Out Hot New Products," *Fortune*, 134(7), 1996, 207-208.

7. Christensen, C., *The Innovator's Dilemma* (New York: HarperBusiness, 2000), see pp. 138-139.

8. Evangelista, R., G. Perani, F. Rapiti, and D. Archibugi, "Nature and Impact of Innovation in Manufacturing Industry: Some Evidence from the Italian Innovation Survey," *Research Policy*, 26(4,5), 1997, 541-536.

9. See, for example, McDonald, D., "Ewe and Your Money: How to Profit from Discoveries," *Money*, 26(4), 1997, 71-72. Also see Strock, O., *Engineering for Profit* (Boca Raton, FL: CRC Press, 1994). See, Razgaitis, R., *Early-Stage Technologies: Valuation and Pricing* (New York: John Wiley & Sons, 1999). In particular, see Method Five: Advanced Valuation.

10. See, for example, McDonald, 1997, *op. cit.*; and Canavan, J., "The Seemingly Impossible Task of Staying Up with Technology," *Information Strategy*, 15(4), 1999, 40-43; and see Campbell, R., "Does Technology Deliver?", *Bankers Monthly*, 109(3), 1992, 17-23.

11. By categorizing the values in Figure 14.4 into "sales from new products" and "cost savings," I have created a duality that can be traced to Michael Porter and his proposed strategies for competitiveness. Porter distinguished between product differentiation, focus (identification of buyer group or target segment), and cost competitiveness. Product differentiation would thus benefit from S&T and innovative characteristics, whereas S&T may also contribute to cost savings. See Porter, M., *Competitive Strategy* (New York: Free Press, 1980).

12. See, Harbert, T., "A Tale of Two Mobile Telephone Makers," *Electronic Business*, 26(5), 2000, 88-98.

13. See interviews with Nokia's CEO Jorma Ollila in, for example, *Industry Week*, "Nokia Corporation: CEO Sees Exceptional Growth," 249(4), 2000, 54-56; and see Zizzo, T., "Nokia Continues to Dominate Cell Phone Market," *Electronic Business*, 26(2), 2000, 38-40.

14. See, for example, Cooper, R., S. Edgett, and E. Kleinschmidt, *Portfolio Management for New Products* (Reading, MA: Addison-Wesley, 1998). Also see Klavans, R., *Identifying the Research Underlying Technical Competitive Intelligence: Keeping Abreast of Science and Technology* (Columbus, OH: Battelle Memorial Institute, 1997).

15. See, for example, the case of the information technology industry, in Moschella, D., *Waves of Power: The Dynamics of Global Technology Leadership, 1964-2010* (New York: Amacom, 1997); and see Kemerer, C., (Ed.), *Information Technology and Industrial Competitiveness: How It Shapes Competition* (Boston: Kluwer Academic Publishers, 1997). Also see, in the case of R&D, compilation of the practices of 18 companies who introduced new products globally, in Bouteller, R., O. Gassman, and Zedtwitz, M., *Managing Global Innovation: Uncovering the Secrets of Future Competitiveness* (New York: Springer-Verlag, 1999).

16. See an excellent narrative of how GE developed and marketed its CAT scanners, in Lynn, G., "Marketing of Medical Technology: GE's Computerized Axial Tomography (CAT Scanning)," in Geisler, E., and O. Heller, *Management of Medical Technology: Theory, Practice, and Cases* (Boston: Kluwer Academic Publishers, 1998), pp. 469-502. Also see Walter Robb's discussion of such risky decisions in: Robb, W., "Is Your Corporate Lab Taking Enough Risk?", *Research-Technology Management*, 43(3), 2000, 31-33.

17. Lynn, 1998, *op. cit.*, p. 488.

18. The decision, as with most decisions of this kind, was also based on their understanding the technology, and the peculiarities of their relevant market, however sketchy such knowledge might have been. See, for example, Laupacis, A., D. Feeny, A. Detsky, and P. Tugwell, "How Attractive Does a New Technology Have to be to Warrant Adoption and Utilization? Tentative Guidelines for Using Clinical and Economic Evaluations," *Canadian Medical Association Journal*, 146(4), 1992, 473-481. Also, in a survey of market forecasting, researchers concluded that the successful introduction of "high-tech" innovative products could be credited to the use of qualitative rather than quantitative forecasting methods. The latter were deemed more useful in "low-tech" product introductions. See Lynn, G., S. Schnaars, and R. Skov, "Survey of New Product Forecasting Practices in Industrial High Technology and Low Technology Businesses," *Industrial Marketing Management*, 28(6), 1999, 565-571.

19. See the early conceptualization in Utterback, J., and L. Kim, "Discontinuities in Product and Process Innovation," paper presented at the ORSA/TIMS Joint National Meeting, Milwaukee, Wisconsin, October 15, 1979.

20. See the insightful analysis of this phenomenon in Thompson, D., "Branching Hasn't Changed Much," *MC Technology Marketing Intelligence*, 20(4), 2000, 90-98. Debra Thompson discussed in this paper the case of Internet technology, but her conclusions are applicable across other industries and products. Also see the case of Internet search engine competition and new technology in Ince, J., "Searching for Profits," *Upside*, 12(5), 2000, 92-104. The author argued that understanding "how to service the complex needs of the corporate customer" is a more important factor for success than technological superiority.

21. See, for example, Kawasaki, G., *Rules for Revolutionaries: The Capitalist Manifesto for Creating and Marketing New Products and Services* (New York: HarperBusiness, 2000).

22. See, for example, the case of human-computer interface in Turk, M., and G. Robertson, "Perceptual User Interfaces," *Communications of the ACM*, 43(3), 2000, 32-34. Also see Ramsey, R., "How Much Technology Is Too Much?—Strategies for Humanizing a High-Tech Workplace," *Supervision*, 61(1), 2000, 3-5. And see Pedersen, C., and M. Lind, "Conceptual Design of Industrial Process Displays," *Ergonomics*, 42(11), 1999, 1531-1548.

23. Sciulli, L., "How Organizational Structure Influences Success in Various Types of Innovation," *Journal of Retail Banking Services*, 20(1), 1998, 13-18. Also see Moorman, C., and R. Slotegraaf, "The Contingency Value of Complementary Capabilities in Product Development," *Journal of Marketing Research*, 36(2), 1999, 239-272.

24. See, Menanteau, P., and H. Lefebvre, "Competing Technologies and the Diffusion of Innovations: The Emergence of Energy-Efficient Lamps in the Residential Sector," *Research Policy*, 29(3), 2000, 375-389. Also see Thomas, L., "Adoption Order of New Technologies in Evolving Markets," *Journal of Economic Behavior & Organization*, 38(4), 1999, 453-482. The study of the computer disk drive industry found that technologies would be more likely adopted by large firms when they do not make existing products obsolete. Conversely, new entrants adopt technologies when they do make existing products obsolete.

25. See, for example, Occiuto, M., and B. Dickes, "People are Key to Technology Adoption," *National Underwriter*, 103(21), 1999, 538-548; and Agarwal, R., and U. Prasad, "Are Individual Differences Germane to the Acceptance of New Information Technologies?", *Decision Sciences*, 30(2), 1999, 361-391.

26. See, for example, Lau, R., "How Does Research and Development Intensity Affect Business Performance?", *South Dakota Business Review*, 57(1), 1998, 4-12. Also see, in the broader framework of new product development, Calantone, R., and A. di Benedetto, "An Integrative Model of the New Product Development Process," *Journal of Product Innovation Management*, 5(3), 1988, 201-215; and see Deshpande, R., J. Farley, and F. Webster, "Corporate Culture, Customer Orientation, and Innovativeness in Japanese Firms: A Quadrad Analysis," *Journal of Marketing*, 52(1), 1993, 23-28.

27. See Buckley, J., *Going for Growth: Increasing Shareholder Value Through R&D* (New York: McGraw-Hill, 1997), in particular Chapters 3 and 5. Also see Rotman, D., "Hoechst Drives R&D Effort Closer to Businesses," *Chemical Week*, 151(21), 1992, 28-33.

28. See, for example, von Meier, A., "Occupational Culture as a Challenge to Technological Innovation," *IEEE Transactions on Engineering Management*, 46(1), 1999, 101-114. The author addressed the issue of diverse perspectives of technology in the case of electric power distribution. She recommends that managers "consider these diverse perspectives carefully when planning technological innovation" (p. 101). Also see Gerchak, Y., and M. Parlar, "Allocating Resources to R&D Projects in a Competitive Environment," *IIE Transactions*, 31(9), 1999, 827-834.

29. There is a vast literature on this topic. See, for example, Lefebvre, L., A. Langley, J. Harvey, and E. Lefebvre, "Exploring the Strategy-Technology Connection in Small Manufacturing Firms," *Production and Operations Management*, 1(3), 1992, 269-285. Also see Parker, A., "Impact on the Organizational Performance of the Strategy-Technology Policy Interaction," *Journal of Business Research*, 47(1), 2000, 55-64. And see the seminal work on corporate decision regarding R&D and strategy in Rubenstein, A., *Managing Technology in the Decentralized Firm* (New York: John Wiley & Sons, 1989).

30. See, for example, Comstock, G., and D. Sjolseth, "Aligning and Prioritizing Corporate R&D," *Research-Technology Management*, 42(3), 1999, 19-25. In this paper the authors described the role of corporate R&D at Weyerhauser, a forest products company. They discussed the shift in the role of R&D from supporting corporate strategy of diversification into new businesses, to that of supporting sustained growth and success of the core business. In both these roles the underlying thesis was that R&D has the ability to support and to contribute to successful implementation of the corporate strategy.

31. See, for example, Souder, W., D. Sherman, and R. Davies-Cooper, "Environmental Uncertainty, Organizational Integration, and New Product Development Effectiveness: A Test of Contingency Theory," *The Journal of Product Innovation Management*, 15(6), 1998, 520-533.

32. For additional readings see Iansiti, M., *Technology Integration: Making Critical Choices in a Dynamic World* (Boston: Harvard Business School Press, 1997). Also see Sanchez, R., "Strategic Product Creation: Managing New

Interactions of Technology, Markets, and Organizations," *European Management Journal*, 14(2), 1996, 121-138.

33. Christensen, 2000, *op. cit.*

34. See, for example, Meyer-Krahmer, F., and G. Reger, "New Perspectives on the Innovation Strategies of Multinational Enterprises: Lessons for Technology Policy in Europe," *Research Policy*, 28(7), 1999, 751-776. Also see Neufville, R., "Dynamic Strategic Planning for Technology Policy," *International Journal of Technology Management*, 19(3-5), 2000, 225-245; and see Mansell, R., "Strategies for Maintaining Market Power in the Face of Rapidly Changing Technologies," *Journal of Economic Issues*, 31(4), 1997, 969-989.

35. See, for example, Price Waterhouse, *The Paradox Principles: How High-Performance Companies Manage Chaos, Complexity, and Contradiction to Achieve Superior Results* (New York: McGraw-Hill, 1995).

36. See, for example, Augsdorfer, P., *Forbidden Fruit: An Analysis of Bootlegging, Uncertainty, and Learning in Corporate R&D* (New York: Ashgate Publishing Company, 1996). In particular, see pp. 71-136. Also see Branscomb, L., and J. Keller (Eds.), *Investing in Innovation* (Cambridge, MA: MIT Press, 1998); and see Presley, A., and D. Liles, "R&D Validation Planning: A Methodology to Link Technical Validations to Benefits Measurement," *R&D Management*, 30(1), 2000, 55-65.

37. There is a vast literature on this topic, which encompasses the management of industrial and corporate R&D. See, for example, Cooper, R., *Winning at New Products: Accelerating the Process from Idea to Launch* (Reading, MA: Addison-Welsey, 1993). Also see Rubenstein, A., *Managing Technology in the Decentralized Firm* (New York: John Wiley & Sons, 1989); and Griffin, A., and J. Hauser, "Integrating R&D and Marketing: A Review and Analysis of the Literature," *Journal of Product Innovation Management*, 13(3), 1996, 191-215. Also see Leonard-Barton, D., "Core Capabilities and Core Rigidities: A Paradox in Managing New Product Development," *Strategic Management Journal*, 13(4), 1992, 111-125.

38. See, for example, how companies deal with these issues in Teece, D., "Capturing Value from Technological Innovation: Integration, Strategic Partnering, and Licensing Decisions," *Interfaces*, 18(3), 1988, 46-61. Also see Wind, J., and U. Mahajan, "Issues and Opportunities in New Product Development: An Introduction to the Special Issue," *Journal of Marketing Research*, 34(1), 1997, 1-11; and see Nevins, T., G. Summe, and B. Uttal, "Commercializing Technology: What the Best Companies Do," *Harvard Business Review*, 68(3), 1990, 154-163.

39. See Cusumano, M., Y. Mylonadis, and R. Rosenbloom, "Strategic Maneuvering and Mass-Market Dynamics: The Triumph of VHS over Beta," *Business History Review*, 66(1), 1992, 51-64.

40. See Cahill, D., S. Thach, and R. Warshawski, "The Marketing Concepts and New High-Tech Products: Is There a Fit?", *Journal of Product Innovation Management*, 11(4), 1994, 336-345.

41. Kortge, D., and P. Okonkwo, "Simultaneous New Product Development: Reducing the New Product Failure Rate," *Industrial Marketing Management*, 18(4), 1989, 301-307.

42. See, for example, Murphy, C., and D. Khirallah, "Ready, Set, Fail," *Information Week*, 784, May 1, 2000, RB15-RB18.

43. See Morrison, G., "DEC Targets Mid-Range," *Electronic News*, 43(2196), 1997, 16-18. Even though DEC developed the "Alpha" processor with Mitsubishi and Samsung, it failed to generate new products that would be able to be successfully launched into the highly competitive personal computers market.

44. See, for example, Hauser, M., "Organizational Culture and Innovativeness of Firms—An Integrative View," *International Journal of Technology Management*, 16(1-3), 1998, 239-255. Also see Claver, E., J. Llopis, D. Garcia, and H. Molina, "Organizational Culture for Innovation and New Technological Behavior," *Journal of High Technology Management*, 9(1), 1998, 55-68; and, Koch, C., "The Ventriloquist's Dummy? The Role of Technology in Political Processes," *Technology Analysis & Strategic Management*, 12(1), 2000, 119-138.

45. See, for example, DiBenedetto, A., "Identifying the Key Success Factors in New Product Launch," *Journal of Product Innovation Management*, 16(6), 2000, 530-544.

46. See, for example, Swan, J., and S. Newell, "Managers' Beliefs about Factors Affecting the Adoption of Technological Innovation: A Study Using Cognitive Maps," *Journal of Managerial Psychology*, 9(2), 1994, 3-13. The authors found that factors considered in the literature as important in adoption of innovations were not considered to be important by managers when assessing the causal relationship between adoption and effects of a technological innovation. Also see Adams, G., and V. Ingersoll, "Culture, Technical Rationality, and Organizational Culture," *American Review of Public Administration*, 20(4), 1990, 285-298. The authors argued that there is a managerial "metamyth" which is a set of beliefs in technological progress. Also see the speech by the CEO of the pharmaceutical company Merck in: Gilmartin, R., "Innovation, Ethics, and Core Values: Keys to Global Success," *Vital Speeches of the Day*, 65(7), 1999, 209-213.

47. See the case of Black & Decker in Graber, D., "How to Manage a Global Product Development Process," *Industrial Marketing Management*, 25(6), 1996, 483-489. B&D had 35 percent of annual sales from products no older than three years.

48. D'Aveni, R., and R. Gunther, *Hypercompetition: Managing the Dynamics of Strategic Maneuvering* (New York: Simon & Schuster, 1994). Also see D'Aveni, R., "Waking Up to the New Era of Hypercompetition," *The Washington Quarterly*, 21(1), 1998, 183-1905.

49. See Veliyath, R., and E. Fitzgerald, "Firm Capabilities, Business Strategies, Customer Preferences, and Hypercompetitive Arenas," *Competitiveness Review*, 10(1), 2000, 56-82.

50. See, for example, Blundell, R., R. Griffith, and J. van Reenen, "Market Share, Market Value, and Innovation in a Panel of British Manufacturing Firms," *The Review of Economic Studies*, 66(228), 1999, 529-554. Also see Sutton, J., *Technology and Market Structure* (Cambridge, MA: MIT Press, 1998).

51. See Cohn, M., "On Webaholism and Other High-Tech Addictions," *ComputerWorld*, 34(2), 2000, 29-31. Among these addictions Cohn listed: parkaholism—where people circle the office parking lot in search of the "best" spot;

postaholism—where people accumulate, hoard, and keep office supplies without any immediate need for them; and Webaholism—where people cannot stay way from logging on to the Internet for shopping, reading the news, e-trading, and simply surfing aimlessly.

52. Armour, S., "Technically, It's An Addiction. Some Workers Finding It Hard to Disconnect," *USA Today*, 21 April, 1998, 4B-6B.

53. See, for example, Foegen, J., "Information Addiction?", *Business and Economic Review*, 44(1), 1997, 29-30. Also see Reed, L., "Domesticating the Personal Computer: The Mainstreaming of a New Technology and the Cultural Management of a Widespread Technophobia, 1964-2000," *Critical Studies in Media Communication*, 17(2), 2000, 159-185.

54. I used the adjective "tantalizing" to recall the fate of Tantalus, King of Lydia, who, in Greek mythology, was condemned by the gods to inhabit luscious gardens yet have water and fruit distance themselves from his reach, thus suffering from unending hunger and thirst. The analogy to the technology race is evident.

55. See, for example, Helpman, E., *General Purpose Technologies and Economic Growth* (Cambridge: MA: MIT Press, 1998), in particular, see pp. 15-84.

56. See Eriksson, C., and T. Lindh, "Growth Cycles with Technology Shifts and Externalities," *Economic Modeling*, 17(1), 2000, 139-170.

57. See, for example, Christensen, C., "The Rigid Disk Drive Industry: A History of Commercial and Technological Turbulence," *Business History Review*, 67(2), 1993, 531-588.

58. Specific data for 1998-2000 were not available to the author at the time this chapter was written.

59. See, for example, Tossey, G., *R&D Trends in the US Economy: Strategies and Policy Implications* (U.S. Department of Commerce, National Institute of Standards and Technology, 1999).

60. See, for example, Geisler, E., "Key Output Indicators in Performance Evaluation of Research and Development Organizations," *Technological Forecasting and Social Change*, 47(2), 1994, 189-204. Also see Nelson, R., "Modeling the Connection in the Cross Section Between Technical Progress and R&D Intensity," *Rand Journal of Economics*, 19(3), 1988, 478-485.

61. See, for example, Bovet, D., and J. Martha, *Value Nets: Breaking the Supply Chain to Unlock Hidden Profits* (New York: John Wiley & Sons, 2000). The authors argued that there are six modes by which value is created in the firm's interface with components of its value chain: (1) customers are mainly contacted by the firm's website; (2) orders are sent directly to suppliers of the firm, via the Internet; (3) the firm has its suppliers ship goods directly to the firm's customers; (4) through "management by exception" the firm only deals with complicated orders; (5) the firm is able to consolidate its operations, warehouses, and distribution centers; and (6) service is provided to customers and suppliers without the need for the firm's employers to be involved. With regard to this last item, also see, Geisler E., "Artificial Management Coming of Age: The Case of B2B and Hypercompetition," working paper, Stuart Graduate School of Business, Illinois Institute of Technology, September, 2000.

62. See, for example, Storey, C., and C. Easingwood, "Types of New Product Performance: Evidence from the Consumer Financial Services Sector," *Journal of Business Research*, 46(2), 1999, 193-203. The authors found that for new products to be highly successful, they need to generate direct economic value as well as benefits to the company. Also see Russell, C., "Seeking Strategic Advantage with Technology? Focus on Customer Value," *Long Range Planning*, 19(2), 1986, 50-58; and see Young, R., "TPT-LCDs Increasing Market Share Through Technological Innovations," *Research & Development*, 40(6), 1998, 72-77.

63. This law is further discussed in more detail in Chapter 16.

16

HOW SOCIETY CREATES AND EXPLOITS VALUE FROM SCIENCE AND TECHNOLOGY

The noted humanist Desiderius Erasmus wrote in his masterpiece *The Praise of Folly*:

> Now, to turn to the arts and sciences, what rouses men to invent and exploit such extraordinary (as they suppose) exercises, if it isn't desire of reputation? They put long hours and agonized effort into the pursuit of fame—I can't imagine how they conceive of it, but nothing could be more inane. Now aren't these the most foolish of mortal men? To be sure, you can enjoy, thanks to their folly, all the good things they produce, and you don't even have to be as crazy as they are—which is the best thing of all.[1]

Erasmus had a keen eye and his observation of artists and scientists, albeit with a touch of irony, would not miss the mark even today. As we continually and increasingly "enjoy all the good things they produce," we are now aware of the value that science and technology produces, thanks to the effort of so many who engage in it. This value, in its various forms, is received and enjoyed by social organizations.

This chapter describes the mechanisms by which social organizations, and society at large, exploit S&T and the benefits that it generates. The chapter starts with the definition of society's components and constituents. It broadly describes the forces that shape its direction, organization, and the allocation of resources to its various functions. Considering the complexity of the social scene, the chapter also addresses the contributions of S&T to social welfare and societal evolution. The notion of "Shared Outputs" is introduced, and the Law of Preponderant Diffusion of S&T is also discussed.

This chapter continues the unfolding analysis of the theme of this book: S&T generates value, both economic and social, that is diffused in companies and social institutions, and that significantly benefits the human condition.

THE NATURE OF SOCIETY AND SOCIAL ORGANIZATIONS

In order to address the topic of how S&T is exploited by society, it is necessary to define what society is and what the institutions are within it that are impacted by S&T. In this chapter, society is defined in a very broad way, accurately enough to form a conceptual framework that will help to describe the processes of diffusion and exploitation of S&T in social organizations. Sociologists, political scientists, and even organization scientists may find this definition and the resultant framework perhaps too simplistic, let alone obvious.

But the focus of this chapter is on the processes and mechanisms by which S&T is introduced into social institutions, how it affects them, and how they benefit from it by exploiting the value generated by S&T outcomes. To this limited end the chapter embarks on an elementary circumscription of the set of key components that participate in this phenomenon.[2]

The impacts of S&T will be considered here from two distinct perspectives. The first is the processes and mechanisms by which S&T contributes to *social institutions* and organizations. These include organizations in the various functions of societal endeavor, such as defense, environmental protection, space exploration, and health. The second perspective addresses the processes and mechanisms by which S&T contributes to, and is exploited by, *society* in general, considered as the representation of the overall "public good."[3]

What Are Social Organizations and What Do They Want From S&T?

Before we look at what social organizations are and what they wish and expect from S&T, we need to distinguish between social *organizations* and social *institutions*. The former are the organizational frameworks created by societies to achieve social, political, economic, and humanitarian objectives. They serve as a formal channeling of human activities within a social context. Examples are social service agencies at the municipal, county, and state levels, government departments and services, and charitable organizations.

Social institutions are somewhat different. They are the embodiment of social preferences and the underlying description of society's main experiences. When these are crystallized in the form of a structure whose existence defies the action of time, and is transmitted across generations—social institutions are thus created. Examples include sexism, racism, religion, equality, and citizenship.[4]

Thus, social organizations may be created to carry out desired actions that are institutionalized in society. For example, the Department of Defense exercises some of the experiences that are embedded in institutionalized militarism, with its objective to defend the country and to maintain and perpetuate the ability to make war.

Social organizations compose all of the activities in society that are geared toward "everybody's business," meaning of general interest not necessarily confined to the needs or interests of an individual, organization, or a specific group.[5] They are involved in functions serving the public interest, its well-being, and its many needs. These functions are, for example, national defense, education, welfare for those unable to subsist by themselves, social services, public transportation (including construction and maintenance of a network of roads, airports, and sea and fluvial ports), law enforcement, administration of the public government, maintaining the legislative and judicial functions, environmental protection, regulations of economic activities, and similar activities.

The organizations that carry out the social functions of a modern society have desires, needs, and expectations from S&T. These are summarized in Figure 16.1.

What social organizations want from S&T can thus be divided into three categories: mission and objectives, internal functioning, and intangible factors. Social organizations have a mission to accomplish and objectives to meet. They operate within the framework of parent agencies, constituents, and social forces that shape their agendas and fund their activities. Therefore they expect S&T to assist them in accomplishing these objectives.

For example, the Occupational Safety and Health Administration (OSHA) functions under the mission to improve and safeguard the rates of workforce safety and health, to reduce morbidity and mortality due to accidents on the job, and to ensure a safe work environment for all Americans. OSHA would then require that S&T contribute to the achievement of these objectives. Similar to private firms, the accomplishment of the mission of the agency also insures its survival on a functioning social organization (and government entity).[6]

A different set of needs and expectations is focused on internal processes, efficiency factors, and cost saving and cost cutting. Like their private counterparts, social organizations expect S&T to help them achieve improved efficiency of operations, higher productivity of their units, and better allocation of their scarce resources.

Figure 16.1
Needs and Expectations of Social Organizations from S&T

ILLUSTRATIVE NEEDS AND EXPECTATIONS FROM S&T
A.   Related to *mission and objectives* of the social organization, such as: accomplishing the mission of the agency or department; doing so within budgetary constraints; satisfaction of recipients of services; satisfaction of the legislative organs; meeting expectations of other constituencies (e.g., White House, civic groups); meeting performance standards (e.g., GPRA), and contributions to higher order national and societal goals.
B.   Related to *internal functioning*, such as: efficiency of operations; using "best available technology"; effective and optimized employment; efficient allocation of scarce resources; improved administration and management procedures and methods; cost-savings and cost-cutting; and improved inter-organizational coordination and cooperation.
C.   Related to *intangible* factors such as: prestige; maintaining traditions; working toward institutionalized behavior of the organization and its function; recognition by public.

Finally, intangible factors such as prestige, maintaining traditions, and recognition by funding bodies and the public at large are also important expectations from S&T. When the space agency fails in a launch of one of its rockets or shuttles, prestige and the long tradition of successful explorations are threatened. S&T is expected to assist in maintaining the high level of these factors, and the position of the agency in public administration. Such a position has important implications on the continuing level of public funding, and on ancillary phenomena such as recruitment of top employees by the agency.

WHAT SOCIETY WANTS FROM S&T

As seen above, social organizations want S&T to contribute to needs that are practical, immediate, and useful, in a way that is similar to the needs of private firms who operate in competitive markets. Society at large expects different benefits and contributions from S&T. What society wants are higher-level, conceptual, and long-term benefits. Figure 16.2 shows some of these needs and expectations.

What society wants is an *organized* form of catering for the common good, by having peace, economic prosperity, justice, and the ability and mechanisms to keep and to perpetuate them.[7] Many of these needs and goals

Figure 16.2
Needs and Expectations of Society at Large from S&T

ILLUSTRATIVE NEEDS AND EXPECTATIONS FROM S&T*

A. Related to *Common Good* ("Nobody's Business"), such as:
•Maintenance of the system of government
•Legislating capabilities
•Civil rest and stability
•Economic prosperity
•National defense
•Environmental protection
•National prestige
•Justice
•Energy adequacy
•Explorations (space, oceans, human genes)
 	
B. Related to *Public Benefits* ("Everybody's Business", affecting
   individuals' lives)
•Healthcare delivery (availability and affordability)
•Transportation
•Welfare (social services, economic support)
•Taxation and allocation and redistribution of resources
•Full employment
•Housing (availability and affordability)
•Law enforcement
•Adequate local services
•Education
•Regulatory function
•Monetary availability and stability
•Administration of justice (availability and affordability of a system of
  courts)
•Administration of national and local affairs (creating and maintaining a
  public bureaucracy)

Not necessarily in any order of importance. This list is illustrative and not exhaustive.

are ethereal, but they represent an overarching aim to which a civilized society should aspire.

At the more empirical level, society at large also expects S&T to contribute to the overall delivery, effectiveness, availability, and affordability of such public services as health care, housing, transportation, education, and law enforcement.   Both the conceptual and the more empirical needs and expectations of society at large are the guiding principles and overall objectives by which social organizations operate. S&T therefore contributes to societal needs and goals by contributing to the working of social organizations. S&T thus helps society to maintain itself and to improve the human condition.

HOW SOCIAL ORGANIZATIONS EXPLOIT S&T

Social organizations are the mechanism or conduit by which S&T is exploited for social purposes and value is thus extracted for social good. There are three main forms by which social organizations exploit S&T: (1) national or publicly supported S&T, (2) agency-specific laboratories, and (3) exploiting S&T from all other (nonsocietal) sources.

National or Publicly Supported S&T

The United States supports S&T at the national level through a variety of mechanisms. Direct funding of S&T via federal agencies is done by grants, dedicated programs, and federal collaborative effort. In the area of basic or exploratory science, the National Science Foundation is a key instrument in the support of investigator-initiated research by the use of a merit system of resources allocation.

The Clinton-Gore administration suggested five goals for S&T to maintain a relevant link to key national objectives:

1. Maintain leadership across the frontiers of scientific knowledge.
2. Enhance connections between fundamental research and national goals.
3. Stimulate partnerships that promote investments in fundamental science and engineering and effective use of physical, human, and financial resources.
4. Produce the finest scientists and engineers for the twenty-first century.
5. Raise scientific and technological literacy of all Americans.[8]

On the other side of the Capitol, the House of Representatives Science Committee advanced the steps needed to achieve the vision that

> The United States of America must maintain and improve its preeminent position in science and technology in order to advance human understanding of the universe and all it contains, and to improve the lives, health, and freedom of all peoples.[9]

There are three steps. The first was to facilitate and encourage basic science. The second called for the application of scientific discoveries to new products and processes and to solutions to social challenges. The third was to improve the educational background and system.[10]

Over the period 1960-1968, publicly supported S&T amounted to about half of all the national investments in R&D, including industry, universities, and government laboratories. This share has fluctuated downward, so that in 1998 it amounted to somewhat below a third. Figure 16.3 shows U.S. R&D expenditures for selected years.

As expected, the share of public funding of *basic research* has been higher. From a high of 70 percent in 1980, the public share in 1998 was a bit over half (see Figure 16.4).

The meaning of this decline and its implications can be summarized in two complementary phenomena. The first is a substantially reduced role of the Federal government in the nation's S&T (from 65% in 1960 to 29% in 1998, a cut by over a half!). The second phenomenon is the shift in the burden of investments from public to private funding of American S&T. Industry picked up the slack and doubled its share in support of the nation's S&T (from 33% in 1960 to 66% in 1998).

The implications from these phenomena are threefold. Publicly supported S&T has become more utilitarian, in that resources are not only reduced but allocated to more politically driven objectives and areas of investigation.

Figure 16.3
Share of Federal Investments in U.S. R&D in Selected Years

Calendar Year	Total US R&D Expenditures[1]	Federal Government[1]	Industry[1]	Share of Federal Government (%)[2]
1960	58,922	38,312	19,407	65%
1970	86,102	49,161	34,280	57%
1980	104.975	49,785	51,284	47%
1990	162,435	65,884	89,084	40%
1995	170,432	58,804	103,251	34%
1998	201,573	59,388	132,789	29%

Source: National Science Board, *Science and Engineering Indicators-2000* (Arlington, VA, 2000), Appendix Table 2.6.
[1]*In millions of constant 1992 dollars.* [2]*Rounded to nearest integer.*

Figure 16.4
Share of Federal Investments in U.S. Basic Research in Selected Years

Calendar Year	Total US Expenditures for Basic Research[1]	Federal Government[1]	Industry[1]	Share of Federal Government (%)[2]
1960	5,526	3,412	1,472	62%
1970	11,791	8,207	1,742	69%
1980	14,627	10,318	2,131	70%
1990	24,399	15,060	5,073	62%
1995	26,890	15,817	6,230	59%
1998	33,609	17,955	10,038	53%

Source: National Science Board, *Science and Engineering Indicators-2000* (Arlington, VA, 2000), Appendix Table 2.10.
[1]*In millions of constant 1992 dollars.* [2]*Rounded to nearest integer.*

Second, the figures for the late 1990s do not agree with the pronouncements of the administration or Congress about maintaining the preeminent position of American S&T. Because industry invests primarily in "relevant," hence short-term, S&T, longer-term effort with social consequences tends to suffer —in the absence of a sustained level of federal support.

Third, industry's investments in S&T that filled the gap left by reduced federal support cannot fully replace public investments in S&T. Even when the Law of Preponderant Diffusion is considered, there are differences in the social effects of publicly supported versus industrial S&T. Industrial S&T may have its outcomes diffused in social organizations, but publicly supported S&T is diffused faster and more effectively. Therefore, society at large suffers when public investments in S&T are dramatically reduced.

Agency-Specific Laboratories

A substantial portion of total R&D expenditures by the federal government are directed toward agency-specific laboratories. This is a network of over 700 S&T laboratories, conducting research and development in areas relevant to the funding agency. For example, laboratories of the Department of the Army conduct R&D in weapons, night vision, clothing and food for ground troops, forms of sustainable habitat, chemical warfare, and similar topics.[11]

The S&T developed by these laboratories is not only geared toward the specific mission and objectives of the parent agency, but also constitutes a warehouse of knowledge and technology in the specific areas of the agency. Hence, many of these laboratories conduct high-quality R&D and are considered premiere institutions of S&T worldwide.[12]

The primary objective of these laboratories is to assist the parent agency and to supply it and its programs with S&T support. Such effort is carried out internally, by S&T performed at the laboratories, and by outsourcing to other performers, such as universities, industry, and specialized consulting organizations.

Exploiting S&T from Other Sources

The third form by which social organizations exploit S&T is by adopting and utilizing outcomes from S&T developed by other sources, such as academia and industry. Technological innovations generated by industrial firms are routinely transferred to the social arena. For example, innovations in technology of automobiles, such as telecommunication equipment and navigation by satellites, have been incorporated by law-enforcement organizations.

By and large, social organizations are a major procurer of S&T. In areas such as transportation, energy, education, and health care, several organizations adopt a variety of S&T generated by universities and industry.[13] A good portion of this transfer occurs when private companies serve as contractors for social organizations. S&T is transferred from the company via interactions of its staff with the technical people and units of the respective social organization.[14]

WHAT SOCIETY WANTS AND WHAT S&T CAN DELIVER

What society (through social organizations) wants from S&T and what S&T can deliver is summarized in Figure 16.5. The figure shows the impact of intervening factors, such as diffusion processes and the existence of constraints on the delivery of social value from S&T. The figure also shows the generation of *actual* value created in the social context.

What S&T Can Deliver

As Figure 16.5 shows, S&T delivers several broadly defined outcomes to society. S&T may generate new industries (such as telecommunication and computers), and spur the creation of new employment opportunities. S&T outputs may also provide solutions, albeit sometimes on a temporary basis, to pressing social problems, such as in healthcare delivery, energy demand, transportation, and defense.

Figure 16.5
What Society Wants From S&T and What S&T Can Deliver

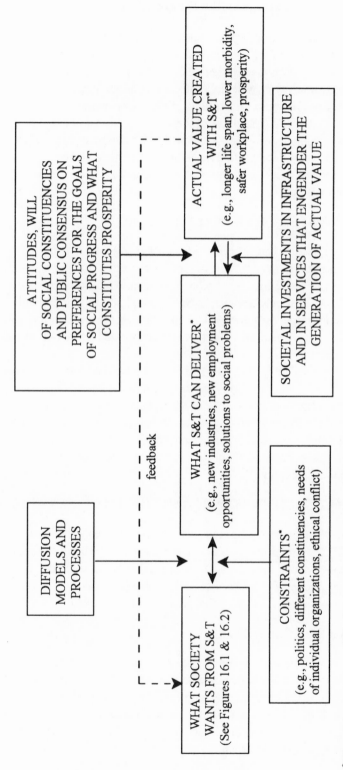

ATTITUDES, WILL
OF SOCIAL CONSTITUENCIES
AND PUBLIC CONSENSUS ON
PREFERENCES FOR THE GOALS
OF SOCIAL PROGRESS AND WHAT
CONSTITUTES PROSPERITY

ACTUAL VALUE CREATED
WITH S&T*
(e.g., longer life span, lower morbidity,
safer workplace, prosperity)

SOCIETAL INVESTMENTS IN INFRASTRUCTURE
AND IN SERVICES THAT ENGENDER THE
GENERATION OF ACTUAL VALUE

WHAT S&T CAN DELIVER*
(e.g., new industries, new employment
opportunities, solutions to social problems)

feedback

DIFFUSION
MODELS AND
PROCESSES

CONSTRAINTS*
(e.g., politics, different constituencies, needs
of individual organizations, ethical conflict)

WHAT SOCIETY
WANTS FROM S&T
(See Figures 16.1 & 16.2)

*Illustrative outcomes. This list is not complete nor exhaustive.

But, the *actual* value created with S&T for society at large is manifested in desirable outcomes that benefit a major portion of the citizenry, and that greatly contributes to improvement in the human condition. Examples include increased longevity of the population, lower morbidity and a safer workplace, as well as overall prosperity. The achievement of this actual value from S&T is mitigated by societal investments in making S&T outputs deliver such value, and in the public's willingness and consensus on investing in such broader goals of prosperity.

An illustrative achievement of actual and lasting value is *longevity*. In his paper on the aging "boomers," Joseph Coughlin argued that "longevity can be listed as one of the nation's greatest policy achievement."[15] In 1900, the average life expectancy in the United States was about 47 years. A century later, in 2000, life expectancy rose to the upper 70s or even 80s.[16]

Such societal achievements may be partially attributed to the outcomes and consequences from S&T. But, as Figure 16.5 shows, the creation of actual value also benefitted from social investments in the infrastructure of social services, and the attitudes and public consensus on how to invest scarce resources in S&T that engenders these outcomes. Thus, the process by which S&T is transformed into social value is contingent upon the diffusion of S&T, the constraints to the process, and societal priorities.

DIFFUSION OF S&T IN SOCIAL ORGANIZATIONS

For S&T to deliver socially relevant value, there must be diffusion of the outcomes from S&T into the processes of social organizations. Even the ultimate social values (such as longevity) are generated through the workings of social organizations.[17]

The diffusion of S&T occurs in several modes. Rui Baptista[18] has identified three theoretical approaches: (1) epidemic and learning; (2) equilibrium models contingent upon organizational attributes; and (3) strategic interaction through cooperation and joint ventures.

Epidemic Model

This diffusion model assumes a rapid spread of S&T outcomes due to the user's interaction with the generators and previous users of the outcomes. The model also assumes that S&T outcomes (innovations) will spread like diseases, by contamination through direct contact between those already infected (actual users) and potential users.

This model has been criticized on several grounds, such as the passivity of potential adopters and their assumed homogeneity. Other discussions in the literature dealt with issues of the type of decision that organizations make at the point of adopting an innovation. For example, is the adoption a yes-no decision, or is it a gradual incorporation via a series of decisions? This dichotomy can be partially explained by incorporating variables such as preferences of adopters and other individual characteristics that would influence the decision into the analysis.[19]

Equilibrium Models and Organizational Characteristics

As the innovation is absorbed into the organization, risks associated with it are diminished, and profitability emerges, thus leading to a desired equilibrium in the organization's processes. As Baptista explained, these models consider organizational attributes, such as size, experience with similar innovations, and expectations of profitability from the innovation.

Strategic Interaction

The third set of models is the strategic interaction of organizations, via the use of game theory, and other attributes of strategic behavior, such as imitation, cooperation, and preemptive competition. In general, these models assume that innovations are adopted because organizations wish to effectively compete in their environments.[20]

How S&T Is Diffused in Social Organizations

Although the models described above were developed with private firms in mind, they also apply to social organizations. In general, all three models offer viable explanations of how S&T is diffused in social organizations. Essentially, the differences are in perspective and consideration of a given set of variables. Despite criticism of each model, S&T is diffused, in part, as an epidemic disease and, in part, in the postadoption stage, moving toward equilibrium.[21] Strategic interaction also explains why organizations adopt innovation. In this latter case, social organizations—like their industrial counterparts—also compete for resources and recognition from their sponsors and parent agencies. They would, therefore, adopt S&T innovations that would assist them in their competitive effort.

Push or Pull of S&T

A related way of looking at the process of diffusion of S&T in social organizations is to inquire whether S&T has been introduced because of its "push," or because of the "pull" from the social organization.[22] The epidemic diffusion model assumes that when an organization learns of the existence of a technology, it will strive to adopt it.

But there are differences between how private and public organizations behave in the diffusion of S&T innovations. Hansen studied the transfer of knowledge from public to private organizations.[23] He concluded that "public technology policy is greatly influenced by the science push idea." Similarly, because of the various constraints on them, shown in Figure 16.5, public organizations tend to adopt innovations that have already been proven in the private marketplace. These constraints include limits on resources, unwillingness to take risks, and political ramifications.

By and large, the diffusion of S&T innovations is a mix of both the push of S&T and the demand-pull by the adopting organization. An excellent illustration is law enforcement, in which numerous S&T innovations were adopted in the decade of 1980s-1990s. Well-publicized innovations such as the use of DNA in identification of criminal suspects were joined by less dramatic innovations such as The Sticky Shocker wireless projectile, and the back-scatter imaging apparatus to reveal concealed weapons.[24] In these cases, adoption has been the result of the congruence of an identified need (such as safety of officers or better identification of criminals) with the push of the innovation—as it became known to the public entities. Also, social organizations tend to work closely with inventors and generators of the S&T innovation to tailor it to their specific needs. In the course of such effort, improvements may be added to the innovation to the benefits of the public, industry, and the generator of the innovation.[25]

WEB OF DISCOVERY

In his unique book on diffusion of knowledge, the British author James Burke argued that innovations flow throughout history within a web of interactions among inventors and scientists.[26] Burke traces the flow of innovative ideas from antiquity through the middle ages to modern times. He defined such flow as a "journey through knowledge."

This concept of a web of knowledge can also be the notion of "Web of Discovery" and similar constructs. The idea of such a web is the development, flow, and diffusion of S&T and innovations by continually transferring them across people, organizations, time, and countries. This notion is similar to that of the "epidemic model" of diffusion of S&T innovations. For example, in the case of contagious epidemics, public health officials trace the spread of the disease back to "patient zero" with whom the disease originated.[27] Cross-fertilization is a continuous pattern.

In the same vein, S&T innovations are diffused through social organizations to the extent that they create social value, and engender benefits as well as some negative effects to society. Another notion that describes the web of knowledge would be the existence of "communities of science" and corresponding communities in technology. Since the publication of Diana Crane's book, *Invisible Colleges*,[28] there have been several reconstructions of the main theme: knowledge is diffused in scientific communities regardless of the members' organizational allegiances. In its original version, such networks or communities shared similar disciplinary interests, thus exercised intensive interaction. Through these contacts, knowledge about the discipline and findings emanating from R&D activity within the discipline quickly and effectively propagated to the members.[29]

But S&T innovations also diffuse across disciplinary boundaries. The rate of such diffusion and its effectiveness depend on the constraints imposed on the process of transfer among individuals and organizations. The key argument here is that social networks that propagate S&T innovations must not necessarily be confined to disciplinary configurations. Rather, cross-disciplinary and cross-sectional diffusion are normal occurrences, leading to effective propagation.[30]

Web of Innovations and Models of Diffusion

S&T innovations are diffused in various networks in which people and organizations congregate by means of opinion leaders and other individuals who excel in propagating ideas, knowledge, and innovations. Valente and Davis have argued that when community or opinion leaders take charge of transferring innovations, the diffusion process is accelerated, within and between specific networks.[31]

Malcolm Gladwell applied this notion to his thesis on how knowledge and products are diffused in society and the economy through the action of three types of key individuals: connectors (people who know people), mavens (people who know and understand how the enemy works), and salesmen (who sell the idea or product).[32] According to Gladwell, specific knowledge that these laypeople have, and contacts they happen to possess within respective networks, allow them to dramatically accelerate the diffusion process, in a pattern that conforms to the "epidemic" form of diffusion.

This notion is similar to that of "technology gatekeepers" as technology power brokers and key protagonists in the systematic transfer of technology. Such gatekeepers were studied in the 1970s and 1980s, with the objective of investigating the transfer of technology among countries and companies.[33]

The Notion of "Shared Outputs" and the Network Economy

A somewhat different construct is the notion of "shared outputs" or "community of benefits." In the present network economy, individuals and organizations are linked in a web of shared interests and outputs. In addition to value nets that companies operate via the Internet, other members of the economy and society are linked in networks that share benefits.

Consider, for example, a group of people who suffer from a certain disease. In parallel, there is a network of people and organizations that generate S&T with outputs that may impact the "diseased community." The two groups share in the benefits accrued from S&T, thus forming a unified network. Although their interests, goals, aspirations, and political and social agendas may substantially differ, they are members of the same network in view of the "shared outputs" and benefits from S&T that are generated by some and impact others.[34]

As the criteria for membership in the network is the shared outputs and benefits, diffusion of S&T innovations in such networks is accelerated. The reason is the sharing in benefits, rather than agreement on social issues or belonging to similar networks. The link by shared benefits seems to be a much stronger string that binds the network together. Diffusion is thus also occurring in these networks across disciplines and organizational boundaries.[35]

The case of diffusion through the Internet is an excellent illustration of virtual communities that form networks based on "shared outputs" and "shared benefits." These communities network beyond the limitations of social, economic, and political issues, and even beyond a common interest in S&T. Thus, communities of science, communities of practice, and other communities create a working network by virtue of sharing benefits from S&T innovations.[36]

LAW OF PREPONDERANT DIFFUSION OF S&T

In one of his early papers on the diffusion of industrial technology, Edwin Mansfield argued that the speed of diffusion is higher than usually accepted.[37] In social contexts, this phenomenon is even more pronounced, with implications for S&T policy and allocation of S&T resources.

The Law of Preponderant Diffusion of S&T innovations in society can be expressed as follows:

> In social contexts, S&T innovations are diffused preponderantly in successive networks, so that cross-fertilization and subsequent adoption occur in the form of an epidemic model. Therefore, diffusion and utilization occur across social structures and organizations, regardless of the origin or the disciplinary nature of the S&T that generated these innovations.[38]

How does this phenomenon occur and what are its implications? S&T outcomes are readily propagated, particularly in their upstream form of knowledge, prototypes, and other proximal outputs. As these outputs are further transformed by social organizations, the existing network of such organizations will facilitate the rapid propagation of downstream S&T outputs, because they are transferable with little or manageable adaptation effort and costs.

Consider S&T outputs from nuclear research that began within the confines of military organizations. S&T innovations in radiation technology soon propagated to social organizations in the form of "Nondestructive Testing" for pipes, manufacturing, and aircrafts. Other applications include nuclear medicine, agriculture, pest control, and security apparati in airports and public buildings.

During the 20th century the rate of such diffusion patterns greatly accelerated. The propagation of S&T innovations at the end of the 19th century were on the average 50 years, whereas a hundred years later they diffuse into social contexts within less than 10 years.[39] A methodological illustration of this "networking" and cross-fertilization of S&T innovations are the attempts to trace the research origins of selected S&T innovations. For example, the studies of the missile system "Bullpup" and projects "Hindsight" and TRACES that were conducted in the 1960s-1970s showed that civilian (or social) research had been successfully diffused into military applications, and that military research had propagated to social contexts.[40]

S&T outcomes and innovations cannot remain confined to a discipline or an area of S&T activity. Thus, the distinction between, for example, military and civilian research are impractical and insignificant. S&T outcomes have a dynamic of their own when they penetrate the boundaries of social organizations. This is due to the following factors:

1. S&T outcomes don't remain stagnant. They are transport-able and transferrable, thus allowing for a relatively smooth "conversion" between areas of S&T activities.
2. Risk in adoption is reduced as the adoption rate increases. So the more social organizations that adopt the innovation, the lesser is the perceived risk by late adopters.
3. As adoption occurs in social organizations, the more information and knowledge about the S&T innovation is generated, regarding its characteristics, adoptability, advantages, and shortcomings.
4. Social adopters of S&T innovations engage in imitative behavior. They will follow the "leaders" who have adopted innovations at the early stages of their appearance.
5. Information and knowledge about S&T innovations and their adoption by *other* sectors and areas (e.g., military) are continually transferred to social organizations. They are

thus able to follow—in real time—the experiences of other sectors.

6. S&T outcomes and innovations *improve* as they undergo transformations and adaptations in all sectors, including the social contexts in which they are introduced. Such improvements and the associated experience gained from the adoption process make the innovations more amenable to standardization, so that further adoptions by other organizations are substantially facilitated.

Implications for S&T Policy

The key implications from the "Law of Preponderant Diffusion of S&T Innovations" are in the allocation of resources for S&T and in the foundational arguments for evaluation of S&T outcomes. In the case of allocation of resources, the rule is that however we spend on S&T, regardless of the specific area of expenditures, there will be gains to both the target area of investment and all other areas and sectors. This pattern of diffusion will be constrained only by barriers to S&T transfer. But it is my belief that notwithstanding such inherent or imposed limitations on the transfer process, diffusion will occur throughout the various networks of *all* sectors, disciplines, and areas of interest.

In the case of evaluation of S&T outcomes, the implication is built into the need to extend the "value net" of S&T outcomes beyond the *organizational* boundaries of the unit under evaluation. This means that even when we assess S&T outcomes in the commercial firm, we should also consider the diffusion into social systems, the social "spin-offs," and the ultimate contributions of the outcomes of industrial S&T in the social arena.[41]

SOCIAL CHOICES AND ALLOCATION OF RESOURCES FOR S&T

There is a distinct difference between expenditures for social programs and expenditures for socially relevant S&T. When society (through its governing bodies and social organizations) invests in social programs, such as health care, transportation, or education, the expenditures are focused and only diffusable or transferrable to a very small extent. For example, spending on military installations such as missile silos cannot be easily transferred into spending on building schools, nor can the silos be easily transformed into other uses—without substantially additional spending.

Conversely, spending on S&T, per the Law of Preponderant Diffusion, are much more amenable to transferrable in the form of S&T innovations.

The "Transferability Factor" is much higher with S&T outcomes than it is with social programs. Another applicable term is "Conversion Facility," in which case S&T innovations are much more easily converted across disciplines and sectors.[42]

Allocation of Resources for Social Programs

For a long time there has been an ongoing discussion in the United States on the choices society should make and the desired preferences in allocating the nation's budget. In the period 1980-2000, there have been some distinct changes in the choice between defense and nondefense expenditures in the federal budget. Figure 16.6 shows data for the 20-year period.

In the decade of the 1990s, discretionary defense expenditures declined by 33 percent, whereas discretionary nondefense slightly increased by 10 percent. In the same period, entitlements also increased by about 12 percent. Figure 16.6 shows that social choices of the American public have strongly tilted toward spending tax dollars on social programs, with much of the shift due to decrease in military outlays.

Figure 16.6
Defense and Social Spendings by the Federal Government in the United States, in the Period 1980-2000

PROGRAMS	YEAR		
	1980[2]	1990[2]	2000[2]
Entitlements[1]	53.3%	60.1%	67.1%
Defense (Discretionary Spending)	20.3%	20.6%	13.2%
Non-Defense (Discretionary Spending)	21.2%	14.1%	15.5%

Source: National Science Foundation, *Science & Engineering Indicators-2000* (Washington, DC, 2000), p. 2-33.
[1]*Includes Social Security, Medicare, Medicaid, Veterans' benefits, and the interest payment on the national debts. These spendings are mandatory. With the exception of the interest payments and veterans benefits, entitlements are social programs that assist the elderly and low-income citizens.*
[2]*The numbers don't add up to 100%. The remainder are spendings for running the federal government itself.*

Allocation of Resources for Federal S&T

A different picture emerges with respect to allocation of U.S. Federal resources to S&T (R&D). Figure 16.7 shows illustrative expenditures for the period 1998-2000.

In the 1990s there has been a shift in the overall federal budget toward civilian expenditures and social programs, at the expense of defense. But R&D expenditures for national defense maintained their level at about half of all R&D expenditures. In fact, if we consider the distinction between *national* and *social* expenditures, the difference is more pronounced. Thus, combining expenditures for defense, space, and energy—as functions of "national interest," total R&D expenditures are close to 70 percent in 1998 and 2000, and 67 percent in 1999. Expenditures for socially relevant R&D (such as health, transportation, and agriculture) remained at less than 33 percent.

Figure 16.7
U.S. Federal R&D Expenditures for Selected Government Agencies,
1998-2000

(in percentages)

FEDERAL AGENCY	1998	1999	2000[1]
Department of Defense	48.3%	45.7%	50.0%
Space Research and Technology	13.6%	12.6%	11.1%
Health and Human Services	19.02%	20.0%	20.8%
Department of Energy	8.09%	8.6%	8.6%
U.S. Department of Agriculture	2%	2.0%	2.0%
U.S. Department of Transportation	0.92%	0.90%	3.4%
Total for Defense	48.3%	45.7%	50.0%
Total for Nondefense	51.7%	54.3%	50.0%
Total Federal R&D Expenditures	$72.11 billion	$75.35 billion	$75.41 billion

Source: National Science Foundation, *Science & Engineering Indicators-2000* (Washington, DC: National Science Board, 2000).
[1]*Estimated figures.*

The bottom line is that Americans are shifting priorities from defense to civilian (and social) programs—*except* in S&T, where expenditures in the national interest remain almost unchanged. R&D expenditures for defense are about half the total for R&D, whereas they are less than 20 percent of the total federal budget.

What accounts for this discrepancy, and what are the implications for S&T policy at the national level? Do Americans prefer spending for R&D in massive defense and national-interest programs while their choice for non-R&D expenditures is overwhelmingly in the civilian-social sector? What are the criteria used by Americans to arrive at such an unequivocal distinction between R&D and non-R&D expenditures?

Social Choices and the Problem of S&T

In actual dollars, Americans spend more for social programs than any country. Spending for health care is a good example of the nation's choices for its discretionary allocation of tax revenues. In 1997 the United States spent per capita for health care $3,925, almost 70 percent more than Germany, and 125 percent more than Japan.[43] As a percent of the gross domestic product, the United States spent 13.5 percent, versus 10.4 for Germany, 9.3 for Canada, and 7.3 for Japan. Americans are even more generous with allocating resources on health care for the elderly, spending 5 percent of GDP, versus 3.5 in Germany, 3.6 in Canada, and 3.4 in Japan.

But spending for S&T by the federal government follows a different trend, where national interests and defense receive the lion's share of investments in R&D. There are at least two key explanations for the discrepancy, and they are both reflected in the document on science policy published by the National Science Foundation in 2000.[44] In this report the agency stated:

> For more than two decades, surveys have shown that American adults have a high level of interest in scientific discoveries, new inventions, and technologies. Three of four perceive the benefits of scientific research to outweigh its potential harm. But no more than one in five Americans either comprehend or appreciate the value and process of scientific inquiry (p. 2).

This is one explanation why Americans are not insisting on similar patterns of spending for S&T as they do with other federal expenditures. The American public and its representatives in government do not possess special criteria that allow them to make such choices for R&D. As the National Science Foundation has indicated, there is an overall lack of public comprehension and appreciation of what constitutes science and technology.

The second explanation is also mentioned in the NSF document. It argued: "Clearly, we are more adept at measuring dollar inputs than outcomes such as peer-reviewed publications, citations, patents, and honorific awards. *Capturing the full public return on investments in science and engineering research remains illusive"* (italics added).[45] Since there are inherent difficulties in an unambiguous evaluation of returns from publicly funded S&T, there is also a lack of criteria to judge and assess the adequacy of trends and distributions of expenditures.

A third explanation is a combination of the fact that unlike the case of S&T, social expenditures in general are clearly defined, easily understandable, and produce short-term results that affect current aspects of life—and the relative ease with which these then can be framed and articulated for public scrutiny.[46]

This discrepancy reinforces the implications from the Law of Preponderant Diffusion of S&T. Although about half of federal S&T expenditures go to defense programs (and another 20 percent to national interests such as space and energy), the outcomes from this targeted S&T are nevertheless *amply diffused in the social sector.* The fundamental example is the case of bioengineering and genetic S&T. President Clinton succinctly argued: "We should also remember that, like the Internet, supercomputers and so many other scientific advances, our ability to read our genetic alphabet grew from decades of research that began with government funding."[47]

So the implications for S&T policies are to invest in S&T, regardless of its specific end or the sector where outcomes will be adopted. Two basic tenets support this proposition: critical mass and technology transfer. In order to gain socially relevant benefit from S&T conducted in other sectors, such as defense and space, the crucial conditions are to maintain a "critical mass" of S&T investments across disciplines, and to create conditions and background climate that will help in overcoming barriers to the transfer of technology.[48]

S&T innovations are diffused across sectors or fail to be adopted by social organizations by following a process similar to that of private firms. The ability to possess foresight as to the potential value of an innovation or to incur in gross oversight (hence failure to adopt) has been a topic of concern and intellectual struggle by several researchers. Some of those concerns were illustrated in a book of readings, edited in 1997 by Garud, Nayyar, and Shapira, professors at New York University.[49] Several contributors to this volume argued that cognitive frameworks and mental minds of managers toward innovations can be shown to influence the organization's proclivity toward adoption. In his review of this book, Johannes Pennings disputed some of these conclusions.[50] He argued that "when demands for a product decline or a market segment vanishes or substitute ones emerge, it amounts to more than simply a perceptual black spot" (p. 708).

S&T innovations will be diffused and adopted when the market conditions are favorable or dictate it, and when the S&T that led to the innovation was broad enough to support its implementation. This means that enough knowledge was generated to resolve problems that arose during adoption. Examples are connectivity, environmental constraints of pollution, heat generation, and safe, systemic performance, learning and training, and configuration with other technologies. Such problems require interdisciplinary S&T, hence the need for a "critical mass" of investments.[51]

IS THERE A NATIONAL S&T POLICY?

The combination of social choices and the need to create conditions that would encourage transfer of S&T outcomes is a powerful argument for a viable and effective national S&T policy. In a pamphlet on S&T policy, published in 2000, the National Science Foundation (NSF) described the role of policy in the following words:

> The future of science and technology will require more wise policy decisions about how to use the nation's resources to the greatest benefit. Policy is a management tool for nurturing, distributing, and harvesting the creativity of S&T. In choices made daily by decision makers in the public and private sectors, Federal policy clasps the invisible hand of the market. The result is an evolving research economy in science and engineering that continues to spur intellectual endeavor, increase participation by those talented and trained, and capture innovations for the public good.[52]

This quote is an articulated way of stating that there is *no* public S&T policy. Decisions made by federal officials on allocation of S&T resources are compartmentalized within the federal departments. They do not follow a coherent S&T policy, because there is none. Priorities in allocating these resources are set by adhering to a mix of agency requirements, public opinion, and public pressures *du jour*. When a certain public good is considered an urgent priority, S&T funds will be reassigned and channeled toward it. Examples include investments in AIDS research, breast cancer, and genetic research. Whatever there is of a consensus and a semblance of a coherent S&T policy at the national level is activated through allocation of resources and the creation of favorable conditions for S&T creation and transfer.

S&T Policy Activated by Resource Allocation

Allocation of resources at the national level influences the behavior of audiences targeted in the allocation. In a process similar to using tax laws to stimulate or depress certain economic behaviors, allocation of S&T resources by federal agencies sparks interest in given areas and disciplines of S&T, and provides actual means to conduct such S&T activities. When this happens, other areas and topics that are not included in the allocation are, by definition, being deemphasized—even without a clear, coherent, and declared policy statement.[53]

At best, a national S&T policy would be focused on allocations of resources for *science*, as a *technology* policy is an impossible task. Why? Because technological innovations are engendered by scientific discoveries *and* by a complex process of transformations. As shown in Chapters 5-6, and 9-13 of this book, technological innovations emerge in response to a variety of different factors, under a myriad of scenarios. The best that government agencies can do to influence this process is to create conditions that would be favorable to the organizations that perform the transformation of scientific outputs into technological innovations, and those that adopt these innovations.

Allocation of resources for *science* will eventually lead to technologies that emanate from them. For example, in the 1960s the federal government allocated large investments into S&T in space exploration, and in the 1970s and 1980s the shift occurred from space toward environmental R&D. As investments in environmental R&D reached a "critical mass," the outcomes from it increased, and with them a more pronounced outcome of technological innovations they engendered. Although much of the R&D was geared toward supporting the regulatory function of environmental agencies, technological innovations that emerged from environmental R&D were diffused to other sectors.[54]

S&T Policy Activated by Creation of Favorable Conditions

The federal government can influence the direction and success of national S&T in a much more effective manner when it creates conditions that favor and facilitate the conduct of S&T, the adoption of technological innovations, and the process of entrepreneurship that utilizes these innovations to create economic value.[55] At least three modes of action are available to the government. The first is *fiscal* policies, primarily through the use of tax credits for R&D. The U.S. tax code, as well as tax codes in many states, allows for deductions of R&D expenses.[56] But how effective are these fiscal policies in stimulating private S&T? Several studies have concluded that a positive relation exists between fiscal incentives and R&D investments. For example, Billings and Fried found the U.S. tax code "meaningfully" influencing R&D intensity in private-sector companies.[57] Another study explored fiscal policies toward R&D in OECD countries.[58] This study concluded that "a dollar in tax credit for R&D stimulates a dollar of addition R&D" (p. 449).

Monetary policies are another mode of action open to the government in its effort to create favorable conditions for S&T. Examples are direct subsidies and affordable credit lines for start-up companies in selected S&T industries. Unlike the case of social policies, there is a lack of consensus among researchers on the effectiveness of direct support for commercial S&T. Giesecke compared R&D support policies for biotechnology in the United States and Germany.[59] She concluded that direct and targeted support is less effective than broader support that helps create what she calls "preferable economic ecology."

A third mode is via *bankruptcy* or insolvency *legislation.* Due to legislative activity in 1999-2000 in the United States Congress that was aimed at drastic modification in the bankruptcy law, the connection to S&T is further explored in the following section.

S&T Policy, Bankruptcy Law, and Technical Entrepreneurship

The U.S. bankruptcy law enacted in 1898 was primarily established to assist interstate commerce and to strive for uniformity in American enterprise, hitherto constrained by a myriad of unequal and debilitating laws in many states. A century later, due to pressures from the financial services industry, Congress decided to tighten allowances for debt-forgiveness.[60]

What is the connection between S&T and bankruptcy laws? Without going into the legal and political details of the discussions in Congress, the provisions of the U.S. bankruptcy law in the past century have created a climate supportive of risk-taking and technological entrepreneurship. Foremost, these provisions of debt-forgiveness allowed society to share in the risks associated with new business initiatives, especially S&T enterprises. They allowed the *spreading of the risk*, thus offering an important incentive that facilitated the creation of risky new ventures. In essence, society gave S&T entrepreneurs a "social boost," allowing them to transfer some of the risk to the overall population. In the end, when S&T entrepreneurs abound (some succeed, others fail)—everybody wins in such a system.[61]

By changing these conditions, the revisions in the bankruptcy laws create a new playing field. It becomes a much tougher environment for entrepreneurs. Society undermines the innovative spirit by taking away the social boost that the sharing of the risk had provided in the previous legislation. Although hard-core technology entrepreneurs will continue to take risks, many potential innovators will be deterred from entering the "race."

The best illustration of the reluctance of entrepreneurs to play in a hostile environment is the former Soviet Union and its satellites in Eastern

Europe. The lack of encouraging policies and risk-sharing may account for the few entrepreneurs that have emerged in these countries.

Financial managers in the United States who have lobbied for changes in bankruptcy laws seem to have little understanding of the innovation process. They have supported an idea that seems financially sound, yet is damaging to the delicate balance of the allocation of social resources, risk, and technological entrepreneurship.

Allocation of Resources by States

State and local governments in the United States and in other countries have recognized the role of science and technology in regional and local development. Unlike federal allocation criteria that emphasize national objectives, states and localities are primarily interested in economic growth and the creation of jobs. Traditionally these governments supported S&T via three complementary strategies: direct investments and fiscal incentives, science and technology parks, and the creation of technology corridors.

Direct investments and fiscal incentives are two sides of the same coin. States attract S&T laboratories and companies by providing infrastructure, tax rebates and "holidays," and by creating an overall climate favorable to S&T in general and to S&T entrepreneurs in particular. For example, the state of Sao Paulo in Brazil established the State Research Foundation (FAPESP) in 1960.[62] The foundation is funded by the state, receiving annually 1 percent of all the state's tax revenues. In early 2000, scientists from FAPESP announced breakthroughs in DNA research.[63] The foundation supports research via peer review, in a mode similar to that employed by the U.S. National Science Foundation.

In the U.S., all 50 states have programs aimed at attracting and nurturing S&T efforts. Most of these programs are managed and funded by the state's department of economic development or similar functions. In the 1990s, estimates of annual support of S&T by states approached $1 billion.[64]

Science and technology parks are another form of state support for S&T. In cooperation with universities and private industry, state and localities support the establishment of S&T corridors and S&T parks. Corridors are stretches of land where high-technology companies and laboratories conjugate, with public support that helps to create the infrastructure and provides fiscal incentives. Examples are Route 128 in Boston, the Illinois corridor west of Chicago, and Silicon Valley south of San Francisco.

Science parks include "incubators" for small entrepreneurial S&T firms. These parks are usually clustered near universities, so they enjoy the intellectual content and facilities of the university.[65] States and localities support such parks in the belief that they enhance the local university, attract private capital, and ultimately create jobs when the company leaves the incubator and normally remains in the region.

Many industrialized countries have established science parks and technology corridors. Japan's Tsukuba "Science City" is an example of a regional and national effort to congregate academics and company researchers in one location, somewhat similar to the Los Alamos effort during the Second World War.[66] Peking University established a science park in Beijing.[67] Taiwan established the Hsinchu Science Park.[68] Sweden formed the Linkoping Foundation for Small Business Development and Finland established the Spinno Program.[69] Other examples are Brazil's Park Alfa, in the southern city of Florianopolis, Western Australian Technology Park, and the technology park of the University of Twente in the Netherlands.[70]

These programs and initiatives vary in scope, size of investments, disciplinary areas of S&T, and the roles that states, localities, and national governments play in their founding and support. But they share some common attributes: mainly the desire to exploit S&T so as to extract from it benefits that would contribute to economic growth and creation of employment opportunities.

How Successful Are State Initiatives?

Are such state and regional initiatives successful, and do they indeed contribute to economic and other benefits? Irwin Feller conducted several studies of the performance of state S&T programs.[71] He concluded that states consider these programs economic investments, therefore they tend to concentrate on performance measures that reflect their impact on economic variables, such as growth and employment. But, in most cases, states fail to adequately assess the outcomes from S&T initiatives because they lack specific and measurable objectives for these investments due to the complexity of the S&T process and the difficulties in relating S&T outputs to economic activity.[72]

The best assessments of S&T by states show some impacts on the region's economic growth pattern. But these results are not sufficient to produce conclusions that could adequately be used in policy-making and decisions on what to do with S&T initiatives and how much they contribute to the state's economy.

HOW SOCIETY ACTUALLY EXPLOITS S&T

In previous sections of this chapter I explored the various means by which society and its institutions extract value from S&T. Although by using standard economic metrics S&T has not proven to be a resounding success (particularly in the case of research parks and similar endeavors), there are other benefits to be considered.

Individual Artifacts

Four categories of such benefits come to mind. The first in order of complexity and comprehensiveness of their impact on society is the effect of *individual artifacts* created by S&T. The telephone, computer, printing press, electrical power and electrical tools, the steam engine, crop rotation, antibiotics, nuclear instruments, the wheel, jet propulsion, and the shaft in wagons drawn by horses are illustrations of individual artifacts that provided social benefits. Each produced some good that benefitted social institutions and society at large in such areas as transportation, health care, construction of homes and roads, communication, and improvements in commerce, security, and similar social needs.[73]

Ultimate Social Objectives

A second category consists of benefits from S&T that contribute to *achieving the ultimate objectives* of human societies and social institutions. If the aims of such entities are to maintain the cohesion of the society, to feed, clothe, and protect its members, to raise the young and to pass on to them the values and traditions of the society, then S&T contributes to achieving these objectives. When S&T outcomes provide improvements in agriculture, locomotion, education, and safety of members, society is not only better off but also better able to survive. Improvements in transportation allow for a timely and rational distribution of agricultural surplus, thus assuring the survival of members who live far from fertile lands, or who have suffered major natural disasters that prevent them from growing adequate amounts of food.

There is, of course, an economic value to these contributions and some causal chain that leads from the S&T output to the ultimate societal goals. But the classification here of S&T benefits simply suggests the link that S&T would have to ultimate social goals. However we achieve these goals, S&T plays an important role in preserving, protecting, and ameliorating the social context and the social experience.[74]

Revolutions and Transformations

Impacts of S&T on society also appear in the more aggregate form of transformations in the ways and means members interact and social institutions conduct their activities. When such transformations are disruptive, leading to a marked departure from existing norms and practices, we have revolutionary transformations. Taken in the context of their historical appearance, innovations such as gun powder, jet propulsion, and the integrated circuit in effect "revolutionized" the workings of society.

How can we define the actual impact of S&T so that transformations in society can be attributed to its outcomes and contributions? Figure 16.8 lists the social dimensions that need to be impacted by S&T in order for transformations to occur.

When S&T engenders changes in culture, beliefs, and practices, a transformation may occur in society that would permanently alter its makeup and basic attributes. The printing press was an innovation that changed not only the way in which books were produced, but directly contributed to deep changes in European culture, its religious landscape, and the social intercourse of its inhabitants. After the 16th century Europeans had ample access to

Figure 16.8
Dimensions of Society Impacted by S&T
in the Creation of Social Transformations

DIMENSION OF SOCIETY	EXAMPLES OF THE NATURE OF IMPACTS
•**Beliefs**	Changes in societal beliefs about nature, politics, economics, etc.
•**Culture**	Changes in cultural elements such as traditions, attitudes, and rituals
•**Practices**	Changes in a variety of practices in politics, economics, religion
•**Social Intercourse**	Changes in methods and approaches to legal issues, language, fashions
•**Means of Production**	Changes in the make-up and distribution of means of production
•**Scientific Approach**	Changes in how society views the world—and its phenomena
•**Segments Affected**	Which segments of society are affected? Differences between changes in the young versus older segments.
•**Role of S&T**	Changes in the degree of importance society places on S&T

Not necessarily in order of importance.

inexpensive and increasingly ubiquitous information and knowledge in the form of printed books, pamphlets, newspapers, and similar variants. This change influenced the spread of political, economic, social, and philosophical ideas, and helped to create changes in the existing practices, notions, and approaches to society's experience and the human condition.[75]

A 1999 survey asked a thousand scientists to name the most important invention of the past millennia. The printing press received many votes for being directly responsible for such phenomena as literacy and the political and social revolutions of the past several centuries.[76]

These transformations, some in a disruptive form of revolution, beg the question: How much should S&T impact social dimensions to create meaningful and sustained transformations? As described in Chapters 14 and 15, S&T produces effects that are often "late bloomers." Because of the intricacies of implementation, adoption of innovations, and factors influencing technology transfer, some innovations may duly engender visible social change only after they have been extensively used by social organizations over a long period of time. The printing press did not immediately create such changes as the spread of democratic ideas, nor did the automobile change the American landscape into a "motorized society" soon upon its introduction.

The impacts of S&T are cumulative and are diffused preponderantly, so their *total* effects measure a combination of factors that accrue over time. Transformations "beget" (generate) additional changes. Printing presses increased literacy, which then led to popular and massive diffusion of ideas, notions, stories, information, and knowledge. These, in turn, impacted society's attitudes toward science and technology and provoked a change in the way common citizens viewed their world, their leaders, and their social surroundings. The "quantities" of these effects and their inputs to subsequent transformations are impossible to measure with adequate precision.

Intangibles

A third category of benefits of S&T are the intangible effects on the members and institutions of society. These are effects that can be viewed as "by-products" of S&T and the impacts of innovations. Four such impacts are possible. First, S&T outputs give hope to the average members of society. They provide confidence in human achievement, and help to alleviate the negative effects of desperation and alienation.

Second, S&T has replaced magic as an explanation of nature. By propagating the use of the scientific method, S&T has made scientific reasoning a more popular approach to problems of humanity. This is exemplified in popular sentiments toward advanced medicine, where parents agree to innoculate their children against age-old childhood diseases— although the parents themselves possess little knowledge or education.[77]

A third category is the answers that S&T provides for people who are simply curious and ask questions, such as Why? How? and When? about the universe and about life itself. How else can we explain the tremendous success and lasting influence of Stephen Hawking and his description of astrophysics, relativity, the nature of the universe, and the history of time.[78] Hawking first published his book in 1988, and has since delighted countless readers with what the *New York Times* reviewer called "an ability to illustrate highly complex propositions with analogies plucked from daily life."[79]

The fourth category includes the *potential* solutions that S&T may offer to perennial social and economic problems facing human societies: hunger, poverty, disease, mortality, morbidity, inequality, and a myriad of other human frailties. All of these intangibles are resistant to measurement and precise assessment, take long periods to appear and to produce visible effects, and are diffused throughout the social experience.

SUMMARY

Society benefits from S&T in various complementary ways. Some direct benefits occur by the effects of S&T innovations on the immediate state of health, education, transportation, and similar social phenomena. Such innovations make a strong impact on social conditions. The average quality of life rises as a result of these S&T innovations, and the human condition is improved.

But S&T innovations also contribute to the transformations in society, and to longer-term effects on such societal dimensions as culture, systems of belief, and overall social intercourse. For example, S&T produced innovations in telecommunication, so that geographical distances have practically shrunk and instantaneous communication has become a reality. This contributed to sharp increase in work-at-home practices, shopping on-line rather than visiting a physical store, and living with networks of electronic mail.

S&T has also generated negative outcomes, such as environmental threats, erosion in social traditions, and individual problems of alienation. Is S&T harboring potential solutions to these problems caused by S&T? Perhaps, as I discuss in Chapter 18, there are solutions that appear as S&T outcomes, but cannot or will not be implemented due to a variety of reasons, other than scientific or technological.[80] Perhaps S&T contains the seeds for curing the ailments and problems it produces. Yet the benefits accrued to society and the human condition far outweigh the side effects and the negative by-products of S&T innovations.[81]

How Society Exploits S&T: Key Propositions

Society exploits S&T in both the immediate effects on the population and social dimensions, and the longer-term benefits that crystallize in social progress and transformation. How much has S&T contributed to societal welfare and to social progress? Clearly this is a difficult, perhaps impossible question to answer. Companies may attempt to compute the returns from S&T, but at the level of society such computations may not be very enlightening. Statistics on morbidity, mortality, infant mortality, educational achievements via testing, and similar social variables may provide an indication of the benefits from S&T.

Thus, decline in mortality and morbidity, improved nutrition and health care, better education, and other such impacts of S&T make the human condition more viable, livable, or any similar adjective.

Proposition 1: Society exploits S&T and generates value from it by gaining immediate as well as long-range benefits in all dimensions and areas of social relations.

Proposition 2: S&T provides benefits to society and to its members by affecting positively and cumulatively: perceptions, attitudes, values, practices, and the perspectives on life and social activities.

Proposition 3: In the final analysis, despite the negative impacts and side-effects from S&T, society is much better off because of the value created by S&T.

Proposition 4: Value created by S&T in society is manifested in improvements and progress in such dimensions as health, transportation, housing, communication, nutrition, education, and public safety.

Proposition 5: The rate of propagation of S&T innovations in society has continually and greatly accelerated during the 20th century. Diffusion of these innovations is today five times faster than in 1900.

Proposition 6: The more a society invests public resources in S&T, the more it will have the tools to ameliorate social conditions and resolve social problems. Having the tools is not an assurance that they will be implemented for the public good.

Proposition 7:   The Law of Preponderant Diffusion of S&T posits that S&T outcomes will diffuse in society, regardless of the sector of social endeavor where S&T investments are made.

Proposition 8:   By impacting societies, S&T is a crucial factor in determining the rate and trajectory of the progress and the destiny of societies, hence dictating their different evolutionary paths.

Chapter 17 explores proposition 8, and addresses other issues in the effect of S&T on society. By themselves, each S&T innovation contributes to one aspect of social life. But, cumulatively, S&T innovations create an immense value for society and its members, allowing for progress and the betterment of social conditions. From the first moment that a cave dweller wandered outside the cave and wondered why the world is the way it is—and what to do about it—S&T became a conduit to forge stable societies and to enable human progress.

NOTES

1. Erasmus, D., *The Praise of Folly and Other Writings* (New York: W.W. Norton & Company, 1989), translated by Robert M. Adams. The paragraph is from p. 27.

2. For a more comprehensive view of society and social institutions see, for example, Nash, J., and J. Calonico, *Institutions in Modern Society: Meanings, Forms, and Character* (New York: General Hall Incorporated, 1990). Also see Jackson, J. (Ed.), *Institutions in American Society: Essays in Market, Political, and Social Organizations* (Ann Arbor: University of Michigan Press, 1990); and Castoriadis, C., *The Imaginary Institution of Society* (Cambridge, MA: MIT Press, 1998).

3. See the continuing debate on what constitutes "public good" in, for example, Kaul, I., M. Stern, and J. Grunberg (Eds.), *Global Public Goods: International Cooperation in the 21st Century* (New York: Oxford University Press, 1999). Also see Sullum, J., *For Your Own Good: The Anti-Smoking Crusade and the Tyranny of Public Health* (New York: The Free Press, 1998); and see Davidson, S., and S. Sommers, *Remaking Medicaid: Managed Care for the Public Good* (San Francisco: Jossey-Bass, 1998).

4. See, for example, Scott, R., *Institutions and Organizations* (Thousand Oaks, CA: Sage Publications, 1995). Also see Skolnick, J., and E. Currie, *Crisis in American Institutions* (Reading, MA: Addison-Wesley, 2000), in particular see pp. 413-440.

5. The notion of "everybody's business" is as vague as "public good." In the course of advertising their ideas, many interest groups resort to the employment of this notion as a descriptor of their unique issue. See, for example, Aaronson, S., *Trade is Everybody's Business* (New York: Close Up Foundation, 1995); Townsend, P., and J. Gebhardt, *Quality is Everybody's Business* (Boca Raton, FL: CRC Press, 1999).

The English writer Daniel Defoe (1660-1731) wrote a didactic book, published in 1775, with the title *Everybody's Business Is Nobody's Business*.

6. See, for example, MacLeon, M., J. Anderson, and B. Martin, "Identifying Research Priorities in Public Sector Funding Agencies: Mapping Science Outputs to User Needs," *Technology Analysis & Strategic Management*, 10(2), 1998, 139-155. This study of the U.K. Natural Environment Research Council criticized allocation of research funds based solely on scientific needs and peer review. The study advocated increased focus on users in the public sector.

7. See, for example, Norberg-Bohm, U., "Stimulating 'Green' Technological Innovation: An Analysis of Alternative Policy Mechanisms," *Policy Sciences*, 32(1), 1999, 13-38. The author discussed the design criteria for public policy that would promote radical technological innovations which would contribute toward a more desirable ecosystem.

8. Clinton, W., and A. Gore, *Science in the National Interest* (Washington, DC: Office of Science and Technology Policy, 1994), p. 7.

9. U.S. House of Representatives Science Committee, *Unlocking Our Future: Toward a New National Science Policy*. (A report to Congress, September 24, 1998, available on the Internet at: *http://www.house.gov/science/science_policy_report.html*).

10. *Ibid.*, p. 12.

11. There is a vast literature on the history, operations, structure, and performance of the network of national S&T laboratories. See, for example, Crow, M., and B. Bozeman, *Limited by Design: R and D Laboratories in the U.S. National Innovation System* (New York: Columbia University Press, 1998).

12. For example, Argonne and Los Alamos in high energy physics (they belong to the Department of Energy), Night-Vision (Department of the Army), and the USDA laboratory in Peoria, Illinois.

13. See, for example, Gosnell, J., *et al.*, "Lessons Learned from Reinvention Labs in the Department of Defense," *The Armed Forces Comptroller*, 43(4), 1998, 5-10. Also see Alic, J., "Technical Knowledge and Technology Diffusion: New Issues for US Government Policy," *Technology Analysis & Strategic Management*, 5(2), 1993, 369-383.

14. See the excellent review of the technology transfer literature in Bozeman, B., "Technology Transfer and Public Policy: A Review of Research and Theory," *Research Policy*, 29(4,5), 2000, 627-655. Also see Molas-Gallart, J., and T. Sinclair, "From Technology Generation to Technology Transfer: The Concept and Reality of the 'Dual Use Technology Centers'," *Technovation*, 19(11), 1999, 661-671.

15. Coughlin, J., "Technology Needs of Aging Boomers," *Issues in Science and Technology*, 16(1), 1999, 53-60.

16. Coughlin also argued that the paradox of longevity is the failure of the country to have made adequate investments in the infrastructure to support this "older" yet active segment of the population. This issue is discussed later in this chapter under the topics of social choices and priorities in allocation of resources for S&T.

17. See, for example, Krishna, V., "Science for Citizens," *The UNESCO Courier*, 52(5), 1999, 35-36. Krishna, who heads the Center for Studies in Science Policy in India, argued that there is a need for a new "social contract" between science

and society, and for the creation of what he calls "institutional safety nets." His arguments rest on the proposition that science provides social relief via its action in social organizations. Also see Georghiou, L., and D. Roessner, "Evaluating Technology Programs: Tools and Methods," *Research Policy*, 29(4/5), 2000, 657-678.

18. Baptista, R., "The Diffusion of Process Innovations: A Selective Review," *International Journal of the Economics of Business*, 6(1), 1999, 107-129.

19. See Chatterje, R., and J. Eliashberg, "The Innovation Diffusion Process in a Heterogeneous Population: A Micromodelling Approach," *Management Science*, 36(6), 1990, 1057-1079.

20. See, for example, Yuan Pu, S., "Expert Systems Diffusion in British Banking: Diffusion Models and Media Factor," *Information & Management*, 35(1), 1999, 1-8. Also see Mahajan, V., and Y. Wind, *Innovation Diffusion Models of New Product Acceptance* (New York, HarperBusiness, 1986); and see the seminal book, Rogers, E., *Diffusion of Innovations* (New York: Simon & Schuster, 1996).

21. See, for example, Karahanna, E., D. Straub, and N. Chervany, "Information Technology Adoption Across Time: A Cross-Sectional Comparison of Pre-Adoption and Post-Adoption Beliefs," *MIS Quarterly*, 23(2), 1999, 183-213. Also see Gruber, H., "The Diffusion of Innovations in Protected Industries: The Textile Industry," *Applied Economics*, 30(1), 1998, 77-83.

22. See, for example, Drury, D., and A. Farhoomand, "Information Technology Push/Pull Reactions," *The Journal of Systems and Software*, 47(1), 1999, 3-10. The authors concluded that for technology-push and demand-pull conditions, there is a need for different strategies and management practices to make diffusion a success.

23. Hansen, P., "Publicly Produced Knowledge for Business: When Is it Effective?" *Technovation*, 15(6), 1995, 387-398.

24. See, for example, Morrison, S., "How Technology Can Make Your Job Safer," *Corrections Today*, 62(4), 2000, 58-61. Also see Coleman, S., "Biometrics: Solving Cases of Mistaken Identity and More," *FBI Law Enforcement Bulletin*, 69(6), 2000, 9-16; and, Taylor, B., "Virtual Private Networking: Secure Law Enforcement Communication on the Internet," *The Police Chief*, 67(6), 2000, 13-14.

25. See, for example, Holden, B., "Driving Forces in Doing Business with the Government: Technology, Teamwork, Trust," *Business Credit*, 102(5), 2000, 56-57. Also see Gallart, J., and T. Sinclair, "From Technology Generation to Technology Transfer: The Concept and Reality of the Dual-Use Technology Centers," *Technovation*, 19(11), 1999, 661-671; and see Palfrey, T., "The Hidden Legacy of Scott: Weapons of Nondestruction and the UK Government Proposals to Control the Transfer of Technology by Intangible Means," *International Review of Law, Computers, and Technology*, 13(2), 1999, 163-181.

26. Burke, J., *The Knowledge Web* (New York: Simon & Schuster, 1999).

27. See, for example, Sharp, P., *et al.*, "Origin and Evolution of AIDS Viruses," *Biological Bulletin*, 196(3), 1999, 338-342.

28. Crane, D., *Invisible Colleges* (Chicago: University of Chicago Press, 1988).

29. See, for example, Schoch, N., and K. Hahn, "Applying Diffusion Theory to Electronic Publishing: A Conceptual Framework for Examining Issues and Outcomes," *Journal of the American Society for Information Science*, 34

(Proceedings of the ASIS Annual Meeting), 1997, 5-13. Also see Laestadius, S., "Biotechnology and the Potential for a Radical Shift of Technology in Forest Industry," *Technology Analysis & Strategic Management*, 12(2), 2000, 193-212.

30. See, for example, Rai, A., "Researching the Organizational Diffusion of Information Technology Innovation," *Information Resources Management Journal*, 11(3), 1998, 3-4. Also see Soule, S., "The Diffusion of an Unsuccessful Innovation," *Annals of the American Academy of Political and Social Sciences*, 566, November 1999, 120-131.

31. Valente, T., and R. Davis, "Accelerating the Diffusion of Innovations Using Opinion Leaders," *Annals of the American Academy of Political and Social Sciences*, 566, November 1999, 55-67.

32. Gladwell, M., *The Tipping Point: How Little Things Can Make a Big Difference* (New York: Little, Brown & Company, 2000).

33. See, for example, Nochur, K., and T. Allen, "Do Nominated Boundary Spanners Become Effective Technological Gatekeepers?" *IEEE Transactions on Engineering Management*, 39(3), 1992, 265-30. Also see DeMeyer, A., "Tech Talk: How Managers Are Stimulating Global R&D Communication," *Sloan Management Review*, 32(3), 1991, 49-59; and see Keenan, W., "Subalterns of Technology: Brokering Techno-Power in Academic Sociology," *The British Journal of Sociology*, 51(2), 2000, 321-338.

34. See, for example, Place, J., "How to Position Yourself in the New Network Economy," *TMA Journal*, 18(6), 1998, 82-85. Also see Achrol, R., and P. Kotler, "Marketing in the Network Economy," *Journal of Marketing*, 63(2), 1999, 146-163.

35. See, Shapiro, C., and H. Varian, *Information Rules: A Strategic Guide to the Network Economy* (Boston: Harvard Business School Press, 1998). Also see Magel, J., and A. Armstrong, *Net Gain: Expanding Markets Through Virtual Communities* (New York: McGraw-Hill, 1997).

36. For example, see Westin, L., B. Johansson, and C. Karlsson (Eds.), *Patterns of a Network Economy* (New York: Springer-Verlag, 1994). Also see Anderson, A., and M. Beckmann (Eds.), *Knowledge and Networks in a Dynamic Economy* (New York: Springer-Verlag, 1999), in particular see pp. 119-150 (Dynamics of International Financial Networks).

37. Mansfield, E., "How Rapidly Does New Industrial Technology Leak Out?" *The Journal of Industrial Economics*, 34(2), 1985, 217-223.

38. Geisler, E., "Law of Preponderant Diffusion of Science and Technology Outcomes in Social Contexts," Working Paper, Stuart Graduate School of Business, Illinois Institute of Technology, September 2000.

39. See the interesting account in James Burke, *The Knowledge Web*, 1999, *op. cit.*, and the description of how ideas and innovation diffuse in social contexts.

40. See the references to these studies in Chapter 13.

41. See the stage model for evaluation of S&T in: Geisler, E., "Integrated Figure of Merit of Public Sector Research Evaluation," *Scientometrics*, 36(3), 1996, 379-395.

42. See, for example, Stiglitz, J., and S. Wallsten, "Public-Private Technology Partnerships: Promises and Pitfalls," *The American Behavioral Scientist*, 43(1), 1999, 52-73. Also see Hillegonda, M., and D. Novaes, "Social Impacts of Technological

Diffusion: Prenatal Diagnosis and Induced Abortion in Brazil," *Social Science & Medicine*, 50(1), 2000, 41-51; and see Cutcliffe, S., *Ideas, Machines, and Values* (London: Rowman & Littlefield, 2000), in particular see pages 44-78 on interdisciplinarity and S&T and society studies.

43. See, for example, Burke, S., E. Kingson, and U. Reinhardt (Eds.), *Social Security and Medicare: Individual Versus Collective Risk and Responsibility* (Washington, DC: Brookings Institution, 2000), pp. 72-74.

44. National Science Foundation, *Science and Technology Policy: Past and Prologue: A Companion to Science and Engineering Indicators-2000* (Arlington, VA: National Science Board, 2000).

45. *Ibid.*, p. 5.

46. See, for example, Reinhardt, U., D. Shactman, and S. Altman (Eds.), *Regulating Managed Care: Theory, Practice, and Future Options* (San Francisco: Jossey-Bass, 1999), pp. 229-228. Also see Johnson, D., "A Reality Check on Entitlements," *The Futurist*, 33(10), 1999, 10-12; and see Levande, D., J. Herrick, and K. Sung, "Eldercare in the United States and South Korea: Balancing Family and Community Support," *Journal of Family Issues*, 21(5), 2000, 632-651; and see Schneider, S., "The Hidden Welfare State: Tax Expenditures and Social Policy in the United States," *The American Political Science Review*, 93(2), 1999, 455-456. This is a review of the book with this title by Christopher Howard, Princeton University Press, 1997.

47. Clinton, W., Speech at the National Medal of Science Award Ceremony, March 14, 2000.

48. There is a vast literature on both conditions. See, for example, Kumar, D., and D. Chubin (Eds.), *Science, Technology, and Society: A Sourcebook on Research and Practice* (Boston: Kluwer Academic Publishers, 2000). Also see Albarran, A., and D. Goff (Eds.), *Understanding the Web: The Social, Political, and Economic Dimensions of the Internet* (Ames, Iowa: Iowa State University Press, 2000); and Johnson, S., *Interface Culture: How New Technology Transforms the Way We Create and Communicate* (New York: Basic Books, 1999). Also see Cross, R., and L. Baird, "Technology is Not Enough: Improving Performance by Building Organizational Memory," *Sloan Management Review*, 41(3), 2000, 69-78.

49. Garud, R., P. Nayyar, and Z. Shapira, (Eds.), *Technological Innovation: Oversights and Foresights* (New York: Cambridge University Press, 1997).

50. Pennings, J., "Technological Innovation: Oversights and Foresights," *Administrative Science Quarterly*, 43(3), 1998, 706-710.

51. Other examples include R&D in health care, where investments in cell research, biochemistry, and genetics are crucial inputs into R&D targeted at specific diseases such as AIDS, diabetes, and Alzheimer's.

52. National Science Foundation, *Science and Technology Policy*, 2000, *op. cit.*, p. 3.

53. For example, tax laws that allow full deduction of interest payments on mortgages stimulate home ownership and are essential to a prosperous housing market.

54. In the late 1990s there were reassessments of environmental S&T and the role of the government in it. See, for example, Kolb, C., R. Loehr, and M. Gopnik,

"Balanced Environmental R&D," *Environmental Science & Technology*, 32(3), 1998, 73-75. The authors cited a report by the National Research Council that called for changes in environmental R&D. Similarly, the Rand Science & Technology Policy Institute suggested that instead of increasing the funding of environmental S&T, the federal government should create the conditions necessary for conducting successful environmental S&T. See, Johnson, J., "Environment and the Bottom Line," *Chemical & Engineering News*, 77(25), 1999, 25-26.

55. In the following discussion I adopt a refined Schumpeterian outlook, described earlier in Chapters 5, 12, and 13.

56. See, for example, Lim, H., and B. Russo, "A Taxation Policy Toward Capital, Technology, and Long-Run Growth," *Journal of Macroeconomics*, 21(3), 1999, 463-491.

57. Billings, A., and Y. Fried, "The Effects of Taxes and Organizational Variables on Research and Development Intensity," *R&D Management*, 29(3), 1999, 289-301. The authors studied 113 companies with data from 1994.

58. Hall, B., and J. Van Reenen, "How Effective are Fiscal Incentives for R&D? A Review of the Evidence," *Research Policy*, 29(4,5), 2000, 449-469.

59. Giesecke, S., "The Contrasting Roles of Government in the Development of Biotechnology Industry in the US and Germany," *Research Policy*, 29(2), 2000, 205-223.

60. See, for example, Hansen, B., "Commercial Associations and the Creation of a National Economy: The Demand for Federal Bankruptcy Law," *Business History Review*, 72(1), 1998, 86-113. Also see Lebaton, S., "House Votes to Make It Tougher to Escape Debt Through Personal Bankruptcy," *New York Times*, May 6, 1999, 28-29.

61. This topic is further addressed in Geisler, E., "S&T Policy, Bankruptcy Legislation, and Technology Entrepreneurship," Working Paper, Stuart Graduate School of Business, Illinois Institute of Technology, May, 2000.

62. See the website: <www.FAPESP.br> (Fundacao de Amparo a Pesquisa do Estado de Sao Paulo). The foundation started operations in 1962.

63. Jones, P., "Brazilian Scientists Adding to Mercurial Rise in National Pride," *Chicago Tribune*, August 23, 2000, Section 1, page 4.

64. See, for example, Coburn, C., *Partnerships: A Compendium of State and Federal Cooperative Technology Programs* (Columbus, OH: Battelle Press, 1995).

65. See, for example, Geisler, E., *The Metrics of Science and Technology* (Westport, CT: Quorum Books, 2000), Chapter 17. Also see Gibb, J. (Ed.), *Science Parks and Innovation Centers: The Economic and Social Impacts* (Amsterdam, Elsevier, 1985); and see, Mowery, D., "State Government Funding of Science and Technology: Lessons for Federal Programs," in: Meredith, M., S. Nelson, and A. Teich (Eds.), *Science and Technology Yearbook* (Washington, DC: American Association for the Advancement of Science, 1991) pp. 241-250.

66. See, for example, Monck, C., D. Porter, and P. Quintas, *Science Parks and the Growth of High Technology Firms* (London: Routledge, 1990); and see, Klofsten, M., and D. Jones-Evans, "Stimulation of Technology-Based Small Firms: A Case Study of University-Industry Cooperation," *Technovation*, 16(4), 1996, 187-193. See, in particular, Gene, G., "Japan's Science City," *The Futurist*, 20(1), 1986, 38-42.

67. See Jun, S., "Peking University of Science Park Shows Great Prospects," *Beijing Review*, 43(20), 2000, 19-20.

68. See Lee, W., and W. Yang, "The Cradle of Taiwan High Technology Industry Development: Hsinchu Science Park (HSP)," *Technovation*, 20(1), 2000, 55-59.

69. Autio, E., and M. Klofsten, "A Comparative Study of Two European Business Incubators," *Journal of Small Business Management*, 36(1), 1998, 30-43.

70. See Cabral, R., "From University-Industry Interfaces to the Making of a Science Park: Florianopolis, Southern Brazil," *International Journal of Technology Management*, 15(8), 1998, 778-799; and see Phillimore, J., "Beyond the Linear View of Innovation in Science Park Evaluation: An Analysis of Western Australian Technology Park," *Technovation*, 19(11), 1999, 673-680.

71. See Feller, I., "Federal and State Government Roles in Science and Technology," *Economic Development Quarterly*, 11(4), 1997, 283-296.

72. See, for example, Cozzens, S., and J. Melkers, "Use and Usefulness of Performance Measurement in State Science and Technology Programs," *Policy Studies Journal*, 25(3), 1997, 425-435. Also see Westhead, P., S. Batstone, and F. Martin, "Technology-Based Firms Located on Science Parks: The Applicability of Bullock's Soft-Hard Model," *Enterprise and Innovation Management Studies*, 1(2), 2000, 107-140.

73. See, for example, Garrison, E., *A History of Engineering and Technology*, 2nd ed. (Boca Raton, FL: CRC Press, 1958). Also see Langdon, W., "A New Social Contract for Science," *Technology Review*, 96(4), 1993, 65-66; and Liban, C., "How Far Will Science and Technology Take Us?" *National Forum*, 80(1), 2000, 6-8.

74. See, for example, Harris, D., and G. Hillman (Eds.), *Foraging and Farming: The Evolution of Plant Exploitation* (London: Unwin Hyman, 1989); and see Pacey, A., *Technology in World Civilization* (Cambridge, MA: MIT Press, 1990). Also see discussion of environmental influences in: Norberg-Bohm, V., "Stimulating 'Green' Technological Innovation: An Analysis of Alternative Policy Mechanisms," *Policy Sciences*, 32(1), 1999, 13-38.

75. See Kumar, D., and D. Chubin (Eds.), *Science, Technology, and Society* (Boston: Kluwer Academic Publishers, 2000); and see Gilmartin, K., *Print Politics: The Press and Radical Opposition in Early Nineteenth Century England* (Cambridge: Cambridge University Press, 1997); and Hedgepeth, J., *The Significance of the Printed Word in Early America* (Westport, CT: Greenwood Press, 1999).

76. Bank, D., "The Nominees for Best Invention," *Wall Street Journal*, January 4, 1999, pg. A13.

77. For example, see Muraskin, W., *The Politics of International Health: The Children's Vaccine Initiative and the Struggle to Develop Vaccines for the Third World* (Albany: State University of New York Press, 1998).

78. Hawking, S., *A Brief History of Time* (New York: Bantam Books, 1998).

79. *Ibid..*, back cover.

80. See, for example, Feenberg, A., *Questioning Technology* (London: Routledge, 1999); and Easton, T., *Taking Sides: Clashing Views on Controversial Issues in Science, Technology, and Society* (New York: McGraw-Hill, 2000). Also see "Visions 21: Our Technology," *Time*, June 19, 2000, pp. 60-116. For innovations

in health care, see for example, Sorid, D., and S. Moore, "The Virtual Surgeon," *IEEE Spectrum*, 37(7), 2000, 26-31.

81. See, for example, Pranzos, N., *Our Cosmic Future: Humanity's Fate in the Universe* (New York: Cambridge University Press, 2000).

17

SCIENCE &TECHNOLOGY, THE ECONOMY, AND SOCIETY: ISSUES, CONTROVERSIES, AND A REALITY CHECK

In the final analysis, we all breathe the same air, we all cherish our children's future, and we are all mortals.

John Fitzgerald Kennedy

S&T is so embedded in our economy and social fabric that no wonder it generates many issues and controversies. In this chapter I will try to sort out some of the more evident, perhaps more vocal, issues. As objective as I have been throughout this book, some personal beliefs will undoubtedly seep into the following pages. S&T influences us all, from the humblest village in the developing world to the inhabitants of mighty skyscrapers in the most advanced metropolises. None of us is immune to feelings about S&T, its nature, and its impacts on our world and our lives.

This book is about the *value* we create with S&T. I approach the notion of value from both the perspectives of the economy and society. But, are we asking adequate questions, or simply accepting the definitions of value used by those who apply and practice S&T?

DEFINING VALUE

For better or worse, industrial companies today define their existence in terms of the value they create for their shareholders. It's a powerful albeit narrow definition of a complex notion of what constitutes a firm. However we expand this definition, S&T ends up being simply a tool or an instrument that helps to generate such value. In fact, my own research on the strategic conception of technology in service companies has shown that even information technology is seldom considered to be of strategic importance.[1]

If S&T is viewed as the means to the creation of economic value for shareholders, are we indeed measuring the entire contribution of S&T to the economy? Also, do we actually know how much or even which value we are computing? Perhaps there is a need to *disaggregate* the definition of S&T from the value of the firm. Although S&T is realized through the workings of the commercial enterprise, its outcomes extend beyond the narrow definition of value created for the owner.

Any new definition of S&T would encompass a broader range of outcomes, impacts, and possibilities. In addition to the notions of "creative destruction" of technological innovations and "destructive technologies" that shake entire industries, S&T should also be defined as the generator of various economic values. As described in Chapter 15, S&T also contributes *economic* outcomes outside the narrow box of corporate value accounting. S&T creates tools, methods, knowledge, and conceptual frameworks that enable managers to exploit strategic opportunities. Thus, S&T contributes not only the actual innovations that are embedded in products and services (which subsequently generate value to shareholders) but also the capabilities needed in complex organizations to effectively compete and survive. This is true for the individual firm, as well as for entire industries, sectors, and the overall economy.

"WAKE-UP CALL"

Reinforcing the earlier statements in the Preface, this is a "wake-up call" to corporations and social policy-makers, social engineers, and social advocates. It's not enough to assess the value of S&T as simply its direct contribution to shareholders' value or to specific social indicators. The definition of S&T value must be expanded to the strategic aspects of S&T in the business environment, and to the comprehensive impacts on the structure of society.

Shareholders, managers, and other stakeholders must view the value of S&T as a complex array of outputs and indicators—way beyond simply creating wealth for shareholders. The question should change from: "How does S&T contribute to the firm's profitability and growth?" to: "*Where is S&T taking us?*" and "*Are we strategically positioned, or will we ever be, in the new market engendered by S&T?*"

Managers must reinvent their strategic outlooks, so that they not only understand and work within the phenomenon of technologies that destroy industries, but especially utilize these technologies to effect changes in their industry.[2] This is what the bookseller Barnes & Noble achieved by "taming" the Internet technology to conquer a solid share of the market, directly competing with the dominance of Amazon.com.

"Taming S&T": Proaction, not Reaction

There is a substantial difference between *coping* with destructive technologies, and totally revamping the definition of *value from S&T*. In the case of coping, companies ride the storm of innovative and destructive technologies.[3] Although successful companies do "everything right," they are still exposed to the destructive power of discontinuous technologies. Hence they struggle to cope and adapt.

By redefining the value gained from S&T, companies are able to "tame" the power of the most destructive technologies. This they do by *proactive* behavior which is a consequence of such redefinition. This chain of events works as follows. Companies now define value from S&T in comprehensive terms by posing the question: "Where is S&T taking us?" This means not only the S&T that we currently possess, but also those that lie over the horizon. That is not as hard to do as it seems *prima facie*. If you are a successful Internet Service Provider alerted to changes in the industry, you may be carefully considering the trends and developments in telecommunication restructuring and repositioning of major players. Yet you may be less prone to monitor developments in voice pattern recognition, which may lead to the creation of a new industry—when combined with progress in telecommunication. That is, over the horizon may lie a single apparatus, to be available in every home, office, or briefcase, containing access to television, telephone, and the Internet—all activated and controlled by voice.

The "taming of S&T" starts with asking: "Where is S&T taking *us*?" instead of: "How can we use S&T to increase (fill the blanks: profits, growth, wealth)?" Adequately answering the first question will help you "tame" S&T and control your future. Answering the second question may mean your demise.

Similarly, there needs to emerge a revolution in the way we assess the *social* value of S&T. As in business, reactive assessments of value are outdated. Proactive assessment means employing a comprehensive view of S&T that transcends specific indicators such as mortality, morbidity, and income.[4] The question that needs to be asked is: "How has S&T contributed to the strength, resiliency, and progress of society and social institutions at large?" Social indicators measure the various attributes of overall social welfare. The value that S&T delivers to society transcends these individual measures, so that a more comprehensive view is taken of S&T value.[5]

Indeed, in the past few decades S&T has produced massive changes in the social fabric. In addition to changes in levels of social indicators (such as longevity),there have also been radical changes in concepts and conventions that are prevalent in social intercourse. The nature of work has been changing—from manual to intellectual—and from capital-driven to information-driven. The nature of time, tenure in employment, allocation of resources, and social justice in such allocation are also being transformed by the outcomes from S&T.

All of this comes with a price that includes negative side effects from S&T—even disasters and confusion. The nature of the price we pay is at the heart of the debate and controversies that accompany the progress of S&T in society.

S&T AS CATALYST FOR CHANGE

In recent times S&T has been a major catalyst for dramatic changes that created irreversible social forces. The introduction of medical technology, for example, has not only generated leaps in healthcare delivery, but has also been the catalyst for discontinuous social trends. With the proliferation of the "pill" in the 1960s, women gained control over their reproductive function, thus leading to a major revolution in the status of women, their increased participation in the workforce, and resultant changes in the structure of the family.[6]

Scientific knowledge and technological innovations have also led to the redefinition of the concept of work. In the late 1990s, advances in telecommunications and information technology have facilitated working conditions across geographical distances. Moreover, social conventions about work, the nature of working, and compensation practices have undergone major restructuring. S&T is now an integral part of the work environment, mastering a different set of requirements and benefits.

Another major social change engendered by outcomes from S&T has been the redistribution of social power and influence among social institutions. Relationships between S&T and politics, S&T and religion, and S&T and legal issues have become pivotal candidates for consideration, restructuring, and controversies. Concepts of individual rights are being negotiated in light of advances in S&T. Our ability to predict a person's health problems as early as at birth has generated heated debates about confidentiality and legal rights. Our ability to practically monitor every aspect of people's lives and movements has also created a host of issues in areas such as legal rights, security and crime-prevention requirements, and the delicate balance between individuals and the authority of government. In all of the above, S&T has been a catalyst for change.[7]

Figure 17.1
S&T as Catalyst for Social Change

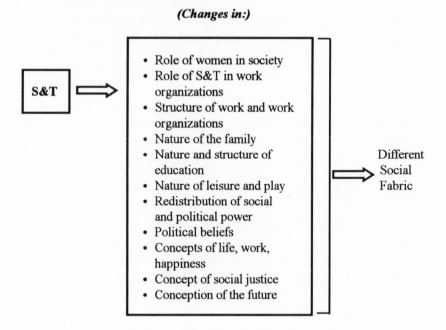

(Changes in:)

- Role of women in society
- Role of S&T in work organizations
- Structure of work and work organizations
- Nature of the family
- Nature and structure of education
- Nature of leisure and play
- Redistribution of social and political power
- Political beliefs
- Concepts of life, work, happiness
- Concept of social justice
- Conception of the future

Different Social Fabric

As social institutions absorb S&T and adapt to the changes thus produced, new and different social norms and structures tend to evolve. They may not be improved, but they are certainly different and they tend to influence each other, so that the multiple impacts are thus magnified. Work, family, social power structure, and leisure are transformed and redefined. They also impact each other, so that the changing landscape of work organizations generates changes in the distribution of social power and social relations, whereas changes in the structure of the family generate not only economic trends but also new modes of leisure, play, education, and political views.

Never before has S&T played such a pivotal role in the redesign of social institutions and social concepts. As individuals we have become "addicted" to S&T, as it invades every aspect of our life. Most of us have very little understanding of its workings and impacts on us and our world. We don't know how to fix our technology nor do most of us comprehend the science that guides it. But we are continually increasing our dependence on technology for even the more mundane activities that guide our existence. So we have become what may be roughly described as *Homo technicus*.

The Notion of *Homo Technicus*

In our postmodern society, S&T has greatly contributed to the development of a social creature we may call: *Homo technicus*. This is a member of society who presently, and in the foreseeable future, inhabits work organizations and other social institutions. Figure 17.2 shows the main attributes or characteristics of this *Homo technicus*.

Some of the attributes in Figure 17.2 show a tendency for such negative effects as social alienation, loss of sense of community, and inability to function without the tools of S&T. But similar arguments have also been proposed in criticisms of industrialization and urbanization.[8] Whenever humans congregate in large urban settings and become dependent on outcomes from S&T (industrialization, postindustrial, or information technology), there is a certain price to pay. Loss of some personal freedoms, sense of alienation and similar constraints on one's time, obligations, and independence seem to accompany trends in the progression of S&T

Figure 17.2
Characteristics of *Homo Technicus*

- Dependency on technology for mundane and routine activities at work and pleasure
- High level of sophistication and urbanity
- Affordable and easy access to information, knowledge, solutions, opinions, news, and ideas
- Proneness to sentiments of social alienation
- Proneness to loss of sense of community
- Development of eclectic terminology, preferences, and avocations
- Heightened interest in, and awareness of, progress in S&T and innovation, and the need to incorporate them in routine applications
- Development of a sense of intolerance for those in society who are not engaged in S&T and its applications
- Transfixed on trends of S&T over the horizon
- Development of a strong sense of belief in the value of S&T and its ability to solve social problems
- Dependency on a continuous flow of S&T innovations in practically all aspects of existence
- Inability to operate on a daily basis without the technology to which it has been accustomed
- Belief in the strong link between healthy economy and progressive society—and S&T
- Belief in the need to increase and improve S&T education

Not necessarily in order of importance.

Homo technicus is a complex notion that includes the benefits from S&T and the social and psychological negative consequences. Moreover, the notion describes a style of living and operating in a social and economic environment that has consistently become more complex and sophisticated. Our existence and successful performance in such an environment requires dependence on the outcomes from S&T. Perhaps for some, *Homo technicus* is a choice but for most it has become a necessity. By not being part of this concept, some members of society are doomed to be left behind, unable to compete and to partake in those benefits that a technologically advanced society has to offer them.

The "Digital Divide"

A good example is the phenomenon of the "digital divide,"[9] broadly defined as the gap between those who have access to the Internet and ancillary technology, and those who have not. The term was first introduced in 1997, following a study that appeared in 1995 conducted by the National Tele-communications and Information Administration of the U.S. Department of Commerce.[10] The gap was originally described as between rural and poor segments of the population in the United States and the rich, urban households. With increased globalization, the term has been expanded to describe gaps among regions, nations, and even continents.

Even though this phenomenon is relatively new, its social and political implications have already stirred a heated debate. There are, in my view, four crucial patterns that are emerging and the subsequent questions they harbor. There is the definition of the divide itself. Is there a divide at all, and if so, is the divide along the key dimensions of geography, race, age, economic and education levels?

Second, is this phenomenon expanding (as many have argued) so that its magnitude makes it increasingly more difficult to close the gap? As economic activities and social functions are diverted to the Internet and telecom-munication technology, those with no access to the technologies are left behind—economically and socially—and the trend will continue, so the distance between the parties expands.

Third, can S&T help to close the gap and offer the cure to the ailments produced by the digital divide? In public discourse on the topic, there have emerged potential solutions. Governments have attempted to engage the private sector to propagate the use of computers in the have-not areas and to build community centers for education and access to the technologies.[11]

Fourth, what are the implications or consequences from the digital divide, if indeed it exists, and are there credible solutions—technological or other means—that can alleviate or even resolve these outcomes? Lack of access to current and future technologies has been deemed to not only accelerate the gap between rich and poor, but also to create two distinct societies. One society is made of sophisticated people who are able to exploit S&T and who therefore enjoy its benefits of political, economic, and military power. The other society lacks this ability and is doomed to persist in a disenfranchised state of little power without enjoyment of the benefits of S&T. Some solutions have been offered, primarily by increasing levels of education and by massive investments by governments.[12]

Homo Technicus and *Homo Simplex*: The Relevant Gap

Differences created by the gap in S&T are among societies and nations, as well as *within* nations and countries. The basic phenomenon is the recent emergence of two types of people: *Homo technicus* and *Homo simplex*. The first was described above and its attributes were listed in Figure 17.2

Homo simplex is a notion of a person who lacks understanding of S&T and its role in the economy and society, does not utilize much of it, or even its emerging variants, and who may not even be aware of such trends and his lack of participation in them. Figure 17.3 shows key differences between the two types of people.

The term *simplex* applies not only to a native of New Guinea or an inhabitant of a hamlet in Central Africa, but also to inhabitants of large cities in advanced nations. Both types of people exhibit attributes that would put them in the category of *Homo simplex*.

Figure 17.3 reveals seven groups of attributes that make up the distinction between the two types: attitudes, awareness, access, use, benefits derived, further incorporation into life's activities, and transfer to the next generation. *Homo simplex* has little or no awareness of S&T, no access to it, utilizes very little of it (particularly emerging technologies), and derives few benefits from it. Two important and often neglected categories are the fact that *Homo simplex* fails to further incorporate S&T into his activities, and fails to channel his offspring out of this category through education and training. Thus, the gap between the two types continues and is widened.

A different assessment would define *Homo technicus* as relatively better fed and clothed, immunized against many diseases, with higher life expectancy, better educated, apt to better communicate with peers, enjoying a variety of social services, enjoying better work conditions and a greater variety of consumer goods with better access to culture, and enjoying a more sophisticated and comfortable habitation. Finally, perhaps more important, doing better—overall—than his parents, and making it possible for his offspring to be better off than he is. Perhaps an index of such *Homo technicus*

Figure 17.3
Differences Between *Homo Technicus* and *Homo Simplex*

HOMO TECHNICUS	HOMO SIMPLEX
• Positive attitudes toward S&T • Transfers attitudes and benefits to offsprings • Awareness of emerging technologies • Awareness of utilization of S&T • Awareness of benefits from S&T • Access to technology • Relatively frequent use • Further incorporation of S&T in routine aspects of life (home, work, and leisure) • Use of distinctive terminology • Derives various benefits from S&T: in education, health care, communication, and transportation • Feels life is enriched by S&T • Inclined to politically support S&T • Awareness and supports the link S&T-Economy & Society	• Lack of clearly defined attitudes towards S&T • To various degrees, unaware of existing or emerging S&T • Generally unaware of the benefits to be derived from S&T • Lacks access to S&T • Unable to incorporate S&T in daily life • Generally ignorant of facts, theories, and the terminology of S&T • Generally lacks access and incentives to access education and training portals to S&T • Generally unable to derive adequate benefits from S&T • Unable to transfer awareness and use to offsprings, hence perpetuating present situation

The different items as shown in the figure are not necessarily arranged in matching pairs.

can be constructed, and the progress by *Homo simplex* on any of these dimensions may be assessed and computed.

So the above attributes of *Homo technicus* and his close ties to S&T may be viewed as "The Measure of Progress." S&T allows us to exist in the current postmodern society. It has become the "Measure of Existence" in a highly dynamic world. Whether progress is a positive notion or brings happiness is a totally different issue. *Homo technicus* exists, survives, and progresses due to S&T. This is the truism of our times.

Perhaps the key outcome from Figure 17.3 is that access or the lack of it alone does not create a lasting gap. There are various differences between the two types of people—thus forming two distinct groups that tend to self-perpetuate—with magnified social and economic consequences. S&T creates a solid *barrier* between *Homo technicus* and *Homo simplex*. This barrier consists of the collapse of communication channels and common interests —in addition to an ownership of S&T and its applications by one group. The other group finds it increasingly difficult to break the barrier.

S&T as Great Equalizer

In a phenomenon similar to *creating* a gap, S&T may also serve as the "Great Equalizer," *closing* existing social and economic laps. This works in the following way. As S&T advances, people and countries who embrace it are able to leapfrog existing plateaus and build up their economic and social position. Examples include Singapore and its leap into a commanding role in global telecommuncation,[13] and India, with its rapid development of the software industry to a degree of world recognition.[14] The chairman of India's Infosys, Narayana Murthy, believes that one feasible solution to India's poverty is to create wealth through technology, instead of merely redistributing existing wealth.[15]

S&T allows for rapid advances for individuals, companies, and countries in a much faster pace than by simply injecting capital and human resources into the desired activity. Without the quantum advances that S&T provides, progress in almost every facet of economic activity would have been dramatically curtailed.[16]

Moreover, when compared with industrialization, S&T in contemporary settings has allowed for a much faster pace of progress. "Catching-up" with industrialization was a process that necessitated at least two generations whereas, currently, S&T allows closing of the gap and the creation of viable industries (particularly in IT) within just several years.

It seems to me that as S&T advances, so does the pace of equalization—assuming that *adoption* and *transfer* processes are adequate and successfully implemented. That is, in those areas of rapid changes (such as information and telecommunication), the pace of equalization is much higher than in sectors where S&T is relatively slower (for example: pharmaceuticals and biotechnology).[17]

So the gap between *Homo technicus* and *Homo simplex*, and the gap that S&T may equalize, are not solely defined in terms of access or use of the Internet. They are the combination of many factors, some of which are described in Figure 17.3.

Both the "gap" and the phenomenon of equalization seem to coexist, side by side. S&T engenders the gap between the two categories of people and nations, but may also contribute to equalization of economic and social gaps. Does this mean that S&T has the solutions to economic and social ills?

Creating and Solving Difficult Problems

The "digital divide" and similar gaps are not created by the new existence or appearance of S&T. Rather, the lack of adequate infrastructure, political and economic support, and related socioeconomic deficiencies (whether national, regional, or local) are the core causes for the emergence of these gaps.

Similarly, S&T can contribute to equalization only if and when there are adequate actions by individual entrepreneurs and corresponding government policies and agencies—all geared toward creation, adoption, and utilization of S&T.[18]

There is a need for a concerted effort that includes favorable conditions and aggressive action by individuals and organizations. There must be supportive legislation that favors entrepreneurship and was enacted with a belief in S&T and its potential benefits. Individuals and governments must work not as adversaries, but in conjunction toward a common objective, namely to create S&T and to distribute its existence as widely as possible.

S&T by itself does not create socioeconomic problems nor does it solve them. It's the implementation of S&T (its adoption, adaptation, utilization, and extraction of benefits) that contributes to socioeconomic problems such as gaps, environmental degradation, and sociological anomalies (alienation, desperation, aggression).

ISSUES AND CONTROVERSIES

S&T plays a dual role in society and the economy, both dividing and equalizing people and organizations.[19] Such duality makes it even more difficult to examine the key issues, such as negative consequences of S&T and ethical considerations.[20] In this section I limit the examination to two categories of issues: (1) harmful side effects from S&T, and (2) ethical considerations.

Negative Consequences from S&T

In addition to being a catalyst for social and economic changes, S&T also contributes to hazards related to the environment. It has long been argued that environmental degradation occurs and that it can be traced to our use (or "overuse," "misuse") of S&T. Cases of global warming and the continuous deforestation of Amazonia and the Far Eastern tropical forests are major examples of this damage.[21]

John Ashton and Ron Laura have argued that S&T innovations are so pervasive in the environment that they continually generate many ailments and devastating chronic conditions.[22] They listed the damage presumed from mobile telephones to electricity, microwave ovens, and pollutants in our water and air supplies. They considered S&T in light of what they described as "The Paradox of Progress," and argued that the price paid for technology by society was way too high.[23]

Although referred by some as being "neo-Luddites," Ashton and Laura exemplify a growing number of scholars who document and lament the perils and actual harm to the global environment and to the safety and health of the world's population.[24] Such concerns are voiced not necessarily in opposition to S&T as an activity, but rather as a call to assess and consider choices, consequences, and options.[25]

But even if the criticism of S&T is directed toward a better understanding of the interrelations of life and the environment and to make more informed choices about S&T, the criticism is still misdirected. Some consequences of S&T are inherent in its utilization, regardless of how careful or conscientious the implementer. *Social* changes in work, leisure, education, and social stratification are almost inevitable outcomes of increased S&T in society and the economy.[26]

On the other side of the spectrum are those consequences that receive the most attention, yet, in my view, are approached in a misguided way. These are particularly the effects (attributed to S&T) on the environment, on safety and health, and on nonsocial attributes of work environments, education, and the quality of life (such as the gaps discussed above).

Implementation, Not S&T

My view on this issue starts out by asserting that I am not disputing the accuracy nor the validity of the scientific evidence on such phenomena as global warming, destruction of the tropical forests, and pollution of air and water. As dramatic as the impacts may be, especially in cases of technology disasters, S&T by itself is *not* the culprit in this story. The very existence of S&T innovations and their pervasive ubiquity in our lives today are *not* precursors of environmental ills and the alleged degradation in human health and safety.[27]

Rather, implementation and application of outcomes from S&T play a key role in creating hazards and damage to the environment and other global conditions. Two examples come to mind. The first is plutonium, the man-made element with a half-life of 24,000 years. This element is artificially produced from uranium. Its major risk is radiological, in addition to its toxicity. Plutonium emits alpha radiation and, when ingested, causes cancer.[28]

Plutonium can be safely maintained, albeit dangers of its use by terrorists as mass poison always exist. Although plutonium is an excellent illustration of the outcome of S&T, adequate safeguards with its use have kept the world safe from its harmful effects since it discovery over 50 years ago.[29]

Another example are the waters of several European spas which contain heavy minerals such as lead. Recent findings suggest that the composer Ludwig Van Beethoven suffered from lead poisoning after recurrent visits to these spas. The natural existence of harmful elements in the environment creates hazards to biological systems, regardless of the level of S&T in a society.

Social and economic institutions who utilize S&T and its innovations have the ultimate choice in how well, how safely, and how responsibly they are going to put them to use and employ them in their activities. Business companies have a choice in how they pollute the environment, and government organizations have a choice in how much regulatory controls they are willing to exercise in order to check, reduce, or even eliminate any possibility of pollution. Society at large has a choice between economic imperatives and pollution prevention, namely, at what cost should zero pollution be feasible, and is society willing to take "acceptable risks?"[30]

Scholars such as Ashton and Laura would probably argue that regardless of how social and economic institutions decide to act, the consequences from S&T are real and present, and we need to confront them and resolve these problems. True, but solutions are not the sole domain of S&T, just as the problems are not due to the mere existence of S&T.[31]

Solutions to the negative consequences of S&T cannot and should not be confined to reduction in S&T or elimination of it—entirely or selectively. Nor are the potential solutions the purview of *more* S&T, so that "technology can cure what technology has caused." None of these extreme solutions is feasible, as both the "Neo-Luddites" and "hypertechnocrats" are simply out of touch with reality.[32]

The answers lie somewhere between such extremes and depend on cooperation among the producers of S&T, its users in the economy and society, and the social institutions that regulate both of them. Some technology is needed to create feasible solutions, and some *new* S&T needs to be engendered for a variety of solutions. But only a concerted effort can decrease the risks from the outcomes and uses of S&T.

CONFLICT: S&T AND SOCIETY

It's easy to advocate cooperation between producers of S&T, society, and economic organizations. It's quite a different story to resolve the conflicts that seem to exist between S&T and society. Three kinds of conflict are the key ingredients in a somewhat chaotic relationship: political conflicts, economic conflicts, and ethical conflicts.

Political Conflicts

Consider the *political* conflict that emerged in South Africa in mid-2000 regarding the status of the Human Immunodeficiency Virus (HIV) and AIDS.

Scientists estimate that about 10 percent of the population in South Africa carries HIV, the precursor to full-blown AIDS.[33] Yet President Thabo Mbeki argued that the link between HIV and AIDS has not been established, and that the existing "Western" cocktails of drugs (proven effective in the U.S. and Europe) are not safe. He went further to assert that his country will not acquiesce to the catechism of the industrial world. President Mbeki has refuted pharmaceutical S&T with political reasoning, with perhaps disastrous consequences for his nation.

Political considerations can and do interfere with the allocation of resources for S&T, and with the subsequent use of S&T outcomes and innovations. Good examples are the pharmacological products connected with abortion, such as RU-486, and the use of stem cells in research. In both instances, political stances have hindered the progress in utilization and application of these technologies.[34] After the Food and Drug Administration authorized the use of RU-486 in the United States and the federal government allowed stem-cell research, the political adversaries continued their arguments for and against these aspects of S&T.[35] In the case of stem-cell research, the Catholic Archbishop of New York has denounced such research as "evil," whereas scientists, such as Irving Weissman from Stanford University, strongly argues that "it would be a tragedy if we don't find a way to resolve these issues."[36]

There are few, if any, feasible solutions to such openly adversarial conflicts between S&T and political opinions. Not so much because S&T is based on reason and emotional detachment (whereas politics and religion are based on cognitive, emotional, and inflexible stands), but also because S&T (in the form of its producers, scientists) is as much a paradigmatic and emotional activity. Scientists and technologists strongly believe in their craft, the correctness of their craft, and the positive role they play in society.[37]

So the conflicts *are* reduced to the emotional level of who is on the *right* side of the issue. Political institutions who fund and regulate S&T feel obligated to take a stand (albeit politically motivated), as do scientists and technologists. Both sides believe they are acting for the "good of society." But both positions are the product of a mix of motives and influences. Political organizations are driven by power, diverse opinions of constituents, and the desire to perpetuate the political institutions. Scientists are motivated by professional factors such as allegiance to a discipline or program of research, personal triumphs, and a sincere desire to make life better for all.[38]

Economic Conflicts

S&T and societal entities conflict on yet another level: the role that economics plays in the creation and utilization of S&T innovations. Three cases come to mind. The first is the patenting of the outcomes from genetic research.

As the mapping of human genes was essentially completed at the turn of the 21st century, the S&T portion has reached a stage in which utilization and economics have begun. The human genome project has been a partnership between the publicly funded National Human Genome Research Institute (NHGRI) and private companies. This cooperation was reflected in the consortium created to identify single nucleotide polymorphisms (SNP): the genetic elements that are responsible for the biological differences among humans. Almost half of the known SNPs had been identified by this consortium. In addition to the NHGRI, major pharmaceutical and biotechnology companies also participated in this concerted effort.[39]

Such major breakthroughs, developed with private industry's support, have unbounded commercial opportunities for healthcare diagnostics and cures, as well as other applications in law enforcement, education, and defense. Patenting of these discoveries is the initial step in their commercial exploitation. As soon as such patenting began, conflicts arose due to concerns by various organizations.

The Case of Cannavan Disease. A revealing example was the lawsuit filed in November 2000 by parents of children who suffered and died from Cannavan disease, which is a rare degeneration of the brain. In a Chicago court, parents argued that researchers discovered the gene responsible for the disease and had been patenting it. By doing so, the parents argued, the researchers are limiting the testing for the disease. The Genome project has been called "The Forces of Good" by Eric Lander of MIT and "The Language of God" by Francis Collins of the NHGRI. The Cannavan lawsuit reiterates the conflict between private ownership and restricted commercial benefits to the few and the needs of the many in the "public good."

The key question in this case (and generally for other genes, tests, and therapeutics) is: can and should private ownership of a human gene allow a few to charge for its use in diagnostics or therapeutics when public funds were also used in its discovery and where patients donated their trust, blood, and other items that permitted such discoveries? In other words, do these discoveries belong to society at large or to the *business* concerns who are exploiting them?

Economic conflicts of this kind are at the core of the commercial use and exploitation of S&T innovations. There is a fine line between society's wish to own and exploit innovations for the public good versus the need to employ private enterprise in both the generation of these innovations and their effective utilization.[40]

The Case of "Orphan Drugs." The second example of economic conflicts is the issue of "orphan drugs." Because of economic considerations, pharmaceutical companies devote little or no resources to exploring cures for rare diseases—those which have few patients, hence a small to insignificant market for the drugs.[41] Several industrialized countries have attempted to create laws and incentives that would allow the public to "adopt" such rare diseases, and to encourage drug makers to explore these cases. In the United States the Orphan Drug Act of 1983 specifically proposed incentives for pharmaceutical companies to target diseases that affect fewer than 200,000 American patients. In 1999, the European Union also enacted its Orphan Drug legislation for fourteen European countries.[42]

The Case of Biotechnology Crops. A third and similar example is the diffusion of biotechnology crops for children in the developing world. Although there are about 100 million children who suffer from malnutrition, they are poor constituencies in the area of international business. Biotechnologically engineered foods can be a major force in fighting hunger in poor countries. Yet economic considerations (sometimes also laced with political issues) seem to prevent the adequate and widespread implementation of these S&T innovations.[43]

Ethical Conflicts

In a way, every conflict that arises between S&T and society involves ethical considerations. I could devote the remainder of this book and perhaps another volume altogether to discussions of ethical issues of this conflict. But, in the interface between S&T and society, this issue will be condensed into the following section.[44]

As I see it, there are at least three levels of conflict between S&T and society: allocation of resources, uses and abuses of S&T outcomes, and ancillary issues. Even before S&T begins, there are ethical issues involving the allocation of resources for S&T initiatives. Funding for certain types of research routinely comes under scrutiny by the public, opinions vary in both their intensity and S&T so targeted. Fueled by interest groups as well as deeply rooted convictions and beliefs, there have been social pressures to prevent, increase, or reallocate funding to medical research such as fetal stem cells, AIDS, and breast cancer. Similarly, pressures have been (and continue to be) mounted against research that may lead to discriminating conclusions.

Uses and possible abuses of S&T outcomes and innovations are also a field of conflict. Social entities oppose uses of S&T outcomes that lead to environmental degradation and health and safety hazards for the population. In November 2000, writer Patrick Tierney criticized the outcomes from three decades of anthropological research in the Amazon region of Brazil.[45] Tierney argued that such research decimated the Yanomami tribes by inserting into their culture deadly diseases (such as measles), and hunting and fishing equipment. These "gifts" incited other tribes in the rain forest (who did not receive them) to violence. Moreover, Tierney maintained that the Yanomami, peaceful by nature, were cajoled by researchers to act violently for the photographers and journalists who accompanied the expeditions.

There are, of course, differences in the ethical issues raised by outcomes from science and those from applications of technology. Outcomes from science are generally open to dispute because they are not as embedded in the economy and society as are technological innovations. Tierney's accusations are being heatedly disputed by other scientists. Yet arguments about technological innovations are usually about the *degree* of damage, not whether the damage has occurred.

For example, incidents such as Three Mile Island, the Love Canal in upstate New York, and the Exxon *Valdez* have factually occurred. What remains to be determined is the extent of the damage and the ethical implications for future utilization of these technologies.

We also need to distinguish between *uses* and *abuses* of S&T in the social context. Accidents that occur with standard and bona fide use of technology are fundamentally different from misuse and abuse of the technology. Uses of genetic engineering technology in diagnosing disease and identifying criminals, for example, are ethically different from misusing this technology for applications in selected sectors of the population—classified by race, mental illness, or national origin—in order to affect changes in their genetic composition. By the same token, pathogenes are routinely used to create vaccines, but most nations have banned the creation and use of pathogenes for military use in "germ warfare."

In the late 1990s the issues of cloning and the commercial use of human tissue have soared in publicity and have raised serious ethical questions. Should the outcomes from genetic engineering be used to clone humans, in addition to the cloning of animals? The topic was popularized as "designer being," made to the specifications of potential buyers. The turning of human life into a commodity raised objections from many quarters. Among the topics in the debate were such dichotomies as uses for life saving versus "cosmetic" purposes, and the potential misuses and abuses of this technology by unscrupulous people, bent on simply amassing fortunes or for criminal intent.[46]

Another level of S&T-society conflict are ancillary issues such as the treatment of animals in scientific experiments and the secondary effect of routine applications of S&T innovations. These issues cover a broad range of concerns in medicine, biological research, social research, and even anthropological and archeological investigations. Excavations of ancient burial grounds have generated religious, ethical, and national sentiments that called for halting the research efforts.

Resolving the Conflicts

Can these conflicts be resolved to the satisfaction of all concerned: scientists, technologists, and social entities? There seem to be three key approaches to generally dealing with these conflicts. The first is through discussions and dissemination of ideas. Each side tries to teach, cajole, explain, and disseminate its position. Arguments are exchanged in various forms, such as the public arena, the media, the political arena, and through activities targeted at the propagation of a position, including boycotts and demonstrations.

Ascending in the level of resolution, some conflicts are brought to a solution (albeit usually temporary) in that resources are allocated or reallocated to research deemed more ethical, "socially responsible," and in line with the positions of opponents. For example, companies will increase resources for R&D targeted at certain diseases, or similarly, companies will discontinue use of animals in the testing of their products.

When all else is insufficient, the government will enter the picture through legislation and regulation. Primarily designed to better define the playing field, government intervention may also establish strict rules that control the development and usage of S&T innovations.[47]

The Implications of S&T-Society Conflicts

In the final analysis some conflicts are resolved, while others remain on the front burner for many years. Many conflicts are focused on one issue, thus can be addressed by both parties in a reasonable manner. Other conflicts involve broader issues of economics, ethics, or even the survival of S&T as an activity. In these cases the government's role is paramount in reflecting the will of the majority of the population in establishing guidelines and rules for the conflict.

S&T-society conflicts have a dual role to play. First, they add flexibility, dynamics, and passion into the public debate. They help to clarify issues and to bring controversies to the public arena. They make the public aware of issues and concerns that involve S&T. Although the vast majority of the population has little knowledge of S&T, these debates help to simplify (sometimes oversimplify) the issues and their implications.

Another role these conflicts play is in providing inputs to the S&T community and fostering the public's function as monitors of S&T and its outcomes. Whether by means of government intervention or public display of emotions concerning S&T issues (such as cloning or use of genetically engineered foods), there emerges a process by which S&T outcomes are closely scrutinized—to the ultimate benefits of society.

However, these conflicts also weaken the S&T effort and are, in many instances, destructive. As pressures mount on scientists and technologists, their incentives to create tend to diminish, leading to the abandonment of important programs and to a decline in performance and productivity.

In my view, there must be a true balance of power between S&T and society. Equal forces tend to generate the dynamics and passion of public debate—without the negative implications of weakening the S&T effort or in diminishing the monitoring function of social organizations. Conflicts of the types described above will continue to be the hallmark of S&T in a free society. They play important roles, yet have few textbook solutions. Ultimately, they must be assessed against the benefits that society derives from S&T.

Five Propositions to Creating Value from S&T

Considering the critical role that S&T plays in economic and social progress, and the various interests of social entities, the following are steps that can be taken to accentuate and facilitate the creation of value from S&T.

Proposition 1:   Society should establish and maintain conditions that will allow S&T producers adequate independence and resources — bounded by a minimalist approach to safety and projected risks.

Proposition 2:   Conflicts between S&T and society should be resolved by allowing first for a balance of power between S&T producers and their supporters, and those detractor forces in society and the economy that oppose S&T.

Proposition 3:   The dichotomy S&T-business should be reduced or even gradually eliminated. Society must accept the awarding of economic incentives and rewards to producers of S&T—in addition to noneconomic incentives such as challenge, fame, and personal satisfaction.

Proposition 4:   Entities in the economy and society who exploit S&T must gain a better understanding of the array of benefits that S&T provides. They should appreciate the overall systemic contributions from S&T and the cumulative impacts of innovations.

Proposition 5:   Value from S&T should be measured along a varied set of dimensions, variables, and benefits. A better coordination is needed between assessments of S&T by economic and social organizations.

These propositions apply equally to S&T performed by business enterprises and government organizations. They call for an approach that promotes S&T but negates extreme positions.

THE REAL DILEMMA

S&T is everybody's business, not confined to the scientists and technologists who generate it, or the organizations that utilize it. But this statement implies that there is a strong link between those who generate S&T and those who exploit it. Such a link represents the real dilemma we are facing.

The dilemma, as I see it, is almost a paradox, and can be expressed as follows:

In order to promote and foster outputs, outcomes, and innovations from S&T, there is a need for incentives and relaxed interference from outsiders in the process of S&T creation. Yet the more incentives (monetary, fiscal, legal, etc.) are provided by society, the more it wishes to impose boundaries, restrictions, and control over how S&T is funded, created, and exploited.

The key to the dilemma is the link between S&T and business enterprises. These two are strange bedfellows. No other area so clearly illustrates this strange partnership as S&T at the cutting edge, where the playing field has not yet been defined. Scientists in biotechnology and medical research who also have financial interests in the outcomes from this research face criticisms from peers and the public alike.[48] Yet, monetary incentives have always served as boosters of S&T creativity in those areas of importance to society. An excellent example is the resolution of the problem of measuring longitude at sea.[49] In 1714 the British Parliament established a reward of 20,000 pounds (over 10 million current dollars). This incentive led to the development of the chronometer.

The more the area of S&T is exploratory and at the cutting edge of discovery, the higher the potential for business applications and associated profits. Some scientists are lured by these incentives. Ethical issues of conflict of interests (as in the case of breakthrough medical research involving patients) create strong barriers between the conduct of science and its commercial exploitation—*by the same people*. Some S&T entrepreneurs argue that scientists should not be prohibited from enjoying—first hand—the fruits of their discovery, by being on "the ground floor" of commercial exploitation of outcomes from their research, as long as there is full disclosure of such dual efforts.[50]

Should S&T producers be allowed to partake in the commercial exploitation of their endeavor? Economic gains are a powerful incentive, and I believe that they should so benefit, with very few exceptions—albeit with strict guidelines. In this era of rapid S&T growth and achievements, the image of the scientist as a poor scholar who languishes in the laboratory in his/her white or grey coat has long been discarded. Scientists can and should be allowed to own a stake in the business applications of their creation, just as companies obtain rights to their intellectual property and artists' rights to their art.[51] In special cases where patients are involved and there may be conflicts between provision of care and business decisions, strict rules should be devised by the parties involved in such research.

A REALITY CHECK

A revealing discussion appeared in the July 2000 edition of *Wired Magazine* following an article by Bill Joy in the April edition of the magazine.[52] Joy was cofounder and chief scientist of Sun Microsystems. He argued that as more enabling technologies, such as robotics, genetic engineering, and nanotechnology are introduced into society for commercial widespread exploitation, humanity may not be able to control these technologies. He contended that we are not assessing the risks from these technologies in any meaningful manner, and that essentially we have made a Faustian bargain: we accept the power these technologies give us in exchange for the destruction of our biosphere and our humanity.

Joy also lamented that once we have opened these Pandora's boxes, it's impossible to put the evils back in the box, thus pushing back the clock of S&T progress. Responses to Joy's article may be grouped along purely partisan lines: those who wholeheartedly agreed with him and those who strongly disagreed.

But dangers, threats, and risks always exist in every human endeavor—S&T is no exception, nor is it the rule. Any such discussion, however alarmist, of the risks involved with breakthrough and enabling S&T should also take into account the benefits that have already been received and those that may accrue and result from such S&T.[53]

We are back to the "Real Dilemma." In order to promote S&T that benefits humanity and its social institutions, we need to reduce interference and controls over the processes, as well as its applications. All of this would be subject to the risks involved. Evidently, some risks cannot be predicted and may be the result of the *cumulative* effects of various S&T outcomes.

Society and the economy are intertwined with S&T. The best possible scenario for coexistence and a shared prosperous future is not to increase control over S&T, but to provide adequate conditions that will allow it to progress at its own rate, while maintaining a balance between incentives and boundaries—based on the analysis of benefits versus risks.

S&T is essential to our lives and to our form of civilization. We should not fear it, nor idealize it. We should view it for what it is: a tool devised by humans to create value and benefits to our society and economy. Just as we have established laws and rules and ethical principles that have controlled and domesticated the basic instincts of human ferocity, violence, and fear—thus creating lasting civilizations—so can we master the very S&T we create and exploit. The answer to any neo-Luddism is for all to see. It shines in the eyes of a child who is cured from a dreaded disease by the outputs from medical S&T. It is embedded in the smile of a crippled worker whose limb has been restored to full function, and it is glowing in the face of the grandparents who lived long enough to see the grandchildren accessing in one hour more information than even existed in their time.

NOTES

1. See, for example, Geisler, E., "How Strategic Is Your Information Technology?" *Industrial Management*, 36(1), 1994, 31-33; and Geisler, E., "Strategic Perspectives of Artificial Management and Organizational Rationality," *Journal of Information Technology Management*, 6(4), 1995, 45-53. Also see Geisler, E., "Strategic Management of Information Technology: Empirical Findings in Three Service Sectors," Portland International Conference on the Management of Engineering and Technology (PICMET), Portland, OR, July 25-29, 1999.

2. See, for example, Hamel, G., "Opinion: Strategy Innovation and the Quest for Value," *Sloan Management Review*, 39(2), 1998, 7-14. Gary Hamel argued that the goal of successful management is "not to earn more than your cost," but "to capture a disproportionate share of industry wealth creation" (p. 8). He recommended innovating the strategic approach to growth to institute revolutionary discontinuities in the industry.

3. Christensen, C., *The Innovator's Dilemma: When New Technologies Cause Great Firms to Fall* (Boston: Harvard Business School Press, 1997).

4. Several methodological issues may also emerge, such as the use of indices of multiple indicators. See, for example, Thompson, J., "The Reinvention Laboratories: Strategic Change by Indirection," *American Review of Public Administration*, 30(1), 2000, 46-68. Also see Brown, J., and P. DuGuid, *The Social Life of Information* (Boston: Harvard Business School Press, 2000).

5. See, for example, Mensch, G., and R. Niehaus (Eds.), *Work, Organizations, and Technological Change* (Boulder, CO: Perseus Books, 1987). Also see Scheer, C., "The Pursuit of Techno-Happiness," *The Nation*, 260(18), 1995, 632-638. The author argued that Americans deal with happiness by considering the future laden with

technological achievements "rather than dealing with the problems of today." See Garson, D., *Computer Technology and Social Issues* (Hershey, PA: Idea Group Publishing, 1995); and see Fukuyama, F., *The Great Disruption: Human Nature and the Reconstitution of Social Order* (New York: The Free Press, 1999). In this book Fukuyama argued that a new social order is unraveling as a result of the technological transformation of the past few decades. In reference to the "postindustrial" society, Fukuyama argued that moral and social values are also changing to fit the technological changes of our times.

6. See Kohlstedt, S. *et al.* (Eds.), *Bodytalk: Rhetoric, Technology, Reproduction* (Madison: University of Wisconsin Press, 2000). This book illustrates the impacts of technology on the female role in society. The authors discuss ownership of knowledge about contraception and birth, control over the function, and changes that occurred in how society defines normal and abnormal sexual behavior. Also see Clarke, A., *Disciplining Reproduction: Modernity, American Life Sciences, and the "Problem of Sex"* (Berkeley: University of California Press, 1998).

7. See, for example, Epstein, R., *Principles for a Free Society: Reconciling Individual Liberty with the Common Good* (Boulder, CO: Perseus Books, 1998). In particular, see Chidambaram, L., and I. Igurs (Eds.), *Our Virtual World: The Transformation of Work Play, and Life Via Technology* (Hershey, PA: Idea Group Publishing, 2001); and Dorf, R., *Technology, Humans, and Society: Toward a Sustainable World* (New York: Academic Press, 2001). In this book Richard Dorf explores the possibilities of engineering technologies that will be favorable to conservation of resources and a sustainable environment.

8. See, for example, Ware, N., *The Industrial Worker, 1840-1860: The Reaction of American Industrial Society to the Advance of the Industrial Revolution* (Chicago: Ivan R. Dee Publisher, 1995); and O'Brien, P., and R. Quinault (Eds.), *The Industrial Revolution and British Society* (Cambridge: Cambridge University Press, 1994). Also see Rosenband, L., "Social Capital in Early Industrial Revolution," *The Journal of Interdisciplinary History*, 39(3), 1999, 435-457. In particular, see Kobrin, S., "Back to the Future: Neomedievalism and the Postmodern Digital World Economy," *Journal of International Affairs*, 51(2), 1998, 361-386. The author argued that the third industrial revolution is now under way and that the global reach of technology will create problems for territorial sovereignity of nations.

9. See the emerging literature on this subject. For example, Bolt, D., and R. Crawford, *Digital Divide: Computers and Our Children's Future* (New York: TV Books, 2000). Also see the mostly journalistic discussion of this topic in, for example, Fatah, H., "The Digital Divide: Politics or a Real Problem?" *MC Technology Marketing Intelligence*, 20(9), 2000, 82-88. The author argued that the problem is not in funding as in lack of marketing messages to the untapped segments of society. Also see Leach, J., "Crossing the Digital Divide," *American Demographics*, 22(6), 2000, 9-11; and Chanda, N., "Asian Innovation Awards: The Digital Divide," *Far Eastern Economic Review*, 163(42), 2000, 50-53. The author equated the disparity in access to technology to the gap between rich and poor nations. Also see Davenport, T., "The Other Digital Divide," *C10*, 13(18), 2000, 62-64. Davenport is the author of many publications on management of knowledge systems in organizations. Here he contended that organizationally, the important "divide" is between the information

technology professionals and the business executives who fund and utilize these technologies. Differences in cultures, perceptions, even terminologies threaten the effectiveness of utilizing information technologies to their full capacity.

10. See, Holderness, M., "Falling Through the Net," *New Statesman & Society*, 8(374), 1995, 24-27.

11. See, for example, Armstrong, A., "Missing the Boat," *Government Executive*, 32(9), 2000, 92-94.

12. See, for example, Hoffman, T., "Leaders: Education Key to Bridging Digital Divide," *ComputerWorld*, 34(37), 2000, 14-16.

13. See, for example, Wilde, G., "View From the Top: Singapore," *Telecommunications*, 34(9), 2000, 25-26.

14. See Bristow, D., "India May Eclipse China in IT," *Far Eastern Economic Review*, 163(31), 2000, 29-31. Also see Chanda, N., "Gates and Gandhi," *Far Eastern Economic Review*, 163(34), 2000, 60-63.

15. InfoSys Technologies Ltd. was founded in 1981. In 2000 it had over 6,000 employees, and had sales of over $250 million per year. See Borrell, J., "A World-Class Company in India," *Upside*, 12(10), 2000, 142-150.

16. See, for example, Tunzelmann, G., *Technology and Industrial Progress* (New York: Edward Elgar, 1997). Also see Mokyr, J., *The Lever of Riches: Technological Creativity and Economic Proress* (New York: Oxford University Press, 1992).

17. Although this phenomenon may be related to issues of market competitiveness of fast advancing versus slower technologies, the issue is not sectorial competition but the closing of gaps in access, usage, and enjoyment of the fruits from S&T.

18. See, in the case of information technology, how attitudes change after adoption, in Karahanna, E., D. Straub, and N. Chervany, "Information Technology Adoption Across Time: A Cross-Sectional Comparison of Pre-Adoption and Post-Adoption Beliefs," *MIS Quarterly*, 23(2), 1999, 183-213. The authors studied Windows technology in one company and found that pre-adoption attitudes are broader than those of post-adoption users who are concerned primarily with instrumentality.

19. For an excellent discussion of the dual role technology plays in *organizations*, see Orlikowski, W., "The Duality of Technology: Rethinking the Concept of Technology in Organizations," *Organization Science*, 3(3), 1992, 398-427.

20. Economists refer to "Duality Theory" as the theory postulated by Ronald Shephard in 1953, in which he identified four duality theorems of direct and indirect cost and revenue functions. See extensions of his theory in Fare, R., and J. Logan, "Duality Theory and Value Constraint," *Scottish Journal of Political Economy*, 40(3), 1993, 330-336. Also see Fare, R., and D. Primont, "The Unification of Ronald W. Shephard's Duality Theory," *Journal of Economics*, 60(2), 1994, 199-209.

21. There is a vast literature on these issues. See, for example, Hodson, L., and R. Uhorchak, "Emerging Technologies: Hazards Assessments Find Same Old Problems," *Professional Safety*, 45(4), 2000, 34-37. Also see the social impacts of technological disasters, in Gunter, V., M. Aronoff, and S. Joel, "Toxic Contamination

and Communities: Using an Ecological-Symbolic Perspective to Theorize Response Contingencies," *Sociological Quarterly*, 40(4), 1999, 623-640; and see Cutter, S., "Societal Responses to Environmental Hazards," *International Social Science Journal*, 48(4), 1996, 525-536; and Cohen, M., "Technological Disasters and Natural Resource Damage Assessment," *Land Economics*, 71(1), 1995, 65-76.

22.   Ashton, J., and R. Laura, *The Perils of Progress: The Health and Environment Hazards of Modern Technology and What You Can Do About Them* (New York: St. Martin's Press, 1999).

23.   Ashton is a food researcher from Australia and Laura was a Professor of Education in the United Kingdom (Newcastle). They used many examples specific to Australia (such as incidence of skin cancers), but overall their arguments may be applicable to other continents and countries.

24.   See, for example, Lees, D., and C. Barrett (Eds.), *Tradeoffs or Synergies: Agricultural Intensification, Economic Development, and the Environment* (New York: Oxford University Press, 2000).   Also see Stiller, D., *Wounding the West: Montana, Mining, and the Environment* (Lincoln: University of Nebraska Press, 2000); and see Hull, J., *Sweet Poison: How the World's Most Popular Artificial Sweetener Is Killing Me—My Story* (San Francisco: New Horizon Press, 1998).

25.   A good example is Studt, T., "Technological Conscience," *Research & Development*, 41(10), 1999, 7-9.

26.   See Lipset, S., and R. Marcella Ridler, "Technology, Work, and Social Change," *Journal of Labor Research*, 17(4), 1996, 613-628.

27.   See, for example, Cutcliffe, S., *Ideas, Machines, and Values: An Introduction to Science, Technology, and Society Studies* (Lanham, MD: Scarecrow Press, 2000); especially Chapter 5, pp. 108-136. Also see Grin, J., and A. Grunwold (Eds.), *Vision Assessment: Shaping Technology in 21ˢᵗ Century Society: Towards a Repertoire for Technology Assessment* (New York: Springer-Verlag, 2000).

28.   See Sutcliffe, W., *et al.*, *A Perspective on the Dangers of Plutonium*, Lawrence Livermore National Laboratory, April 14, 1995, document UCRL-JC-118825.

29.   With the exception of its use in nuclear bombs, one detonated over Nagasaki and others in tests throughout the "cold war" years.

30.   See, for example, Draper, W., *Environmental Epidemiology: Effects of Environmental Chemicals on Human Health* (New York: American Chemical Society, 1994). Also see Lee, S., *The Throwaway Society* (Danbury, CT: Franklin Watts Publishers, 1990).

31.   Evidently, the range of issues and consequences from S&T are many and encompass a very broad area of intellectual activity. This chapter is only an illustrative coverage of selected issues, controversies, and potential solutions.

32.   See, for example, Postman, N., *Building a Bridge to the 18ᵗʰ Century: How the Past Can Improve Our Future* (New York: Alfred Knopf, 1999). Also see Nye, D., *American Technological Sublime* (Cambridge, MA: MIT Press, 1994); and see Newman, O., and R. deSoyza, *The American Dream in the Information Age* (New York: St. Martin's Press, 1999).

33.   See the story in Solopek, D., "Soviet Specter Haunts South Africa Forum in AIDS," *Chicago Tribune*, July 9, 2000, Section 2, pp. 1, 6.

34. Although some arguments in the cases may have originated from religious or ethical principles, they ultimately manifested themselves as political pressures. See, for example, Segestrale, U. (Ed.), *Beyond the Science Wars: The Mining Discourse About Science and Society* (Albany: State University of New York Press, 2000). Also see Star, S. (Ed.), *Ecologies of Knowledge: Work and Politics in Science and Technology* (Albany: State University of New York, 1995). Also see Sullivan, A., "RU 4 Life," *The New Republic*, 223(16), 2000, 12-15.

35. See, for example, Malcolm, T., "Approval of Abortion Bill Meets Criticism Praise," *National Catholic Reporter*, 36(44), 2000, 9-12. Also see Mangan, K., "Archbishop, Scientists Spar over Stein Cells," *The Chronicle of Higher Education*, 47(11), 2000, A31-34.

36. Managan, *ibid.*, p. A31. This issue may become moot, as recent discoveries offer hope that we can extract stem cells from fat cells, rather than from fetuses.

37. See Friedrich, M., "Debating Pros and Cons of Stein Cell Research," *JAMA*, 284(6), 2000, 681-682. Also see, in particular, Segerstole, U., *Defenders of the Truth: The Battle for Science in the Sociobiology Debate and Beyond* (New York: Oxford University Press, 2000).

38. For example, see Conceicao, P., D. Gibson, M. Heitor, and S. Shariq (Eds.), *Science, Technology, and Innovation Policy* (Westport, CT: Quorum Books, 2000). Also see Campanario, J., "Peer Review for Journals as it Stands Today—Part 2," *Science Communication*, 19(4), 1998, 277-306. The author discussed self-interest, favoritism, and connections among scientists as biases in the peer review system. Regardless of these biases, Companario argued that peer review is essential for quality control of scientific outputs.

39. Among the members were Aventis-Pharma, Bayer AG, Bristol-Myers Squibb, Celera Genomics, Hoffman-LaRoche, Glaxo-Wellcome, Novartis, Pfizer, Pharmacia, Smithkline Beecham, Motorola, IBM, Stanford University, and Washington University. See, for example, Davis, K., *Cracking the Genome: Inside the Race to Unlock Human DNA* (New York: The Free Press, 2000). Also see Zilinskas, R., and P. Balint (Eds.), *The Human Genome Project and Minority Communities: Ethical, Social, and Political Dilemmas* (Westport, CT: Greenwood Press, 2000).

40. This is an on-going issue yet to be clearly defined or resolved by society. My opinion and other potential solutions are in the section on "The Real Dilemma."

41. See, for example, Thamer, M., N. Brennan, and R. Semansky, "A Cross-National Comparison of Orphan Drug Policies: Implications for the U.S. Orphan Drug Act," *Journal of Health Politics, Policy, and Law*, 23(2), 1998, 265-290. Also see Potvin, F., "Orphan Drugs: Small Changes Can Make a Big Difference," *The Exceptional Parent*, 28(7), 1998, 24-33.

42. See Weber, W., "European Parliament Raises Awareness for Patients with Rare Diseases," *The Lancet*, 356(9240), October 28, 2000, 1504-1507.

43. See, for example, Hohn, T., and K. Leisinger (Eds.), *Biotechnology of Food Crops in Developing Countries* (New York: Springer-Verlag, 2000).

44. There is, of course, a vast literature on the ethical conflicts between S&T and society. See, for example, Winston, M., and R. Edelbach, *Society, Ethics, and Technology* (Belmont, CA: Wadsworth Publishing Company, 1999). This is a

fundamental text on the subject. Also see, Chadwick, R. (Ed.), *The Concise Encyclopedia of the Ethics of New Technologies* (New York: Academic Press, 2000). Professor Chadwick of the University of Lancaster in the United Kingdom has assembled various papers on the ethical foundations for the generation of policies and the enactment of legislation for ethical utilization of innovations.

45. Tierney, P., *Darkness in El Dorado: How Scientists and Journalists Devastated the Amazon* (New York: W. W. Norton & Company, 2000).

46. See, for example, Andrews, L., and D. Nelkin, *Body Bazaar: The Market for Human Tissue in the Biotechnology Age* (New York: Crown Publishing Group, 2001). Also see Andrews, L., *The Clone Age: Adventures in the New World of Reproductive Technology* (New York: Henry Holt & Company, 2000); and Kaplan, A., and G. McGee (Eds.), *The Human Cloning Debate* (Berkeley, CA: Berkeley Hills Books, 2000).

47. See, for example, Grossman, M., and A. Andres, "Regulation of Genetically Modified Organisms in the European Union," *The American Behavioral Scientist*, 44(3), 2000, 378-434.

48. See, for example, Philipkoski, K., "Science + Business: A Bad Mix," *Wired News*, 21 February, 2000. Also see Snow, C. P., *The Two Cultures* (New York: Cambridge University Press, 1993); and Linehand, J., *The Engines of Our Ingenuity: An Engineer Looks at Technology and Culture* (New York: Oxford University Press, 2000).

49. The story of the clockmaker John Harrison and his creation of the chronometer is told in Sobel, D., *Longitude: The True Story of a Lone Genius Who Solved the Greatest Scientific Problem of His Time* (New York: Penguin, 1996).

50. See interview with Cyrus Harmon, President of Neomorphic, in Philipkoski, 2000, *op. cit.*

51. Clearly S&T producers who work *for* companies have specific agreements with their employers regarding their rights to the intellectual property they produce.

52. Joy, W., "Why The Future Doesn't Need Us," *Wired Magazine*, April 2000, pp. 237-262.

53. See, for example, the story in *Time* magazine on inventions and the future, in the December 4, 2000, issue.

18

SCIENCE &TECHNOLOGY, THE ECONOMY, AND SOCIETY: THE FUTURE

Inventions reached their limit long ago, and I see no hope for further development.

Sextus Julius Frontinus (ca. 35-103 A.D.)
Engineer of public works for the city of Rome

In 1925, James Guthrie Harbord, then chairman of RCA, gleefully declared: "Radio will serve to make the concept of 'Peace on Earth and good will toward man' a reality."[1] History declared otherwise, and 14 years later the world was thrown into the most savage and destructive war it ever experienced.

As I reiterated throughout this book, science and technology is not, by itself, the solution nor the cause to what ails the human experience. But S&T is inevitable, and it's a tool that provides us with proven benefits, as well as future contributions well beyond our limited experience. In the much contested American presidential election of 2000, the Florida Supreme Court declared: "Although error cannot be completely eliminated in any tabulation of the ballots, our society has not yet gone so far as to place blind faith in machines. In almost all endeavors, including elections, humans routinely correct the errors of machines."[2]

We indeed do place blind faith in machines and we trust our lives to them. Routinely, computers take control of airplanes in flight ("automatic pilots"). Machines monitor and regulate the flow of medications to patients. They control the working of fuel rods in nuclear facilities and coordinate and manage our global financial system.

The future belongs to S&T, and I say so without trepidation. The dominance of S&T in our lives will take shape in both the enormous benefits to our existence, and the changing nature of our surroundings.[3] Human beings are particularly adaptive and they have a powerful tool in the outcomes from S&T. Risks and benefits will flow together in what I consider to be "Serial Intersects."

THE CASE FOR SERIAL INTERSECTS

Adaptation to future outcomes and consequences from S&T will also be largely resolved by S&T. This is the case for serial intersects shown in Figure 18.1. As one negative outcome occurs, another positive outcome intersects with it in a similar time period.

For example, emissions of certain gases puncture the ozone layer of the atmosphere, thus allowing more ultraviolet radiation to penetrate through the ozone protection, hence contributing to a higher incidence of skin cancers. Concomitantly, medical and biological research is closing in on finding a cure for cancer and, in the future, perhaps even a vaccine. For each threat there will be a balancing array of solutions provided by S&T—at about the same trajectory of time and flow. What some outcomes and consequences from S&T may hinder or hurt, other outcomes from S&T may help to restore.

Figure 18.1
The Law of Serial Intersects of Threats and Benefits from S&T

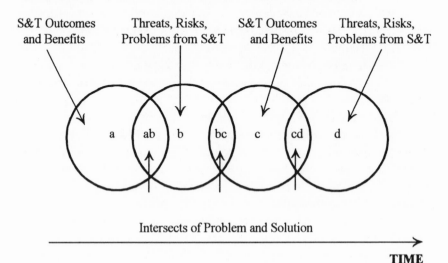

The Serial Intersects are not a guarantee for solving all threats, risks, and problems from S&T. In the future there may be individual cases of unresolved damage to people and our biosphere. But, in the broader perspective of future events, S&T will generate more benefits, and will attenuate more negative events than damages it will cause—directly or indirectly.[4] In the final analysis, the benefits will far outweigh the negatives.

THE CASE FOR "3 Es"

To paraphrase the famous statement in 1927 by Al Jolson at the dawn of sound in movies: "We ain't seen nothin' yet." The revolutionary innovations created thus far by S&T are only the beginning of a true golden era of S&T progress.[5]

These revolutions will be similar to the quest of physicists to uncover the theory that explains everything. While looking for the building blocks of the universe, they came across Higgs bosons (a particle or pattern of strong vibration).[6] When empirically detected, this discovery will not only help in explaining the nature of why physical objects have mass, but will open the door to an entirely new field of scientific explanations and discoveries. Each question answered initiates a set of new questions, cumulatively adding to our stock of S&T.

Elitism

But as S&T increasingly permeates our existence, a phenomenon will unravel, composed of 3 Es: elitism, education, and empowerment. Elitism means the reinforcement of those groups in society and the economy with access to and understanding of S&T and its value. Gaps, such as "digital gap" and overall "S&T gaps," will grow so that value from S&T will be unequally concentrated in the hands of the few, in a form parallel to concentration of land and capital in earlier history.

Moreover, the value and benefits from S&T will be exponentially multiplied. As S&T accumulates, so will its benefits, bestowed on selected segments of society and the economy. Whereas benefits from capital and industrialization increased linearly, benefits from S&T will be many times more pronounced.

Consider the amount of time it took for an innovation in the industrial or even postindustrial era to be fully exploited in the marketplace compared with the amount of time in the information era. The shorter the time, the faster value is accumulated, and the deeper and more powerful the gaps between those who enjoy this value and those who do not.

Education

In the future, education will not only be the means to enjoy the benefits from S&T, but the *only* way. At the dawn of the 20th century, the average person needed minimal knowledge of reading and elementary math as sufficient requisites for survival. A century later one needs the amount of education provided by high schools and even college, namely 12-16 years of schooling.

In the future, education will be much more condensed during these years, and what we now call "graduate" education or postbaccalaureate will be a necessity. As labor and capital lose their luster to knowledge and the increased role of S&T, education, training, and constant updating will become a crucial ingredient to aspire, let alone belong, to the new elite.

Empowerment

The third element of this phenomenon is the empowerment of S&T producers. The current clear demarcation between producers of S&T and those who exploit it will rapidly disappear. Scientists and technologists will enjoy more than the protection of patents. Enterprises such as Microsoft, America on Line, and Intel will be the norm, not the exception. Inventors-owners will be the run-of-the-mill members of the new elite, and their power will extend to policy-making as well.[7]

Today, more than ever, inventors can go directly to the marketplace where their risky ideas may be funded—whereas in prior times they needed the approval and the support of rulers and major financiers. This schism will melt away as resources generated from S&T outcomes will be used to generate more S&T—where the allocation is done by former S&T producers themselves.

THREATS AND FEARS

We should not fear the future in which S&T is supposed to play such a major role. Rather, the fear is not in S&T nor its outcomes—but in ourselves. We should be cognizant of the threats from misuse or abuse of the outcomes of S&T. In particular, we should be aware of their use in religious and ethnic conflicts, and by those who are driven by irrational and antisocial passions.

There is a vast difference between the passion that fuels scientists and technologists and that which drives users of the outcomes from S&T. The former are focused on the activity itself, whereas users (or abusers) are desirous to employ such S&T in the pursuit of their interests—as tools to achieving extemporaneous goals.

"Spoils of the Egyptians"

To an extent, exploiting S&T in general is justified by a concept similar to the doctrine of St. Jerome, as related to the study of the classics by medieval scholars.[8] The Children of Israel took spoils with them as they were liberated from the bondage in Egypt. By the same token, medieval scholars could study—selectively—the works of pagan authors.

Users of S&T can thus selectively exploit the outcomes from S&T, just as the Children of Israel and medieval scholars had done. Some use it for the pleasure of knowledge, others for different reasons with consequences beyond those envisioned by the users and their supporters. The dangers lie not in S&T and its outcomes—but in those who exploit them and their objectives.[9]

HUMANS AND MACHINES

Is there an inherent struggle or conflict between humans and the machines they build as outcomes from S&T? In my view, such conflict is merely the product of fear of the unknown, and fear that humanity will lack the capability to safely utilize S&T.

Human-machine interaction is more like a *partnership* than a tug-of-war. Imagine your first time at the wheel of a car. Enthralled by trepidation of the need to control dozens of horses that are embedded in the engine and tons of metal that are ready to roll at high speed, you felt the power of technology in the hands of a novice. Yet, education and experience have turned the machine into an obedient tool for locomotion and pleasure.

Ultimate control can and will always remain with humans. Although the science fiction literature enjoys the rebellion of machines (such as "Hal" the computer in *2001—A Space Odyssey*), alarmists and neo-Luddites such as Sun Microsystem's Bill Joey, are engaged in the wrong battle. The threat is not in the technologies, but in ourselves, the masters and users. Are *we* up to the task? Can we ascertain that the utilization of S&T outcomes will be a responsible and humanitarian effort? This is the key issue of controlling "runaway" technologies.

WHERE DO WE GO FROM HERE?

In my view there are benefits and riches beyond our wildest imagination in the future we and our descendants will enjoy with S&T. The pattern is clear: S&T will continue its path of progression and will increasingly permeate our lives.[10]

Will the future then be "more of the same?" Probably so, albeit with a more systematic impact of S&T on every aspect of our existence. Will more and better S&T be the answer to "bad" or harmful S&T? Probably so, but with more discretion as to what and how it should be applied to which problem. As S&T proliferates, society will become more adept at dealing with it, curing its shortcomings, and selecting the "good" from the "bad."[11]

Why will this happen? Because the rate of discovery is astonishingly high, but concerns about the future use of technological innovation is also growing.[12] Fueled by the continuing arguments from scientists and technology for improved controls, society will strive for rational delimitations of misuses and the prevention of evil uses of S&T outcomes.[13]

What Are We Losing?

The future as I described it here will also mean the loss of several assets we now enjoy in our society. Loss doesn't necessarily imply that such assets will entirely disappear. In most cases they will be diminished or "bruised."

Examples are some freedoms of an open society many enjoy in the free world. Personal freedoms such as confidentiality and a certain measure of anonymity will be severely diminished. The relatively rapid pace of today's life will seem like a slow pace, compared with what the future holds. With instant information transfer and analysis, and with machines interacting with machines (on our behalf) at unimaginable speeds, the pace of routine life will be staggeringly high.

We are also bound to experience a different world of pleasures and enjoyment, and a different sense of adventure. Today's virtual reality will be magnified to cater to dreams beyond today's conception.

Beware of · · ·

As I reiterated earlier in this book, the future of S&T and our future with its benefits and consequences should *not* be a cause for alarm. I am not fearful of S&T but of the frailty and emotional extremes of humans who take charge of S&T. Our "contract" with S&T has been, and will continue to be, first and foremost a partnership, and beyond it a bold yet assured effort by humanity to strive for a better life.[14]

We should be aware not of lack of controls over the outcomes from S&T but of the possible misappropriation of these outcomes. The real danger lies not in the nature of S&T to be created, but in the harmful motives and convoluted aims that some people and groups devise for, and with, S&T. Humanity and society are too good, resilient, and promising to allow the bad to subjugate and displace the good.

NOTES

1. Ehrlich, E., and M. DeBruhl, *The International Thesaurus of Quotations* (New York: Harper Perennial, 1996).

2. Quoted in the *Chicago Tribune*, November 21, 2000.

3. See, for example, Liban, C., "How Far Will Science and Technology Take Us?" *National Forum*, 80(1), 2000, 6-8. Also see Coates, J., J. Mahaftie, and A. Hines, *2025: Scenarios of U.S. and Global Society Reshaped by Science and Technology* (Winchester, VA: Oakhill Press, 1996).

4. See, Holtzman, N., L. Andrews, A. Motulsky, and J. Fullerton (Eds.), *Assessing Genetic Risks: Implications for Health and Social Policy* (Washington, DC: National Academy Press, 1999).

5. See, for example, Johnston, S., "We Ain't Seen Nothin' Yet," *Information Week*, November 27, 2000, pp. 190-191.

6. Greene, B., *The Elegant Universe: Superstrings, Hidden Dimensions, and the Quest for the Ultimate Theory* (New York: Vintage Books, 2000).

7. The economic and sociological implications from these predictions need further elaboration, perhaps in a follow-up book, and particularly by other scholars to whom I extend this challenge.

8. See, La Monte, J., *The World of the Middle Ages* (New York: Appleton-Century-Crofts, 1949).

9. See, for example, Drucker, P., *Management Challenges for the 21st Century* (New York: HarperCollins, 1999). Also see Kaku, M., *Visions: How Science Will Revolutionize the 21st Century* (New York: Doubleday & Company, 1998); and Berman, M., *The Twilight of American Culture* (New York: W.W. Norton & Company, 2000).

10. See, for example, Knoke, W., *Bold New World* (Los Angeles, CA: Kodansha America, 1997). Also see Postman, N., *Technopoly: The Surrender of Culture to Technology* (New York: Vintage Books, 1993); and see Scheer, C., "The Pursuit of Techno-Happiness," *The Nation*, 260(18), 1995, 632-636.

11. See, for example, Martin-Brown, J., "Rethinking Technology in the Future," *Environmental Science & Technology*, 26(6), 1992, 1100-1106.

12. See Mahurin, M., "Twenty Ideas That Will Rule Research in the Next Twenty Years," *Discover*, 21(10), 2000, 88-91.

13. See, for example, Radder, H., "The Governance of Science: Ideology and the Future of the Open Society," *Science, Technology, & Human Values*, 25(4), 2000, 520-527.

14. See, Guston, D., "Retiring the Social Contract for Science," *Issues in Science and Technology*, 16(4), 2000, 32-36.

EPILOGUE

The journey you took with me in this book traveled in controversial waters of what value is created by S&T, how this value comes into existence, and what its implications are. Whatever your initial beliefs about S&T, you will now perhaps join me in the astonishment felt about the accomplishments of S&T.

Social institutions and economic entities do indeed derive immense value from S&T. They exploit these innovations to create wealth and to achieve prosperity. As we enjoy these riches, it behooves us to make it possible for others in our time, and those who will follow us, to have the same or better role in the franchise of growth and well-being that S&T can provide our economy and society.

In the first half of 2001, the "boom" of technology stocks (particularly Internet companies) took a downturn in what analysts called a "bust." Many "DotCom" firms could not survive and were either terminated or laying off employees. Even more traditional technology companies began trimming their workforce due to the slowing economy. Winstar Communications laid off almost half of its force. AOL Time Warner trimmed 2,400 jobs. Motorola laid off 15 percent of its worldwide workforce. Dell Computers cut 4 percent, and Schwab trimmed 9 percent of its jobs.

Does this "boom" turned "bust" indicate a reversal of fate and faith in technology as the future prospect of the economy? In my view these developments are simply the reverberations of the economy and society in view of the adoption processes of technologies developed in the 1990s. Overall, the journey of science and technology continues uninterrupted.

This journey contained numerous modes by which science and technology impacted the human experience. This book, in particular, examined and even highlighted such powerful outcomes and benefits. Let us continue to enjoy the fruits of scientific discoveries and technological achievements—as they are the product of immense intellectual effort of many generations before us. But let us also be vigilant, insofar as science and technology—tools of progress—may often be misused and, intolerably, made harmful to our world and ourselves We are the recipients of such a vast gift given to us by many brilliant minds in conjunction with the effort of many entrepreneurial people. As recipients, we also bear the responsibility of ensuring that the patrimony of past scholars remains a positive force in our lives. If we succeed, we will turn the torch over to our children. If we fail, there will be none to receive, nor to remember. Science and technology are marvelous, yet perilous gifts. They carry much good, laced with challenges and responsibilities. I strongly believe that we are up to the task!

SELECTED BIBLIOGRAPHY

This is a selected list of readings that are deemed relevant to the topics in this book. The list is not an exhaustive array of references. It merely serves to introduce the reader to the relevant literature.

American Chemical Society Staff, *Science in the Technical World: Medical Technology* (New York: W. H. Freeman Company, 2001).

Archibugi, D., and J. Michie (Eds.), *Trade, Growth, and Technical Change* (New York: Cambridge University Press, 1998).

Auletta, K., *World War 3.0: The Microsoft Trial and the Battle to Rule the New Economy* (New York: Random House, 2001).

Boer, P., *The Valuation of Technology: Business and Financial Issues in R&D* (New York: John Wiley & Sons, 1999).

Bowers, C., *Let Them Eat Data: How Computers Affect Education, Cultural Diversity, and the Prospects of Ecological Sustainability* (Athens, GA: The University of Georgia Press, 2000).

Boyle, D., *The Sum of Our Discontent: Why Numbers Make Us Irrational* (London, UK: Texere Publications, 2001).

Busch, M., *Trade Warriors: States, Firms, and Strategic-Trade Policy in High-Technology Competition* (New York: Cambridge University Press, 1999).

Cairncross, F., *The Death of Distance* (Boston, MA: Harvard Business School Press, 2001).

Castells, M., *The Rise of the Network Society* (New York: Blackwell Publishers, 2000).

Choi, S., and A. Whinston, *The Internet Economy: Technology and Practice* (New York: Smartecon Publishing, 2000).

Coates, J., J. Mahaffie, and A. Hines, *2025: Scenarios of US and Global Society Shaped by Science and Technology* (Winchester, VA: Oakhill Press, 1996).

Colton, J., and S. Bruchey (Eds.), *Technology, The Economy, and Society: The American Experience* (New York: Columbia University Press, 1987).

Cooke, P., and K. Morgan, *The Associational Economy: Firms, Regions, and Innovation* (New York: Oxford University Press, 1999).

Cutliffe, S., and C. Mitcham (Eds.), *Visions of STS: Counterpoints in Science, Technology, and Society Studies* (Albany, New York: State University of New York Press, 2001).

Dodgson, M., *The Management of Technological Innovation: An International and Strategic Approach* (New York: Oxford University Press, 2000).

Dorf, R., *Technology, Humans, and Society: Toward a Sustainable World* (New York: Academic Press, 2001).

Dowd, K., *Beyond Value at Risk: The New Science of Risk Management* (New York: John Wiley & Sons, 1998).

Evans, P., and T. Wurster, *Blown to Bits: How the New Economics of Information Transforms Strategy* (Boston, MA: Harvard Business School Publishing, 1999).

Floyd, C., *Managing Technology for Corporate Success* (Hampshire, United Kingdom: Ashgate Publishing Company, 1997).

Gates, B., *Business at the Speed of Thought: Using a Digital Nervous System* (New York: Time-Warner, 1999).

Geisler, E., *The Metrics of Science and Technology* (Westport, CT: Quorum Books, 2000).

Gibson, D., P. Conceicao, and M. Heitor (Eds.), *Science, Technology, and Innovation Policy* (Westport, CT: Quorum Books, 2000).

Goel, R., *Economic Models of Technological Change: Theory and Application* (Westport, CT: Quorum Books, 1999).

Henwood, F., and. N. Miller, *Technology and IN/Equality: Questioning the Information Society* (London: Routledge Publishers, 2000).

Higgs, E., A. Light, and D. Strong (Eds.), *Technology and the Good Life?* (Chicago, IL: University of Chicago Press, 2000).

Kleinman, D. (Ed.), *Science, Technology, and Democracy* (Albany, NY: State University of New York Press, 2000).

Kumar, D., and D. Chubin (Eds.), *Science, Technology, and Society: A Source Book on Research and Practice* (Boston, MA: Kluwer Academic Publishers, 2000).

Lall, S., *Competitiveness, Technology, and Skills* (London: Edward Elgar, 2001).

Lewis, M., M. Branscomb, and J. Keller (Eds.), *Investing in Innovation: Creating a Research and Innovation Policy that Works* (Cambridge, MA: MIT Press, 1999).

Lienhard, J., *The Engines of Our Ingenuity: An Engineer Looks at Technology and Culture* (New York: Oxford University Press, 2000).

Link, A., and J. Scott, *Public Accountability: Evaluating Technology-Based Institutions* (Boston, MA: Kluwer Academic Publishers, 1998).

Lopez, R., and A. Piccaluga (Eds.), *Knowledge Flows in National Innovation Systems* (London: Edward Elgar, 2001).

Matheson, D., and J. Matheson, *The Smart Organization: Creating Value Through Strategic R&D* (Boston, MA: Harvard Business School Press, 1997).

Moore, G., *Crossing the Chasm: Marketing and Selling High-Tech Products to Mainstream Customers* (New York: HarperCollins Publishers, 1999).

Mothe, J. de la, and J. Niosi (Eds.), *The Economic and Social Dynamics of Biotechnology* (Boston, MA: Kluwer Academic Publishers, 2000).

Naisbitt, J., D. Philips, and N. Naisbitt, *High Tech/High Touch: Technology and Our Accelerated Search for Meaning* (London: Nicholas Brealey Publishers, 2001).

Nooteboom, B., *Learning and Innovation in Organizations and Economics* (New York: Oxford University Press, 2000).

Okina, K. (Ed.), *Monetary Policy in a World of Knowledge-Based Growth* (New York: St. Martin's Press, 2001).

Organization for Economic Cooperation and Development, *Policy Evaluation in Innovation and Technology: Towards Best Practices* (Geneva, Switzerland: OECD, 1998).

Panth, S., *Technological Innovation, Industrial Evolution, and Economic Growth* (New York: Garland Publishing, 1997).

Razgaitis, R., *Early-Stage Technologies: Valuation and Pricing* (New York: John Wiley & Sons, 1999).

Saviotti, P. and B. Nooteboom (Eds.), *Technology and Knowledge: From the Firm to Innovation Systems* (London: Edward Elgar, 2000).

Schiller, D., *Digital Capitalism: Networking the Global Market System* (Cambridge, MA: MIT Press, 2000).

Shaw, J., *Telecommunications Deregulation and the Information Economy* (Boston, MA: Artech House, 2001).

Shy, O., *The Economics of Network Industries* (New York: Cambridge University Press, 2001).

Sunstein C., *Republic.Com* (Princeton, NJ: Princeton University Press, 2001).

Tapscott, D., A. Lowy, and D. Ticoli, *Digital Capital: Harnessing the Power of Business Webs* (Boston, MA: Harvard Business School Press, 2000).

Tassey, G., *The Economics of R and D Policy* (Westport, CT: Quorum Books, 1997).

Vanderburg, W., *The Labyrinth of Technology* (Toronto, Canada: The University of Toronto Press, 2000).

Volti, R., *Society and Technological Change* (New York: Worth Publishers, 2000).

Ward. M., *Virtual Organisms: The Startling World of Artificial Life* (New York: St. Martin's Press, 2000).

Williams, C., *Technology and the Dream: Reflections on the Black Experience* (Cambridge, MA: MIT Press, 2001).

Wilson, S., *Information Arts: Intersections of Art, Science, and Technology* (Cambridge, MA: MIT Press, 2001).

Wolf, J., and N. Zee, *The Last Mile: Broadband and the Next Internet Revolution* (New York: McGraw-Hill Companies, 2000).

INDEX

About the Author

ELIEZER GEISLER is Professor of Organizational Behavior, Stuart Graduate School of Business, Illinois Institute of Technology, Chicago. With a doctorate from Northwestern's Kellogg School and with more than 80 scientific publications and five books, three published by Quorum, Dr. Geisler specializes in the evaluation and measurement of science and technology, the strategic management of technology and medical technology specifically. Dr. Geisler has also served as Chair of the College of Innovation Management and Entrepreneurship, a division of INFORMS, and as editor for various journals in his fields.